Demographic Change in Uruguay

DIRECTIONS IN DEVELOPMENT
Human Development

Demographic Change in Uruguay

Economic Opportunities and Challenges

Rafael Rofman, Verónica Amarante, and Ignacio Apella,
Editors

WORLD BANK GROUP

1 2 3 4 19 18 17 16

ISBN (paper): 978-1-4648-0844-9
ISBN (electronic): 978-1-4648-0845-6
DOI: 10.1596/978-1-4648-0844-9

Cover design: Debra Naylor, Naylor Design, Inc.

Library of Congress Cataloging-in-Publication data
Names: Rofman, Rafael, editor. | Amarante, Verónica, editor. | Apella, Ignacio, editor.
Title: Demographic change in Uruguay : economic opportunities and challenges / edited by Rafael Rofman, Verónica Amarante, and Ignacio Apella.
Description: Washington, DC : World Bank, [2016]
Identifiers: LCCN 2016023082| ISBN 9781464808449 (pdf) | ISBN 9781464808456
Subjects: LCSH: Demographic transition—Uruguay. | Uruguay—Population. | Uruguay—Economic conditions.
Classification: LCC HB3577 .D464 2016 | DDC 304.6/209895—dc23
LC record available at https://lccn.loc.gov/2016023082

Contents

Boxes

Figures

Tables

Foreword

Uruguay's development progress in recent decades includes falling mortality and fertility which is changing the age structure of the population. This aging of the population will continue in coming years and motivates the reflections in this book.

These demographic trends are good news: falling fertility reflects Uruguayans' ability to control the size of their families, and its aging is a potent indicator of development. However, we cannot ignore that a change of such magnitude poses significant challenges along various dimensions: on the long-term horizon through 2100, the economically active population will fall, with diverse impacts on the labor market and public accounts. This book explores the potential effects of the demographic change on social protection, the demand for health care and education services, the functioning of the labor market, and the macroeconomic environment. It considers the institutional changes and rules needed to respond to this new reality.

The two editing organizations behind this book—the World Bank and ECLAC—consider it to be a priority for Uruguay to identify policies that ensure that per capita output grows in a context of population aging, with very low or even negative demographic growth rates. Additionally, it is important to guarantee that institutions offer the appropriate mechanisms so that this growth is distributed equitably.

The book combines our efforts to enrich the discussion the country should have about these topics, in the belief that the rigorous analysis of prospects is fundamental to the construction of successful strategies for facing the challenges. We hope that the book contributes to the realization of the strategies necessary to face the coming changes, putting the economy on a path of sustained growth that guarantees well-being for all.

Alicia Bárcena
Executive Secretary
Economic Commission for Latin America and the Caribbean (ECLAC)

Jesko Hentchel
Country Director, Argentina, Paraguay, and Uruguay
The World Bank

Preface

This book was written under the auspices of a joint project between the World Bank and the Economic Commission for Latin America and the Caribbean, coordinated by Rafael Rofman, Verónica Amarante, and Ignacio Apella.

Authors include Verónica Amarante (chapters 1 and 7), Ignacio Apella (chapters 1, 4, 8, and 10), Marisa Bucheli (chapter 3), Juan José Calvo (chapter 2), Maira Colacce (chapter 7), Carlos Grau (chapter 5), Cecilia Llambí (chapter 6), Fernando Lorenzo (chapter 9), Rafael Rofman (chapters 1, 4, and 8), Sara Troiano (chapter 3), Maren Vairo (chapter 6), and Gonzalo Zunino (chapter 9).

Valuable contributions and comments received from Rodrigo Arim, Oscar Centrángolo, Fernando Filgueira, Jamele Rigolini, and Emily Sinnott supported the book's development.

We would especially like to thank Augusto de la Torre (Chief Economist, Regional Office for Latin America and the Caribbean, World Bank) and Margaret Grosh (Manager, Social Protection and Employment for Latin America and the Caribbean, World Bank) for their comments, guidance, and direction.

The book's 10 chapters analyze the potential economic and social impact of the demographic transition in Uruguay. The introduction summarizes findings, chapter 2 presents demographic forecasts through 2100, and chapter 3 estimates the National Transfer Accounts and the consumption and labor income profile by age group. Chapters 4, 5, and 6 analyze the potential impact of the demographic transition on the pension, health care, and education systems, respectively, depending on different public policy options. Chapter 7 studies the dynamics of the labor market in a context of population aging and the potential impact on the economically active population. Chapter 8 analyzes the demographic situation in an international context. Chapter 9 studies Uruguay's macroeconomic performance and the potential impact of aging on output growth, and chapter 10 summarizes the principal paths to economic growth in these contexts.

We hope that reading this book opens up space for ideas and public policy debates in the medium and long terms, and also that it is enjoyable.

About the Editors

Rafael Rofman is a Program Leader at the World Bank, coordinating all programs in social sectors developed in Argentina, Paraguay, and Uruguay. He has worked on social protection and pension policy in many Latin American countries as well as in other regions of the world. He graduated as an economist from the University of Buenos Aires, and received an MA in social demography from the University of Lujan and a PhD in demography from the University of California at Berkeley. Before joining the World Bank, he held positions in Argentina, both in academic institutions and government agencies, including Head of the Research Unit at the Supervision of Pension Funds and adviser to the Minister of Economy and to the Secretary of Social Security. He is the author of many studies on adult mortality, social security, and pension reform, including a recently published book on expanding old-age income protection coverage in 14 Latin American countries. He has been a university professor at the University of Buenos Aires, Torcuato Di Tella University, and the University of Lujan, among others.

Verónica Amarante holds a master's in economics from Universitat Pompeu Fabra and a PhD in economics from the University of Sussex. She has been working at the Economic Commission for Latin America and the Caribbean, United Nations, since 2012, first at the Social Development Division and then as the Director of the Office in Montevideo. Prior to that, she worked for 15 years as a researcher at Instituto de Economía, Universidad de la República. Her main research interests are in labor markets, poverty, inequality, and social policies. She has written and researched extensively on these topics for Uruguay and Latin America.

Ignacio Apella is an economist for the Social Protection and Labor Global Practice at the World Bank. He graduated as an economist from the University of Buenos Aires and received an MA in economics from the University of Buenos Aires. Since joining the World Bank, he has worked mainly on social protection, pension policy, labor economics, and health economics in several Latin American countries, including Argentina, Bolivia, Chile, El Salvador, and Mexico. Before joining the Bank, he was a researcher at the Center for the Study of State and Society for almost 10 years and Vice Director at the Department of Economics at the University of Buenos Aires. He is the author of many studies on social security and pension, health economics, and industrial organization in private pension funds. His most recent publications are two books: one on expanding income protection coverage for the elderly in 14 Latin American countries and the other on the potential economic impacts of the demographic transition in Argentina. He is also a professor of microeconomics at the University of Buenos Aires.

Abbreviations

AFAPs	Social Security Savings Fund Administrators (Administradoras de Fondos de Ahorro Previsional)
ANEP	National Administration of Public Education (Administración Nacional de Educación Pública)
BCU	Central Bank of Uruguay (Banco Central del Uruguay)
BGR	benefit generosity ratio
BPS	Social Security Bank (Banco de Previsión Social)
ECH	Continuous Household Survey (Encuesta Continua de Hogares)
ECLAC	Economic Commission for Latin America and the Caribbean
FONASA	National Health Care Fund (Fondo Nacional de Salud)
GDP	gross domestic product
GER	gross enrollment ratio
IAMC	Collective Medical Assistance Institutions (Instituciones de Asistencia Médica Colectiva)
IASS	social security assistance tax (Impuesto de Asistencia a la Seguridad Social)
IMESI	specific internal tax (Impuesto Específico Interno)
INE	National Institute of Statistics (Instituto Nacional de Estadística)
IRPF	individual income tax (Impuesto a las Rentas de las Personas Físicas)
IVA	value added tax (Impuesto al Valor Agregado)
MEC	Ministry of Education and Culture (Ministerio de Educación y Cultura)
MIDES	Ministry of Social Development (Ministerio de Desarrollo Social)
MSP	Ministry of Public Health (Ministerio de Salud Pública)
NER	net enrollment ratio
NTAs	National Transfer Accounts
OECD	Organisation for Economic Co-operation and Development
PANES	National Plan for Attention to the Social Emergency (Plan de Atención Nacional a la Emergencia Social)

SDR	school-age dependency ratio
SINADI	National Information System (Sistema Nacional de Información)
SR	support ratio
TDR	total dependency ratio
TFP	total factor productivity
UdelaR	University of the Republic (Universidad de la República, Montevideo)

CHAPTER 1

Demographic Change and Social Policies in Uruguay

Rafael Rofman, Verónica Amarante, and Ignacio Apella

Introduction

As in the majority of countries around the world, the population of Uruguay is undergoing demographic transition that is gradually aging the population, with fewer children, more elderly, and an overall trend toward stabilization of the population structure. This process is the result of two, socially very positive phenomena: a decrease in mortality among all age groups and a reduction in fertility, which increasingly is because Uruguayans can choose the size of their families.

The demographic trends of recent decades, which are expected to continue in the medium term, will have significant ramifications for Uruguay's economic development and well-being. And the demographic changes they imply involve significant macroeconomic and institutional challenges. If the central objective of public policies in Uruguay is to ensure sustained improvement in well-being and to promote economic growth and the appropriate distribution of its benefits, then the principal challenges will be to identify the policies that ensure that per capita income grows and institutions offer the appropriate mechanisms so this growth is distributed equitably.

This book's analysis was performed using the National Transfer Accounts model as a starting point. The methodological foundation of the model is simple: beginning with empirical data collected by household surveys or other instruments, it is possible to estimate the income and consumption profile for each age group in a population, both as an aggregate and disaggregated on the basis of types of consumption (such as spending on education or health care) and separating public consumption (paid by government) from private (directly paid by households). It is also possible to create a model that distributes the country's income, consumption, and total transfers by age. This can be done by complementing this information with information about transfers and capital flows—both public (as in the case of pension systems, taxes, and transfers to households) and private (such as families' savings and dissaving or intergenerational transfers)—and adjusting the different age profiles such that the amounts aggregated by age correspond to the national accounts.

The chapter then builds on the discussion about the effects of demographic change and the demands it will place on institutions and public policies. It considers the effect that the change in population age structure could have on the different dimensions studied in the first analysis, which could be defined as an "absolute composition effect." Based on this scheme, the chapters of the book then discuss the possible implications of the demographic changes for the economy, fiscal situation, and population well-being; the institutional changes the changes will create; and policy reforms that could help adapt institutions to the new population reality.

The Uruguayan demographic transition is also an opportunity. The country is now enjoying a demographic dividend in which its age structure, proportionately, represents its highest working-age population in centuries. Though temporary, this situation could allow an increase in capital and labor and launch sustained economic growth. For this to happen, it is necessary to generate institutional, financial, and fiscal conditions that promote larger savings and investment, increase the productivity of the economy, and sustain per capita gross domestic product (GDP) growth.

Population aging could also increase the fiscal needs of social sectors such as pension and health systems. Although reforms may contain this increase, it is important to identify the main sources of growth and the distribution mechanisms to meet the new demands.

This chapter summarizes the main findings of the book. The next section briefly presents Uruguayan demography, identifying the principal trends since the middle of the last century and the forecasts for the rest of the current century. The third section analyzes the income and consumption profiles of the population through 2013 and how the demographic evolution could impact the life-cycle deficit and the level of resources destined for the social sectors, public and private. The fourth section details the situation in health care, education, and social protection, analyzing their determinants and expected evolution. The fifth section discusses issues related to the labor market and the trends in participation rates among the different population groups. The sixth section discusses principal macroeconomic effects and the impact of aging on economic growth prospects, and the last section concludes and identifies areas where public policy interventions may be justified in the medium and long terms.

Uruguay's Demography: 1950–2100

Among Latin American countries, Uruguay began its demographic transition earliest. Already at the beginning of the 20th century, the country exhibited demographic trends similar to those in several European countries, with sustained decline in fertility and mortality. In 1908 fertility was about 6 children per woman, but it dropped to about 3 during the first half of the

20th century; since 1975, the rate began a new decline until it reached current levels near the replacement rate. In mortality, the decline had already begun in the 19th century, pushing life expectancy at birth significantly higher before 1900. The downward trend in mortality was sustained throughout the 20th century (with some slowing in the 1960s), and current life expectancy exceeds 75 years.

In coming decades, forecasts assume that fertility will continue its downward trend until the middle of the century before recovering and stabilizing slightly below the replacement rate; mortality is expected to continue decreasing and, by 2100, life expectancy at birth could reach 86 years (figure 1.1). The drop in fertility should also help reduce poverty, as household size declines among lower-income families.

Under this demographic transition, population age structure gradually changes and population growth slows. The natural increase of the Uruguayan population was around 1 percent per year during 1950–80 (although the net balance was significantly lower due to migration patterns), and later began to decrease. Currently, growth is around 0.45 percent and the population is expected to reach its maximum around 2050 from more than 3.3 million in 2013, after which it will begin to slowly decline.[1]

These trends resulted in earlier and slower demographic aging than in other countries in the region, as well as in middle- and middle-to-high-income countries in general. Demographic transition in Uruguay started later and developed more slowly than in other, more developed countries like Italy and Spain, and

Figure 1.1 Evolution of Fertility and Mortality in Uruguay, 1884–2100

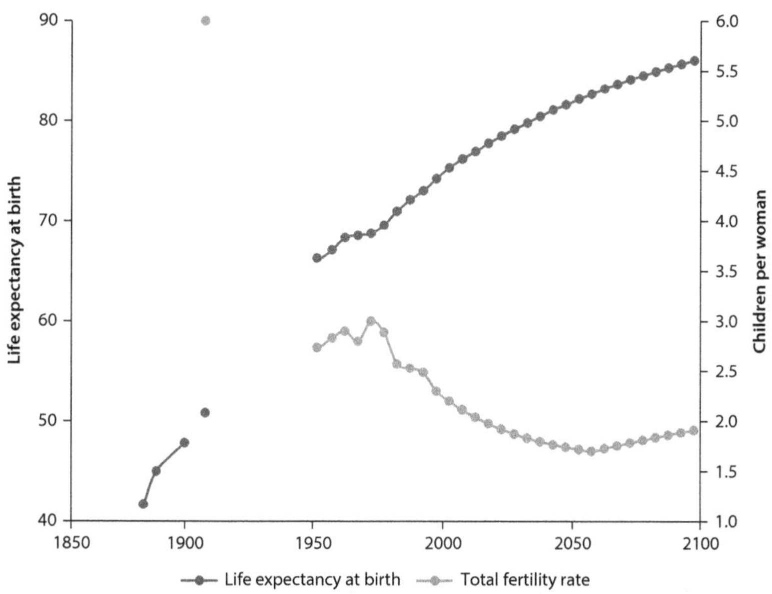

Source: Elaboration based on chapter 2.

Figure 1.2 Median Population Age, Uruguay and Selected Countries, 1950–2100

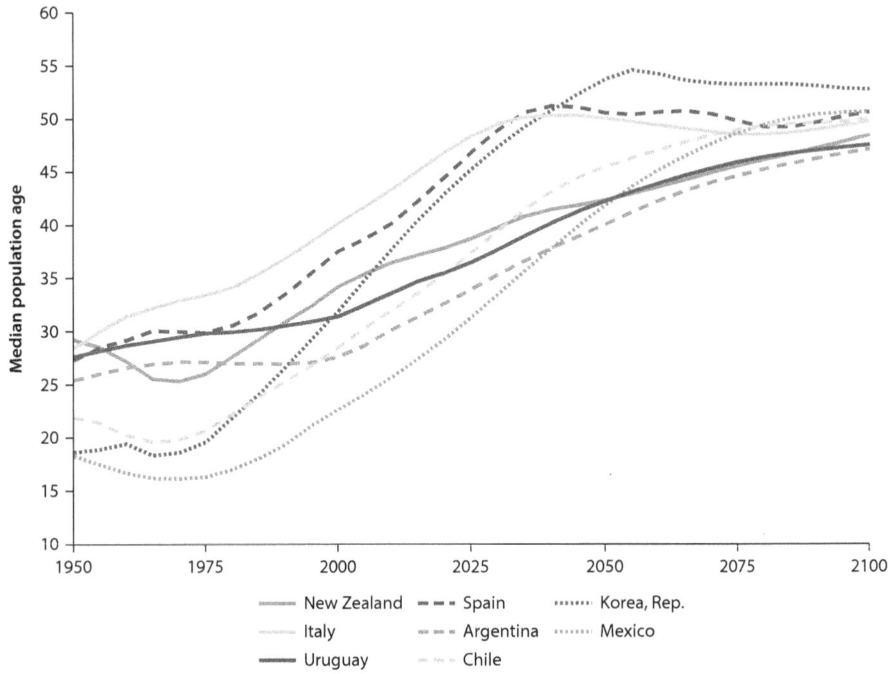

Source: United Nations 2014.

more closely resembles countries like New Zealand at the time (figure 1.2). In this sense, Uruguay is less exposed to the impacts of demographic change than many other countries around the world.

The impact of this demographic change is clear in dependency ratio indicators, which show the number of minors below age 15 for every 100 individuals between the ages of 15 and 64 (child dependency ratio), the number of elderly adults (age 65 and above) for every 100 individuals between the ages of 15 and 64 (aged dependency ratio), or the total which is the sum of the two. Figure 1.3 shows the downward trend in child dependency and upward in elderly dependency, for a rising long-term trend in total dependency. The period of temporary decrease known as the demographic dividend occurs in the first decades of this century.

Although the total dependency ratio is a good indicator of demographic trends, its usefulness for evaluating the impact that demography can have on an economy's performance is more limited, given the two basic assumptions on which it is based. First, the dependency rate only takes into account the demographic aspect, assuming that the entire population below age 15 and above age 65 is dependent and that all adults ages 15–65 are active. In reality, the actual participation rates begin to increase during adolescence (although they never reach 100 percent of the population), and decline around retirement age. The second limitation is that the indicator is "static," because it establishes

Figure 1.3 Dependency Ratios in Uruguay, 1950–2100

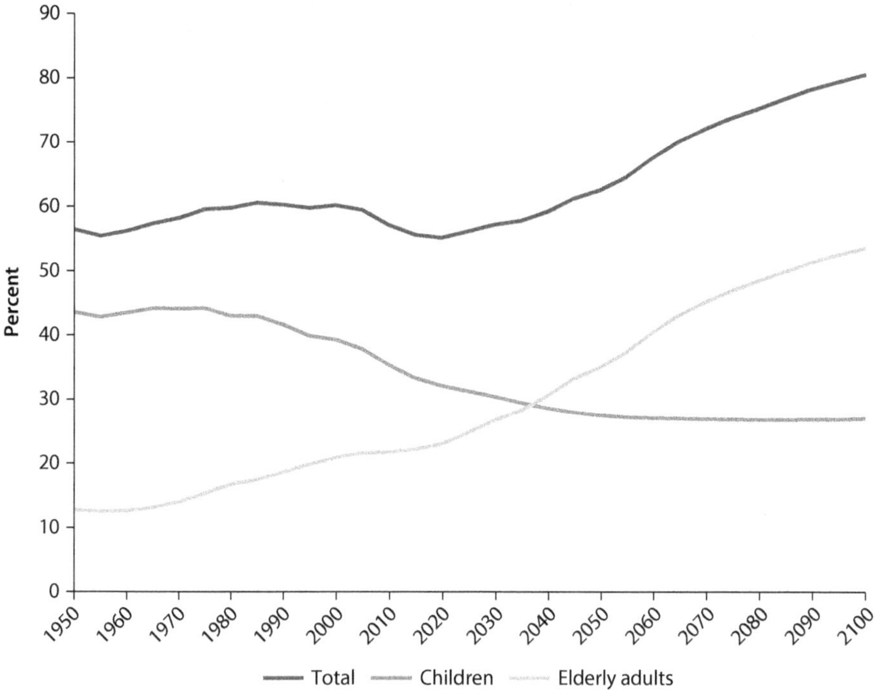

Source: Chapter 2.

cut-off ages at 15 and 65 years old (or any other normatively determined value), without recognizing that, over time, the population tends to change its behavior, and institutions adapt to these new behaviors, thus changing the age of entry into the labor force (due to higher levels of education) as well as exit ages (due to postponement of retirement ages). The following section discusses the first aspect in detail, considering the population's income and consumption profiles by age.

Income and Consumption Profiles and Their Impact on Social Spending

In a simplified model one could assume that members of the population below age 15 and above age 65 are "pure" consumers. That is, they do not participate in production processes for goods and services but, rather, only consume them, and their access to these goods depends on the resources that they receive from transfers or financing, while young adults make up the productive population. However, it is clear that the transition between economic participation and nonparticipation is less deterministic. Individuals exist below age 15 who do participate in the production of goods and services, and the same is true for some individuals over age 65, just as the entire population participates in consumption.

In this context, it is interesting to analyze the problem considering the population not as a dichotomy (consumers and producers), but rather as individuals that consume and produce at the same time. Thus, the relevant point is whether or not these activities create a deficit (meaning the individual would need to receive transfers or use savings to finance his or her consumption) or a surplus (which could be transferred or saved).

Figure 1.4 shows per capita income and consumption profiles by age for Uruguay in 2013. The income profile suggests that, although during the first years of life labor income is zero, it begins to increase slowly after age 15 until reaching a level near its peak at about age 30, when it slows until age 50 and then begins to decrease. In contrast, the consumption profile shows continuous growth throughout individuals' lifetime. As a result of these trends, it is possible to observe three stages in the life cycle: first, a deficit stage (when consumption exceeds income) from birth to age 27; a second surplus stage from age 28 to 57; and a final deficit stage after age 58.

Figure 1.5 shows the same variables, but in aggregate form, and in addition to considering the per capita value, also takes population size into account. The main effect of considering this variable is that the life-cycle deficit among the elderly, which at a per capita level begins to grow consistently after age 52, increases in this case until age 70, but later decreases due to the smaller population size.

Figure 1.4 Per Capita Income, Consumption, and Deficit by Age, 2013

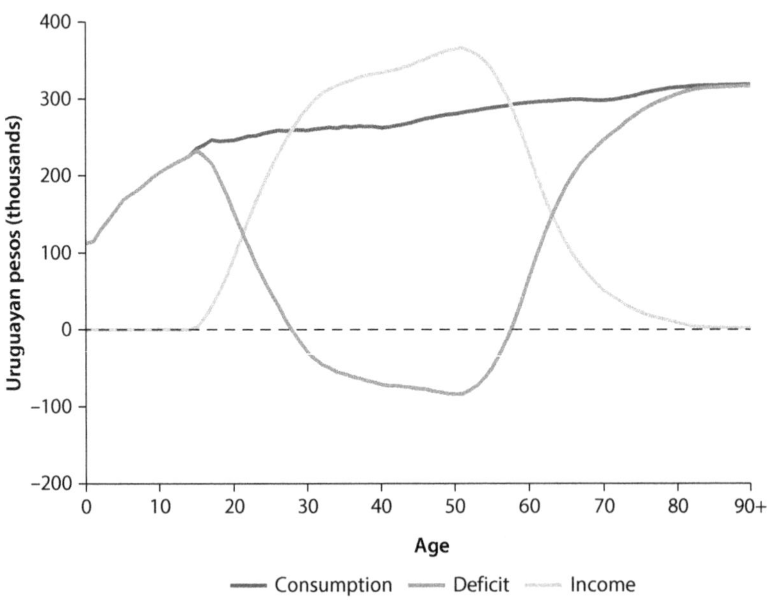

Note: These profiles were estimated based on the National Transfer Accounts methodology, which allows consumption and income patterns to be assigned to different age groups based on observations from household surveys and other sources of administrative data.

Figure 1.5 Aggregate Income, Consumption, and Deficit by Age, 2013

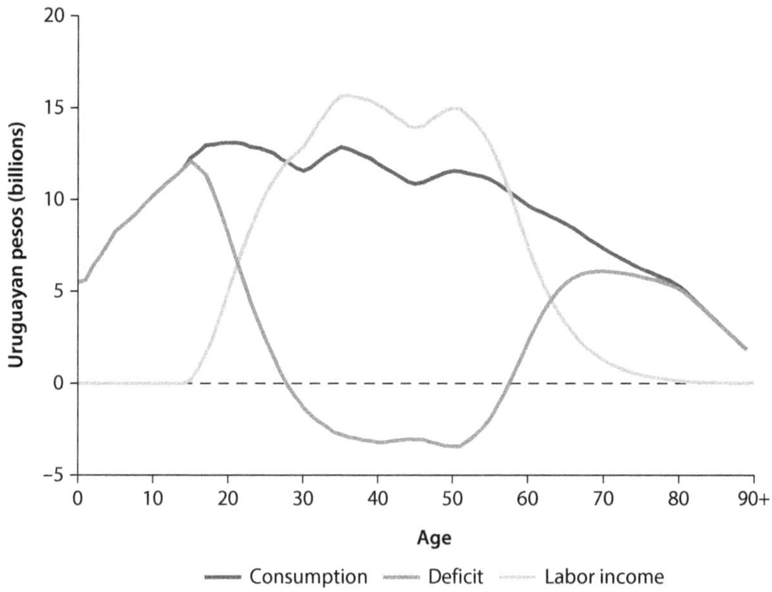

Source: Chapter 3.

The length and intensity of the surplus period show that Uruguay has a smaller space to benefit from the demographic dividend. Figure 1.6 shows the life-cycle deficit by age for Uruguay and selected other countries. Uruguay has (a) a shorter surplus period than countries like the Republic of Korea or China (although similar to other Latin American countries); (b) a lower intensity of this surplus; and (c) a period of deficit among the elderly with a similar length but significantly deeper than all comparator countries.

The surplus period in Uruguay and other countries in the region is not only shorter but also significantly less intense than in high-growth Asian countries. In the case of China, and Korea, the difference between labor income and consumption is significantly higher than that observed in the cases of Uruguay, Argentina, Brazil, and Chile. This shorter and less intense surplus results in less aggregate savings, a problem that affects most countries in Latin America. This weakness in the savings rate is not good news for the ability of countries to take advantage of the demographic dividend.

The economic support ratio, a synthetic indicator of deficit and surplus levels during a lifetime, shows the relation between producers and consumers. The added value of this approach is that it facilitates deeper understanding of the demographic impacts than dependency rates do, as considers the potential participation of individuals in the labor force during their life cycle, their effective participation, and better defines the concept of "effective consumers." This ratio increases as the active population increases, but it also reflects consumption and savings levels, as it is larger when savings are larger. Thus, the

Figure 1.6 Life-Cycle Deficit in Uruguay and Selected Countries by Age as a Proportion of Average Income between Ages 30–49 (closest date available)

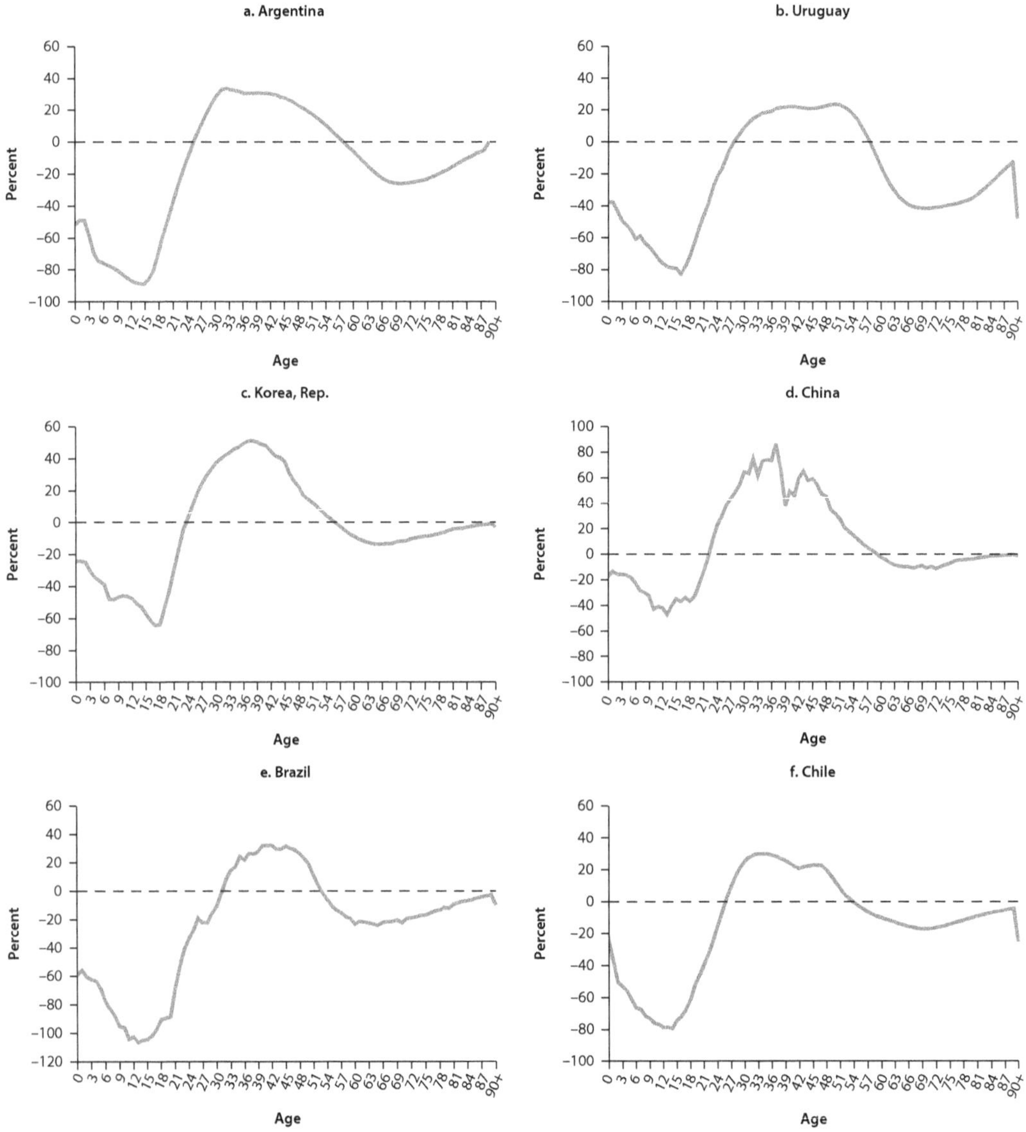

Source: Chapter 8.

ratio shows the balance between income and consumption at the societal level. When aggregate income is identical to consumption, the ratio is equal to 1, and it grows as savings increase. Figure 1.7 shows the levels and a projection of this ratio given expected demographic trends. It is interesting to note that the decline in the support ratio starts later than the increase in the dependency ratio (see figure 1.3), reflecting the different income and consumption patterns in the active population.

Figure 1.7 Economic Support Ratio, 2010–2100

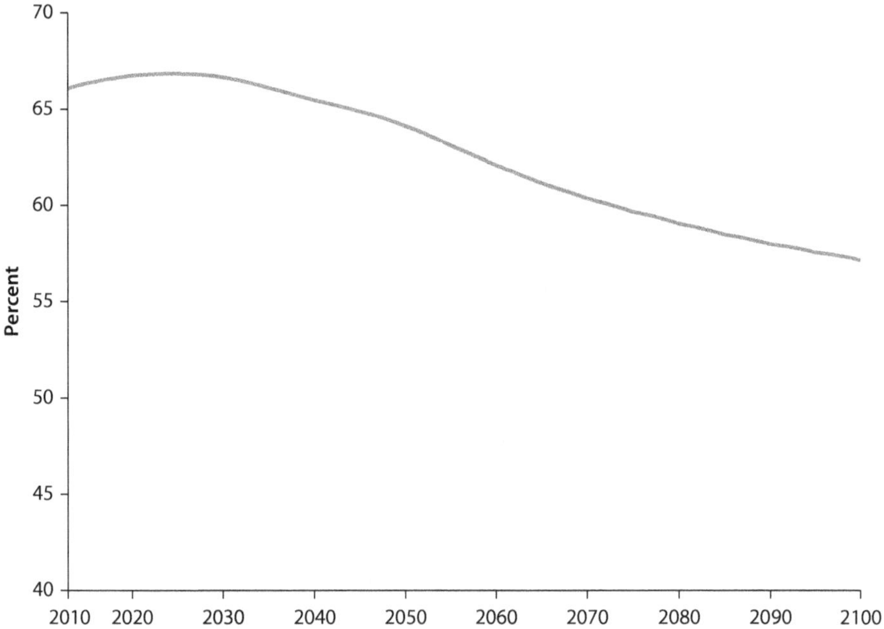

Source: Elaboration based on chapters 2 and 3.

On the other hand, the difference in deficits of children and the elderly is relevant for public policy, as a significant part of these deficits is financed with fiscal resources. Uruguay is among the five countries with the largest bias in favor of transfers to the elderly, with a ratio of 3.3 in transfers to children, after Brazil (3.7), Chile (3.5), and Costa Rica (3.5). A ratio above 1 means that in per capita terms the elderly receive larger transfers than children receive. An aged demographic structure puts pressure on public transfer priorities, tilting them toward the elderly. Most countries with available data have a ratio above 1 (figure 1.8).

The National Transfer Accounts methodology allows us to disaggregate expenditure by component. Figure 1.9 shows the aggregated consumption by age divided into some of its principal components. As can be expected, spending on education, public and private, is concentrated at younger ages, and health care spending slowly rises as age increases. Per capita spending on social protection (essentially, the national pension system, as well as other transfers such as family allowances, unemployment insurance, and the "*Tarjeta Uruguay Social*") is low among youth, but increases rapidly with age. In aggregate terms, social protection spending decreases rapidly at the most advanced ages due to the smaller size of the population. Figure 1.9 shows the aggregate consumption and transfers in the same social sectors.

The disaggregation by age of public and private resources destined for the main social sectors, combined with the information from population projections, produces a simulation of the potential demographic impacts on

Figure 1.8 Relationship between Net Public Transfer per Capita to the Elderly and Children, Uruguay and Selected Countries, Various Years

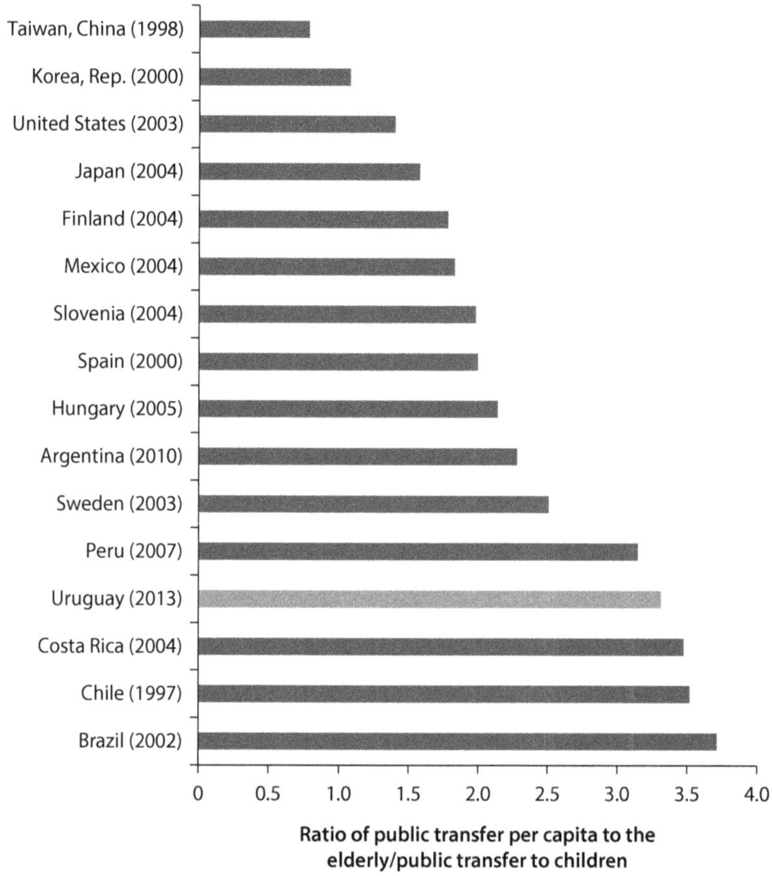

Source: Chapter 8.

these variables. Importantly, this simulation is not predictive, because it is calculated assuming no changes in the way consumption and transfers are organized over the next 85 years, an assumption that is very unlikely to hold over such a long period of time. Conversely, the exercise is useful for considering what the "pure" demographic impact could be.[2] Figure 1.10 shows the results of this exercise.

With no regulatory or behavioral changes, public and private consumption spending on health care could increase during the rest of this century, from 7.8 percent of GDP in 2013 (two-thirds of which is public spending) to 9.7 percent. Conversely, education spending should exhibit an inverse trend, due to the decrease in the number of children in the population. Thus, this spending would decrease from 5.8 percent of GDP in 2013 (63 percent from the public sector) to around 4.2 percent in 2100. Finally, the resources designated for financing social protection (which include the Banco de Previsión Social's pay-as-you-go

Figure 1.9 Per Capita Consumption and Transfers in Social Sectors by Age, 2013

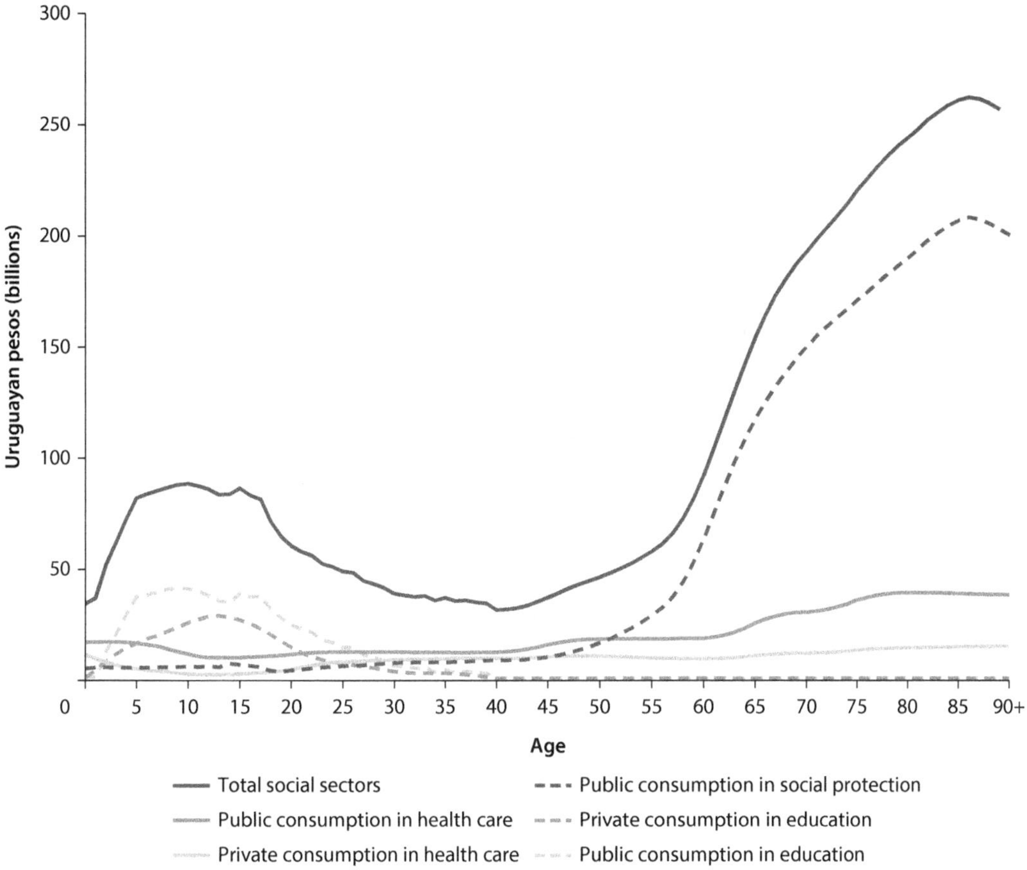

Source: Chapter 3.

pension system, the parastatal funds, other social protection programs in the public sector, and benefit payments from the funded scheme [Administradoras de Fondos de Ahorro Previsional (AFAPs) and insurance companies in the private sector]) would increase from 11 percent of GDP in 2013 (almost entirely accounted for by public spending) to 18.6 percent in 2100 (with around 25 percent in private sector spending).

Figure 1.10 shows that, in aggregate terms, the percentage of GDP destined for basic social services (health care and education) and social protection will increase from a little less than 25 percent in 2013 to around 32 percent in 2100.[3] Essentially as a result of the effect of the 1996 pension reform, the need for fiscal resources will tend to decrease during the next two decades, but once the transition to the new regime is completed near the end of the 2030s the rate of spending increase will accelerate. At the same time, the resources from the private sector will tend to grow during the first decades, as the importance of the private pension system increases, leveling off at around 9 percent of GDP after 2050.

Figure 1.10 Consumption and Transfers in Social Sectors, 2013–2100

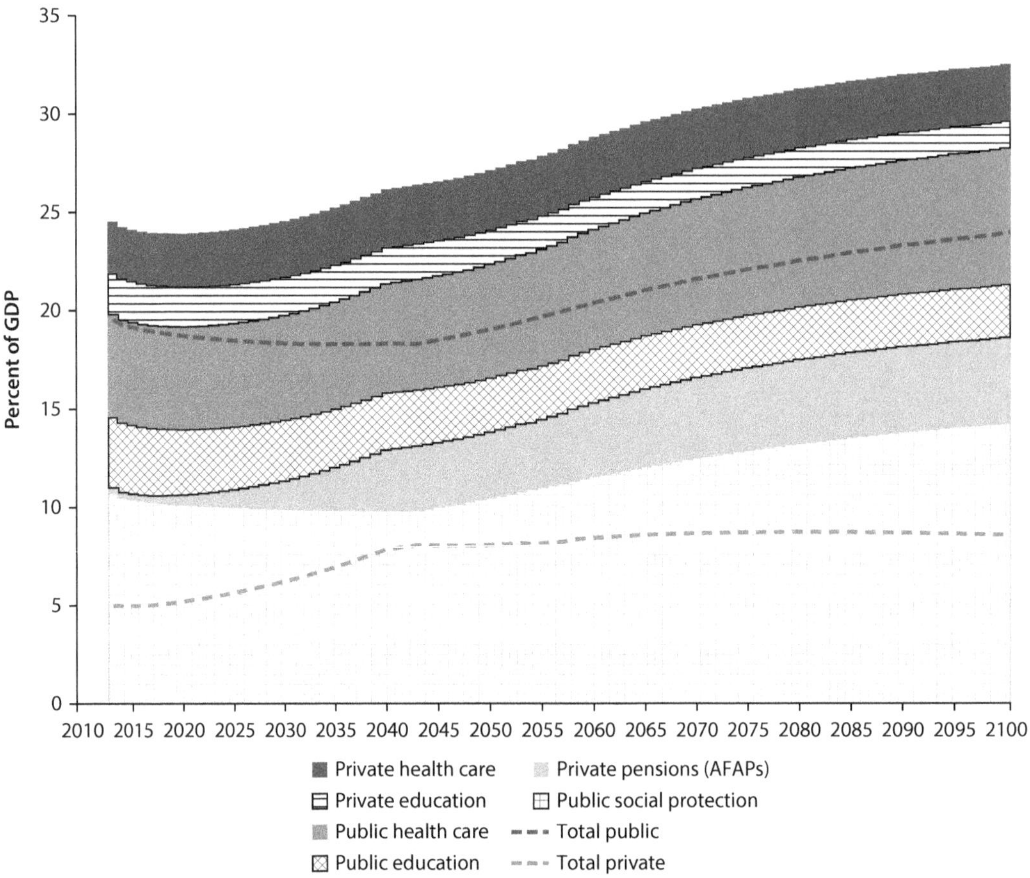

Source: Elaboration based on chapters 3, 4, 5, and 6.
Note: AFAPs = Administradoras de Fondos de Ahorro Previsional (Social Security Savings Fund Administrators).

The Social Sectors' Challenge in a Context of Population Aging

The discussion in the previous section presents the possible evolution of the resources required to maintain social services at the current levels until the end of the century, whether financed with public or private funds. However, it is clear that these services' characteristics will change over time, for reasons arising from the demographic shift itself (such as the epidemiological transition in the health sector or the fall in the number of school-age children and youth). This section offers some considerations based on these topics, which are discussed in detail in chapters 4–6.

The three sectors considered in this discussion present specific analytical challenges. On the one hand, social protection policies have undergone deep reform since the mid-1990s, when an individual funded scheme was introduced. The scheme transferred part of the financial management of the pension system to the private sector, in addition to modifying some of the system's basic parameters to make it more restrictive. In 2008, a new reform revised some of these changes and eased access to contributory retirement benefits. At the same time, at the end of the 1990s a process of increasing access to some social protection benefits began, such as family allowances, which meant that some children whose parents were not employed in the formal labor market could receive a transfer. This change in the traditionally Bismarckian focus of the social protection system was expanded in 2004 and 2005 when the current scheme was finalized. This scheme provides transfers that are not directly linked to workers' employment status (essentially family allowances from the Equity Plan and the *Tarjeta Uruguay Social* [Uruguay Social Card]). Thus, in coverage and adaptation of social protection in the last 20 years Uruguay had an initial period of adding restrictions and transferring funding responsibilities to the private sector and a subsequent period of expanding the role played by the public sector (although, in fiscal terms, to a much lesser degree than before), adding transfers to relatively vulnerable families.

The medium- and long-term trend in this sector is clear. In the coming decades the need for resources to fund the pension system will increase continuously, as the number of older adults increases and their relative proportion of the total population also increases due to the aging process. As a result of the 1996 pension reform, it can be expected that in the coming decades public pension spending should remain at current levels or even decrease slightly, but it is interesting to note that this decrease will be broadly made up for by an increase in private sector expenditure. In this sense, the main impact of the reform was not a reduction in coverage or benefit levels (and, consequently, in the financial resources directed to the sector), but rather a partial transfer of the financing mechanisms from the public to the private sector. By 2040, once the transition to the new system is complete, public expenditure will reestablish its upward trend and the private spending growth rate will decrease.

As was pointed out earlier, public funds directed to noncontributory social protection transfers increased significantly in recent years. Although in 1998 just 0.5 percent of GDP was used to fund these programs (mostly an elderly pension program), this percentage increased slightly after the family allowance program for low-income households was created in 1999, and later increased more rapidly with the approval of Law No. 18,227, which introduced the family allowance component of the Social Equity Plan. However, even after incorporating this program it is important to note that spending on noncontributory benefits represents just 10 percent of spending on contributory benefits. This difference is reflected in the structure of spending by age group because the largest part of contributory benefits is assigned to the elderly through the pension system. Figure 1.11 shows the distribution of per capita spending on social protection grouped by age and program, and figure 1.12 shows the aggregate distribution.

The medium- and long-term trend for pension expenditure is increasing, as discussed in the previous section. As figure 1.10 shows, if reforms are not made to the system in the coming decades, the percentage of GDP directed to pensions

Figure 1.11 Per Capita Public Spending on Social Protection by Age and Program, 2013

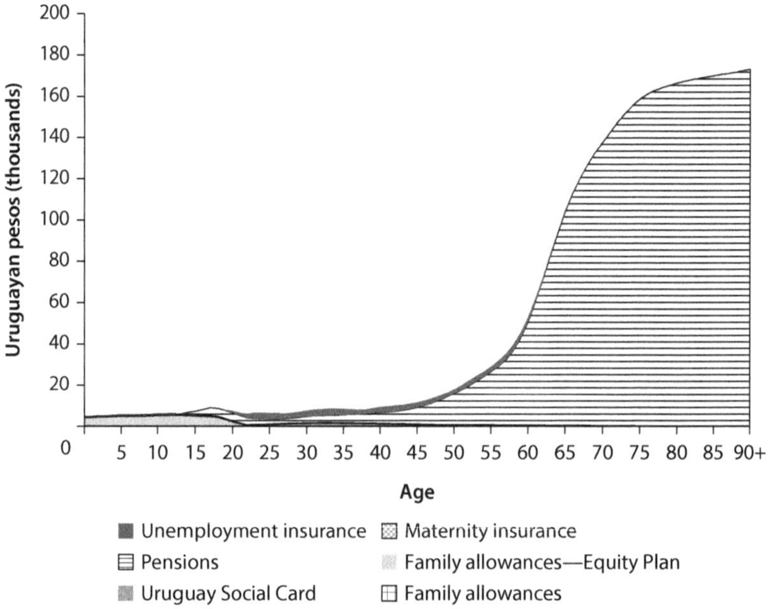

Source: Chapter 4.

Figure 1.12 Aggregate Public Spending on Social Protection by Age and Program, 2013

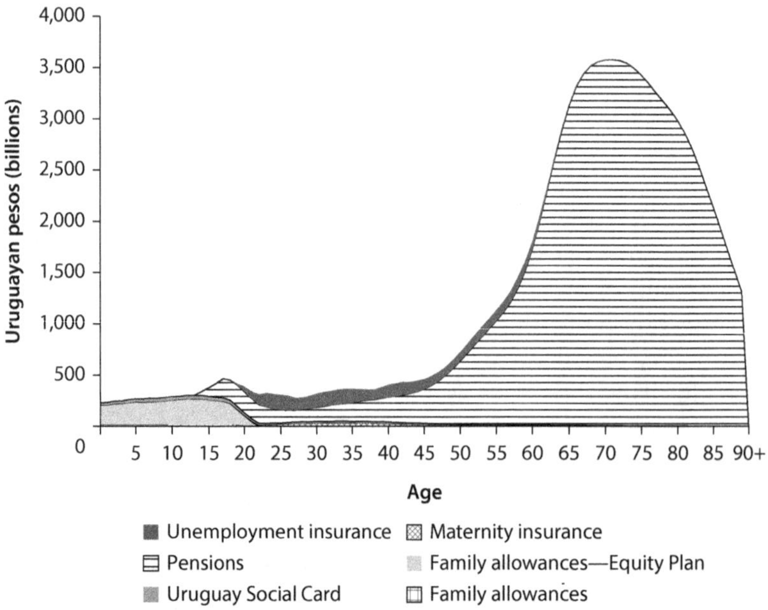

Source: Chapter 4.

in Uruguay will increase from current levels slightly below 10 percent to almost 18.6 percent in 2100. The growth in the early decades will be concentrated in the funded scheme, which will increase from 2 percent of total pensions in 2013 to nearly 27 percent in 2043, and will later stabilize around 25 percent.

In the health care sector, the reform in the insurance system that began around a decade ago entailed a modification to the services' funding mechanisms, with growing participation from the public sector, but no changes to the services' characteristics or cost.

Population aging poses a clear funding challenge for the public sector due to two factors. First, increased demand as a consequence of the greater size of the portion of the population at advanced ages. In this sense, different studies performed in Organisation for Economic Co-operation and Development countries suggest that the highest level of demand for health care services that a person generates is during his or her final decade of life, and within this decade mostly during the final year.

Second, one must add to the higher demand the greater relative cost of health care services in demand as a consequence of the greater complexity of the most prevalent illnesses (chronic and disabling conditions). This final point is further reinforced as the population undergoes an epidemiological transition, moving from a context with high rates of transmissible diseases to a greater prevalence of nontransmissible conditions. Developing countries move from mortality profiles linked to infectious diseases to chronic and noncommunicable diseases such as cardiac problems or cancer-related ailments. On many occasions, the unequal income distribution leads to the coexistence of both scenarios, a dual situation that must be overcome to advance in the social development process.

The magnitude of the increase of the health spending will depend on the health status of those whose life has been extended. Prevention and delaying of chronic and disabling illnesses, and maintaining good health status, will remain the main challenges as the population ages. Additionally, constant technological improvements in diagnostics and treatments, preventive medicine, and the development of new drugs that increase the quality of life and the ability to fight illness, will have an impact on the financial mechanisms for health care coverage.

Clearly, public health policies that tend to reduce morbidity and mortality, such as those that tend to reduce consumption of tobacco and salty foods or that promote healthy lifestyles, extend life expectancy, which entails higher health care expenditure instead of lower. In effect, the health care spending trend dependent on the aging process of the Uruguayan population has been growing, increasing from 7.8 percent of GDP in 2013 to 10.3 percent expected in 2100, and this trend can be expected to continue.

The education sector is where challenges become more interesting because, unlike what can be expected in social protection or health care, the population demanding these services will tend to decrease. As a result, if no changes in coverage or policies are implemented, resources necessary to fund the sector could be expected to decrease (see figure 1.10), because total consumption of education services will fall from 5.8 percent of GDP in 2013 to around

4.2 percent at the end of the century. However, it is reasonable to suppose that the assumption of stability in the levels of coverage and per capita cost is not appropriate because Uruguay currently has a significant school desertion problem, especially during the final years of high school. Moreover, there are clear signals (which have framed the current political debate) in the need to increase the level of investment in basic education.

Demographic decline of student numbers has already begun. As chapter 6 points out, primary school enrollment fell about 11 percent from 2005 to 2013, mostly as population decreases. Increases at the preschool (ages 4 and 5) and the secondary levels currently make up for this downward trend, and at the upper secondary and tertiary levels a complex phenomenon has emerged in which enrollment has increased during periods of economic recession and decreased during boom times. This issue is potentially related to increases in labor demand. However, increases in coverage will only be able to offset the population decrease for a time: according to the various scenarios set out, even in the event of a successful decrease in the coverage gap, total enrollment would only increase by some 50,000 students between now and the end of the next decade, and subsequently begin to decline again in a scenario of universal coverage. This coverage expansion might reduce the incidence of poverty and income inequality, as better education outcomes among those in the lowest income quintile should increase their productivity and hence the potential labor income. A more equal distribution of the accumulated human capital would allow a more equitable income distribution.

In addition to the expansion of coverage, two scenarios deserve to be explored. In addition to the coverage deficiencies concentrated at the secondary level, Uruguay has problems related to learning trajectory delays, meaning that many students take longer than expected to complete their education. This problem begins in the primary level, but is seriously accentuated at the middle and upper secondary levels, when nearly 37 percent of students are above-age for their grade level. Correcting this phenomenon, by decreasing repetition and delays, would result in less aggregate demand for education services, which could partially offset the effect of the increase in coverage. Figure 1.13 shows the trends in total enrollment in education for the three scenarios that in any case will tend to decrease.

The third scenario assumes that not only will coverage increase and delays among students decrease, but also that an effort to increase the quality of education would entail an increase in per-student spending, which would mean that per capita spending would tend to increase. Hence, this final scenario combines the effects of the previous ones.

The differences between the first three scenarios ("pure" demographics, the universalization of coverage, and universal coverage with the elimination of delays) are directly related to enrollment; a fourth scenario also entails an increase in per-student expenditure, which means that the total resources needed for public education would increase by some 50 percent. Figure 1.14 shows the evolution of public spending on education in these four scenarios.

Figure 1.13 Education Enrollment by Simulation Scenario, 2013–2100

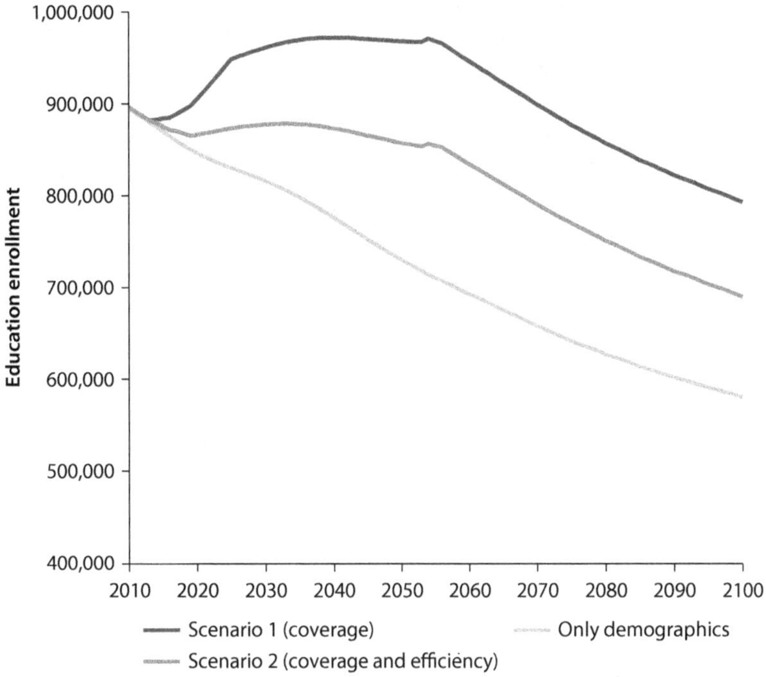

Figure 1.14 Education Expenditure by Simulation Scenario, 2013–2100

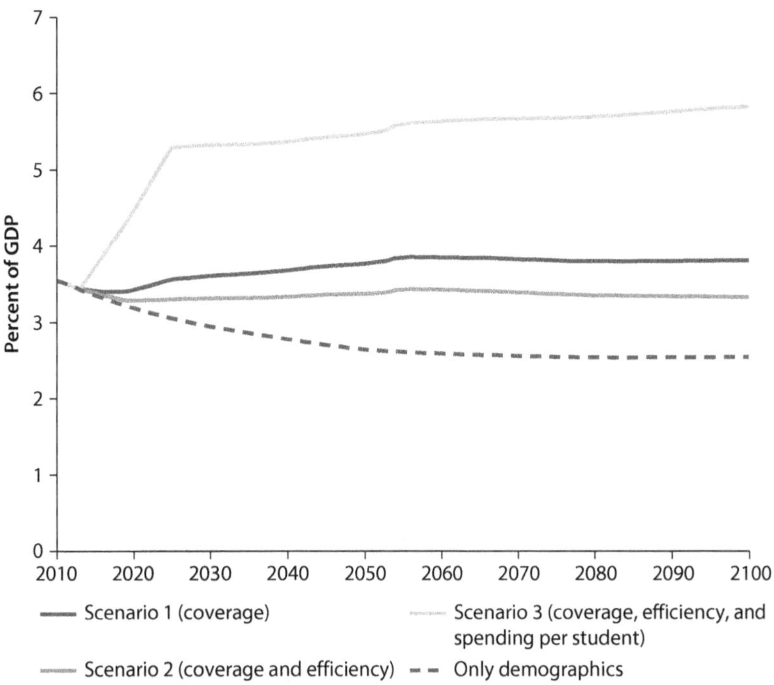

Source: Chapter 6.

However, the medium- and long-term education policy agenda aimed at expanding coverage and quality should consider possible tensions. For example, coverage expansion and quality improvements may require greater financial effort, but amid demographic transition this should not be a big constraint, given the reduction in people at schooling age. The focus on quality would also imply changes in institutions, which could generate debate and resistance from key actors in the sector. The history of proposals, debates, and conflicts around education reforms in Uruguay are evidence of this problem.

Population aging is a gradual but inevitable phenomenon. It is therefore necessary to focus on medium- and long-term policies, as the demographic dividend offers important opportunities to adapt to this new reality. In the design of the pension system, the increasing proportion of elderly will make challenges in generating additional resources to finance benefits more visible. The pension system provides almost universal coverage to the elderly, protecting groups that, without those benefits, would be among the poorest in society. In the medium and long term, population aging will put greater pressure on the public and private resources needed to finance pension benefits. However, it is possible to consider factors that could help relieve that pressure. A potential increase in formal employment would increase the contributory source of financing. Moreover, in a context of healthy aging, where workers choose to remain active in the labor market beyond the legal age of retirement, a gradual increase in the minimum legal age of retirement could be possible.

For the health system, it will be necessary to focus system structure on future challenges, considering the evolving demographic and epidemiological profiles. Given that noncommunicable diseases are emerging as the leading cause of morbidity, disability, and mortality, effective public initiatives should be implemented to address the major risk factors: smoking, physical inactivity, alcohol consumption, and unhealthy diets.

Finally, although resources are freed in the education system as age structure changes, it is important to invest these funds in an effective and strategic way to improve the quality of the services and thus increase the productivity of the future labor force.

The Labor Market

One preliminary conclusion of the discussion so far is that during the coming decades Uruguay will face a significant challenge as resources to finance the social sectors grow and the population in active ages declines (reflected in the projected decrease in the support ratio after the passing of the demographic dividend).

One possible response to this challenge can be found in the labor market. The projections discussed in the second section of this chapter assume that there will not be changes in the population's behavior in labor market participation. It is worth exploring, nonetheless, the possible impacts that changes to this assumption would have. Chapter 7 details the recent evolution and future prospects for the labor market, showing the significant increase in participation rates in recent decades linked to two principal factors: a steady increase in participation rates among women and the postponement of retirement for all.

An analysis of these processes offers insights into the possible evolution of the labor market in the medium term. The increase in women's participation appears to be a process that has been sustained over time and will continue. A significant part of the phenomenon is due to a "cohort" effect, that is, participation is greater as the new generations of women enter the labor market and their economic participation is consolidated. The female participation rate was, at the beginning of the 1980s, just half of that of males, but in 2013 it exceeded 75 percent and exceeded 85 percent among ages 20 and 40. This convergence can be expected to continue and, in a few years, the differences in participation rates between men and women will be minimal. In turn, the age at which young adults enter the labor market has increased, causing participation rates among the youngest groups to fall (among men participation rates for minors under age 18 fell by at least half between 1981 and 2013 and by 15 percent among adults under age 24, and among women the decrease in the participation rate for minors under age 18 exceeded 40 percent) and retirement ages have increased (with participation rates between 20 and 40 percent higher than in 1981 among men aged 55–65 in 2013).

Chapter 7 thus proposes three alternative scenarios. First, it considers how the total participation rate would evolve if the age-specific rates stayed at current levels until 2100. A second scenario assumes that the convergence trend in participation rates by gender will continue, progressively closing the gap until the age-specific activity rates for women reach levels similar to those of more developed countries. Finally, a third scenario considers the impact that a sustained increase in education levels would have on economic participation, assuming that the age-specific participation rates would remain the same for the various groups defined by the highest level of education achieved. Given that the population with more education currently has the highest participation rates, this would increase total rates (figure 1.15).

The differences are clear: in the first scenario the effect of demographic aging would result in a sustained fall in the proportion of the active population, and an increase in women's participation would result in an increase in the participation rate but not of the long-term trend (given that once the gender gap is closed, the demographic effect would take over). However, in the third scenario the increase in the population's education level would increase participation rates less than the gender gap scenario, with a minor effect on the long-term trend. The importance of the future evolution of the participation rate is clear: if no other factors that contribute to economic growth change, then a fall in the participation rate would tend to result in a decrease in the level of production of goods and services, resulting in a serious challenge for Uruguay to maintain output sufficient to satisfy the consumption and welfare needs of its population.

Figure 1.15 Total Projected Labor Market Participation Rates by Simulation Scenario, 2013–2100

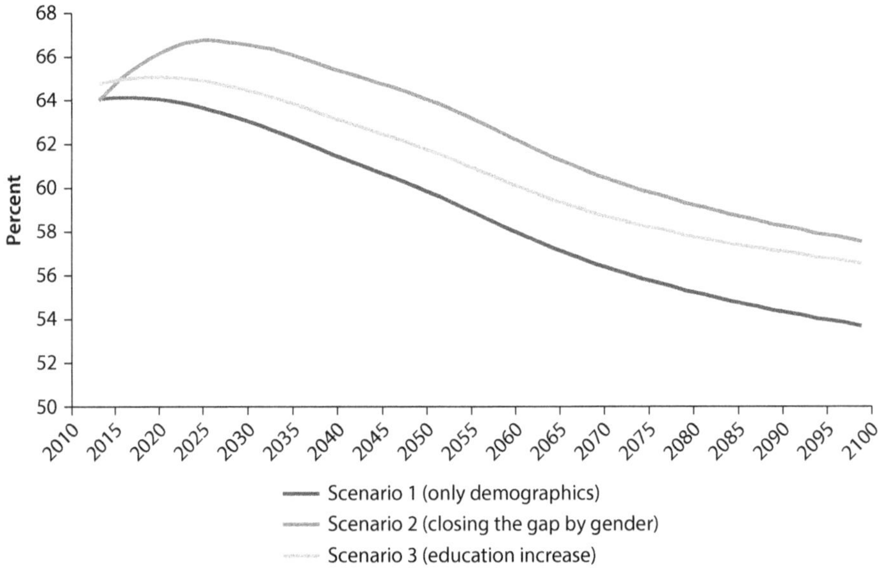

Source: Chapter 7.

The Impacts on Macroeconomics: The Challenge of Productivity

An analysis of the role of the labor force and other factors in Uruguay's economic growth requires consideration of the contribution that each factor makes to total growth. The literature on sources of economic growth is broad and clearly identifies the possible determinants of the level of production in a society. Economic growth depends, fundamentally, on the growth of the endowments of the factors of production (that is, labor and capital) and on changes in the way that production is organized, that is, total factor productivity (TFP), which means the use of the factors in more or less efficient ways. The previous section discussed the situation expected in the labor market in the context of demographic aging. The analysis shows that, even with possible differences in participation of segments of society that currently do not participate in the labor market and could do so if the proper conditions existed, it can be expected that a downward trend in the number of workers as a proportion of the entire population would develop. Consequently, the principal challenge for the macro-economy appears to be finding mechanisms that ensure sustained growth in the endowment of capital as well as TFP in a manner that counters the inevitable reduction in the endowment of labor.

The capital endowment can increase as a function of investment sustained over time. Uruguay has exhibited relatively low internal savings during recent decades, especially in comparison with other countries that have been able to follow more effective growth paths. This level represents an important challenge, especially considering that the demographic dividend represents a window of opportunity to increase the savings level because, as figure 1.7 shows, the support ratio will remain at relatively high levels during the next decade. In this context, it would be possible to direct surpluses to savings and investment, which would generate a virtuous cycle of investment, growth, and savings, known as the "second demographic dividend." In contrast, if significant savings levels are not achieved in the coming years, the risk posed for the economy's sustainability could be significant in the medium and long term, because as the support ratio falls (and consequently the levels of consumption increase relative to household incomes) the trend would be toward a decrease in internal savings in the economy, which could provoke a vicious cycle of falling savings, falling investment, and falling production.

The low gross savings rate in Uruguay (figure 1.16) is related in part to the behavior of the "primary savers," that is, the population group that because of its age finds itself in the stage of life that offers greater opportunities for saving. This is the case with adults who have already passed the family formation stage and the associated transfers of resources to their children, but continue to generate significant income. In Uruguay, consumption in this group is relatively high compared to other countries, regionally and globally, which limits their capacity to save. Figure 1.17 shows how, in ages 40–65, Uruguay maintains the highest levels of consumption relative to income, with very marked differences relative to countries like China, Germany, Japan, and the Republic of Korea, but also higher than other countries in the region, such as Argentina, Brazil, Chile, and Costa Rica.

Figure 1.16 Gross Savings Rate, Uruguay and Selected Countries, 1986–2013

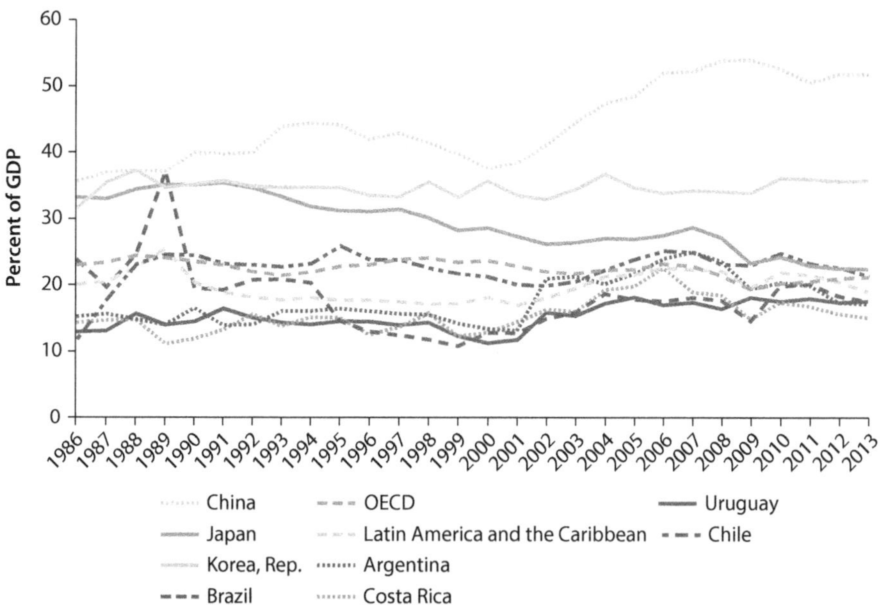

Source: Chapter 8.
Note: OECD = Organisation for Economic Co-operation and Development.

Figure 1.17 Consumption Profiles Ages 40–65, Uruguay and Selected Countries, Available Years

percent of average income ages 30–49

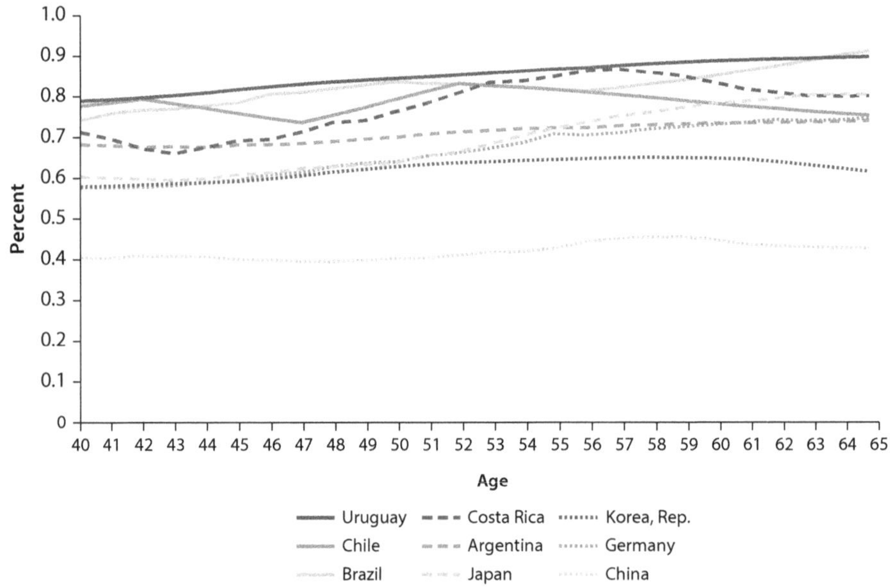

Source: National Transfer Accounts Project, http://ntaccounts.org.

There is implicit tension in the intertemporal consumption choice. Higher consumption in the present may produce a higher utility level or welfare in the short term, but this also implies a lower level of consumption in the future. In a context of aging, high consumption implies lower savings and therefore lower investment. In the medium and long term, this situation limits the capacity to accumulate capital per worker, and consequently restricts the increment of labor productivity and TFP. Therefore, the economy converges to a lower rate of economic growth and future consumption, in a scenario characterized by larger need to finance health and pension expenditures.

The demographic transition and population aging will gradually increase aggregate consumption in the economy, as the proportion of the population considered "net consumers" rises. The elderly have a high marginal propensity to consume and, therefore, the proportion of income consumed increases with age. The increase in net consumers in relation to "net workers" creates a scenario with lower income per capita. In this context, individuals should either reduce their current consumption or accept that the low savings rate will undermine the investment process and, therefore, economic growth in the medium and long term.

The main challenge for public policy is to promote strong investment in the next 15 or 20 years, seeking productivity gains and improvements in production efficiency. Taking advantage of the favorable demographic conditions for investment is one of the most important macroeconomic challenges, with significant implications for economic growth. Productivity improvement is a critical challenge as it has the potential to address some short-term demands without affecting long-term growth. To achieve these improvements, a revision of institutional, fiscal, and financial institutions, rules, and incentives is required.

In this context, a sustained increase in TFP could help sustain economic growth in the medium term. This component varies as a function of characteristics such as the accumulation of human capital (that is, training of workers to allow them to increase their productivity at the same levels of employment intensity and availability of capital resources) and technological characteristics linked to innovation and the organization of the production of goods and services.

A factor decomposition exercise of economic growth in 2004–14 suggests that 56 percent of GDP growth in this period is explained by the variation of productive factor endowments, capital, and labor. The remaining 44 percent is the result of the evolution of TFP.[4] Labor had a particularly important role in this decade, as the labor force grew rapidly thanks to an increase in participation rates and a decline in unemployment, but this performance will not be sustainable in the long term.

Starting from this exercise, the analysis in chapter 9 analyzes the trend of per capita GDP, considering four possible scenarios. The first two assume that labor force changes only due to aging (pure demographic effect) and that TFP's contribution explains a third of economic growth, which is somewhat below the level mentioned in the previous paragraph. The second scenario assumes that TFP contributes 1.5 percentage points to total growth each year, independent of what happens with the other factors. The difference between these two scenarios is critical and has a strong impact on the results of the simulations, because in one it is assumed that a drop in the factors' contribution to growth also affects TFP and in the other TFP is assumed to be independent.

In the third and fourth scenarios the assumptions used in Scenarios 1 and 2 regarding TFP are adopted, but the labor force contribution is expected to change following the third scenario, presented in figure 1.14, with increasing education. Figure 1.18 shows the projection of per capita GDP in each of the four scenarios.

The main driver of differences in these results is the assumption about TFP. In effect, Scenarios 2 and 4 show a clear upward trend for per capita GDP, and the scenarios in which TFP contribution is affected by other factors show a decline or a limited growth in the long term. The simulation clearly shows that, although the aging process will reduce the long-term economic growth trend, a sustained improvement in the endowment of human capital through a higher societal education level and a focus on promoting innovation and technological change to promote TFP growth are two critical objectives where public policy should focus in the coming decades.

Uruguay's recent experience in this area has been very positive, with an estimated contribution of TFP to GDP growth reaching about 2.5 percentage points in recent years. Almost 50 percent of Uruguayan economic growth during the last decade is explained by this mechanism, and one of the principal challenges

Figure 1.18 GDP per Capita by Simulation Scenario, 2015–2100

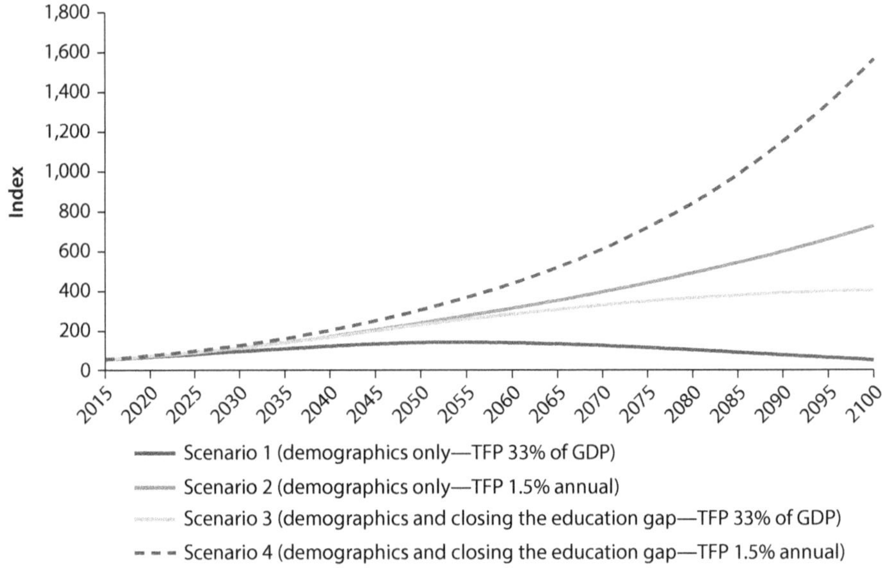

Source: Chapter 9.
Note: Index base 2015 = 100. TFP = total factor productivity.

for society will be to maintain it near current levels in order to guarantee a sustained economic growth path, even in the context of demographic aging.

In this context, the medium-term challenge consists of creating the necessary conditions to incentivize higher investment in human capital as well as research and development, which would allow the economy to constantly improve the organization of the factors of production. In fact, technological innovation, through the creation of mechanized production processes and knowledge, is generally considered an additional factor of production. The progress made in this direction does not just entail the creation of genuinely new knowledge, but also allows for the adoption and adaptation of technological changes created in developed countries. In effect, during the first stage of the process of strengthening the innovation system, activities stand out that are associated with imitative innovation and reverse engineering of inventions created in other countries. This is the case of the Republic of Korea, which began by adapting foreign technologies. To achieve this, the productive sector, with government support, needs to undertake more intensive investment in the development of local technological capacities and to adopt more technologies through license acquisition and transfer agreements for know-how with multinational firms located in the country.

The effective development of these activities depends on the availability of key complementary resources, such as human capital and institutions, and it is therefore necessary to invest locally in learning and innovation, both through the formal education system as well as through continuing education programs.

Conclusions and Policy Challenges

The analysis of the recent demographic situation and expectations for the coming decades in Uruguay clearly demonstrates the effect of the demographic transition that began during the last century and continues today: sustained population aging, with a growing proportion of elderly adults, and a trend toward stabilization and a slow decline in the total population.

These changes are clearly positive as they are the result of two phenomena that show the progress in the population's social and material living conditions: the fall in the levels of mortality—the product of improvements in health care—and in fertility levels, the result of the progressive integration of women into the labor market on increasingly equal terms and the ability for families to effectively control fertility. Nonetheless, these same phenomena have significant impacts on various public policies that may require that the phenomena be revised, as well as on macroeconomic trends that may require the development of alternative growth strategies.

The expected demographic changes will certainly generate additional fiscal pressures in areas like health care and social protection at levels that, as discussed in the pertinent chapters, should be sustainable if they are properly managed. And in the education sector the impact will be unique: the decrease in the population of school-age children and youth (which has been occurring for the last 10 years) will reduce demand for fiscal resources. This means that part of these resources could be directed toward improving the quality of the education system and increasing the accumulation of human capital among new generations or toward financing other priority areas.

In any case, the main challenge for Uruguay in the next few decades will be to sustain economic growth in the context of a diminishing working-age population. This could be partially offset by the expansion of women's economic participation, a process that began several decades ago, as well as a gradual postponement of retirement among older adults (which is also naturally occurring). However, it appears essential to ensure that those that are economically active also maintain a significant pace of growth in their productivity. This will be achieved only through sustained growth of the capital per worker ratio (which in turn requires sustained levels of savings and investment) and the incorporation of innovations and technological developments that facilitate increased production of goods and services for the entire population.

The analysis of the impact of the demographic transition on social expenditure and economic growth should consider an important link between these two dimensions: tax collection. Government revenues are not exempt from the effects of population aging. The current tax structure includes some progressive direct taxes. In a context of economic growth, these taxes would result in increased revenues, with no need for major reforms. Indeed, "progressive" taxes on personal income and social security should raise general revenues as the economy grows. This element is particularly relevant in the analysis, as it could help mitigate some of the pressure on public finances caused by the demographic transition.

Structure of the Book

In the rest of the book, chapter 2 describes Uruguay's long-term demographic context, showing the historical trends and projections of its evolution. Chapter 3 details estimates of the National Transfer Accounts and their application to the Uruguayan case to estimate consumption profiles, labor income, and public transfers by age. Additionally, it presents the simple projections for social sector expenditure, assuming just the effects of demographic changes.

Chapters 4, 5, and 6 describe the recent evolution of social policies in Uruguay related to the social protection, health care, and education systems, respectively. These chapters discuss the probable implications of current policies in a context of demographic transition, proposing alternative scenarios that would allow for the mitigation of the adverse effects and the exploitation of the opportunities offered by the demographic transition.

Chapter 7 analyzes labor market prospects amid population aging, emphasizing two key variables: the participation rate and labor productivity. Chapter 8 briefly describes key indicators of the Uruguayan demographic transition in an international context. Chapter 9 analyzes the potential macroeconomic implications. And chapter 10 briefly discusses the sources of economic growth in the context of aging.

Notes

1. This scenario assumes no migratory movements. Although some migrations should occur in coming decades, it is relevant to note that the migration balances of the last decade have been positive, but at very low levels in a context of economic growth, so it is difficult to foresee a situation where there is a significant migration surplus for extended periods.
2. At the end of this simulation, it was assumed that per capita consumption by age in health care and education would remain fixed over time, and the value of transfers would adjust as the pension system introduced in 1996 matured and a growing population share would begin to receive pension benefits from the funded scheme.
3. The figures presented here for the aggregate values could overestimate the growth trends because they consider spending and transfers together. In effect, at least a portion of private expenditure on health care and education could be financed with resources received by households as public or private social protection, meaning that some amounts could be double counted.
4. The exercise is presented in detail in chapter 9 of this book.

Reference

United Nations. 2014. *World Population Prospects: The 2012 Revision*. New York: United Nations.

CHAPTER 2

Current and Future Uruguayan Demographics

Juan José Calvo[1]

Introduction

Uruguay is distinguished from most Latin American and Caribbean countries for the early beginning of its first demographic transition, during the first decades of the 20th century, putting the country in a very advanced stage of this process. Its rate of population growth slowed prematurely and its age structure grew older as a result, making for slight population growth and eventual stabilization of gross birth and death rates to relatively low levels during the last few decades.

Net international migration into Uruguay has been slightly positive after nearly half a century in negative territory, contributing to slowing population growth rate and accentuating population aging. And a second demographic transition has been under way since the mid-1980s, featuring falling fertility—to below the population replacement rate—a strong increase in the divorce rate, and the occurrence of most births outside of marriage. A growing proportion of single-person households and more single-parent, extended, and mixed families are also issues. And rapid urbanization and significant concentration of the population in the coastal regions, especially in metropolitan Montevideo, also characterize the country demographics and round out the demographic changes (Calvo and Pardo 2014).

This chapter analyzes Uruguay's current and future demographics, emphasizing the evolution of the population's age structure (particularly the aging process) and the characteristics of past and projected demographic changes (birth rate, mortality, and migration). It does all of this within the framework of the country's demographic transition.

The chapter also analyzes how the transition in age structure changes demographic dependency ratios and looks at some of the consequences and challenges this entails, particularly for the labor market and the education, health care, and social security systems. In doing so, we primarily use existing exercises based on estimates and projections of the population by age and gender: official estimates produced by the National Institute of Statistics (Instituto Nacional de Estadística; INE); estimates from specialized international organizations—in particular those of the Population Division of the Latin American and Caribbean Demographic Center at the Economic Commission for Latin America and the Caribbean (ECLAC) and from the Department of Economic and Social Affairs at the United Nations—and alternative forecasts from the Population Program at the University of the Republic (see box 2.1).

Demographic projections all concur that in the coming decades growth will remain slow—a product of low birth and mortality rates and a pace mainly affected by possible changes in international migration. In all scenarios forecast in these projections, aging of the population will continue to deepen (and in all projections, variations are the product of different assumptions about the evolution of birth, mortality, and international migration rates).

Box 2.1 Alternative Demographic Forecasts

What would happen if we were to consider bolder assumptions to forecast population changes in Uruguay?

This question is the basis of an exercise by the Population Program at the School of Social Sciences at the University of the Republic (Calvo and Pellegrino 2011), carried out in the context of a wider debate about the country's development, in which some politicians suggested that a significant population increase was necessary to achieve conditions that would trigger specific productive processes. Expressions like "a Uruguay of 10 million people" and similar phrases insisting that population increase is necessary for development have recently joined a chorus with a long history in a country that has always had a small population.

However, performing alternative forecasts that consider bolder assumptions about reproductive and migratory behaviors provides results in stark contrast with these types of political expressions. Calvo and Pellegrino (2011) forecast the population through 2050, using three scenarios (minimum, trend, and maximum) for fertility and international migration behaviors. Even assuming very optimistic hypotheses for the rebound in fertility and numbers of immigrants, the Uruguayan population would barely surpass the threshold of 4 million inhabitants by 2050, as can be seen in figure B2.1.1.

The only scenario in which the Uruguayan population barely surpasses 4 million assumes, on the one hand, an increase in fertility until returning to the replacement rate (equal to a total fertility rate of 2.1 children per woman) and positive net migration stable around 5,000 people a year from 2015 onward. In contrast, assuming that the downward trend in fertility reaches the threshold generally known as "very low fertility" (equal to 1.5 children per woman) would happen in combination with a return to the pattern of negative net migration, this would accelerate the decrease in the population. In the exercise undertaken, this would occur at the end of the third decade of this century. In summary, with a fixed time horizon of 2050, these forecasts indicate that the Uruguayan population could number somewhere between 3.4 million and 4.1 million people, depending on the assumptions made.

box continues next page

Box 2.1 Alternative Demographic Forecasts *(continued)*

Figure B2.1.1 Evolution of the Population in Three Alternative Demographic Scenarios, 1996–2050

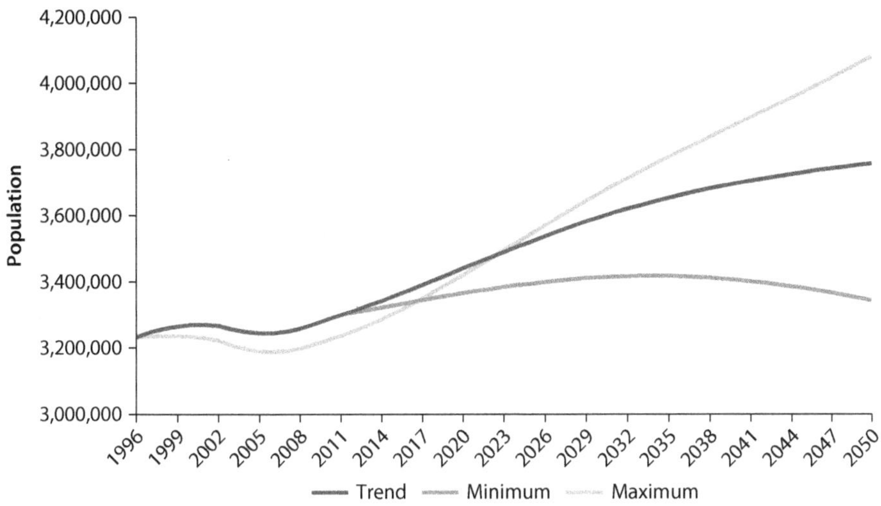

Source: Calvo and Pellegrino 2011.

The population age structures in the different scenarios take very distinct forms, but in all cases the aging trend does not stop, although the intensity is very different in each scenario. In the maximum scenario, all the generations make up a similar proportion of the population, and in the minimum scenario, the fall in fertility to very low rates means that each generation would be smaller than the one which preceded it. In the coming decades, the population of older adults will grow at a much faster pace than the average of the rest of the age groups. By 2030, Uruguay will have a population of 624,000 people aged 65 and older, of which 162,000 will be over 80. And in 2050 these groups will reach 743,000 and 250,000 people, respectively. The population over age 80 will grow at a rate never previously seen. Even though the value of the dependency ratio does not vary substantially in these scenarios (60.7 in the maximum scenario, 58.9 in the minimum), its composition reveals important differences in the relative weight of children and the elderly in the overall population.

Demographics: Past and Present

A Brief History of the Country's Population

Pellegrino (2010) regarded the 19th century (especially its second half) as the period with the fastest population growth, attributing it to European, regional, and African slave immigration. Through almost all of that century, the country was in a pretransition phase, with elevated mortality and birth rates, the latter stimulated by immigrant populations largely of reproductive age.

Figure 2.1 Total Estimated Population, Selected Years

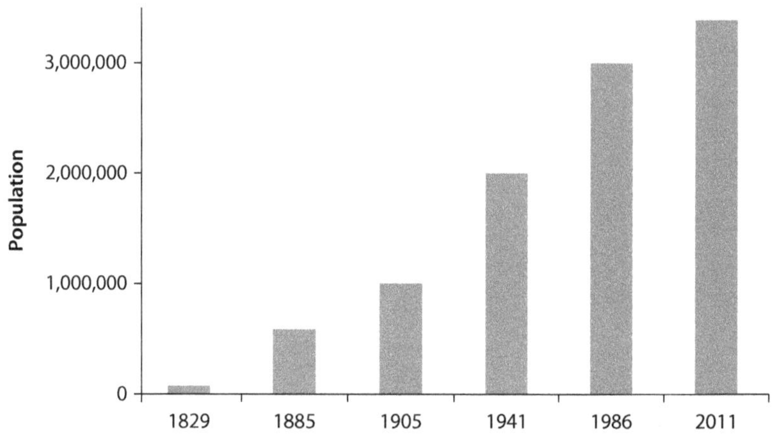

Sources: Based on the series created by Pellegrino 2010 and the final results of the 2011 National Institute of Statistics (Instituto Nacional de Estadística) population census.

In addition to the picture presented in figure 2.1, the first census of the 20th century, in 1908, showed 1,042,686 people. Subsequent censuses recorded a population of 2.5 million in 1963, 2.8 million in 1975, 2.9 million in 1986, and 3.2 million people in 1996. The first census of the 21st century, by INE in 2011, counted 3.3 million people (or about 3.4 million when allowing for undercounting).

During the 20th century, population growth was below the very high rates of the intermediate stages of the demographic transition in the rest of Latin America and the Caribbean. As noted, Uruguay reached the advanced stage of this transition prematurely, a few years later than Spain and Italy reached it, the countries of origin for a significant proportion of immigrants flooding in at the end of the 19th century and the first years of the 20th century. Around 1950, Uruguay's gross birth and mortality rates had fallen significantly and stabilized as a result demographic growth.

The effect of this effect on age structure shaped a population pyramid that was already beginning to show signs of aging (figure 2.2, panels a and b). The decline in the birth rate precipitated the passage from a "very young" population pyramid in 1908 to a clearly older one by 1950. At the base of the pyramids, where the weight of the generations of children and youth rests, the pyramid lost its triangular shape (characteristic of a very young structure) and the middle-age range began to become more significant. At the top of the pyramid, one can already visualize around the middle of the last century the significant number of people aged 65 and older. In addition to slowing population growth, this change in structure is the principal consequence of the demographic transition taking place.

The decline in birth and mortality rates deepened in the following decades. International immigration, a key factor in explaining strong population growth until the early decades of the 20th century, diminished and the economic

Figure 2.2 Uruguay's Population Pyramid, 1908 and 1950

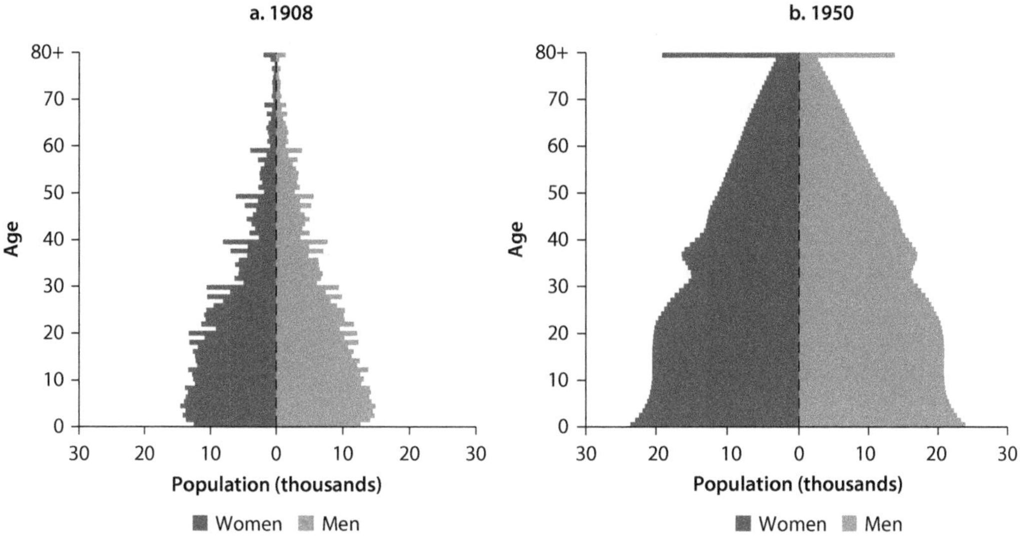

Sources: Panel a: elaboration based on the General Directorate of Statistics 1911; panel b: elaboration based on United Nations 2014.

stagnation and decline that the country began to suffer during the 1960s—with the subsequent political crisis that saw the installation of a military dictatorship at the beginning of the 1970s through the mid-1980s—promoted unprecedentedly large international emigration. With the return to democracy, the country continued, with ups and downs, to send away more migrants than it received until the end of the first decade of the 21st century. The demographic consequences of all of these trends were, primarily, a low growth rate and significant maturing of the age structure (Calvo 2012; Calvo and Pardo 2014). Throughout this period, fertility fell, reaching below the replacement rate in 2004, although still significantly above what would constitute very low fertility (with a rebound beginning in 2012).[2]

A Cursory Description of Uruguay's Current Population

At just 3.4 million people, Uruguay's current population is small, and the country's advanced demographic transition includes a mature age structure (19 percent of the population was 60 years or older in 2015),[3] a low population growth rate, fertility below the replacement rate, and an overwhelmingly urban spatial distribution of the population (95 percent) concentrated significantly in the coastal strip and in the capital and surrounding metropolitan area (Calvo and Pardo 2014). After nearly half a century of negative net international migration, it has recently returned to slightly positive levels.[4]

Beginning in the second half of the 20th century, the natural increase in the population (the difference between births and deaths) has remained low and relatively constant, leaving international migration as the principal factor explaining fluctuations in population growth. As per the 2011 census, the population had grown at an annual rate of 1.9 per 1,000 since the census of 2004 (table 2.1).

Table 2.1 Annual Exponential Rates of Total Population Growth, Selected Intercensal Periods

Intercensal period	*Annual growth (per 1,000 inhabitants)*
1963–1975	6.2
1975–1985	3.6
1985–1996	6.4
1996–2004	3.2
2004–2011	1.9

Source: Calvo and Pardo 2014.

Figure 2.3 Births, Deaths, Natural Increase, and Total Fertility, 2000–12

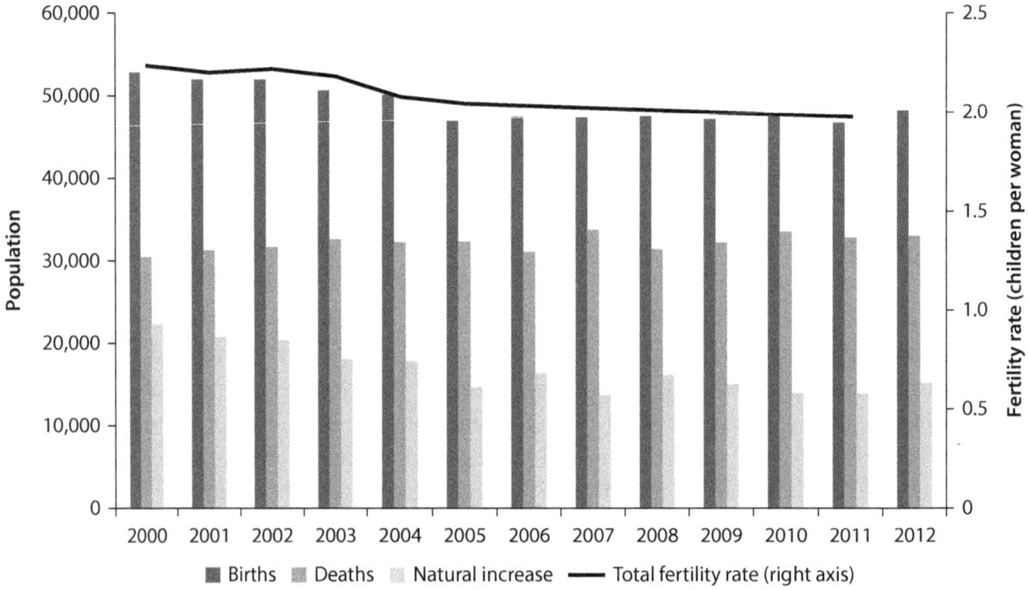

Source: Based on data published by the National Institute of Statistics, available at http://www.ine.gub.uy/socio-demograficos/demograficos2008.asp.
Note: The deaths recorded for 2011 are subject to review and could be modified due to problems found in the records. Data to the latest year with available information.

Figure 2.3 presents the quantity of births, deaths, and the total fertility rate from 2000 to 2012. The number of births fell from almost 52,800 in 2000 to 46,700 in 2011 (increasing in 2012—the most recent official data—to 48,200); this follows the trend over the past several decades, with isolated increases during some years. During the first decade of this century, deaths per year increased from approximately 30,500 to 33,000 in 2012; as a result, the natural increase of the population declined from 22,300 people in 2000 to 15,200 in 2012.

The increase in life expectancy and the effects of international emigration, which was most intense from the mid-1960s through the end of the first decade of the 2000s, have also contributed to Uruguay's aging trend.

According to the 2011 census, children (from birth to 14 years old) comprise 22 percent of the total population. The middle group in the population pyramid, the 15- to 64-year-olds, are active in the labor market and represent 64 percent. This group can be subdivided into youth and young adults (from 15 to 29 years old, 22 percent of the total population) and adults from 30 to 64 years old (42 percent). Older adults (aged 65 and older) are already 14 percent of the population. Even though up to age 21 there are more men, women account for 52 percent of the population, which is the result of the effect of greater mortality among men (among all age groups). Indeed, according to the National Institute of Statistics (2014), male life expectancy at birth was 72.87 years, but 79.95 years for females. The accumulated effect of this excess mortality among males is very evident at advanced ages: the census counted nearly 280,000 women aged 65 and older, compared to around 184,000 men.

Projections under Different Scenarios

The field of population projections poses challenges that on many occasions are insuperable for specialists: even though the methodologies utilized can be very sophisticated, the main challenge is in reasonably determining future scenarios (social, economic, cultural) that determine the elements of demographic change. The greater the time from the last verified data (usually, the population census), the greater the uncertainty and the probability that an estimate will differ from reality. Another important factor is size of the population to be forecast; the smaller it is, the greater the probability that local or singular events will affect the forecast. Uruguay's recent official exercise in demographic projections was carried out in 2014 by the governing organization of the national statistical system, the National Institute of Statistics. Its forecasts, based on their methodological rigor and the newness of the information from which they were created—a recently performed census, reconciliation with vital statistics, consideration of the recent evolution of net migration—are the best suited for making projections. However, for this book, unfortunately their horizon extends to only 2050, which forces us to utilize another set of estimates, created by the Population Division of the Department of Economic and Social Affairs of the United Nations, which extend until 2100. In the comparison between both exercises, the principal difference is in methodology (Uruguay's statistics utilize deterministic methods to project birth rates and fertility, and UN statistics employ probabilistic methods), and, more significantly, in their assumptions about international migration. The national forecasts incorporate recent changes in migration patterns, and the UN numbers predict significant negative net migration over a long period (including even for some previous years that other estimates have shown to have experienced positive net migration). The main consequence for the results is obvious: the UN estimates forecast a smaller population (almost 65,000 fewer people in the 2050 estimate, which is the final year included in the National Institute of Statistics forecast), as well as an older one than in the Uruguayan forecasts.

The United Nations' Population Forecasts to 2100

Given that this work's goal is to analyze some of the economic implications of Uruguay's long-term demographic changes, we have chosen to work mainly using the longer forecasts of the United Nations Population Division.[5]

According to the United Nations, Uruguay's population will peak at 3.64 million people in 2046, beginning to decline that year until it reaches 3.29 million people in 2100 (the same as in 1998) (see figure 2.4). This evolution is explained mainly by low fertility rates and, secondarily, by the forecast behavior of net migration. Nonetheless, changes in total population mask diverse situations among different age groups; the population of children (which reached an historical high in 1999, at almost 816,000) will drop consistently to 493,000 by 2100 (40 percent fewer children than in 1999). And this fall begins 47 years before the total population begins to decline.

In contrast, the number of older adults (individuals aged 65 and older) will increase continuously throughout the entire period and reach more than 976,000 by the beginning of the 22nd century. Within two decades, in the year 2035, the number of children will equal the number of older adults, and from then on the number of elderly will exceed the number of children. The 15–64 age group, which contains the largest share of the economically active population, will increase from 2.18 million in 2013 to reach 2.29 million in 2036, and then will begin to decline until reaching 1.82 million at the end of the century. Therefore, by the middle of the third decade of this century, the population will reach a significant inflection point in the relative weights of the various age groups.

Figure 2.4 Evolution of the Total Population and Major Age Groups, 1950–2100

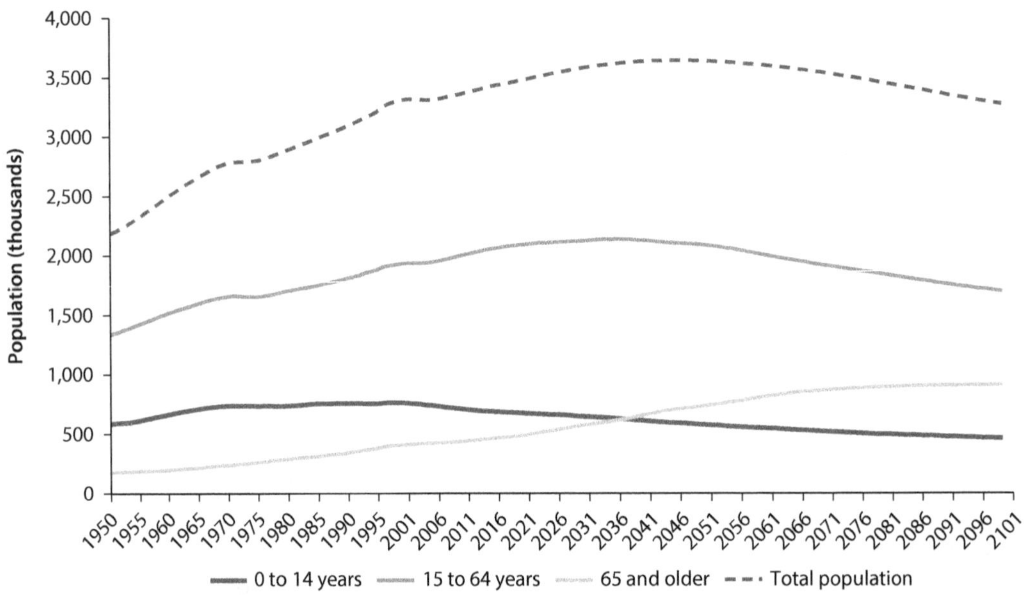

Source: Elaboration based on United Nations 2014.

A more disaggregated analysis utilizing the population pyramids from three years (2000, 2050, and 2100) reveals this profound transformation. The pyramid's base narrows, evening out the relative weight of the different age groups (and as such the pyramid becomes more rectangular) and eventually its shape even partially inverts, becoming wider at the age ranges corresponding to older adults and diminishing the relative weight of the younger age groups (figure 2.5). This effect is a consequence of two factors. First, the prolonged period of low fertility (which narrows the base of the pyramid and produces generations that are the same size instead of larger and larger generations, as was the case prior to the demographic transition). Second, the improvement in mortality evident in increasing life expectancy and over time, raises the pyramid's tip. In the forecasts used, the assumption

Figure 2.5 Population by Age, 2000, 2050, and 2100

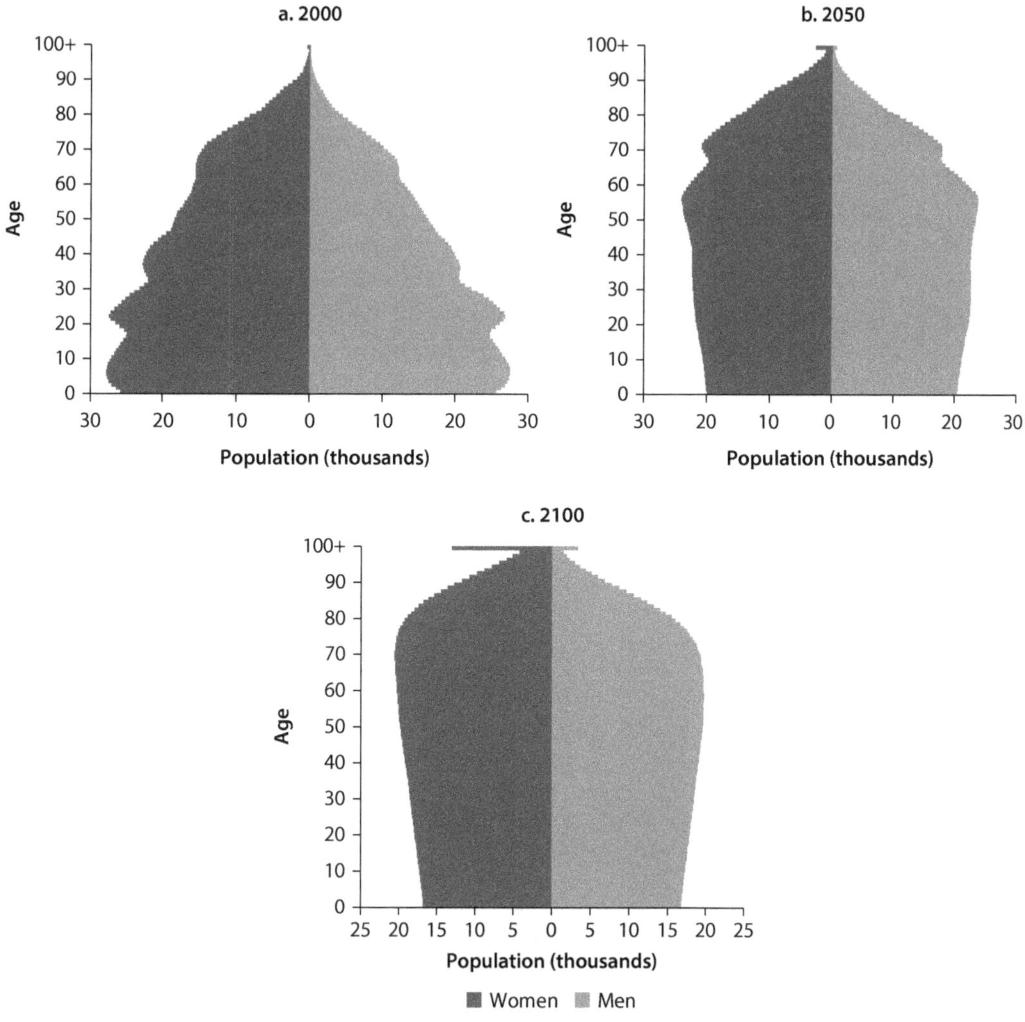

Source: Elaboration based on United Nations 2014.

for migration is that net migration will be negative and volumes will decrease until reaching zero during 2095 to 2100.

Dependency Ratios and the Demographic Dividend

Another manner of analyzing the evolution of the age structure of the population, with an eye on estimating the economic consequences of demographic change, is through the demographic dependency ratios. This method provides a preliminary estimate on the topic; as we will see in later chapters, it is possible to make the analysis more sophisticated through use of other instruments that analyze income and expenditure throughout the life cycle. Nonetheless, as an initial approach, dependency ratios for youth (the ratio of individuals from 0 to 14 years old to those aged 15–64), elderly (the ratio of individuals age 65 and older to those aged 15–64), and the total dependency ratio (the sum of the two previous ratios) provide us with an idea of the potential pressure or load that workers carry to maintain those groups outside and how it could be evolving. This indicator has inherent limitations, including that not all people ages 15–64 are economically active, or employed or, even if they are, may not be employed full-time. Also, not all people included in the dependent age groups are actually dependent. Moreover, one can question whether the age limits that define these groups will remain fixed over time; it is clear that concepts such as childhood, youth, adulthood, and old age have acquired different meanings over time. Individuals now reach old age in better health and with greater abilities than they did in the past (and, presumably, their abilities will continue to improve and will be present at even older ages in the future). Figure 2.6 illustrates the evolution of life expectancy at age 65 (that is, the average number of additional years that an individual who reaches age 65 can expect to live). Although for men of 65, life expectancy was 12.3 years in 1950, they are expected to live 22.3 years past 65 in 2100

Figure 2.6 Life Expectancy at Age 65, by Gender, 1950–2100

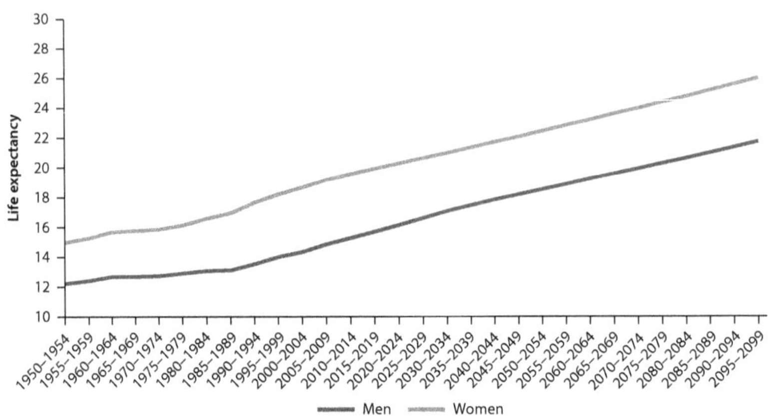

Source: Elaboration based on United Nations 2014.

(gaining 10 more years of life during the 150 years covered in the forecast analysis. Among women, life expectancy at age 65 will increase from 15.2 to 26.8 years.

However, as a general approach to the topic, the dependency ratio allows one to visualize the demographic change in a simple way and reach conclusions about how priorities on several issues intrinsic to public policy could change. Figure 2.7 presents changes in dependency ratio indicators over 150 years.

Several points stand out when considering the evolution of these indicators over time. First, the number of potential dependents relative to potentially active workers oscillates between 57 and 60 per 100 potential workers for nearly a century, from 1950 to 2041, and subsequently begins to grow significantly until the beginning of the 22nd century, the end of the forecast period.

Second, a concavity in the curve is apparent as the result of a temporary decrease that begins around 2000 and continues for 20 years, placing the minimum of the dataset (55.27) in 2019, the moment in which the curve begins to rise again.

Third, it is even more interesting to analyze the evolution of the two component parts of the total dependency ratio. On the one hand, the child dependency ratio remains relatively stable (on average 43 children for every 100 potential workers) from 1950 until the mid-1980s, when a slight decline begins and steepens until it stabilizes around the middle of the 21st century at 27 children per 100 potential workers. On the other, the elderly dependency ratio is stable for a brief period until the mid-1960s (13 older adults for every 100 working-age adults)

Figure 2.7 Dependency Ratio among Children, the Elderly, and in Total, 1950–2100

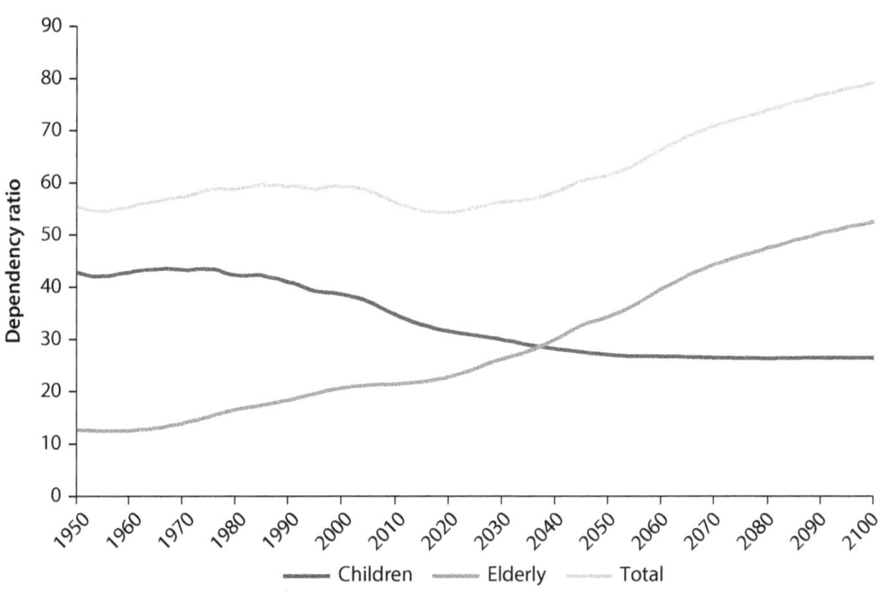

Source: Elaboration based on United Nations 2014.
Note: For every 100 individuals in the 15–64 age group.

and then begins a climb that will not stop until the end of the dataset, reaching a maximum in 2100, when the indicator falls just short of 54 (double the child dependency ratio at that point). In 2037, the elderly dependency ratio passes a significant threshold, when for the first time it is equal to and then surpasses the child dependency ratio, with increasing distance separating the two. Once the child dependency ratio stabilizes, the elderly and total dependency ratio curves become practically parallel.

Are the demographic changes in Uruguay especially unique? The answer is "no," although the specific moments in time, pace, and intensity of the process are certainly products of the country's economic, social, political, and cultural contexts. However, all populations experience a period in which the proportion of working-age adults increases, and this occurs during the second and third stages of the demographic transition (ECLAC 2014). These years are favorable for economic growth because the potential labor force grows more quickly than the dependent population (Bloom, Canning, and Sevilla 2003; Wong and Carvalho 2006).

This situation belongs to the time characterized as the "demographic window of opportunity" or the "demographic dividend" and is primarily the result of declining fertility, which leads to a slowing of demographic growth and, particularly, of the growth rate of the population of children, which descends more rapidly than that of the elderly population, maximizing the growth of the middle group. As the process of decreasing fertility and increasing life expectancy progresses, the growth rate of the elderly population surpasses the shrinkage of the child population and the total dependency ratio again begins to worsen, closing the demographic window of opportunity. Taking advantage of the potential benefits of this period depends in large part on a society's ability to transform the momentary respite in pressure on public coffers and create the conditions for sustainability once population aging begins to exert pressure on spending. This may manifest through increased investment in the younger generations (which become smaller as fertility decreases), especially in education and health care, to improve their future abilities and help tackle some of the challenges that aging will present. Another way of taking advantage of the demographic dividend is to strengthen programs that fight poverty (for example, direct cash transfer programs for poor individuals and households).

Conclusions

In demographic terms, Uruguay is a small, slow-growth country that is experiencing the posttransitional period of the first demographic transition and is quickly progressing through its second demographic transition. The country faces both opportunities and challenges as a result.

Various population forecasts show that the country is headed for a century of increased aging. Regardless of the worry that this situation could create, the aging of the population should be considered good news; it reflects, above all else, the primary demographic impact of improvement of Uruguayan well-being (including better nutrition, education, shelter, dwellings, and health care services, among others) and, more generally, the effective exercise of human rights (particularly those related to health care and sexual and reproductive rights).

The decline in fertility and, to a lesser extent, the increase in life expectancy explain the aging trend. The former leads to a decline in births that precedes the arrival of large contingents of older adults to the population mix. During this time, a window of opportunity opens (the demographic dividend) as demographic dependency ratios turn favorable. This period of time must be taken advantage of with investment in better economic conditions before that window shuts. That is, when dependency ratios return to their upward trend, once aging at the tip of the pyramid outweighs the effect of the decline in the number of children. Improving education for children, adolescents, and youth is one way to do this.

Financial pressures on retirement and pension systems stand out as one of numerous consequences of population aging. So do the increasing costs of national health care systems as the population ages and the need to care for the rising number of elderly in the context of changing family structures and arrangements, gender roles, and labor market demands.

The following chapters of this book will examine some of these aspects in more detail, emphasizing the opportunities and challenges to come in the context of Uruguay's new demographic era and its maturing economy.

Notes

1. Juan José Calvo, University of the Republic. Correspondence to calvo.juanjo@gmail.com.
2. Fertility is at a replacement level when the net reproduction rate reaches a value of 1, approximately equivalent to a value of 2.1 in the total fertility rate. Below this, women of reproductive age are not replaced by future women. When the total fertility rate reaches 1.5, it is standard to refer to "very low fertility."
3. Author's calculation based on projections from the Population Division of the United Nations in *World Population Prospects: The 2012 Revision.*
4. However, the population projections created by the Population Division of the Department of Economic and Social Affairs of the United Nations that are utilized in this chapter and in the rest of the book estimate that net migration is currently negative because the assumptions used for these projections have not been updated with the latest available migration data.
5. As has been mentioned, the principal difference (which is accentuated over time) is that the estimated population is smaller and older than in government forecasts.

References

Bloom, D., D. Canning, and J. Sevilla. 2003. *The Demographic Dividend: A New Perspective on the Economic Consequences of Population Change.* Santa Monica, CA: RAND Population Matters Program, MR-1274.

Calvo, J. 2012. "El Siglo del Envejecimiento Demográfico." Tricentenario: 43–48, MEC, Montevideo.

Calvo, J., and I. Pardo. 2014. "Cuántos y Cómo Somos." Colección Nuestro Tiempo, IMPO Montevideo.

Calvo, J., and A. Pellegrino. 2011. "Tres Posibles Futuros de la Población Uruguaya: Un Ensayo Demográfico." In *La Aventura Uruguaya: El País y el Mundo*, edited by G. Caetano and R. Arocena, 181–204. Montevideo: Editorial Sudamericana.

ECLAC (Economic Commission for Latin America and the Caribbean). 2014. *La Nueva Era Demográfica en América Latina y el Caribe: La Hora de la Igualdad de Acuerdo al Reloj Poblacional*. ECLAC, Santiago de Chile.

General Directorate of Statistics (Dirección General de Estadística). 1911. *Anuario Estadístico de 1908*. Dirección General de Estadística, Montevideo.

National Institute of Statistics (Instituto Nacional de Estadística; INE). 2014. *Estimaciones y Proyecciones de la Población de Uruguay: Metodología y Resultados. Revisión 2013*, INE, Montevideo.

Pellegrino, A. 2010. *La Población en Uruguay: Breve Caracterización Demográfica*. United Nations Population Fund, Montevideo.

United Nations. 2014. *World Population Prospects: The 2012 Revision*. New York: United Nations.

Wong, L., and J. Carvalho. 2006. "Age-Structural Transition in Brazil: Demographic Bonuses and Emerging Challenges." In *Age-Structured Transitions: Challenges for Development*, edited by I. Pool and L. Wong. Paris: Committee for International Cooperation in National Research Demography (CICRED).

CHAPTER 3

National Transfer Accounts

Marisa Bucheli and Sara Troiano[1]

Introduction

Uruguay's demographic transition, because it changes individual economic behaviors and results in each age group, carries important economic implications. Broadly speaking, individuals go through three stages in life. The first is childhood and adolescence, when individuals do not yet generate their own resources and are sustained by the rest of society. A second period begins when the individual enters the labor market earning an income that helps sustain the individual and others, including children and adolescents. The third stage begins at retirement when labor income is lost and individuals begin relying on savings and, once again, transfers from the rest of society.

This description highlights the importance to a society of mechanisms that ensure that the surpluses created by second-stage individuals flow to people in the first and third stages. These mechanisms may be private (for example, when parents provide food to their children) or public (government collecting taxes to provide services and benefits). Ensuring these mechanisms are adequate creates two demographic challenges.

In one, falling birth and mortality rates progressively age the population, and, in its most advanced stage of the demographic transition, reduce the proportion of the population that generates resources. This progressively increases pressure on second-stage individuals to sustain the entire population. In other words, as chapter 2 explains, this change affects the dependency ratio, and as a result, the economic support ratio (between resources created and resources consumed).

Aging also increases the ratio of elderly individuals to children. The mechanisms that ensure transfers to children are distinct from those to the elderly. It is sufficient to observe that children live with adults, forming households which have to make various decisions, including those surrounding how to support each member. Meanwhile, group living situations are less common among individuals in the second and third stages, requiring coordination among households to make transfers among them. When the ratio increases it can mean that the well-oiled mechanisms used to carry out transfers in a society, accustomed to a certain balance between the populations of the elderly and children, may cease to function.

Specifically, public institutions tend to need more time to design, agree upon, and implement the necessary reforms. As a result, the eventual lack of resources to ensure support through the stages of the life cycle, as well as greater intergenerational equity, generally manifests itself in public transfer mechanisms rather than in private ones.

This chapter is interested in three aspects of this situation. It describes the economic life cycle in Uruguay and examines the role of public transfers, especially social spending, as necessary flows to ensure support in the first and last stages of the life cycle. And it analyzes the effect of demographic change on the economic support ratio, on public accounts, and, especially, on public social spending.

The dataset was prepared following the estimation methodology of the National Transfer Accounts System (known as the NTA System) presented in box 3.1. These accounts offer information on income, consumption, and, more generally, economic flows by age, allowing us to analyze ratios between age groups.

Box 3.1 The National Transfer Accounts System Relevance to Public Policy in Uruguay

The National Transfer Accounts (NTA) System was developed as part of an international project started in 2000 by Ronald Lee (University of California, Berkeley) and Andrew Mason (University of Hawaii) to compile information about intergenerational transfers in different countries. Specifically, the NTA System allows disaggregation of its principal components (and subcomponents) by age to understand how families, the market, and the government interact to sustain individuals throughout the life cycle.

Among other applications, the system has been identified as a fundamental source of information in the design of public policies, given that these have distinct impacts (explicit or implicit) on different age groups. For example, as Miller and Castanheira (2013) and Gragnolati and Troiano (2014) point out, public sector expenditure on primary education is mostly concentrated on ages 3–17, with less impact on individuals at other stages of the life cycle. The system accounts for this phenomenon, assigning the expenditure (or benefit) of education to the individuals that truly receive it. Thus, the NTA age profile captures both educational enrollment (which is greater among the 3–17 age group) as well as the benefit received by each student (thereby capturing the differences in the education subsystems).

NTA estimates for Uruguay exist for 1994 and 2006, while the estimates in this chapter refer to 2013, and are constructed based on two datasets. For each category macro-controls are calculated, which consist of the aggregate values of the various components and subcomponents (such as public education consumption, family allowances, labor income) which ensure consistency with the national accounts and official figures published by the relevant institutions. In Uruguay's case, the macro-control values mainly come from the national accounts created by the Central Bank of Uruguay (2013), the Budget Performance information as reported by the General Accounting Office of the Nation (2013), and information from the Social Security Bank (2013). To perform the distribution of the macro-controls by age group,

box continues next page

Box 3.1 The National Transfer Accounts System Relevance to Public Policy in Uruguay *(continued)*

we primarily utilized information from the Continuous Household Survey (National Institute of Statistics 2013) and the Household Income and Expenditure Survey (National Institute of Statistics 2006). Finally, the NTA estimates are consistent with the 2013 population age group estimate carried out by the United Nations (2014).

In general terms, the method for estimating a component follows three steps. First, the average level of consumption or income obtained from the microdata (Continuous Household Survey or the Household Income and Expenditure Survey, depending on the situation) is attributed to each age group (single age groups). Second, a smoothing procedure is performed for each age group for the attributed levels. Third, the aggregate value by age group is calculated, taking into account the total population for each age group, and the data is then rescaled such that the aggregate value coincides with the macro-control. Throughout the chapter, more information is provided regarding the estimation of specific categories.

The Economic Life Cycle

Income and Consumption

In a calendar year, income generation relies on individuals in the middle-age groups. To measure this pattern, figure 3.1 presents average labor income by age in 2013 relative to average labor income for the 30–49 age group. Labor income includes the taxes and contributions paid by workers and employers; in other words, it includes the value of the entire cost of labor (see box 3.2). To calculate the average for each age group, one must account for the entire population; individuals who do not work and do not generate income are calculated as zero income. This explains why the curve has a bell shape. The early zero-income years correspond to the economically inactive years when individuals are children. During adolescence and youth, average labor income grows with age for two reasons: the number of people entering the labor market increases and remuneration per employed person grows. The maximum value is achieved around age 50. From that point on average income falls, mostly as an effect of retirement until it is once again nearly zero at more advanced ages. The general shape is similar to that from 2006, although the maximum point is now at a slightly older age (Bucheli and González 2011). International evidence uncovers similar profiles in all countries, while less developed countries exhibit higher levels of income generation at the early and advanced ends of the age spectrum (Mason and Lee 2011).

Consumption, in contrast, occurs throughout the life cycle, which is reflected in the flatter age group profiles. In the Uruguayan case, the data from 2013 (the estimation methodology is presented in box 3.2) show that consumption increases continuously with age (figure 3.1). The international evidence indicates that in all countries consumption is lower during childhood than during old age, although in general the difference is less significant in developed countries (Tung 2011). In any case, not all countries show sustained growth at older ages, including Uruguay.

Figure 3.1 Per Capita Income and Consumption by Age, 2013
percent of average labor income for ages 30–49

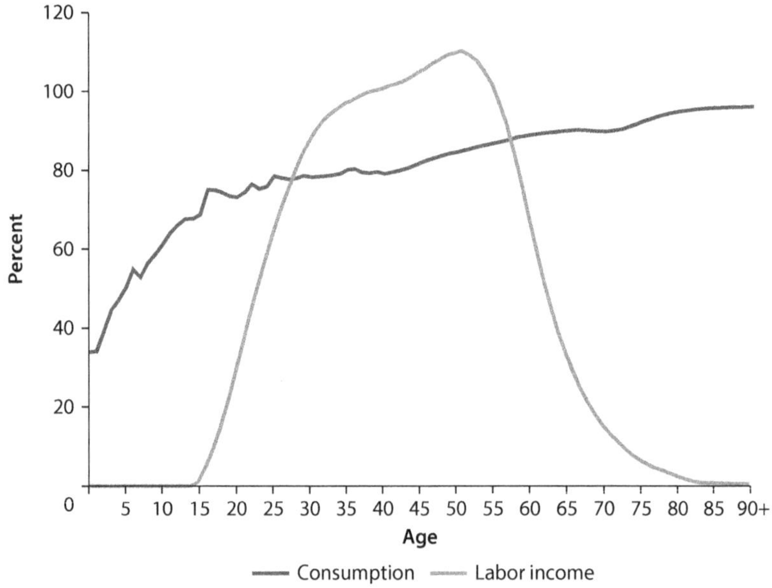

Sources: Elaboration based on National Institute of Statistics 2006 and 2013; Central Bank of Uruguay 2013; and Burdin, Esponda, and Vigorito 2014.

Box 3.2 Estimating Consumption and Labor Income by Age

The macro-controls related to consumption are based on the National Accounts (Central Bank of Uruguay 2013). Public consumption includes production of services from the central and departmental governments, as well as compulsory social security mechanisms (Social Security Bank and other parastatal funds). It does not include investment expenditure, transfers, or market production. To estimate the National Transfer Accounts (NTA) by age, we calculated three components separately: education, health care, and other (remainder). This required estimation of macro-controls for each component.

The consumption macro-control for public education was estimated based on the budget exercise information from the General Accounting Office of the Nation (2013), and considered each of the education subsystems separately. Specifically, it includes all of the services under the control of the National Administration of Public Education, including teacher training, early childhood education managed by the Uruguayan Institute of Children and Adolescents (Child and Family Care Centers Plan), and university education (University of the Republic). To estimate the profile by age group, we estimated per-student expenditure in each subsystem and then assigned those values to each age group based on the attendance statistics obtained from the Continuous Household Survey. In this case, we did not perform any data smoothing to reflect the changes resulting from the different costs at each level of education.

box continues next page

Box 3.2 Estimating Consumption and Labor Income by Age *(continued)*

The consumption macro-control for public health contains three components that we analyzed separately: (a) care services in public establishments (Administration of State Health Services and Police and Military Health Services), (b) mother-child care through the Social Security Bank, and (c) funding provided through the National Health Care Fund (Fondo Nacional de Salud [FONASA]) to the Collective Medical Assistance Institutions, health insurance companies, and private service providers under the auspices of the National Resource Fund. The National Health Council is the source of this information. To estimate the benefit by age group, the equivalent of per-user public expenditure was assigned to each age group using the equivalence scale established implicitly in the FONASA funding scheme (this transfer, known as a "capita," changes according to age and gender). Finally, data smoothing was employed to mitigate spikes in the capitas.

The remainder of public consumption is the difference between the total reported by the national accounts and the estimates established in the processes described in the two previous paragraphs. We assumed that it is distributed equally among the population, so its value by age group is the same for all ages.

To calculate private consumption, we followed the NTA methodology and used figures net of taxes minus grants. The consumption macro-control for education was estimated based on its share of private consumption in 2006, which is the year for which the Household Income and Expenditure Survey is available, corrected to account for changes in the price index and private tuition. The survey was also used to create the profile by age group. For health care, the macro-control was estimated based on Oreggioni and Rivas (2015), which reports household spending on premiums paid to the Collective Medical Assistance Institutions and health insurance companies, co-payments, and direct payments by households for medications and other health care goods and services. The profile is equal to the one showing the funding provided by FONASA, except for direct payments by households, which were estimated based on the profile provided by the Household Income and Expenditure Survey in the "non-sick expenditure" category.

Labor income comprises cash payments, social security benefits, direct taxes paid by workers, and self-employment income. The labor income macro-control is estimated by Burdin, Esponda, and Vigorito (2014) in a work that updated the Income Generation Accounts (the Central Bank of Uruguay stopped publishing this account in 2006). The labor income profiles and their subcomponents are estimated based on the Continuous Household Survey 2013.

To analyze consumption, we obtained information about consumption in education, health care, and other types of consumption, divided into its public and private components. It is necessary to remember that private consumption is the total value of the goods and services purchased by family units, while public consumption reflects the goods and services individuals access through the public sector without having to pay a fee for them.

The consumption profile's upward trend as age increases is the product of the behavior of private consumption. This is clear in figure 3.2, where public and private consumption are presented separately. Moreover, the same figure shows what has been called the "consumption remainder," in other words, consumption

Figure 3.2 Total Public and Private Consumption and the "Consumption Remainder" per Capita by Age, 2013

percent of average labor income for ages 30–49

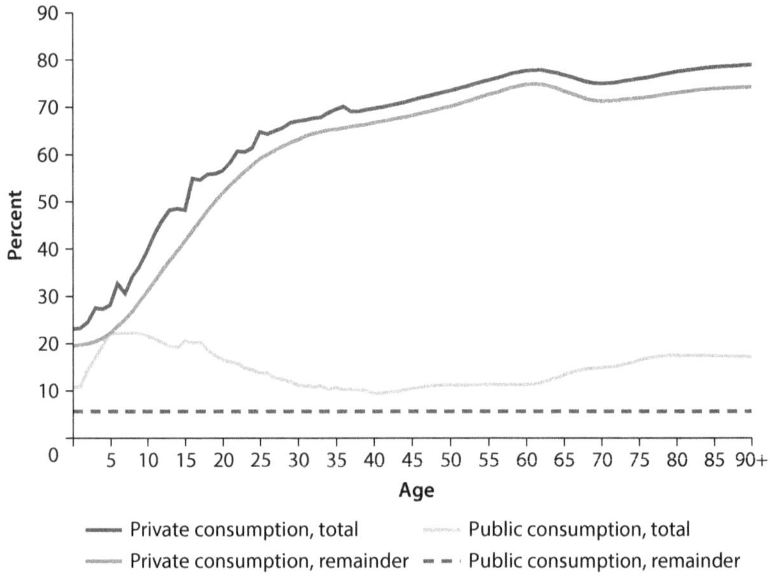

Sources: Elaboration based on National Institute of Statistics 2006 and 2013; Central Bank of Uruguay 2013; and Burdin, Esponda, and Vigorito 2014.

minus health care and education. This allows us to note that the upward trend is particularly the product of the so-called "private consumption remainder," which is the primary component of consumption.

Total public consumption is less than private consumption for all age groups. It is relatively higher during the early years of the life cycle: the public component's proportion is around 40 percent of the total during childhood, but it is notably lower (from 12 percent to 18 percent) at other ages. It falls during middle age and increases again during old age. The significance of public consumption during childhood is primarily explained by education, while the increase in public consumption at advanced ages is due to consumption of health care. Thus, public consumption is redistributed among age groups, with higher spending on children and the elderly than on the working-age population.

Education is one component of human capital investment. In 2013, it represented an estimated 8 percent of total consumption, rising to 20 percent for the 0–29 age group. As an age group that does not generate sufficient income, this means that transfers are crucial for ensuring this investment occurs. A portion of these transfers come through private channels, primarily from other household and family members. These fund private consumption of education, including tuition for private establishments, spending on books and school supplies, payments to private tutors, and so on. Another portion, through public channels funded by taxes, is public consumption of education, which includes current expenditure on public education.

Figure 3.3 shows the age group profiles of public and private consumption of education through age 40. These profiles represent education consumption per person, thus simultaneously reflecting both consumption per student and educational enrollment.[2] Public is always larger than private consumption, and around 65 percent on average for the age groups corresponding to early and primary education. It is lower for ages 13–18, remaining at 58 percent on average, and higher for age groups corresponding to tertiary education, reaching 70 percent for the 19–24 age group. Private consumption is higher for the age groups corresponding to secondary education.

In both 2006 and 2013, Uruguayan society designated 12 percent of labor income to education consumption. This means that the effort measured as a proportion of income was stable. However, a change is observed in the public/private structure: in 2013, 63 percent of consumption in education occurred through public channels, while in 2006, this figure was 47 percent. This change was especially apparent in secondary education, in which private channels were predominant over public channels in 2013. It is important to remember that while public consumption of education is almost totally dedicated to students in the public sector, private consumption of education includes students in both sectors, given that some resources and services (such as notebooks, supplies, and so on) are a family's responsibility regardless of the type of educational establishment.

Health is another important determinant of human capital. Health care consumption is especially intense at advanced ages, however, in contrast with

Figure 3.3 Per Capita Education Consumption by Age, 2013
percent of average labor income for individuals ages 30–49

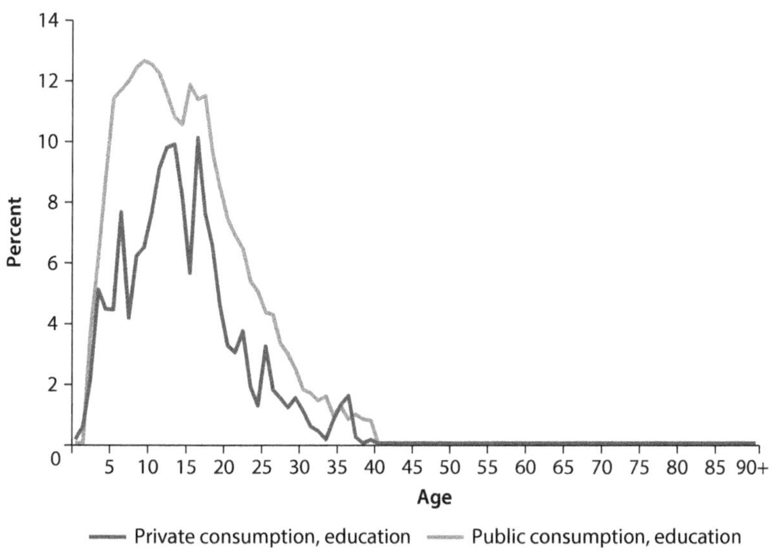

Sources: Elaboration based on National Institute of Statistics 2006 and 2013; Central Bank of Uruguay 2013; Burdin, Esponda, and Vigorito 2014; and the General Accounting Office of the Nation 2013.

education, representing 10 percent of the entire population's consumption and 15 percent of individuals over age 64.

Figure 3.4 presents the consumption profile in health care, differentiating between public and private components.[3] Public consumption refers to the services funded through taxes: it includes direct provision and National Health Care Fund (Fondo Nacional de Salud; FONASA) funding. Private consumption is goods and services financed by individuals: spending in care facilities, payments for medical tests, purchases of medication, and so on. Remember that, in this case as well, average consumption is calculated for the entire population, thereby capturing both the number of and expenditure per consumer.

Sixty-seven percent of health care consumption occurs through public channels. The public sector is more important for the "deficit" age groups: that is, it represents around 70 percent of health care consumption for individuals under age 20 or over age 64. In contrast, 62 percent of spending for those aged 30–49 is private consumption.

Finally, figure 3.5 presents income and consumption aggregated by age. These values are obtained by multiplying the average for each age group (figure 3.1) by the population of each age group, such that the sum of these values represents the country's labor income and consumption. Because the weight of each age group within the population is distinct, the shapes of the income and consumption curves by age in figure 3.1 are different from those in figure 3.5. As a result, we observe two peaks in labor income, one around age 30 and another around

Figure 3.4 Per Capita Health Care Consumption by Age, 2013

percent of average labor income for individuals ages 30–49

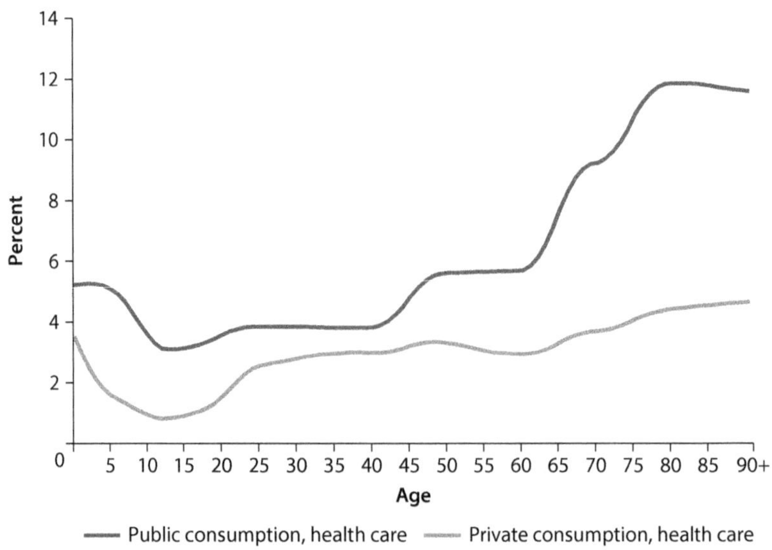

Sources: Elaboration based on National Institute of Statistics 2006 and 2013; Central Bank of Uruguay 2013; Burdin, Esponda, and Vigorito 2014; the General Accounting Office of the Nation 2013; and the National Information System 2015.

Figure 3.5 Income and Consumption Aggregated by Age, 2013

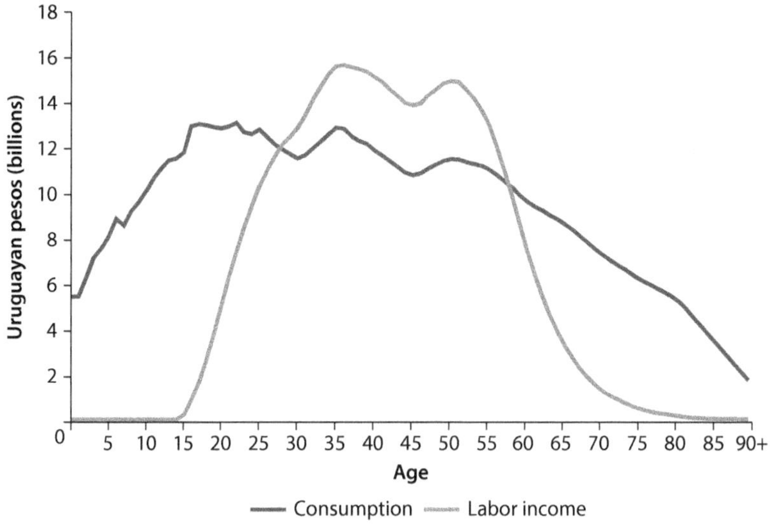

Sources: Elaboration based on National Institute of Statistics 2006 and 2013; Central Bank of Uruguay 2013; Burdin, Esponda, and Vigorito 2014.

age 50. The plateau shape of the aggregated values reflects the absence of individuals from the middle-aged generations, which is a result of Uruguay's substantial emigration (chapter 2). For consumption, the feature contrasting most with the per capita profile is the downward slope of the curve as age increases, which results because age cohorts of older individuals are smaller than those of younger individuals.

The Life-Cycle Balance

The life-cycle deficit describes the situation in which consumption is greater than labor income, in contrast with the life-cycle surplus which occurs when resource generation is more than sufficient to finance personal consumption. Figure 3.6 presents an estimate of the deficit for each age group, in other words, consumption minus income. The positive values signal that a deficit exists, meaning that consumption is greater than income and thus it must be financed. In contrast, the negative values signal that a surplus exists for that age group, creating sufficient resources to be able to finance not only its own consumption, but also that of other age groups. The shape of the curve shows that, in 2013, individuals below age 28 and over age 57 faced a deficit situation and their consumption was financed by the middle-age groups. The per capita deficit is greater for the older age groups than for the younger, but the overall deficit for the older is less because their size is smaller than the younger generations (figure 3.7). Overall, 58 percent of the deficit is generated by individuals below age 28, while 42 percent corresponds to those over age 57.

The deficit and the surplus are sustainable because economic mechanisms, which are more or less formally institutionalized, channel the movement of

Figure 3.6 Per Capita Life-Cycle Deficit by Age, 2013
percent of average labor income for ages 30–49

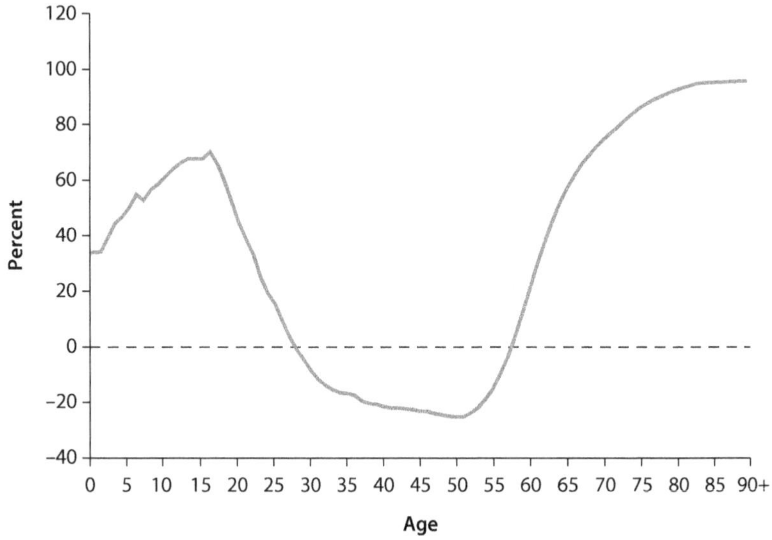

Sources: Elaboration based on National Institute of Statistics 2006 and 2013; Central Bank of Uruguay 2013; Burdin, Esponda, and Vigorito 2014.

Figure 3.7 Aggregate Life-Cycle Deficit by Age, 2013

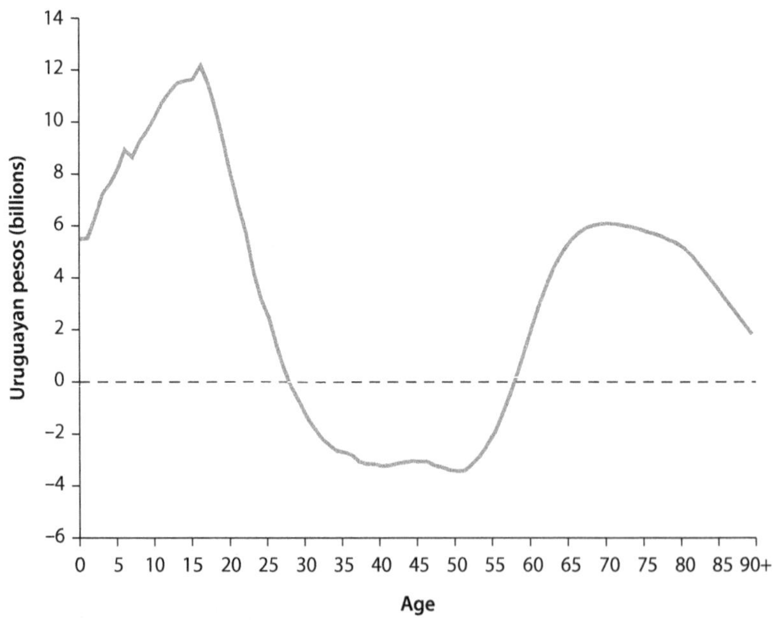

Sources: Elaboration based on National Institute of Statistics 2006 and 2013; Central Bank of Uruguay 2013; Burdin, Esponda, and Vigorito 2014.

resources among age groups. In other words, individuals receive (inflows) and contribute (outflows) resources: the deficit is financed by inflows that are greater than outflows. These movements are channeled through two mechanisms: assets and transfers.

The reallocation of resources through assets occurs in the market. This process refers to income and expenditure derived from asset ownership, such as interest and rent and saving and dissaving, which frequently involve intertemporal exchanges. For example, one way that individuals reallocate resources over time is by purchasing a house when they are economically active (which generates an outflow) and selling it in their later years (creating an inflow).

As opposed to reallocation through assets, the transfer mechanism does not involve the market and does not entail—at least explicitly—an exchange of present or future commitments between recipients and contributors. For example, when parents feed their children or the public sector pays family allowances, a transfer is occurring; in one case it is voluntary and private and in the other it is under the auspices of a public program.

In reallocation through assets, as well as through transfers, the agents may be public or private. This study focuses on the role of the public sector in reallocation through transfers, with the understanding that any reform that seeks to adapt public policies to the changes in the age structure of the population benefits from previous discussions based on quantitative information. This is why we have only performed estimates for this reallocation mechanism. Nonetheless, estimates for previous years have produced some interesting results that deserve comment (box 3.3 presents the estimation method).

In particular, the NTA estimates for 1994 and 2006 indicated that, in Uruguay, private transfers played a principal role in financing consumption during childhood and adolescence, suggesting the importance of family relationships (Bucheli, González, and Olivieri 2010; Bucheli and González 2011). In addition,

Box 3.3 Estimating the Public Transfer Accounts

Public transfers to households (inflows) are divided into in-kind and cash transfers. In-kind transfers are equal to household consumption directly financed by the public sector (public consumption). This is the case for public consumption of education, public health care, National Health Care Fund (Fondo Nacional de Salud [FONASA]) funding for private health care, and the rest of public consumption, for which estimates are presented in box 3.2.

Cash transfers, on the other hand, include social security and assistance benefits. They comprise all the programs under the Social Security Bank (contributory and noncontributory pensions and retirement benefits, and subsidies for illness, unemployment, maternity, and family allowances), retirements and pensions distributed by the Military and Police Funds, as well as the Uruguay Social Card directed toward low-income households and financed by the Ministry of Social Development.

Public transfers from households (outflows) comprise taxes and social security contributions.

the estimates showed that during old age the deficit was mainly financed by income derived from assets and public transfers, while net private transfers were negative. In other words, the elderly received public resources, utilized their assets, and made transfers, most likely to their families. One can make the interpretation that these transfers reinforced the importance of familial bonds in order to reallocate resources to children and adolescents. When consumption during the early stages of life mainly depends on resources generated by older members of the family, the environment at birth acquires greater importance. In contrast, public channels are able to collect resources from the middle-age groups in general, to a greater or lesser degree of progressiveness depending on the design of a country's tax policy, and reallocate them to children and adolescents, making up for differences at birth. Thus, the structure of public and private transfer channels highlights a limitation to overcoming low intergenerational mobility and the inequality of opportunities.

Public transfers constitute an institutionalized and regulated mechanism for resource reallocation. The government collects taxes and contributions, which are utilized to fund its expenditures. This spending takes the form of public consumption (or household consumption directly financed by the public sector) and cash transfers. From an individual's point of view, the government's collections represent outflows while public expenditure represents inflows. Inflows exceeding outflows represent a surplus situation for the public sector, which must be financed by those individuals whose outflows (taxes and contributions) exceed their inflows (public consumption and transfers). As a result, net public transfers (inflows minus outflows) point to a sort of life-cycle balance for the public sector, whose age limits may differ from the limits for the life-cycle balance for the economy as a whole.

Life-Cycle Deficit and Public Transfers

Figure 3.8 presents the life-cycle deficit and net public transfers per capita in 2013. Up to age 19, net public transfers are positive, meaning that the resources received through the public sector are greater than payments made (taxes and contributions) to the public sector. Between the ages of 20 and 62, individuals turn over more resources to the public sector than they receive, while after age 62 the population again becomes a net recipient of public resources.

Figure 3.8 shows that, in per capita terms, net public transfers received by the population at older ages are greater than those received by children and adolescents. This means that children and adolescents make more intensive use of other channels to finance their life-cycle deficit, which one can appreciate from the gap that exists between the life-cycle deficit and net public transfer curves.

Figure 3.9 presents the aggregate values by age group for the life-cycle deficit as well as for net public transfers. Because the cohorts of children and adolescents are more numerous than those of the elderly, the two curves are higher for the younger age groups than for the older ones. In any case, one can still appreciate that the difference between the curves is greater for children and adolescents. In other words, private channels are more important for this age group.

Figure 3.8 Life-Cycle Deficit and Net Public Transfers per Capita by Age, 2013
percent of average labor income for ages 30–49

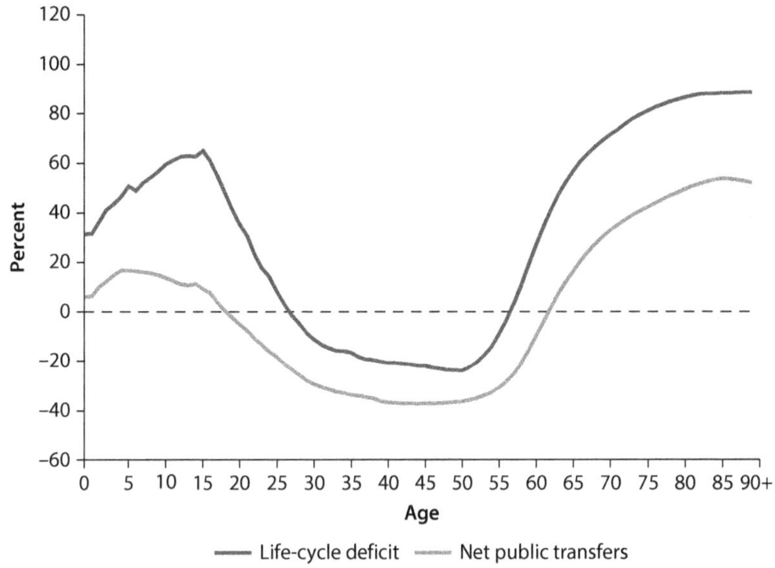

Sources: Elaboration based on National Institute of Statistics 2006 and 2013; Central Bank of Uruguay 2013; Burdin, Esponda, and Vigorito 2014; the General Accounting Office of the Nation 2013; and the Social Security Bank 2013.

Figure 3.9 Aggregate Life-Cycle Deficit and Net Public Transfers by Age, 2013

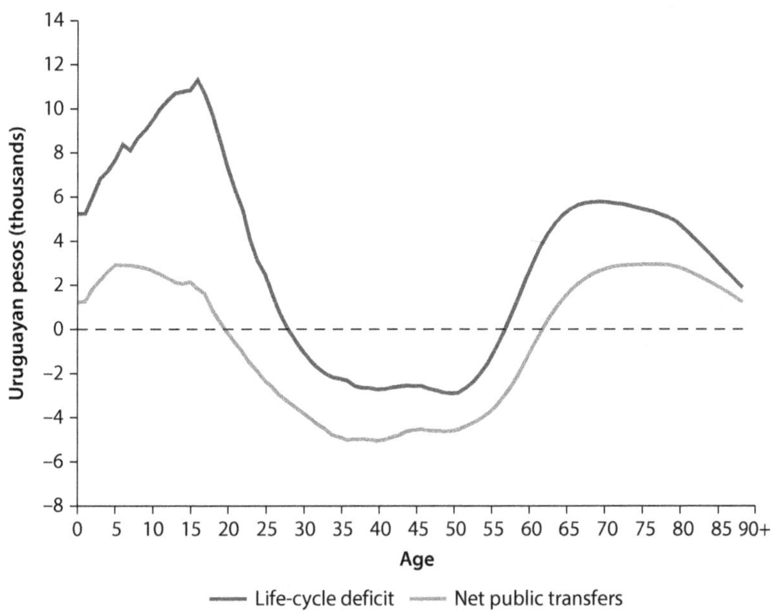

Sources: Elaboration based on National Institute of Statistics 2006 and 2013; Central Bank of Uruguay 2013; Burdin, Esponda, and Vigorito 2014; the General Accounting Office of the Nation 2013; and the Social Security Bank 2013.

These estimates reaffirm the conclusions drawn from 1994 and 2006: public transfers play a noticeably more important role in the later stages of life than in the earlier. Essentially, less than a quarter of the consumption of individuals below age 19 is financed by net public transfers. Meanwhile, 45 percent of the consumption of individuals over age 64 is financed with public transfers. Note that these observations propose a different interpretation of the financing of consumption compared to the one developed in the "Income and Consumption" section on page 43. In that case, we saw that public consumption (in-kind transfers) played a larger role in sustaining children's and adolescents' consumption relative to the elderly. Once the role of cash transfers per population (for example, pensions and retirement benefits, family allowances, and other cash transfer programs) is included in the discussion, as well as the resources that the population turns over to the public sector (taxes and social security contributions), it is possible to capture a complete picture of net public financing offered by the public sector (in-kind and cash public transfers received by the population, taxes, and contributions). Specifically, thanks to retirement benefits and pensions, the elderly find in the public sector a source of essential support for their consumption. On the other hand, even though public consumption represents 40 percent of total consumption by minors, the importance of the public sector in sustaining children and adolescents is diminished because they finance part of public expenditure through the payment of indirect taxes.

Suggestions have been made that this "distribution of responsibilities" between public and private actors has been moderated over time as a result of two processes.

In a comparison between 1994 and 2006, Bucheli, González, and Olivieri (2010) show that the public transfer gap between children and the elderly narrowed during this period. A medium-term process of increasing public consumption in education played a very important role in this. Even though methodological differences between the 2006 and 2013 estimates mean that a comparison between them is not possible,[4] in an analysis of public social spending by age group from 2005 to 2012, the Ministry of Social Development (MIDES; 2014) revealed that this trend had continued.

In addition, average labor income among the elderly has grown in recent decades, allowing them to sustain their own consumption. The increase in labor income has two causes. Greater economic activity at older ages is in part the consequence of generations with a greater proportion of economically active women reaching old age. Moreover, activity is growing as a result of the postponement of retirement (Alvarez and others 2009).

Public Transfers by Age Group

Figure 3.10 presents per capita inflows and outflows for public transfers, which form the curve of net transfers presented in the previous section. It is readily apparent that the inflow is higher among the older age groups than for the rest of the age groups. Those over age 64 receive an average per capita transfer

Figure 3.10 Public Inflows and Outflows per Capita by Age Group, 2013
percent of average labor income for ages 30–49

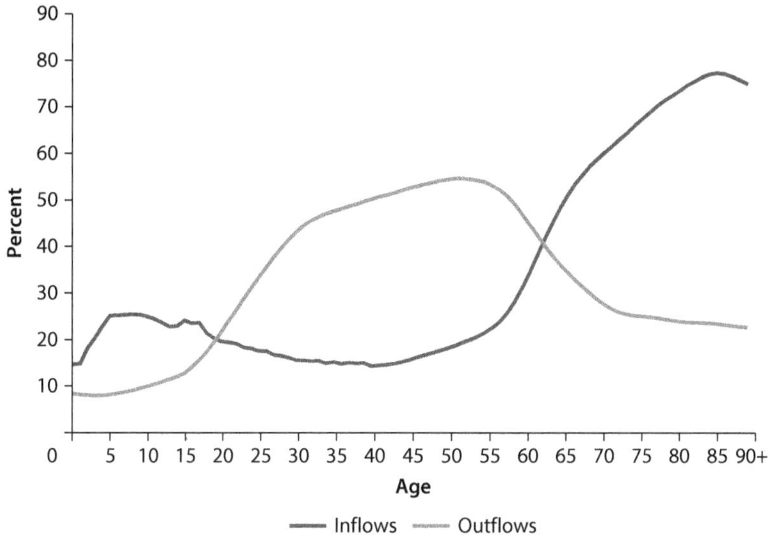

Sources: Elaboration based on National Institute of Statistics 2006 and 2013; Central Bank of Uruguay 2013; Burdin, Esponda, and Vigorito 2014; the General Accounting Office of the Nation 2013; and the Social Security Bank 2013.

3.3 times greater than those under age 21. Meanwhile, the outflow is bell-shaped: resource generation mainly falls on the middle-age groups. As a result of the sizes of the generations or cohorts, at the level of the state's general resources, the differences between age groups are diminished, as figure 3.11 illustrates.

Below, the first section analyzes the categories that comprise the inflows, while the second looks at the components of the outflows.

Inflows

The age pattern illustrated in figure 3.10 indicates that the inflow shows a hump for children, adolescents, and youth. This is the result of public consumption in education, which grows among the younger age groups, reaching its highest peak around age 10, as figures 3.12 and 3.13 reveal. After age 10, public consumption in the education component falls, and even though it recovers around the ages that correspond with the second cycle of middle education, it subsequently continues to fall. Consumption of public education is the most significant inflow during the early years of the life cycle, followed by the rest of public consumption, health care transfers, and finally cash transfers that at this age are practically all from the family allowance program.

Around middle age, the inflow remains stable at low levels. As can be observed in figures 3.12 and 3.13, the principal component is the "public consumption, remainder," followed by health care, and, with a noticeably lower proportion, cash transfers, which mostly consist of subsidies related to employment administered by the Social Security Bank.

Figure 3.11 Aggregate Public Inflows and Outflows by Age, 2013

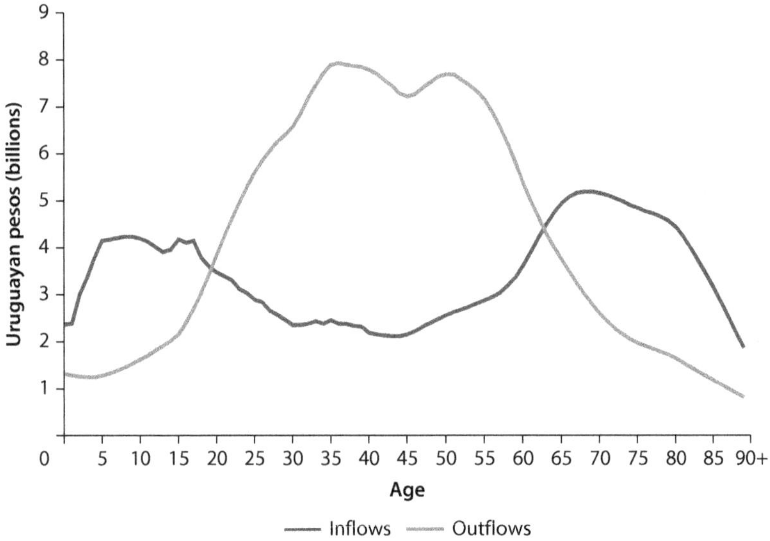

Sources: Elaboration based on National Institute of Statistics 2006 and 2013; Central Bank of Uruguay 2013; Burdin, Esponda, and Vigorito 2014; the General Accounting Office of the Nation 2013; and the Social Security Bank 2013.

Figure 3.12 Components of Public Inflows per Capita by Age, 2013
percent of average labor income for ages 30–49

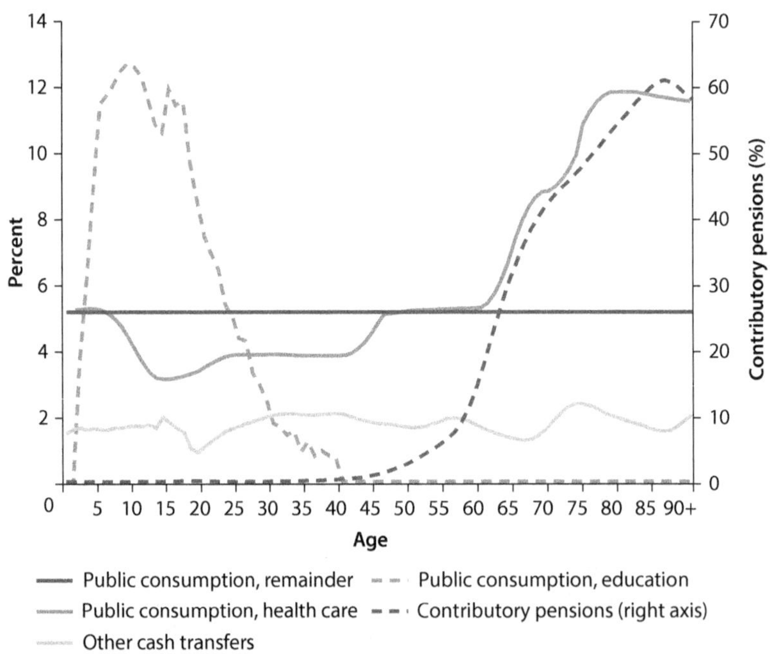

Sources: Elaboration based on National Institute of Statistics 2006 and 2013; Central Bank of Uruguay 2013; Burdin, Esponda, and Vigorito 2014; the General Accounting Office of the Nation 2013; the Social Security Bank 2013; and the National Information System 2015.

Figure 3.13 Components of Aggregate Public Inflows by Age, 2013

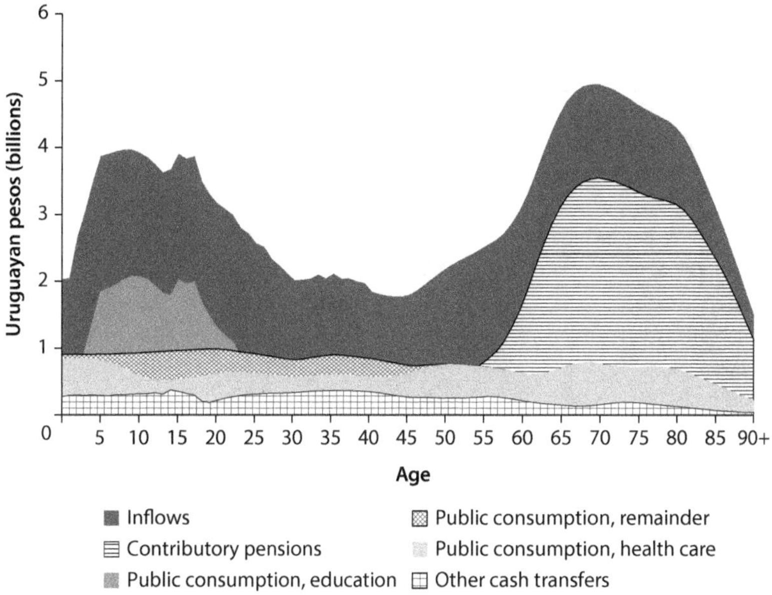

Sources: Elaboration based on National Institute of Statistics 2006 and 2013; Central Bank of Uruguay 2013; Burdin, Esponda, and Vigorito 2014; the General Accounting Office of the Nation 2013; the Social Security Bank 2013; and the National Information System 2015.

After age 50, the inflow grows uninterruptedly, driven by the transfers from retirement programs and, to a lesser extent, by public consumption of health care. The remainder of public consumption is next, followed by the rest of the cash transfers, which for these age groups mostly correspond to the Elderly and Disability Program (noncontributory pensions) administered by the Social Security Bank.

Significant differences exist in inflows of public transfers to the deficit age groups. On one hand, the level of the inflow to older age groups is notably higher than that to the younger. On the other, the makeup of the inflow is different. Table 3.1 allows comparison of the composition of transfers at the two extremes of the life cycle.

The flow to the elderly is mostly in cash (76.5 percent of the total per capita inflow and 75.9 percent of the aggregate), while consumption plays a lesser role (23.5 percent and 24.1 percent, respectively). Just retirement benefits and pensions (contributory and noncontributory) account for approximately 76 percent of total flows. In contrast, the flows to children and adolescents are mostly in-kind (92 percent of the total), particularly in education (45 percent of the total). Family allowances represent just 6 percent of public transfers to this age group. In turn, health care transfers exhibit a different makeup among age groups. Health care consumption has two components: care in public facilities and subsidies for care in private facilities through FONASA. As a proportion of total

Table 3.1 Categories of Public Transfers as Percentages of the Total Inflow

	Per capita as percentage of the total inflow			*Aggregate as percentage of the total inflow*		
	Ages 0–20	*Ages 65+*	*Total*	*Ages 0–20*	*Ages 65+*	*Total*
Total consumption	**91.4**	**23.5**	**43.7**	**91.4**	**24.1**	**57.2**
Public consumption, education	44.8	0.0	8.2	45.0	0.0	14.5
Public consumption, health care	19.5	15.4	18.8	19.4	15.6	20.6
Public care	9.1	5.5	7.1	9.1	5.7	8.1
FONASA funding to private providers	10.4	9.9	11.7	10.3	9.8	12.6
Other consumption	27.0	8.1	16.8	27.0	8.5	22.2
Total transfers in cash	**8.6**	**76.5**	**56.3**	**8.6**	**75.9**	**42.8**
Retirement benefits and pensions	0.9	76.2	53.0	0.9	75.6	37.6
Family allowances	6.3	0.0	0.9	6.2	0.0	1.6
Other social protection, in cash	1.5	0.2	2.4	1.5	0.3	3.6
Total	**100.0**	**100.0**	**100.0**	**100.0**	**100.0**	**100.0**

Sources: Elaboration based on National Institute of Statistics 2006 and 2013; Central Bank of Uruguay 2013; Burdin, Esponda, and Vigorito 2014; the General Accounting Office of the Nation 2013; the Social Security Bank 2013; and the National Information System 2015.
Note: FONASA = National Health Care Fund (Fondo Nacional de Salud).

health care consumption, transfers through subsidies for care in private facilities are higher for individuals over age 64.

Outflows

As was previously mentioned, the outflow by age group has a bell shape both in per capita and aggregate value terms (figures 3.14 and 3.15). As for labor income, within the active age groups one observes a greater proportion of the younger age groups due to the emigration process.

The lowest outflow values occur during childhood and adolescence. As figures 3.14 and 3.15 illustrate, these flows correspond to the payment of indirect taxes that takes place as part of consumption (the value added tax, for example). As individuals enter the labor market, they begin to gain significance in terms of the flows that correspond to social security contributions, other taxes, contributions to FONASA, and direct taxes on individuals. During old age, the second deficit period, the main outflows once again are made up of indirect taxes, in addition to direct taxes on individuals.

The Effects of Demographic Change on the Support Ratio and the Public Accounts

We have waited until now to address the life-cycle deficit from the point of view of how it is financed and the resource flows that make this possible. An interesting perspective emerges based on considering that total labor income represents 66 percent of total consumption. This indicator, which presents the percentage of consumption financed by resources generated during the current period, is an estimate of the economic support ratio.

Figure 3.14 Components of Per Capita Public Outflows by Age Group by Average Labor Income for the 30–49 Age Group, 2013

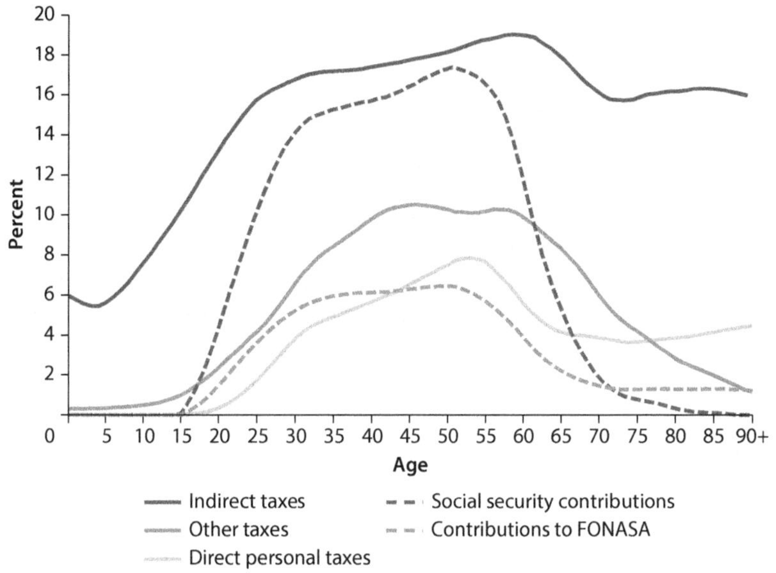

Sources: Elaboration based on National Institute of Statistics 2006 and 2013; Central Bank of Uruguay 2013; Burdin, Esponda, and Vigorito 2014; the General Accounting Office of the Nation 2013; the Social Security Bank 2013.
Note: FONASA = National Health Care Fund (Fondo Nacional de Salud).

Figure 3.15 Components of Aggregate Public Outflows by Age Group, 2013

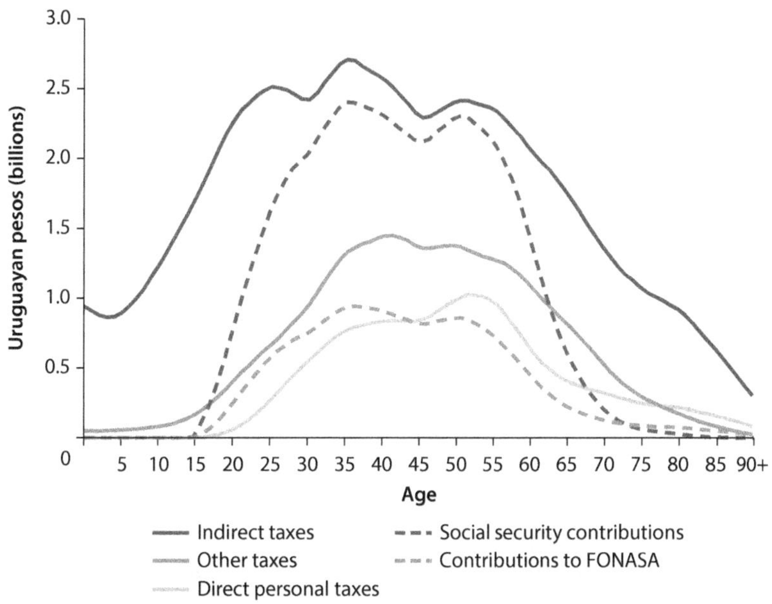

Sources: Elaboration based on National Institute of Statistics 2006 and 2013; Central Bank of Uruguay 2013; Burdin, Esponda, and Vigorito 2014; the General Accounting Office of the Nation 2013; the Social Security Bank 2013.
Note: FONASA = National Health Care Fund (Fondo Nacional de Salud).

Traditionally, the support ratio is measured through the dependency ratio, that is, the proportion of working-age individuals. In this manner, one attempts to measure to what extent the productive population is sufficiently numerous to be able to economically sustain the entire society. As chapter 2 discusses, the purely demographic indicator exhibits some defects associated with the fact that productivity and the propensity to consume vary according to age. Mason and Lee (2006, 2007) propose fine-tuning the measurement of this indicator, both in its numerator and its denominator. The authors seek to make the numerator representative of the effective generation of resources (observed in economic terms), not the potential generation of resources (based on demographic measurements). To achieve this, they propose adjusting the working-age population by average income for each age group. In turn, they seek to make the denominator capture the use of these resources; thus, they propose adjusting the population to reflect average consumption for each age group.

In summary, the support ratio is defined here as the ratio of income to consumption, which allows for an "economic" measurement versus a purely "demographic" view of dependency. Thus, one way of analyzing the effect of demographic change on the support ratio consists of forecasting the income/consumption ratio, assuming that per capita income and consumption by age group maintain their 2013 values, while changing the number of individuals in each age group according to population forecasts. In this way, the support ratio forecast varies solely as a result of demographic changes, allowing us to analyze future challenges that are the result of population dynamics. The analysis of this exercise is presented in the section "The Support Ratio." Subsequently, in the "Public Social Spending" and "Fiscal Support Ratio" sections, we employ an analogous method to analyze the effects of demographic change on public social spending and on the fiscal support ratio (defined as the outflow/inflow ratio for public transfers).

The simulations presented in this section make the following assumptions:

1. The income, consumption, and transfer profiles by age group remain constant,[5] leaving the discussion of how they might vary and the effect of these variations for chapters 4, 5, 6, and 7. This allows us to isolate the effect of the demographic transition from other social and economic changes.
2. The averages for labor income, consumption, and other transfers by age group grow at the same rate.[6] An arbitrary value of 2.5 percent is assumed for this growth rate. In other words, the average labor income for an individual of age x in year t will be 2.5 percent higher than that of an individual of age x in year $(t-1)$. This value is consistent with similar forecasts in developing countries (Miller and Castanheira 2013).
3. Finally, to forecast gross domestic product (GDP), we assumed that the proportion of labor income was N, in constant GDP, which was equal to the value observed in 2013 (49.9 percent). This assumption is consistent with an economy that maintains a Cobb-Douglas production function in a steady state.

Note that the combination of these assumptions offers some advantages. In particular, if income, consumption, and transfers grow at the same constant rate and labor income's proportion of GDP is also constant, it is not necessary to make direct estimates of the GDP growth rate through 2100, given that GDP can be derived from the growth in labor income. In any case, the arbitrary value chosen in this case (2.5 percent per year) implies that the economic growth rate will be consistent with the rate estimated by the International Monetary Fund (IMF; 2014) for Uruguay during 2012–19, and is situated around the average rate observed during the last 30 years (see chapter 7). Additionally, it is important to point out that, given that all income and transfers grow at the same rate, according to assumption 3 the forecasts of public expenditure as a percentage of GDP are robust for any value that is assumed as the growth rate.

The present, purely analytical exercise, even if simplistic, allows us to obtain an approximation of the magnitude of the effects of demographic change on the results of social policies. To that effect, while the economic and political future can be difficult to predict, demographic trends represent a gradual, certain change. For that reason, the current forecast's goal is not to obtain a set of exact numbers related to income, consumption, and social expenditure for every moment in time, but rather to reflect the importance of taking into account a predictable factor like the demographic transition in the design and impact of public policies.

The Support Ratio

An important concern that emerges after reviewing the demographic transition is related to the ability of the working population to finance those who are economically dependent on them while the age structure is changing and the average age is increasing. Grouping individuals into the categories of workers or dependents based on arbitrary age limits (such as those suggested by international standards, for example, which consider all adults over age 65 to be dependents) hinders this type of discussion insomuch as it does not allow one to reflect on the implications of changes in socioeconomic behavior, which can be expected in terms of productivity, labor market participation, and educational system retention, among others.

Additionally, a purely demographic dependency ratio assumes that the ability to generate income and the propensity to consume are homogeneous within the working-age and dependent groups of individuals. However, factors like unemployment, salary, and propensity to consume differ among age groups, as is reflected in labor income and consumption by age group estimates.

Based on these considerations, and utilizing the NTA estimates, the economic-support ratio (SR) is defined as the ratio between the quantity of effective workers and effective consumers. According to Mason and Lee (2007), if we define $x_{a,t}$ as the number of individuals at age a at moment t, ω as the maximum age one can reach, γ_a as per capita labor income at age a, and φ_a as per capita consumption at age a, we can then define effective producers or workers (L_t) and effective consumers (N_t) as is defined in equations 3.1 and 3.2:

$$N_t = \sum_{a=0}^{\omega} \varphi_a x_{a,t} \tag{3.1}$$

$$L_t = \sum_{a=0}^{\omega} \gamma_a x_{a,t} \tag{3.2}$$

Note that the number of effective workers (and consumers) depends on the per capita income (or consumption) for each age group, as well as the number of individuals in each cohort. Therefore, the economic support ratio is defined as:

$$SR_t = L_t/N_t \tag{3.3}$$

This indicator allows one to account for the differences in consumption and income among age groups.[7] In practical terms, the economic support ratio is calculated here based on the ratio between income and aggregate consumption (public and private, which does not include cash transfers), given that these variables reflect, on one hand, the labor income and consumption profiles by age group, and, on the other, the age structure of the population. Consequently, changes in the age structure of the population produce changes in the economic support ratio.

Figure 3.16 presents the simulation of the support ratio during 2013–2100, utilizing the population forecasts presented in chapter 2, based on the aforementioned assumptions. It demonstrates that as the window of opportunity closes, the support ratio also falls.

Another way to visualize the effect of population aging is to calculate the aggregate life-cycle deficit as a percentage of consumption and forecast it, changing just the population. This indicator reflects the number of net effective workers per consumer (that is, the difference between aggregate labor income and aggregate consumption, divided by aggregate consumption). Given that this indicator is a measure of the deficit or surplus of the aggregate life cycle, it takes on negative or positive values depending on age. In other words, because each age is associated with the condition of being either a net producer or consumer, by changing the weight of each age group in the total population, the aggregate life-cycle deficit also changes.

Figure 3.17 shows the calculation of this indicator for 2013, 2050, and 2100. As mentioned, the simulation assumes that the income and consumption profile by age group remains constant and equal to the estimate for 2013. Thus, the aggregate life-cycle deficit by age group changes over time solely as a result of demographic change or, in other words, because of the changes in the size of each cohort.[8] We observe that the aggregate life-cycle deficit (as a percentage of consumption) decreases in the first deficit stage but increases in the second deficit stage, while the middle-age group's surplus remains relatively stable.

Figure 3.16 Evolution of the Economic Support Ratio, 2013–2100

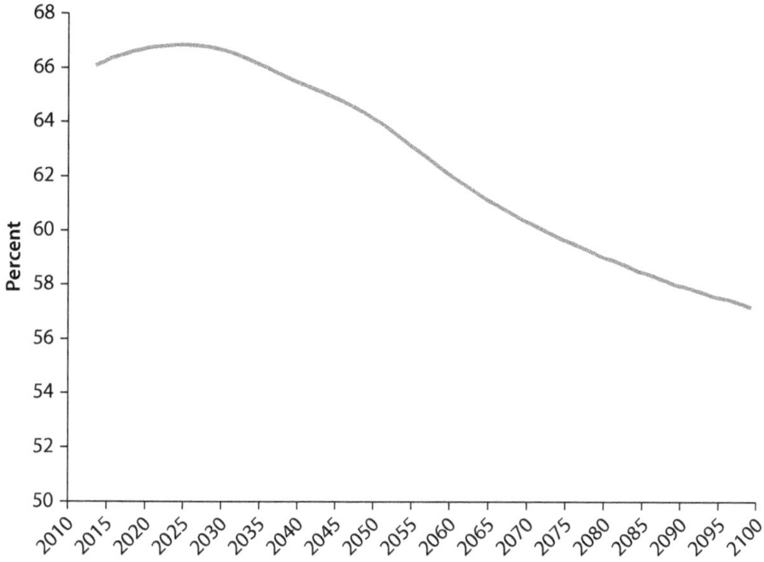

Figure 3.17 Life-Cycle Deficit/Consumption by Age Group, 2013, and Simulations for 2050 and 2100 Aggregate Values

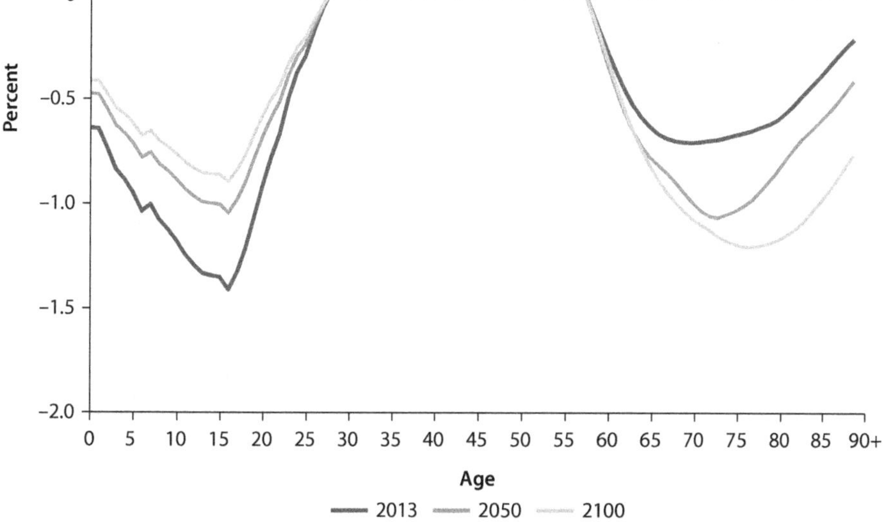

Figure 3.18 Evolution of the Life-Cycle Deficit/Aggregate Consumption for Three Age Groups, 2014–2100

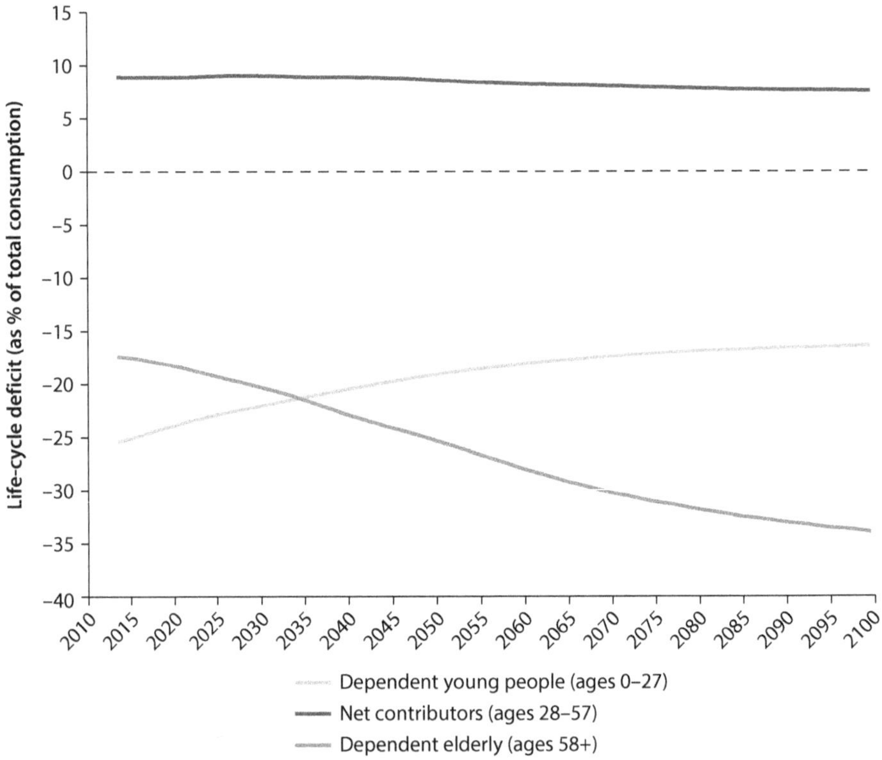

The analysis of the aggregate life-cycle deficit allows for a better understanding of the distinct forces behind the support ratio's downward trend, as illustrated in figure 3.16. Figure 3.18 presents the forecast of the indicator separately for three age groups: the first deficit period (under age 27), the surplus group (28–57), and the second deficit period (58 and older). The results suggest that the support ratio's fall is mainly due to the negative contribution of an ever more numerous group of dependent elderly persons, which more than offsets the reduction in resources required to support the lower proportion of dependent young people. The contribution from net workers remains stable, although it falls slightly due to the increase in the group's average age.

Public Social Spending

Social spending represents one of the most important components of public expenditure. In strategic terms, the centrality of social spending is the result of its role as the "expression of the public commitment to the population's well-being" (MIDES 2014). In quantitative terms, MIDES reported that in 2012, this component of public expenditure exceeded 250 billion Uruguayan pesos (MIDES 2014), representing some 25 percent of GDP and 75 percent of total public expenditure. The estimate made in this chapter for public transfers attributable to social ends (education, health care, and cash transfers) differs from MIDES' estimate because the former is concentrated in some specific sectors (it does not include dwellings, water, sewer, and other nonconventional social spending for example) and only considers in-kind (public consumption) and cash transfers, leaving out investment. Thus, these transfers added up to something more than 220 billion Uruguayan pesos in 2013, representing approximately 19.4 percent of GDP.

The goal of the current section is to study the effect of demographic change on the various social components of public transfers. Specifically, policies such as education, health care, retirement benefits, and family allowances target distinct age groups. Consequently, each of these components will be affected differently by the progress of the demographic transition. The following paragraphs present the results of the forecasts to show the impact of purely demographic changes, leaving the discussion of eventual changes in behaviors favored by these changes and by the implementation of new policies for the sectoral chapters.

The methodology used by Miller and Castanheira (2013) was adapted for the forecasts. The aggregate benefit of each of the social programs is defined as:

$$B_t = \sum_{a=0}^{\omega} b_a x_{a,t} \tag{3.4}$$

where b_a is respectively the per capita benefit in education, health care, retirement benefits and pensions, and the remainder of social protection transfers to age group a. As box 3.1 presented, this parameter captures both the average benefit amount as well as the coverage of each program. To study the effect of demographic change, we assume that the per capita benefit for each age group remains at 2013 levels, with the exception of retirement benefits and pensions. An ad hoc modeling exercise is utilized for the pension system. It accounts for contributors' transition from a public distribution system managed by the Social Security Bank to an individual capitalization scheme with public-private management in which the Retirement Savings Fund Administrators (*Administradoras de Fondos de Ahorro de Pensiones*) play a central role. This transition has been in progress since the 1996 pension reform, and thus the preexisting policy informs this exercise. The assumptions and parameters utilized for this simulation are defined in chapter 4.

Figure 3.19 presents the results of this simulation in terms of GDP, broken down into four components: education, health care, retirement benefits, and pensions (contributory and noncontributory), and the remainder of cash transfers (in Social Security Bank benefits to active beneficiaries, family allowances, and the Uruguay Social Card distributed by the MIDES).

In education, as Uruguay progresses through the demographic transition, the fiscal effort required to maintain current coverage and per-student expenditure is reduced, driven by a decrease in the target population. In other words, as the

Figure 3.19 Public Social Transfers in Uruguay, 2013–2100

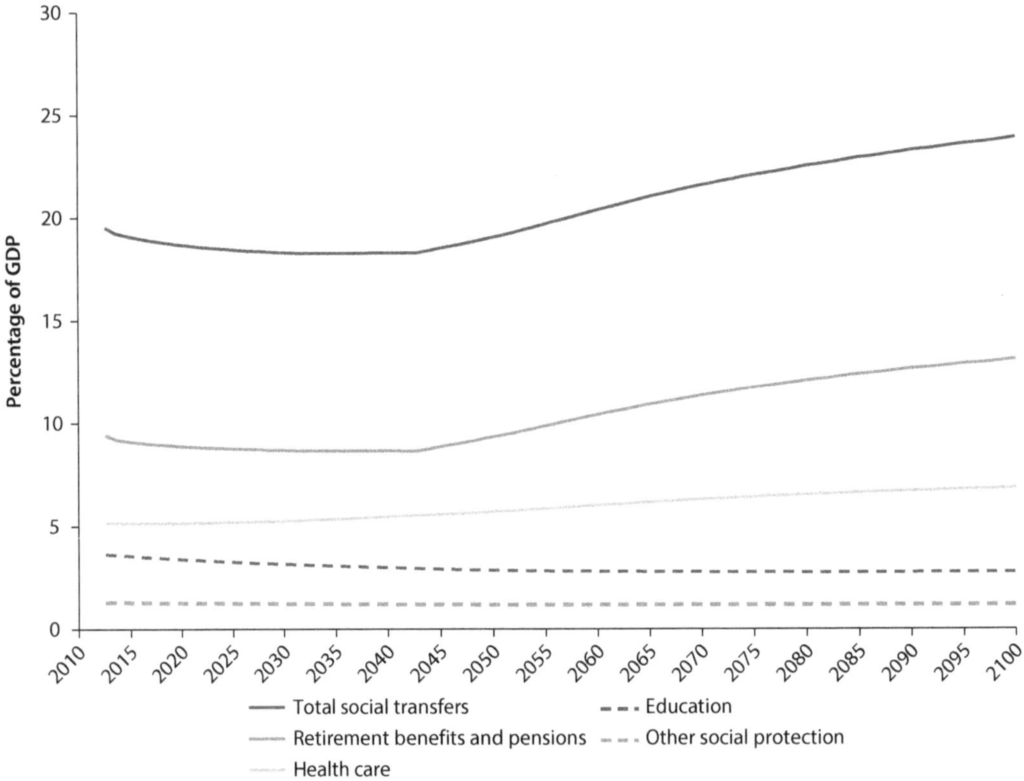

number of younger cohorts falls, aggregate expenditure in education falls, freeing up resources that can be used to improve investment within the sector (increased coverage and/or increased per-student expenditure) or can be used to cover emerging needs in other sectors. According to this simulation, which demonstrates just the effects of the demographic change, approximately 0.9 percent of GDP could be freed up between 2013 and 2100. The size of this gain is limited as a result of the already advanced state in which Uruguay finds itself in the demographic transition in the base year.

The health care sector, in contrast, will face fiscal challenges due to changes in the demographic structure. The simulation implies that health care consumption financed by the public sector will grow from approximately 5.2 percent of GDP in 2013 to 6.8 percent in 2100. Even though the target population in this sector includes all age groups, differences in health care spending among age groups exist. Specifically, as has been previously described, health care spending is higher among older age groups. Thus, an increase in the average age of the population will result in increased fiscal effort in the sector. Note that if the public/private ratio of services offered to the elderly remains the same, this increase will be reflected above all in increased FONASA financing to private providers and, to a lesser extent, in the use of public health care services.

Social protection and assistance transfers, with the exception of retirement benefits and pensions, comprise a markedly heterogeneous set of programs over the age groups they target. On one hand, family allowances are designed to support the development of children up to age 18, while unemployment and illness insurance clearly target working-age individuals. Maternity benefits complete this set; they are aimed at women of ages 20–45. Meanwhile, the Uruguay Social Card targets low-income households.

Expenditure on this type of transfer is notably less than for other categories of social spending, which means that changes of any significant size in terms of GDP are not visible. Essentially, the resources destined for these transfers will remain approximately constant (from 1.3 percent of GDP in 2013 to 1.2 percent in 2100), indicating that the positive effects of a decrease in the relative weight of the younger age groups will be offset by the negative effect of an increase in the older age groups.

Finally, contrary to what one might intuitively expect in a context of demographic aging, public sector expenditure on retirement benefits and pensions will fall until approximately 2040/2045 due to the gradual shift of a portion of pension payments from the Social Security Bank to the Retirement Savings Fund Administrators. The incorporation of the individual capitalization scheme will allow public spending on pensions to decrease from 9.4 percent of GDP in 2013 to 8.6 percent in 2043. Subsequently, as the new mixed regime matures, the demographic component will become more significant, and will drive growth in expenditure on retirement benefits and pensions, until reaching 13.1 percent of GDP in 2100. These results do not establish an alarm related to the eventual stress that an older population will cause for the pension system in the medium term.

The results suggest that the fiscal weight of public social transfers in terms of GDP will remain approximately constant and may even decrease during the next four decades. In effect, from the point of view of the public accounts, the resources that are freed up during the transition from a purely public pension system to the current mixed system, combined with the decreased fiscal effort required by the education sector, will be more than sufficient to offset the negative fiscal effects of population aging. Beginning in the second half of the century, spending on social transfers will begin to rise, reaching 24 percent by 2100.

In relative terms, the health care sector will become the most significant sector in total public transfers, especially during the first half of the century. In the forecast, financing of health care consumption will grow from 27 percent of total public social transfers in 2013 to 30 percent in 2050. On the contrary, maintaining per-student expenditure and coverage in the education sector at current levels will require fewer fiscal resources. As a result, the elderly will remain the most favored group for public transfers, given that they represent not just the entire beneficiary population for retirement benefits, but also the population that uses the most health care services. While in 2013 net beneficiaries among the elderly population (ages 63+) captured 40 percent of total social benefits distributed by the public sector, in the forecast this group will receive 53 percent of the total inflows in 2050 and 63 percent in 2100.

Thus, the demographic change allows a rethink of the eventual reassignment of resources among sectors because resources will be freed up in some sectors, while others will require increased fiscal effort. Nonetheless, it must be kept in mind that each type of transfer requires a different institutional structure to be set up by the state. As a result, the eventual reassignment of resources among sectors will have not just fiscal implications but also consequences for their administration. In addition, demographic change affects public resources, which is analyzed in the next section.

The Fiscal Support Ratio

After observing the evolution of social spending in the education, health care, and retirement and pensions sectors, it is fair to ask how public transfers will evolve as a whole (inflows to households), and, moreover, what changes can be expected in outflows. Where the support ratio provides a measure of workers' ability to support the economically dependent population, the fiscal support ratio captures the sustainability of the public transfer system, taking into account the current collections structure and expenditure per age group. Within the public sector, the population is also divided into contributors and beneficiaries. Thus, following the same logic utilized to determine the support ratio, the number of effective contributors (U_t) and effective beneficiaries (Q_t) is defined as:

$$U_t = \sum_{a=0}^{\omega} \beta_a x_{a,t} \tag{3.5}$$

$$Q_t = \sum_{a=0}^{\omega} \alpha_a x_{a,t} \tag{3.6}$$

where β_a and α_a are the per capita outflow (tax pressure) per age group and the per capita inflow (benefit received through public in-kind or cash transfers) per age group, respectively.

Just as with the support ratio, one way of visualizing the effect of population aging on public transfers is to calculate $(Q_t - U_t)/Q_t$, keeping tax pressure and the per capita benefit per age group constant, while changing the sizes of the cohorts according to the population forecast. Remember that our calculation differs from this general method because it takes into account that a portion of the new contingents of dependents belong to the mixed system, which means that, in the forecast, the average benefit per dependent varies from the 2013 level.

This indicator exhibits positive values if the age group is a net recipient of public resources; conversely, it exhibits negative values when an age group contributes more than it receives. Because each age group is a net contributor or recipient in 2013, as the relative sizes of the cohorts are modified, the values of

Figure 3.20 Net Public Transfers/Inflows by Age Group, 2013, 2050, and 2100

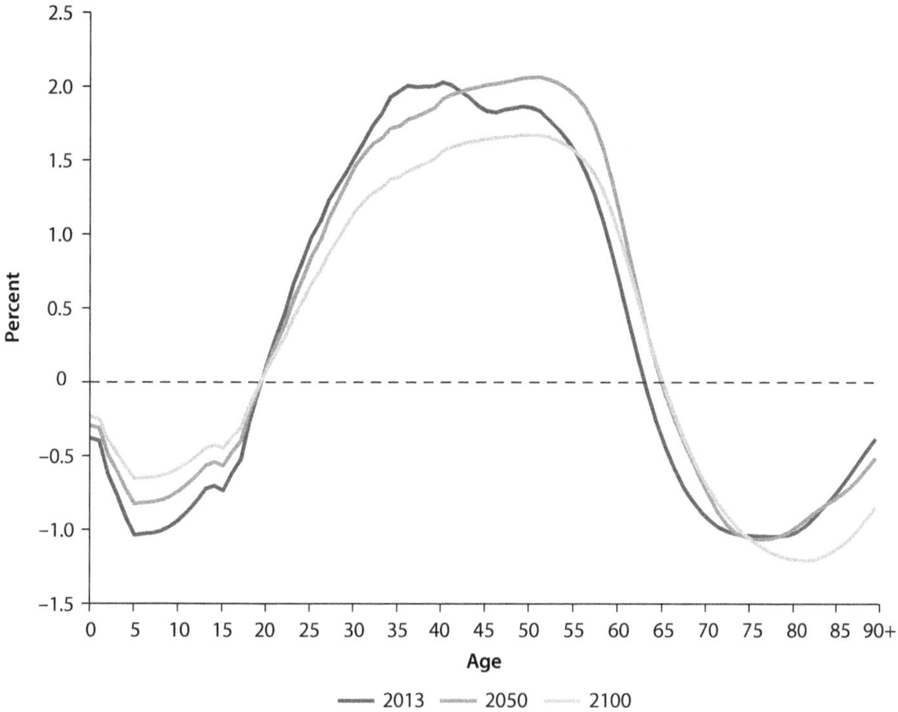

the net aggregate transfers also change. Figure 3.20 shows their values for 2013 and the forecasts for 2050 and 2100. As a result of the decrease in the youth population, the net resources received by these age groups are diminished. However, one does not observe a significant increase in the net resources captured by the older age groups because the simulation accounts for the reduction of the public pension system's coverage. In fact, this situation translates into an increase in the age at which individuals switch from net contributors to net recipients: 63 years old in 2013, and 65 in 2050 and 2100. Finally, the middle-age groups increase their net contribution in 2050, but by 2100 it falls below the 2013 level.

The fiscal support ratio (FS) can be defined as:

$$FS_t = U_t/Q_t \tag{3.7}$$

This ratio tells us what proportion of public transfers can be directly financed by collections of taxes and social contributions, without considering other ways of obtaining resources, such as market production, debt, or external financing.

Figure 3.21 shows a forecast of the support ratio, keeping the average inflow and outflow for each age group stable while adjusting the population. In this scenario, up until 2040–2045 resources from net contributors more than offset the effect of population aging. This growth in the FS is exhausted for two reasons: the demographic change and the end of the transition period of the social

Figure 3.21 Evolution of the Fiscal Support Ratio, 2013–2100

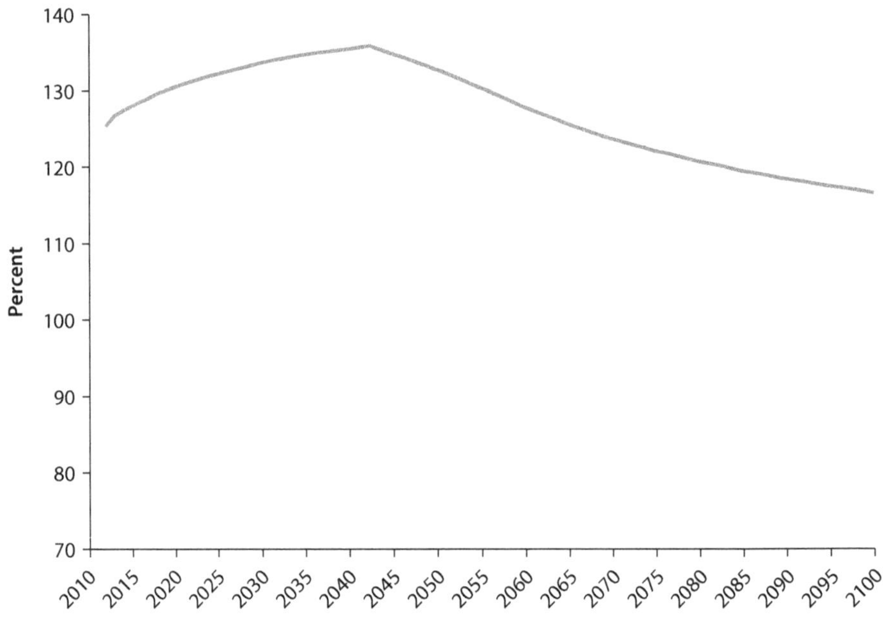

security reform. Thus, in the second half of the century, the FS begins to deteriorate to an ever greater degree as Uruguay progresses through the demographic transition. In contrast with the economic support ratio, the FS benefits less from the decrease in the proportion of young people in the population, given that this age group's consumption is mostly financed by private, intrafamily transfers.

Conclusions

This chapter makes an initial presentation of an information system specially designed to analyze how the life-cycle deficit is financed. In particular, this system shows how public and private consumption, labor income, and transfers to and from the public sector change with age. As a result, the changes that one can expect in the age structure of the population and especially its aging in general have fundamental economic and social implications for Uruguay. As the country progresses through the demographic transition, public policies must adapt to account for the changes that the transition will create in the composition and productivity of the labor force, the fiscal space, and the demands placed on social sectors (education, health care, and social protection and assistance), among others. Although it is obvious, this fact is not well recognized in the analytical debate of public policies in Uruguay, mostly due to the lack of detailed information regarding the age-specific changes in inflows and outflows throughout the life cycle. The information presented in this chapter allows us to overcome this obstacle and offers the foundation for a rigorous and wide-ranging discussion of the effects of the demographic transition that is developed throughout this book.

The estimates for 2013 in particular indicate that, in Uruguay, public transfers play a notably more significant role in financing the deficit in the later stages of life than in the early stages. As a result, we find evidence of a pattern of "allocation of responsibilities" by which households take primary responsibility for financing children's and adolescents' consumption, while the public sector has a more significant role in sustaining the elderly. Public sector transfers differ by age group in more than just quantitative terms. While children and adolescents receive support principally through public consumption, that is, through in-kind transfers, older adults receive most of their transfers in cash. Finally, while children and adolescents are the target population in the education sector, the elderly are the most intensive users in the health care sector.

The information generated is utilized to analyze the impact of demographic aging on the economic support ratio and on the public channels of financing for the life-cycle deficit, highlighting public social spending. The forecasts of the support ratio, the fiscal support ratio, and social spending are made using certain assumptions that in general terms consist of maintaining age group profiles of variables as in the current levels. This is the case for productivity, propensity to consume, tax collections, and public expenditure (with the exception of the changes that the 1996 social security reform created for the average pension in the future).

Remaining chapters consider changes in the said variables in order to analyze the most plausible scenarios. However, it is important to keep in mind that even though the assumption that these variables will remain constant is not representative of the future, it is useful for taking such a scenario as a baseline so that we can isolate the effects of purely demographic changes from other effects.

The simulations suggest that the magnitude of the effect of demographic change is not alarming. In terms of the support ratio, the simulation shows a fall after the mid-2030s; in terms of the fiscal support ratio, values below current levels appear from the 2060s on. Pressure on social spending is contained at the beginning and increases from the 2040s on. Two changes have effects during this decade: the demographic transition and the end of the transition begun with the 1996 Social Security Reform. All of the above indicates that Uruguay has time to adjust its policies to deal with the challenges that the population aging process entails.

Nonetheless, it is important to begin an informed debate, in particular in order to fully understand the tensions that will present themselves as a result of the changes in the relative requirements of the public social sectors. The increase in retirement benefits and pensions is not surprising if one assumes that the retirement age will not change while the number of older adults rises. This increase is accompanied by the growing role of health care spending, which results because the elderly are the most intensive consumers of these services. In contrast, the education spending forecast indicates that resources will be freed up due to a decrease in the school-age population, assuming that coverage remains at current levels. In conclusion, demographic changes may offer opportunities to reach various policy objectives, depending on the strategy the country chooses.

Notes

1. Marisa Bucheli, Department of Economics, School of Social Sciences, University of the Republic, and Sara Troiano, World Bank, Social Protection and Labor Global Practice and Pompeu Fabra University-Johns Hopkins University Public Policy Center, Barcelona, Spain.

   The authors wish to thank Gabriella Miraballes (Central Bank of Uruguay), Giselle Jorcin and Laura Rivas (Ministry of Public Health), and Andrea Vigorito (Institute of Economics, School of Economic and Management Sciences, University of the Republic) for their support in the estimation of the macro-controls.

   Correspondence to marisa.bucheli@cienciassociales.edu.uy and stroiano@worldbank.org.
2. Following suggestions from the NTA System, no smoothing was applied to the profiles in education because the discontinuities observed in consumption by age group in this sector are not typically random, but rather are associated with entry and exit ages for the different educational levels.
3. Note that even though in order to estimate health care consumption by age group we used the FONASA capita values, the smoothing procedure absorbs some of the differences. In particular, the capita for individuals less than one year old is very elevated, which is not reflected in the profile presented in figure 3.4.
4. In the 1994 and 2006 estimates, family allowances were assigned to the head of the household, who, in any case, utilized them to make a private transfer to the minors in his or her care. In the 2013 estimates, family allowances were allocated directly to minors, meaning that a direct comparison with the 2006 estimates is not possible. In addition, the equivalency scale for health care expenditure is different in 2013 compared to previous estimates.
5. For a discussion of how reasonable it is to assume profiles that are constant from the base year in these simulations, see Mason and Lee (2006).
6. For a justification of this assumption, see Lee and Edwards (2002) and Miller and Castanheira (2013).
7. Note that, in the case of labor income, the estimate of the profile by age group reflects both salary by age group as well as the labor market participation of each cohort in the base year.
8. Note that the null values for the life-cycle deficit are the same as in figure 3.1.

References

Alvarez, I., N. da Silva, A. Forteza, and I. Rossi. 2009. "El Retiro de los Trabajadores Uruguayos y la Seguridad Social." *Revista de Economía* 16 (2): 147–84.

Bucheli, M., and C. González. 2011. "Public Transfer Flow between Generations." In *Population Aging and the Generational Economy: A Global Perspective*, edited by R. Lee and A. Mason, 434–45. Cheltenham, UK: Edward Elgar Publishing.

Bucheli, M., C. González, and C. Olivieri. 2010. "Transferencias del Sector Público a la Infancia y Vejez en Uruguay." *Notas de Población* 90: 163–84.

Burdin, G., F. Esponda, and A. Vigorito. 2014. "Desigualdad y Sectores de Altos Ingresos en Uruguay: Un Análisis en Base a Registros Tributarios y Encuestas de Hogares para el Período 2009–2011." Documento de Trabajo 06/2014, Instituto de Economía,

Facultad de Ciencias Económicas y de Administración, Universidad de la República, Montevideo.

Central Bank of Uruguay (Banco Central del Uruguay). 2013. *Cuentas Nacionales 2013*. http://www.bcu.gub.uy/Estadisticas-e-Indicadores/Cuentas%20Nacionales.

General Accounting Office of the Nation (Contaduria General de la Nación). 2013. *Ejecución Presupuestal 2013*. Vol. III: Funcionamiento e Inversiones, and Vol. IV: Recursos.

Gragnolati, M., and S. Troiano. 2014. "Las Finanzas Públicas frente al Envejecimiento en Argentina." In *Los Años No Vienen Solos: Oportunidades y Desafíos Económicos de la Transición Demográfica en Argentina*, edited by M. Gragnolati, R. Rofman, I. Apella, and S. Troiano, 119–40. Buenos Aires: Banco Mundial.

IMF (International Monetary Fund). 2014. *World Economic Outlook: October 2014*. Washington, DC: IMF. http://www.imf.org/external/pubs/ft/weo/2014/02/weodata/index.aspx.

Lee, R., and R. D. Edwards. 2002. "The Fiscal Impact of Population Aging in the U.S.: Assessing the Uncertainties." In *Tax Policy and the Economy*, edited by J. Poterba, 141–81. Cambridge, MA: MIT Press.

Mason, A., and R. Lee. 2006. "Reform and Support Systems for the Elderly in Developing Countries: Capturing the Second Demographic Dividend." *Genus* 62 (2): 11–35.

———. 2007. "Transfers, Capital, and Consumption over the Demographic Transition." In *Population Aging, Intergenerational Transfers and the Macroeconomy*, edited by R. Clark, A. Mason, and N. Ogawa, 128–62. Cheltenham, UK: Edward Elgar Publishing.

———. 2011. "Population Aging and the Generational Economy: Key Findings." In *Population Aging and the Generational Economy: A Global Perspective*, edited by R. Lee and A. Mason, 3–31. Cheltenham, UK: Edward Elgar Publishing.

MIDES (Ministry of Social Development). 2014. "Estimación del Gasto Público Social por Edad y Sexo: Principales Resultados 2005–2013. Informe de Actualización." Draft, Montevideo.

Miller, T., and H. Castanheira. 2013. "The Fiscal Impact of Population Aging in Brazil: 2005–2050." *Revista Brasileira de Estudos de População* 30: S5–23.

National Institute of Statistics (Instituto Nacional de Estadística). 2006. "Encuesta Nacional de Gastos e Ingreso de los Hogares, Años 2005–2006." http://www3.ine.gub.uy/anda4/index.php/catalog/42.

———. 2013. "Encuesta Continua de Hogares 2013." http://www.ine.gub.uy/microdatos/microdatosnew2008.asp#ech.

National Information System (Sistema Nacional de Información). 2015. *Estado de Resultados de las IAMC, 2012 y 2013*. http://www.msp.gub.uy/publicaciones/direcci%C3%B3n-general-del-sistema-nacional-integrado-de-salud/econom%C3%ADa-de-la-salud/sistema.

Oreggioni, I., and L. Rivas. 2015. "Cuentas Nacionales de Salud 2009-2010," Ministerio de Salud Pública de la República Oriental del Uruguay y Organización Mundial de la Salud. http://www.msp.gub.uy/sites/default/files/INFORME%20Cuentas%20Nacionales%20de%20Salud%202009-2012%20FINAL.pdf.

Social Security Bank (Banco de Previsión Social). 2013. *Boletín Estadístico 2013*. http://www.bps.gub.uy/1920/boletin-estadistico.html.

Tung, A. 2011. "Consumption over the Lifecycle: An International Comparison." In *Population Aging and the Generational Economy: A Global Perspective*, edited by R. Lee and A. Mason, 136–60. Cheltenham, UK: Edward Elgar Publishing.

United Nations. 2014. *World Population Prospects: The 2012 Revision*. New York: United Nations.

CHAPTER 4

Social Protection in a Demographic Transition

Rafael Rofman and Ignacio Apella[1]

Introduction

The population of Uruguay is one of the oldest in Latin America, a profile similar to some European countries. Demographic transition has driven a sustained increase in the population over age 65, from 8 percent of people in 1950 to 14 percent in 2010, and this will continue until 30 percent of the population will be over age 65 in 2100. Given this context, concerns have emerged about the impact of demographic change on the social protection system.

The increase in the population over age 65 in many countries around the world has provoked interest in this trend's impact on some dimensions of social security. Population aging not only increases the number of potential beneficiaries for social security, but also reduces the number of potential contributors, which creates uncertainty around the fiscal and economic sustainability of these systems. The answers to these challenges appear to involve the combination of an effort to increase available resources (through continuous economic growth and expanding the sources of collections) and a review of social security system parameters, whether the product of independent changes in a population's behavior (as appears in Uruguay in workers deciding to delay their retirement) or normative changes.

The analysis in this chapter shows that the current social protection system in Uruguay has, like most other countries, a strong age bias that concentrates resources among the elderly at the expense of other groups, like economically active adults or children. This situation gives rise to debates about the system's intergenerational equity and economic efficiency, debates which cannot be resolved with a technical analysis, but instead respond to a society's policy preferences.

In this context, the goal of this chapter is to study the impact that demographic transition may have on social protection spending and how it is distributed among age groups. We also investigate the relationship between types of social protection programs, the age of the target beneficiary population, and the incidence of poverty.

Long-term forecasts are necessary to assess how the system will react to expected changes in economic, political, and demographic conditions. These forecasts are not designed to predict the future, but rather to evaluate the system's prospects, given certain reasonable hypotheses regarding the long-term evolution of some determinant variables.

Social Protection in Uruguay

Social security is usually defined as the set of programs and policies that guard against the effects of specific risks related to loss of household income, through schemes that require participants to contribute to funding. In general terms, social security is instituted to provide certainty and insure individuals against the risk of income losses or spikes in spending related to retirement in old age or as a result of disability, illness, accident, or death.

In turn, social protection covers a broader sector than just social security, including traditional contributory social security programs and noncontributory transfer schemes. Noncontributory programs in Latin America have traditionally had very limited reach, in budget as well as coverage. In recent years, a change in this trend for social protection systems has occurred as these programs have become progressively more important. In Uruguay, the implementation of the Equity Plan (Plan Equidad) and the loosening of eligibility requirements for beneficiaries of social security are clear examples of the expansion of coverage to the part of the population excluded from the formal labor market and living in situations of poverty or vulnerability.

Uruguay was among the pioneers in Latin America in implementing social security schemes at the end of the 19th century, along with Argentina, Brazil, Chile, and Cuba. At the start, the Uruguayan social security system offered coverage only to some government officials, before it was expanded to all members of the public sector. It was not until the 1950s that these benefits reached all workers. During this time, "parastatal funds" were also created. These are institutions that offer protection to specific groups of workers, such as bankers, notaries, university professionals, and, more recently, members of the police and armed forces.

Risks covered by the social security system include loss of income resulting from old age, disability, and death, as well as unemployment. In addition, cash transfers through family allowances are part of Uruguay's social security system, although the family allowance does not attempt to insure income against a specific risk but has the goal of increasing disposable income in households with children.

Traditionally, these programs have been conceived as contributory in nature. Coverage accordingly is directly linked to the scale of formal employment in the labor market. The rise in informality and labor insecurity during the 1990s limited the reach of social security coverage.

Uruguay, as with most countries in the region, is characterized by what is known as a "truncated welfare system." In this, the formal sector of the economy contributes to social security and in return receives insurance against risks, but a significant percentage of workers employed outside the formal labor market face serious limitations on their access to protection. In this context, in the late 1990s Uruguay began to implement programs for workers (and their families) excluded from the formal labor market, which did not link benefits to contributions.

The Social Security System

The Uruguayan social security system has developed in several distinct phases. The first phase began at the end of the 19th century, when the government awarded disability benefits to soldiers who had fought in the independence wars, survivor benefits for their widows, and retirement benefits to civil servants.

In 1919, the Pension Scheme for Public Utilities Employees (Caja de Jubilaciones y Pensiones de Empleados y Obreros de los Servicios Públicos) was created. It incorporated workers at public utilities, such as telegraphs, railroads, streetcars, telephone companies, running water, and gas providers. In 1954, once most private sector workers had been included in the social security system, the passage of Law No. 12,138 established guidelines for including anyone performing lawful, paid work in coverage administered by the Industry and Commerce Retirement and Pension Fund (Caja de Jubilaciones y Pensiones de Industria y Comercio), provided they were not covered by other retirement systems, and gave the social security system legal status in a universal coverage scheme.

During the second half of the 20th century, the funds began to go into deficit and were forced to rely on government funding. These financial difficulties were already evident in the 1960s. They were the product not just of population aging and the systems maturing, but also of the disordered incorporation of different economic sectors, the introduction of new benefits without an adequate funding strategy, and the absence of any technical management of financial resources.

In 1967, the Social Security Bank (Banco de Previsión Social; BPS) was created as an autonomous institution, administratively and financially independent of central government. The goal of the BPS was to organize the social protection system's operations. Existing funds were merged into the bank, while eligibility criteria and benefit levels were unified. Nonetheless, the social security system continued to generate financial deficits, which required the state to transfer budgetary resources to ensure that retirement and pension benefits could be funded.

In 1995, as part of a trend in other countries of the region, Law No. 16,713 was passed. The law created a mixed retirement system comprising two pillars: a pay-as-you-go regime administered by the BPS, and an individually funded scheme for commercial enterprises under the auspices of the Retirement Savings Fund Administrators (Administradoras de Fondos de Ahorro Previsional; AFAP). Participation in the pay-as-you-go regime continued to be compulsory for all workers, while the funded scheme was compulsory for high-income workers and voluntary for middle- and low-income workers. As a result of this strategy, most workers in Uruguay participate in both schemes.

This reform, implemented due to serious concerns about the high cost of the system, also included several parametric changes, such as the unification of the retirement age between men and women at age 60, an increase in the number of years for contributions from 30 to 35, an increase in the reference period for benefit determination from the final 3 to the final 10 years of salaries, as well as a reduction in the promised replacement rates. These parametric reforms tightened the criteria for access to benefits and reduced their value.

Funding for the social security system comes from several sources: contributions from covered workers (15 percent of their salaries), employer contributions (7.5 percent of salaries), and the state through designated taxes and transfers to subsidize the BPS deficit. Public funds cover one-fifth of the BPS retirement and pension payments, according to Filgueira and Hernández (2012). Retirement and pension payments for the individually funded scheme are paid exclusively from workers' contributions and the financial return on accumulated capital.

In 2008, in an attempt to expand the social security system's coverage, the government reduced the contribution years required to access retirement benefits from 35 to 30 years, while maintaining the minimum retirement age at 60. The government also loosened requirements for access to retirement benefits at more advanced ages, offering a reduced benefit to workers of age 70 and older who had made at least 15 years of contributions. With this new program, a progressive scale was adopted that allowed individuals to access benefits at advanced ages, trading years of age for years of contributions: age 69 and 17 years of contributions; age 68 and 19 years; age 67 and 21 years; age 66 and 23 years; and age 65 and 25 years of contributions.

Finally, the 2008 reform recognized the distinct status of women in the labor market. The reform established that women with children would receive the equivalent of a year of contributions for each child born or adopted (up to age five) for the purposes of calculating retirement age. Based on this provision, for example, mothers with five adopted or natural children may retire at age 55.

Unemployment Insurance

Unemployment insurance protects workers from the risk of income loss related to job loss. It provides coverage to all formal salaried workers and is funded by social security contributions made during the working life.

From 1981 until the end of 2008, workers on unemployment benefit received a uniform amount of up to six months, equivalent to 50 percent of their average salary during their last 6 months of employment. The benefits could not be less than 50 percent of the national minimum wage, nor more than eight times the minimum wage. At the end of 2008, a reform established a decreasing replacement rate: starting at 66 percent of the minimum wage during the first month and falling to 40 percent by the sixth month. A further six months of coverage were provided for people over age 50 who had been laid off.

The Family Allowance System

The family allowance regime was created in 1942, with the passage of Law No. 10,449, as an income transfer program for workers in the industrial and commercial sectors. To receive the benefit workers were required to contribute to social security and children had to be complying with school attendance requirements from ages 6 to 14.

In 1950, the Central Council of Family Allowances (Consejo Central de Asignaciones Familiares) was created with representation from employers, workers, and the state. The compensation funds' principal function was to collect contributions and pay benefits. Compensation was generated by the funds and in the event of a deficit they could request the respective compensation from the council. In 1954, family allowance benefits were expanded to rural workers, and in 1958 to unemployed workers in the industrial and commercial sectors.

During the 1960s, children and minors in the care of retirees, and pensioners from the Industry and Commerce Fund, the Rural Workers Fund, and seniors were added as beneficiaries, according to Sierna (2007). Children of public servants and those of retirees from the Banking Fund were included, among others.

From 1973, the Central Council of Family Allowances and the compensation funds started to centralize the regime, and within a few years, the council became the only authority in the system. In 1979, the council and the funds that depended on it were restructured as the Directorate of Family Allowances under the Ministry of Labor and Social Security.

Rising unemployment and an increase in labor informality during the 1990s gradually excluded a significant proportion of the population. The combination of fiscal pressures and the decrease in coverage created the need to target income transfer programs to the poorest and most vulnerable people.

Changes to the regime transformed it from a system originally conceived for workers covered by social security to a benefit targeted to households composed of low-income workers, and elderly individuals excluded from the social security system who had children in their care, according to Arim, Cruces, and Vigorito (2009).

In1995, Law No. 16,697 modified the family allowance regime, basing benefits on household income. The benefit amount was equal to 16 percent of the minimum wage for contributors with income less than or equal to six times the minimum wage. For workers with income between six and ten minimum wages, the benefit was 8 percent. Finally, the benefit was not provided to workers with incomes greater than ten times the minimum wage.

Three income transfer initiatives stand out during 2000–10: the 2004 reform to the family allowance regime; the "Citizen Income" component of the broader National Plan for Attention to the Social Emergency (Plan de Atención Nacional a la Emergencia Social; PANES) in 2005 and 2007; and the creation of the family allowances regime within the Equity Plan in 2008.

Law No. 17,758 was passed in 2004 as a means of achieving universal transfers to households. It changed the nature of the family allowance benefit, delinking it from the contribution requirement and expanding it to all households with income of less than three times the minimum wage, including those not covered under previous laws. The benefit for these households was set at 16 percent of the minimum wage.

PANES was created in 2005 through Law No. 17,869. This initiative consisted of a set of social policies aimed at very low-income households. The target population comprised the poorest 20 percent of people below the poverty line.

The program, conceived as a temporary two-year intervention from 2005–07, had two big goals. The first, with a short time horizon, was to provide assistance to poor households through cash transfers (called the Citizen Income; Ingreso Ciudadano) and food transfers, as well as interventions to improve the conditions of homes. The second, long-term, goal was to accumulate human capital in households and help people return to the labor market through training, education, and social and labor participation. The Citizen Income component consisted of a fixed conditional cash transfer of Ur$1,360 per month, regardless of the size of the household. Participation was contingent on children and adolescents up to age 14 attending school, and on children and pregnant women receiving health checkups.

A new variation of transfers to children was introduced in 2008 to succeed PANES. The Family Allowances Plan (Asignaciones Familiares) from the Equity Plan was designed to provide income transfers to the population under age 18 living in vulnerable conditions. Vulnerability was estimated through a means test implemented by the BPS. Households receiving the Citizen Income benefit at the end of 2007 were passed directly into the new Family Allowances system if their socioeconomic status was below an established threshold.

The previous noncontributory family allowance regimes disappeared gradually, as beneficiaries passed into the new Equity Plan. The transfer amount varies according to a scale that considers age and educational achievement, paying more to adolescents who are ready to enter secondary studies.

Uruguay Social Card

As with many of the instruments designed to reduce the incidence of poverty between 2005 and 2007, the National Nutrition Plan (Plan Alimentario Nacional; PAN) began as a component of PANES. In May 2006, this program consisted of a cash transfer through a bank card, called the PANES Card, and was meant to be used to buy food, cleaning, and personal hygiene supplies for households living in poverty. The target population comprised those households in poverty with children in their care and/or pregnant women.

Implementation of the Equity Plan from 2008 saw the original PANES Card switch from the sole administration of the Ministry of Social Development (Ministerio de Desarrollo Social; MIDES) to becoming a tool of national government, through the Central Interinstitutional Commission of the Nutrition

Component in the Social Cabinet (Comisión Interinstitucional Central del Componente Alimentario del Gabinete Social), made up of representatives from MIDES, the MTSS-INDA (Ministerio de Trabajo y Seguridad Social-Instituto Nacional de Alimentación), the MSP (Ministerio de Salud Pública), and the ASSE (Administración de los Servicios de Salud del Estado).

The Uruguay Social Card is a prepaid magnetic strip card used to buy foodstuffs, personal, and household items, and also products and services that contribute to social inclusion and integration.

The program's target population is households in a state of indigence or which are vulnerable to it, prioritizing those with children. To achieve this, the program uses a targeting instrument that allows the government to determine to an exacting degree whether a household meets the criteria for being a beneficiary. This instrument is called the Critical Deficiencies Index and consists of a means testing index that weights various nonmonetary household characteristics that reveal the degree of vulnerability. In 2015, the value of a single transfer varied from Ur$684 to Ur$1,839, depending on the number of minors in the household. In turn, households considered among the 30,000 most vulnerable receive double the standard benefit, ranging from Ur$1,368 to Ur$3,678.

Income Transfers and Poverty

Even though wage income represents the principal component of household resources, transfer programs play an important role in poverty reduction and income distribution policies. The gap between income distribution and poverty indicators before and after taxes and transfers can be explained in part by differences in tax systems, but the role of public spending is important. This expenditure includes social protection policies.

In most countries in the region, the principal objective of social protection is to replace labor income (in the case of retirement and pension systems or unemployment insurance) to ensure a basic income (in the case of targeted income transfer programs) or consumption (transfers of goods), and even to promote the accumulation of human capital (as in the case of cash transfer programs made on the condition that the recipient attend some form of education or training).

Even though their common objective is to ensure households do not go without income, these transfers vary, based on eligibility mechanisms for beneficiaries. For example, pension programs are aimed at the older adult population with the goal of substituting labor income during old age; family allowance transfers consist of a transfer designed to increase disposable income among households with children; and unemployment insurance transfers seek to support young adults with employability problems. In other words, in many cases it is possible to identify a connection between the specific objectives of social protection programs and the age of the beneficiaries.

The pattern of resource distribution gains greater relevance when considering the changing profile of poverty through the household's life cycle. Poverty for each age group depends on the pattern of transfers and consumption throughout the life cycle, which follows three phases. At the beginning, during childhood, individuals face a deficit since they do not have the ability to generate income and require funding from the adults who care for them. During a second phase as they enter the labor market, income exceeds consumption, giving rise to the possibility of generating savings and accumulating assets. Finally, they pass through the third phase, during which they decrease their assets and retire from the labor market.

This classification is important for the analysis of the incidence of poverty, since different stages of the life cycle require different policy responses. As an example, while the incidence of poverty in an initial phase could be the consequence of young adults finding it difficult to generate sufficient surpluses to fund their own consumption and that of their children, an individual who barely rises above the poverty line in the second phase and therefore cannot accumulate significant savings could find it difficult upon retirement from work if social security schemes do not provide sufficient resources to help.

The following arithmetical exercise, covering 2001 and 2013, has as its goal obtaining an estimate of the importance of social protection transfers in combating the incidence of poverty. Using the Continuous Household Survey as the principal information source, the exercise consists of calculating the incidence of poverty and the poverty gap depending on individuals' ages, and considering total household income with and without social protection transfers. The estimates do not include the effects of transfers on the behavior of household members, which is assumed to be unchanged whether or not transfers occur. As a result, the analysis is unavoidably biased, but it allows us to identify any trends in the incidence of poverty among different age groups in Uruguay.

Figure 4.1 shows the percentage of individuals in poor households in 2001 and 2013, divided by five-year age groups and identifying the impact that eliminating each type of social protection transfer program would have. It is apparent that in 2001 poverty affected 30 percent of the population, but also that without transfer programs, this would have increased to 50 percent. The main program that holds back poverty is the social security system, which explains why the impact simulated here is concentrated among older adults. In 2013, the incidence of poverty was significantly lower (9 percent) than in 2001, and this is true for all age groups. As in 2001, income transfers from the social protection system played a central role in diminishing poverty in 2013—without these programs the percentage of individuals belonging to poor households would have reached 25 percent. This impact is greater than the effect observed in 2001 as a result of the expansion of social protection coverage through noncontributory programs during the first decade of the new millennium.

It is interesting to note that social protection policies are not just important during each period in reducing poverty, but they have also helped decrease the incidence of poverty since the beginning of the last decade.

According to a study prepared by the World Bank (2015), these policies explain 13 percent of the fall in poverty during that period, while the rest of the reduction is explained by improvements in the labor market (especially real salaries).

Figure 4.2 presents the poverty gap; that is, the average percentage of income needed to raise income to the poverty line, by age group and type of transfer. In 2001, individuals living in poverty needed, on average, 10 percent of the value of the poverty line in order to reach it. Furthermore, poor children had a gap of 21 percent, while for young adults it was 10 percent and for the elderly the gap was 3 percent. The results allow us to appreciate the importance of social protection programs not just for reducing the incidence of poverty, but also for reducing

Figure 4.1 Percentage of Individuals in Poor Households by Age Group and Transfer Type, 2001 and 2013

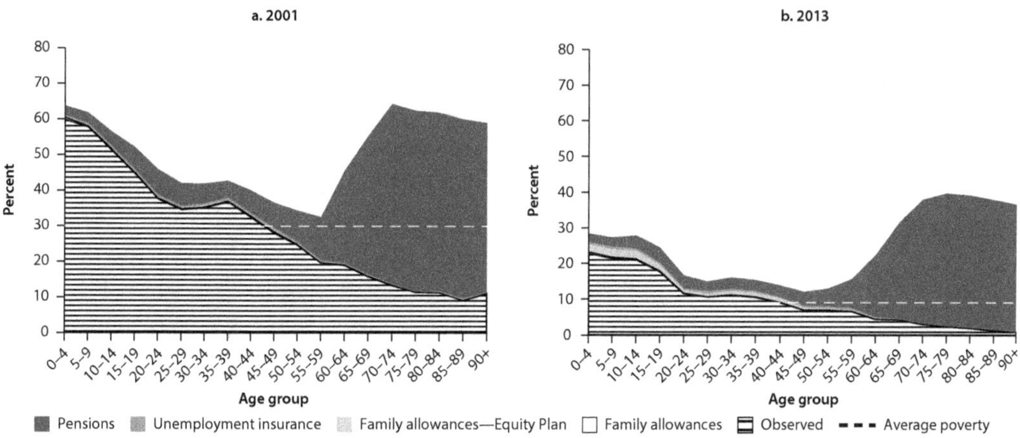

Source: Elaboration based on National Institute of Statistics household surveys (Instituto Nacional de Estadística, Encuesta Continua de Hogares).

Figure 4.2 Poverty Gap by Age Group and Transfer Type, 2001 and 2013

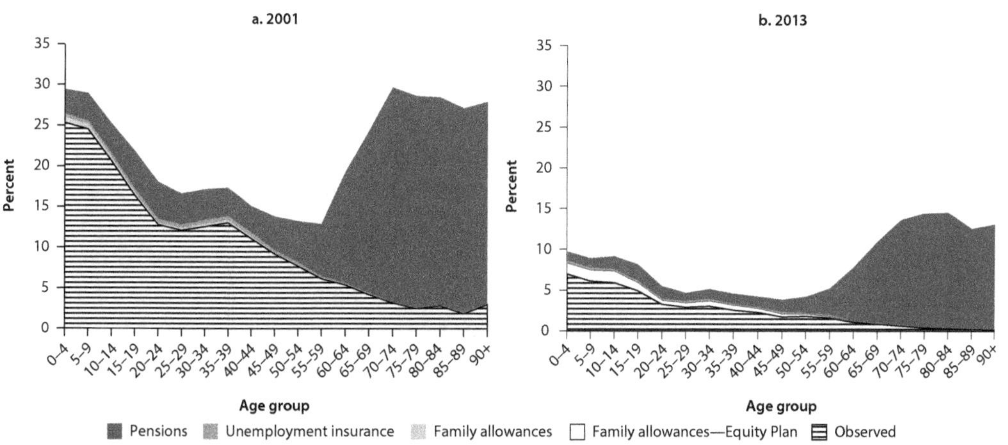

Source: Elaboration based on National Institute of Statistics household surveys (Instituto Nacional de Estadística, Encuesta Continua de Hogares).

the gap for individuals whose income remains below the line. This is particularly notable among the elderly, a group that without transfers from the social security system would have had a poverty gap of 28 percent in 2001 and 13 percent in 2013. For family allowances, the effect is important although less significant. This type of transfer increases disposable income among young households. As such, its impact on poverty reduction and closing the poverty gap is felt among children and also among young adults.

The results demonstrate that social protection is very important as a tool for reducing the impact of poverty. The expansion of social security coverage along with the generosity of benefits, and consideration of the composition of beneficiary households, enable significantly more impact on poverty reduction, especially on the elderly. Additionally, family allowances, both the traditional version and the Equity Plan, achieved a decrease in the incidence of poverty, especially among children.

Profile of Social Protection Beneficiaries in 2013

Social protection benefits in Uruguay are concentrated in two large age groups: children and the elderly. This concentration appears to be an adequate response to the distribution of poverty, as reflected in figure 4.1. It is evident from this distribution that the incidence of poverty is greatest among these two age groups, due in part to individuals in both groups passing through deficit phases in the life cycle; in other words, their consumption exceeds their labor incomes. Figure 4.3 presents the profile of social protection beneficiaries by age and type of transfer received for 2013.

In 2013, a little more than 480,000 children were beneficiaries of family allowances, with 25 percent receiving traditional allowances and 75 percent receiving family allowances from the Equity Plan. Additionally, this age group benefited from the Uruguay Social Card, which reached approximately 79,000 households, equivalent to 271,000 people.

Moreover, social security benefits reached not just the elderly, but also other age groups because the social security system entitles covered individuals not only to retirement benefits, but also to disability and survivor benefits. Nonetheless, the greatest concentration of beneficiaries is in the over-60 age group.

In 2013, social protection cash transfers, excluding operating costs, reached Ur$119 billion, equivalent to 10.5 percent of gross domestic product (GDP). Figure 4.4, based on the distribution of beneficiaries by age group, and type of program, presents the profile of total social protection transfers for 2013.

Figure 4.4 shows that the adult population over age 60 receives 75 percent of social protection spending, principally the result of retirement and pension transfers. In turn, children are beneficiaries of 5 percent of the expenditure. This asymmetry in the distribution of social protection resources is related to the difference in the average benefits provided by each program. During December 2013, the average social security benefit was Ur$14,000, while traditional and Equity Plan family allowances were Ur$225 and Ur$960, respectively.

Figure 4.3 Beneficiaries by Social Protection Program and Age, 2013

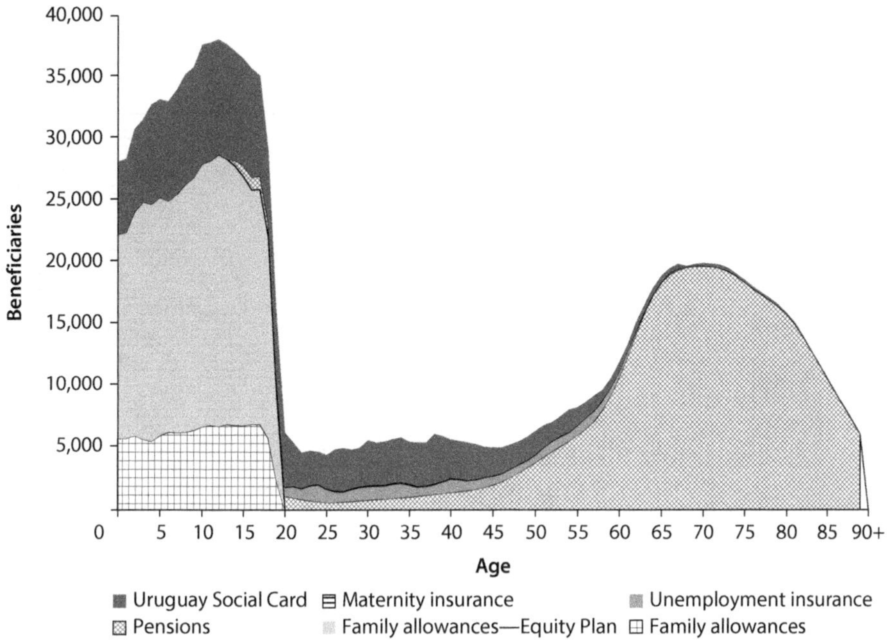

Sources: Elaboration based on information from the National Institute of Statistics (Instituto Nacional de Estadística) and the Social Security Bank (Banco de Previsión Social).

Figure 4.4 Total Expenditure on Social Protection by Age Group and Program, Single-Year Age Groups, 2013

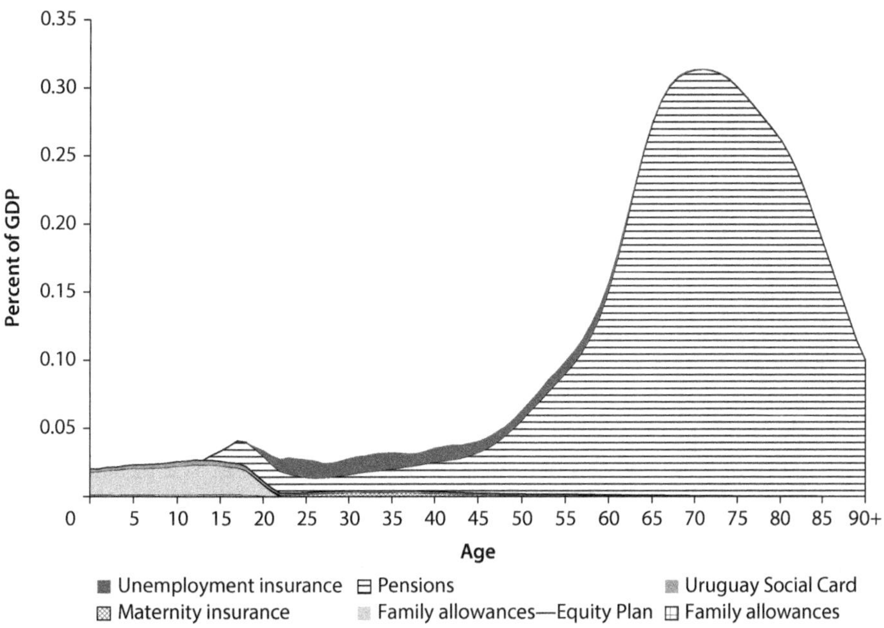

Sources: Elaboration based on information from the National Institute of Statistics (Instituto Nacional de Estadística) and the Social Security Bank (Banco de Previsión Social).

Figure 4.5 Per Capita Social Protection Expenditure by Age Group and Program, 2013

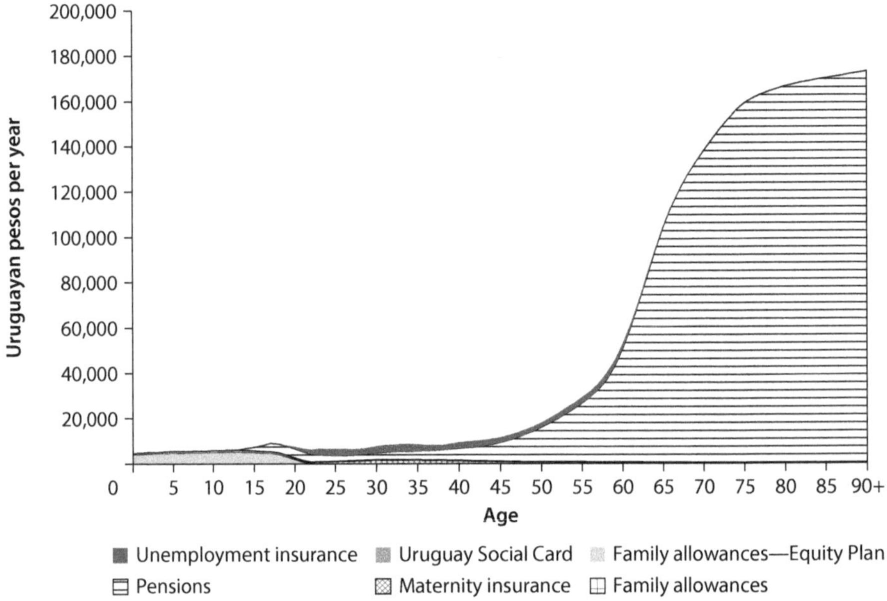

Sources: Elaboration based on information from the National Institute of Statistics (Instituto Nacional de Estadística) and the Social Security Bank (Banco de Previsión Social).

Although total social protection expenditure per age group exhibits a strong bias toward older adults, the effect is even more notable if one considers per capita expenditure. Figure 4.5 allows us to observe the strong spending bias in favor of older adults who receive transfers worth an average 30 times greater than those for children and young adults. This difference results from the combination of the high value of retirement benefits relative to transfers to children and the greater coverage of social protection among older adults.

The differences reflected in figure 4.5 give rise to debate about the intergenerational equity of the system. The discussion has two dimensions.

On one hand, it is clear that older adults benefit significantly from transfers, although it is possible that part of this difference is offset when older adults use a portion of these resources to finance consumption by their children and grandchildren. Even if this were the case, one still must question if a social protection policy is reasonable if it exhibits such a strong bias.

On the other hand, it could be possible to judge the apparent inequality as not that important if viewed through the lens of a cohort analysis. The principal arguments for this point would be that: (a) throughout the life cycle all age cohorts pass through childhood and old age, which means that eventually everyone benefits from this model; and (b) older adults receiving these benefits have made contributions, both through social security contributions, and through their labor and payment of general taxes throughout their lives, which means that these transfers are essentially the result of the efforts they have made in previous decades.

The latter argument is related to the idea that social security benefits constitute income as a type of deferred wages. This vision proposes that, given the current configuration of the social security system—funded by wage-based contributions and from general taxes—workers make contributions during their economically active period as a way of postponing some income for use during their retirement. In any case, it would appear that, beyond the normative discussion of intergenerational equity that this data should provoke, it is important to also consider the issue of efficiency. Even assuming that the cohort focus is more correct and, consequently, the impact of intergenerational transfers is reduced over the long term, it is worthwhile to consider the social utility of delaying the largest part of public transfers to households to promote the accumulation of human capital and economic and social development to the final stage of the life cycle. Making a transfer earlier in the life cycle could facilitate the accumulation of human capital through, for example, increased expenditure on education, which would result in improved living conditions through the entire cycle and increased aggregate productivity in the economy.

The Future of Social Protection

Based on the breakdown of transfers per age group and the type of programs discussed earlier, the following section considers the spending trend for social protection cash transfers during 2013–2100, working from some assumptions of the long-term behavior of the intervening variables.

Methodology

The expenditure by each social protection transfer program, except for the pension program, at any moment in time is defined in equation 4.1:

$$G_{p,t} = \sum_{x=0}^{+90} b_{p,x,t,} \cdot N_{t,x} \cdot \alpha_{p,x,t} \tag{4.1}$$

Where:

$G_{p,t}$ represents total expenditure by program p, during period t.

$b_{p,x,t}$ is the average benefit received by beneficiaries in age group x, from program p, at time t. This value is adjusted over time using the same growth rate as GDP per capita.

$N_{t,x}$ is the population in age group x, at time t.

$\alpha_{p,x,t}$ is the percentage of the population of age group x covered by program p at time t.

The programs included in the forecast are: retirement benefits and pensions administered by the BPS; the funded regime and the parastatal funds; traditional and Equity Plan family allowances; unemployment insurance; maternity insurance; and the Uruguay Social Card.

Given that it is preferable to prioritize a long-term vision and a structural analysis of the social protection system under relatively stable conditions, we have chosen to present a scenario with annual GDP growth that depends on the evolution of the returns to labor and their proportion of GDP. We assume that these returns grow an average of 2.5 percent per year and their relative proportion of GDP is constant at 49 percent. Additionally, even though each program exhibits particular characteristics, we have assumed that the coverage of the target population remains constant for all of them, $\alpha_{p,x,t}$. Finally, we use the United Nations Population Division's population forecast.

The spending forecast for the social security system deserves special consideration because it is necessary to consider its multipillar character, in which a pay-as-you-go scheme with obligatory affiliation administered by the BPS coexists with the individually funded Social Security Savings Fund Administrators regime. The average benefit paid by the pay-as-you-go scheme $\bar{b}_{R,t}$ is simulated as the product of the theoretical substitution rate of said scheme (γ_t) and the average wage for a formal worker ($\bar{w}_t$).

$$\bar{b}_{R,t} = \gamma_t \cdot \bar{w}_t \tag{4.2}$$

This substitution rate was 60 percent[2] in 2013 and is expected to converge around 45 percent at the beginning of the 2040s when the new multipillar pension scheme is consolidated and most retirees will receive benefits through the mixed system.

On the other hand, the simulation for benefits spending by the Social Security Savings Fund Administrators requires us to forecast the accumulated funds for each active worker. For simplicity's sake, and without loss of generality, we assume that the real return from investing the accumulated funds (r) is equal to 1.5 percent per year; the commission charged by the administrator, c, is equal to 2.8 percent; and the individual contribution, s, remains constant over time (15 percent).

Thus, F_{jt} is defined as the retirement and pension fund for worker j during period $\bar{t}$ as:

$$F_{j\bar{t}} = (s-c)\sum_{t=1}^{\bar{t}} w_{jt}(1+r)^{\bar{t}-t} \cdot \beta_{jt} \tag{4.3}$$

where w_{jt} is the wage for worker j for each period t, and β_{jt} is equal to one if the individual participates in the formal labor market or set at zero for any other case.

The annual benefit that the individual receives is equivalent to the ratio between the total accumulated resources in his fund at age 60 and the actuarial factor corresponding to age 60, $a(60)$[3]

$$\bar{b}_{C,t} = \frac{F_{j,60}}{a(60)} \tag{4.4}$$

It follows that total expenditure on retirement and pension benefits provided by the individually funded system is expressed as:

$$G_{C,t} = \sum_{x=60}^{+90} \bar{b}_{C,t} \cdot N_{t,x} \cdot \alpha_{t,x} \cdot \varphi_{t,x} \tag{4.5}$$

Where $\phi_{t,x}$ is the percentage of beneficiaries in the funded scheme. Following the methodology used in Dassatti and Mariño (2014) we estimate that the proportion of retirees in both regimes increases over time, reaching its maximum value at the beginning of the 2040s at approximately 89 percent.[4]

Empirical Results

In our first exercise, we estimate the trend for total social protection spending using the system's current parameters. Figure 4.6 presents the forecast trajectory for retirement and pension expenditure as a percentage of GDP for each financial regime.

Based on the assumptions made, if the current rules are not modified, the aging process will significantly increase the financial effort that the economy as a whole will have to make to sustain spending on retirement benefits and pensions.

Social security spending in the pay-as-you-go scheme drops slightly until the end of the 2020s, reaching 8.8 percent of GDP. This phenomenon is associated with a reduction in the substitution rate, which is the result of the growing proportion of beneficiaries in the funded regime. Nonetheless, once the system has matured, the pay-as-you-go scheme's expenditure starts to rise again as a result of population aging, increasing to 9.5 percent of GDP in 2050 and 13.4 percent in 2100.

It is important to consider trends related to the funded regime in addition to those for fiscal conditions. Essentially, the benefits to be paid directly by the

Figure 4.6 Total Expenditure on Retirement Benefits and Pensions, 2013–2100

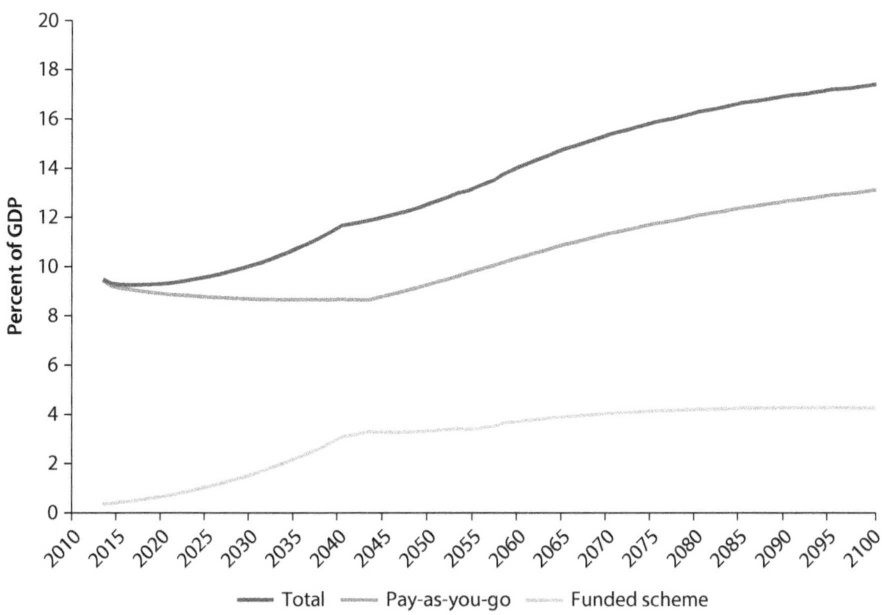

Social Security Savings Fund Administrators or through insurers have no direct relevance for the public accounts, but they are relevant in terms of the effort society as a whole must make to generate the resources to be transferred to older adults. The benefits paid by the funded regime are forecasted to grow exponentially until the beginning of the 2040s, then grow at a fairly constant rate, until reaching 3.3 percent of GDP in 2050 and 4 percent in 2100. The existence of these two sections in the individually funded scheme's overall spending trend is explained by the growing number of beneficiaries during the first stage of the system's consolidation, which later stabilizes and follows the demographic trends.

Consequently, the social security system as a whole could require around 12.8 percent of GDP in 2050 and 17.1 percent in 2100, which is a clear challenge for the entire economy because if the goal is to maintain the current rules of operation, the economy will have to provide a greater portion of its product to fund this set of transfers.

The projected evolution of expenditure in other programs follows demographic trends, as we do not assume changes in coverage or benefit levels. Thus, figure 4.7 shows how payments of traditional and Equity Plan family allowances will be declining, given the fall in the relative size of the population of children and adolescents. The same will occur in the case of unemployment and maternity insurance due to the falling proportion of the population that is

Figure 4.7 Expenditure on Family Allowances, Unemployment Insurance, and Maternity Insurance, 2013–2100

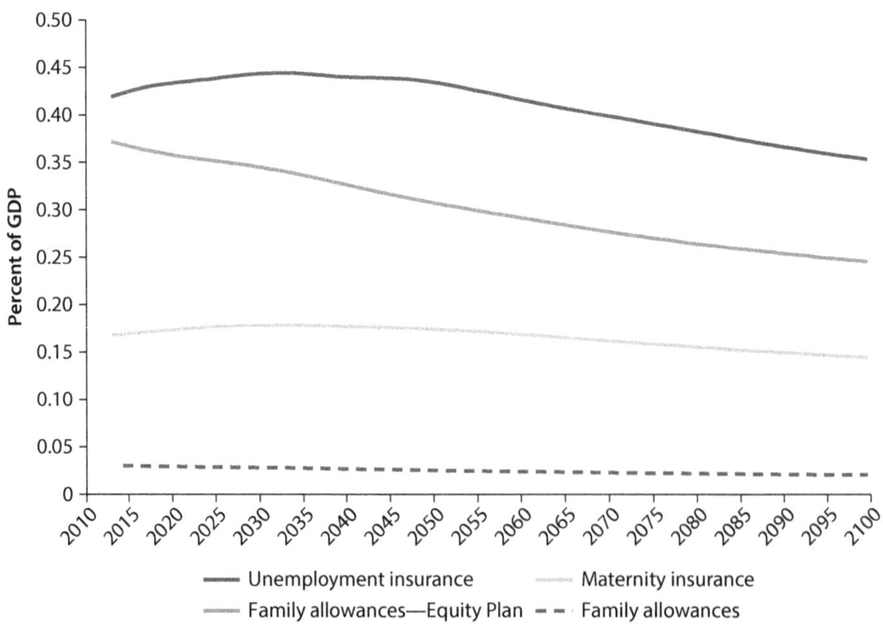

of working age. The relative significance of spending on this set of programs will continue to be minor (and will even decrease) relative to social security spending.

Total public expenditure in the sector (that is, including the six programs previously discussed), which reached 10.7 percent of GDP in 2013, will tend to increase in the coming decades, as figure 4.8 shows. If the social security system maintains its current rules, it will reach nearly 13.9 percent of GDP in 2100, which will represent a significant strain, not just on fiscal resources which the State will have to confront by combining various sources of alternative financing, but also on the economy as a whole, especially considering that, adding in the retirement benefits and pensions paid by the funded regime, the total amount will be around 18.6 percent of GDP.

The transition to an older population creates pressure as the number of people dependent on the income of others increases. In effect, the money spent by the social security system in its entirety (pay-as-you-go and funded) is growing during the entire period under study. Although public expenditure decreases during the first stage, due to the transition to the mixed system, from the 2040s onward the aging of the population adds to demand for spending by the pay-as-you-go regime once the transition phase is complete.

These forecasts mean that, in the coming decades, Uruguayan society must identify effective responses that ensure the sustainability of the social protection system. The options are clear. On one hand it will be essential to ensure sustained

Figure 4.8 Total Social Protection Expenditure (Public Spending and Funded Social Security), 2013–2100

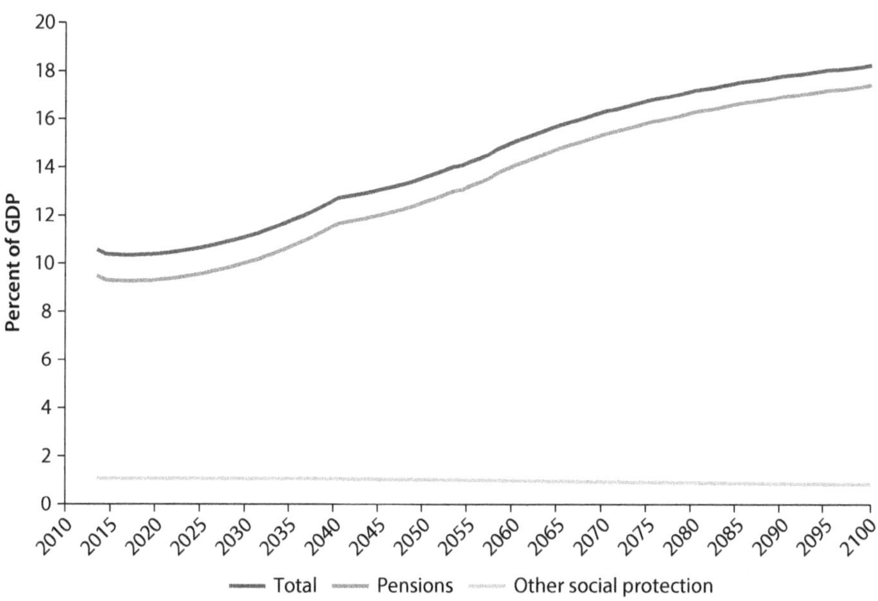

growth in the economy, which will allow for the creation of greater resources. On the other hand, one can hope that behavioral changes in the population or normative adjustments will allow the social security system to adapt to the new demographic reality.

According to Alvarez et al. (2010), the retirement age among men remained stable between 1996 and 2004, while among women it increased by almost four years. Meanwhile, Colombo (2012) estimates that between 2004 and 2011 the retirement age among men increased by one year and 0.5 years among women, reaching ages 63.6 and 61.9 years, respectively. These increases, even after considering the impact of the 2008 reforms, which led to a slight fall in average retirement ages, demonstrate a natural trend of increasing retirement ages. This phenomenon could continue if a legal framework that incentivizes it were to be put in place.

Additionally, it may be assumed that the social security system could create financial incentives for delaying retirement, as some experts have proposed (Stock and Wise 1990; Gruber and Wise 2002). The gain is composed of two components: the present value of wages from working longer, combined with a higher future social security benefit associated with a "premium" for the additional contribution periods acquired and the lower number of years during which a worker who delayed retirement would be paid the expected benefit.

This incentive occurs naturally in the funded regime, insomuch as a longer contribution period favors the creation of a larger retirement and pension fund, which along with the same number of years as a beneficiary means that a higher benefit would be provided. In addition, given the mixed nature of the Uruguayan social security system, it is assumed that the same financial gain is offered to the benefits paid by the pay-as-you-go regime.[5]

Under an alternative scenario, the effective retirement age could be raised one year for every ten years beginning in 2020. The idea behind this alternative is to maintain postretirement life expectancy at current levels. Currently, the average life expectancy for a man at age 64 is 19 years, while for a woman at age 62 it is 24 years. Demographic forecasts indicate that by 2020 this will be the life expectancy for the age 65 men and the age 63 women, and so forth every ten years. Certainly, this is simply a possible scenario; one that enables us to evaluate the impacts of changes in the system, and we do not intend for it to have any predictive value.

Figure 4.9 presents the trend for expenditure on retirement benefits and pensions for each financial regime from 2013 to 2100, comparing the previously described base-case scenario with the alternative that assumes a progressive increase in the retirement age.

In general terms, one observes that although total expenditure on retirement benefits and pensions will continue to rise slightly throughout the period of study, in the alternative scenario its level is well below the estimate based on current criteria. Accordingly, total expenditure on retirement benefits and pensions would reach 10.8 percent of GDP at the beginning of the 2040s

Figure 4.9 Total Expenditure on Retirement Benefits and Pensions, 2013–2100

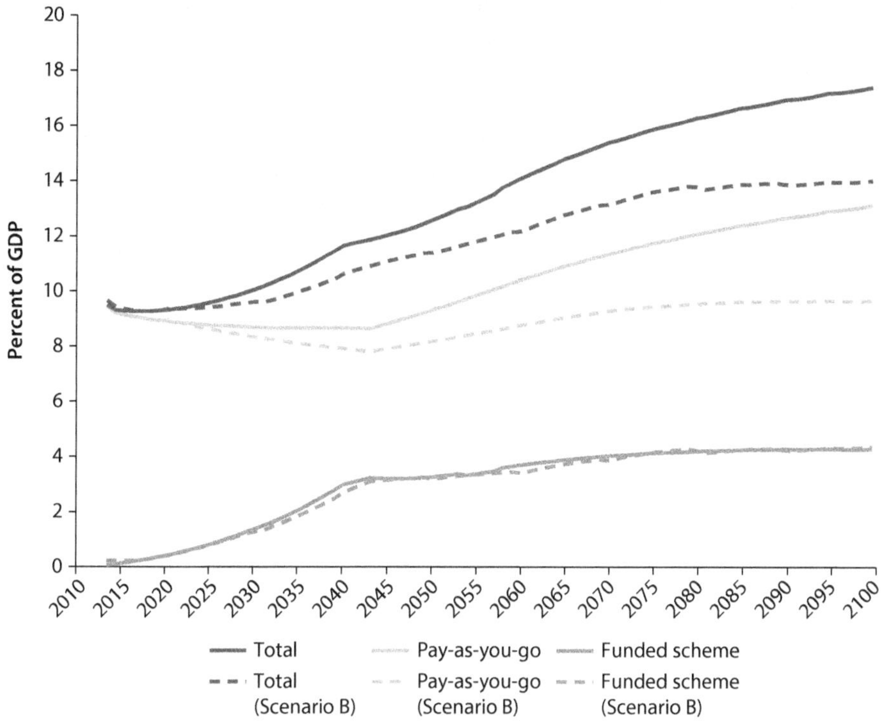

Note: Scenario B with a gradual increase in the retirement age.

(one percentage point less than it would reach in the current context). This gap would increase over time, with total expenditure reaching 14 percent of GDP in 2100, 3 percentage points less than in the base-case scenario.

This trend is explained by the potential evolution of the pay-as-you-go regime's expenditure, while total spending by the funded system is nearly unchanged. The reason for the latter is the compensation generated during the delay in retirement and the increased accumulation of retirement and pension funds it entails, along with the greater benefit generated from the actuarial calculations performed. In turn, the pay-as-you-go system's spending decreases because even though a scenario is simulated in which additional years of contributions with increased benefits are recognized, this adjustment is not actuarially balanced and therefore creates savings for the system.

Conclusions

Even though Uruguay is still moving through its demographic window of opportunity as a relatively young country, population aging poses concerns related not only to the actuarial sustainability of the social protection system, but also to its fiscal and economic sustainability. Such concerns primarily originate in the retirement and pension system.

In anticipation of predicted demographic shifts, in 1995 a structural reform to the social security system was adopted with the incorporation of an individually funded pillar. Parametric adjustments were also implemented, reducing the state's financial exposure. These included the unification of the retirement age between men and women at age 60, an increase in the number of contribution years from 30 to 35, the modification of the salary base for benefit calculations, and a reduction in the substitution rates expected. The creation of a mixed pension system and the applied parametric changes pursued a well-defined goal: to reduce financial pressure over the medium and long term on a pay-as-you-go regime that had been compromised by the aging of the population.

According to the estimates of spending trends that have been presented in this chapter, it is plausible that such a goal could be achieved. Nonetheless, pressure over the economic sustainability of the programs that fund the elderly population's consumption continues unabated.

Overall, total expenditure on social protection programs (that is, including the six programs discussed here), which in 2013 reached 10.7 percent of GDP, will increase in coming decades. If the current rules for the social security system were maintained, that would increase to nearly 13.9 percent of GDP in 2050 and 18.6 percent in 2100. This trend is clearly defined by the evolution of expenditure on retirement benefits and pensions, which will represent 12.7 percent of GDP in 2050 and 17.8 percent in 2100.

The pay-as-you-go regime's social security spending will decline until the end of the 2020s, when it will reach 8.8 percent of GDP, in the transition to the mixed scheme introduced in 1996. However, once the system matures, if no other changes are made, the pay-as-you-go regime's expenditure will return to its upward trend as a result of population aging, reaching 9.3 percent of GDP in 2050 and 13.1 percent in 2100. In turn, the funded regime's spending will grow exponentially until the beginning of the 2040s, when it will taper off to a constant rate with spending reaching 3.3 percent of GDP in 2050 and 4.3 percent in 2100.

In any circumstance, a period of growing spending requirements will begin in the 2020s. This is linked to the end of the demographic dividend, which in any case has not been very intense, and consequently an increase in retirees relative to the economically active young adult population.

However, some changes in personal behaviors could smooth, and even offset, the effect of population aging on the dependency of older adults. In some countries in the region older adults are increasingly postponing retirement. According to CELADE (Centro Latinoamericano y Caribeño de Demografía), a constant increase in the economic participation of older adults is predicted, especially among workers between ages 65 and 79 (Rofman and Apella 2014). This behavior represents a natural extension of the retirement age and would reduce financial pressure on the social protection system.

Under the assumption of an increase in the retirement age (an additional year for each decade), which keeps life expectancy at the time of retirement stable, spending on social protection would undergo a significant change. Even though total expenditure on retirement benefits and pensions continues to grow over the coming years, its pace is far lower than the estimate based on current parameters. In effect, expenditure on retirement benefits and pensions would reach 10.8 percent of GDP at the beginning of the 2040s (one percentage point less than it would reach with no change to the retirement age) and the gap would increase at a constant rate, reaching 14 percent of GDP in 2100 compared to 17.4 percent for the estimate under current conditions.

The discussion in this chapter enables us to identify three dimensions for attention. First, population aging does not just mean an increased number of older adults, but also a relative reduction in the size of the young adult population. This phenomenon brings two distinct features to bear on the fiscal and economic sustainability of social security. The increase of the retirement-age population entails greater demand for benefits from the system, while the reduction in the number of young adults entails a reduction in contributions destined to fund benefits. Structural reform of the social security system in the mid-1990s reduced the demand for fiscal resources in the medium and long term by implementing an individually funded pillar and introducing some parametric modifications. Nonetheless, if the current rules remain, the effect of the reform will be exhausted during the 2040s, when social security expenditure will again begin to increase as a percentage of GDP. Moreover, the individually funded pillar's benefits also require financing (although not from fiscal resources), meaning that older adults' total demand for resources will grow continuously.

The challenge for the social security system is to create the conditions necessary to ensure a flow of contributory and fiscal resources, as well as economic surpluses to be transferred through the funded regime that will enable the system to maintain the adequacy of current coverage. In this context, it appears essential to create the conditions for an economic situation where, at the very least, per capita GDP is stable or growing even as the total dependency ratio increases. It is also essential that it promotes institutional arrangements that fit the country's demographic and social processes. In other words, the demographic pressure predicted in the coming decades should be matched by an increase in disposable resources (from sustained growth of the economy) and some of the critical parameters in the social security system should also be reviewed.

During the last decade the average effective retirement age has increased as workers have changed their behavior. If this trend were to continue, through an improvement in health conditions, increased accumulation of human capital, and a legal framework that incentivized postponing retirement, some of the previously mentioned risks could be solved. It would appear to be reasonable to loosen some of the retirement age rules and revise benefit replacement rates, with the goal of giving workers more incentive to remain in the labor force.

Finally, population aging poses concerns related to the degree of intergenerational equity created by transfers through the social protection system. This chapter shows that social protection is strongly focused on older adults, with less spending reaching economically active adults and children. This situation could be considered unequal in intergenerational terms as well as economically inefficient, given that if more resources were concentrated during the phase of human capital accumulation, one could expect all of society to benefit as worker productivity increased. That said, the inequality problem is offset in the medium term because all generations move through the different phases of the life cycle. In any case, it is not possible to define an objective scale of intergenerational transfers that could be considered as being optimal. The choice to prioritize funding for one population group or another is defined by social preferences, which is a choice to be made through existing political and institutional mechanisms.

Notes

1. Rafael Rofman and Ignacio Apella, World Bank, Social Protection and Labor Global Practice. The authors would like to thank Oscar Centrángolo for his valuable comments. Correspondence to rrofman@worldbank.org, iapella@worldbank.org.
2. This substitution rate is the ratio between the average retirement benefit and the wages of a formal worker, as observed in BPS statistics. Since the forecast also considers pensions, the substitution rate for pension benefits is estimated from what percentage of a typical retirement benefit they are equivalent.
3. $a(60)$ is an estimate of the actuarial factor calculated from the mortality table for each gender using the individual's age and an annual interest rate of 1.75 percent.
4. We assume that social security coverage will not change over time. In other words, both labor formality and social security inclusion policies designed to achieve universality will remain unchanged.
5. It is estimated for each additional year of contributions that while the same number of years of life during retirement is maintained, the variation in the retirement and pension fund allows for a 6 percent increase in the average benefit.

References

Alvarez, I., N. da Silva, A. Forteza, and I. Rossi. 2010. "El Retiro de los Trabajadores Uruguayos y la Seguridad Social." Presented at IX Jornadas de Investigación de la Facultad de Ciencias Sociales, Universidad de la República, Montevideo, September 13–15.

Arim, R., G. Cruces, and A. Vigorito. 2009. "Programas Sociales y Transferencias de Ingresos en Uruguay: Los Beneficios No Contributivos y las Alternativas para Su Extensión." Serie Políticas Sociales 146, División de Desarrollo Social, CEPAL, Santiago de Chile.

Colombo, C. 2012. "Análisis de las Principales Características de las Altas de Jubilación de los Años 2002 al 2011." Comentarios de Seguridad Social 35, BPS, Montevideo.

Dassatti, C., and N. Mariño. 2014. "Maduración del Sistema Previsional: Proyecciones y Agenda." Draft. http://www.bcu.gub.uy/Comunicaciones/Jornadaspercent20depercent20Economa/t_dassatti_cecilia_2014.pdf.

Filgueira, F., and D. Hernández. 2012. "Sistema de Protección Social en América Latina y el Caribe: Uruguay." Colección Documentos de Proyectos, CEPAL, Santiago de Chile.

Gruber, J., and D. Wise. 2002. "Social Security Programs and Retirement around the World: Micro Estimation." NBER Working Paper 9407, National Bureau of Economic Research, Cambridge, MA.

Rofman, R., and I. Apella. 2014. "La Protección Social Argentina en un Contexto de Transición Demográfica." En *Los Años No Vienen Solos: Oportunidades y Desafíos Económicos de la Transición Demográfica en Argentina,* edited by M. Gragnolati, R. Rofman, I. Apella, and S. Troiano, 143–68. Buenos Aires: World Bank.

Sierna, M. 2007. "La Evolución del Sistema de Seguridad Social en el Uruguay (1829–1986)." Serie Documento de Trabajo 07, Instituto de Economía, Facultad de Ciencias Económicas y de Administración, Universidad de la República, Montevideo.

Social Security Bank (Banco de Previsión Social [BPS]). 2010. "Proyección Financiera del Sistema Previsional Contributivo Administrado por el Banco de Previsión Social." www.bps.gub.uy.

Stock, J., and D. Wise. 1990. "Pensions, the Option Value of Work, and Retirement." *Econometrica* 58 (5): 1151–80.

World Bank. 2015. *Notas de Política. Uruguay: Desafíos y Oportunidades 2015–2020.* Montevideo: World Bank.

CHAPTER 5

Population Aging and Challenges for Health Care

Carlos Grau[1]

Introduction

Rising life expectancy, although an important indicator of well-being, tends to raise the public transfers (such as through pensions) and, not surprisingly therefore, increase public spending and complicate fiscal sustainability.

And even as life expectancy rises, health authorities still worry about risk factors that can undermine population health, including tobacco consumption, obesity, overly salty diets, and sedentary lifestyles, among others. Health policies that mitigate these risks improve quality of life, but they also generally increase health care spending throughout the life cycle.

This chapter describes the organization of Uruguay's health care sector and the country's epidemiological characteristics, then analyzes the sectoral environment to identify the principal determinants of cash inflows and outflows. Finally, it forecasts long-term health care spending.

The forecasts incorporate the impact of demographic and other expected changes on the system's institutional setup. Specifically, they consider the impact of inclusion of retirees and pensioners in the National Health Care Fund's (Fondo Nacional de Salud [FONASA]) financing system, possible changes in how the budget is determined for public health care services, and the eventual reduction in the cost of co-payments. These changes amplify the impact of population aging on health care spending, compounding challenges to the long-term sustainability of fiscal policy.

A Brief Description of Uruguay's Health Care System

Health care in Uruguay comprises public and private sectors. The State Health Services Administration, the principal public actor,[2] is mostly funded by the national budget, but also from health care premiums paid by FONASA. FONASA's funding comes primarily from social employee and employer security contributions, and general revenues cover any imbalances.

Table 5.1 State Health Services Administration Coverage, August 2014

Type of coverage	*Number of individuals*	*Percent*
Free	778,042	61.5
FONASA	409,780	32.4
Police Health Care and Military Health Care	76,707	6.1
Total	**1,264,529**	**100**

Source: State Health Services Administration, www.asse.com.uy.
Note: FONASA = National Health Care Fund (Fondo Nacional de Salud).

Currently, the State Health Services Administration covers a little more than one-third of the country's population, or about 1.2 million people (table 5.1). Of its beneficiaries, 61.5 percent are entitled to benefits without making a direct economic contribution; 32.4 percent are insured by FONASA, that is, they contribute a portion of their salary to fund the sector; and the remaining 6 percent corresponds to services provided to individuals covered by other public providers, Police Health Care, and Military Health Care.

The principal actor in the private sector is the group of Collective Medical Assistance Institutions (Instituciones de Asistencia Médica Colectiva [IAMCs]), which cover 64 percent of the population. These are private institutions; however, their principal source of financing comes from public funds from FONASA. Currently, approximately two-thirds of the population receives health care services from the IAMC sector.

The population entitled to care under the IAMC subsystem breaks down as follows: 90 percent are FONASA members (about 58.2 percent of the population); 5 percent are individual members, which means that they pay directly out-of-pocket; and 5 percent are collective members, who are entitled to benefits as a result of agreements between the IAMCs and other institutions.

The number of the IAMCs' individual and collective members (private financing) has decreased over time. Conversely, the relative participation of financing from public funds has increased, making them ever more important to the fiscal sustainability of the system. Current regulations provide for the inclusion of new collective groups to the public financing system under FONASA, which means that this trend will continue in the coming years.

The principal sources of income for the IAMC system include the health care premiums as a function of the number and type of members covered under FONASA. The health care premiums are financed with funds mainly from social security contributions made by employees and employers, with taxes playing a minor role.

The health care premium combines a prepaid component called a "capita" the value of which varies by gender and age, but is the same for all institutions, and a component that varies with the degree to which a set of care goals set by health care authorities are accomplished. The scale of current capita values is shown in table 5.2 and figure 5.1.

Table 5.2 Relative Capita Values by Age Group, 2014
men ages 20–44 = 1.0

	<1	*1 to 4*	*5 to 14*	*15 to 19*	*20 to 44*	*45 to 64*	*65 to 74*	*>75*
Male	6.456	1.890	1.120	1.011	1.000	2.058	3.955	5.208
Female	5.515	1.781	1.011	1.444	2.124	2.516	3.440	4.297

Source: Ministry of Public Health, http://www.msp.gub.uy/sites/default/files/Jornadas_MecPagos_1.pdf.

Figure 5.1 Relative Capita Values by Age Group, 2014
men ages 20–44 = 1.0

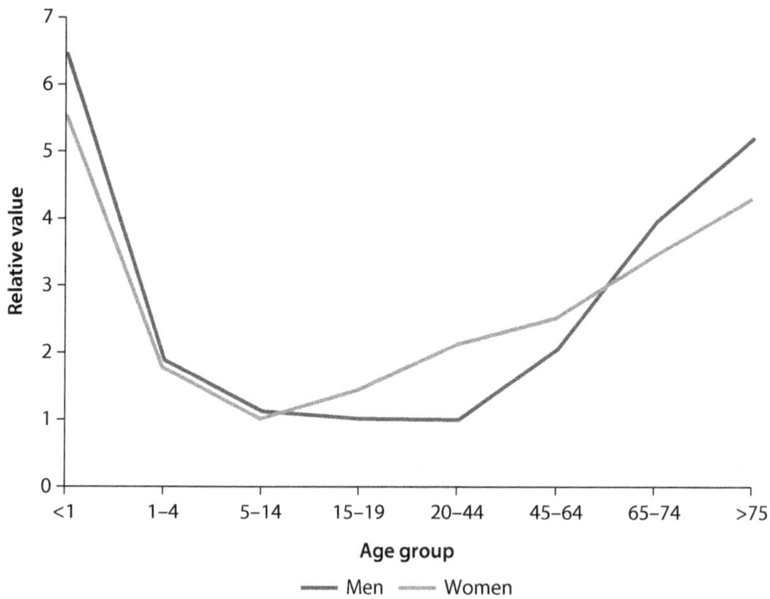

Source: Ministry of Public Health, http://www.msp.gub.uy/sites/default/files/Jornadas_MecPagos_1.pdf.

Currently four care goals exist that are associated with: (1) follow-up and checkups for children and women, (2) primary care physician, (3) the elderly, and (4) human resource model reform.

The health care premiums represent almost 80 percent of the IAMCs' operating income. In turn, 92 percent of income from health care premiums comes from capitas, and the remaining 8 percent corresponds to the care goals (table 5.3).

The other significant component of the IAMCs' income comprises co-payments, which are divided into two categories called orders and tickets. The former are paid upon requesting an appointment with a professional, whether at a clinic or a house call. Tickets correspond to the delivery of medicines or performing diagnostic tests requested by the attending doctor during an appointment. Co-payments are not applied for services received while an individual is checked in to a hospital or clinic.

The relative proportion of orders in the institutions' income has been decreasing as the result of a policy implemented with the goal of reducing access barriers

Table 5.3 Structure of the IAMC Income, 2010–13
percent

Description	*2010*	*2011*	*2012*	*2013*
Individual memberships	14.1	12.1	8.8	5.0
Collective members	10.1	8.2	5.5	4.2
Capitas	59.5	61.7	68.0	73.1
Goals	5.0	5.0	5.2	5.9
Orders	2.3	2.2	1.9	1.7
Tickets for medicines and diagnostics	7.7	7.9	7.9	8.0
Substitute for moderating rates	0.3	0.4	0.5	0.7
Fiscal Credit Law No. 18,464	1.0	2.6	2.2	1.5
Total	**100.0**	**100.0**	**100.0**	**100.0**

Source: Elaboration based on information from the SINADI (Sistema Nacional de Información; National Information System).
Note: IAMC = Collective Medical Assistance Institution (Institución de Asistencia Médica Colectiva).

by decreasing the cost of co-payments. Currently orders account for 1.7 percent of total operating income in the sector, and tickets account for 8.0 percent.

Reducing the value of orders had two effects. First, private funding was replaced by public funding as the income that the IAMCs lost as a result of reducing the cost of co-payments was generally offset by increases in the value of the capitas. Second, it provoked an increase in service utilization rates, and consequently increased spending in the sector.

Rules of the Game in the Health Sector

The evolution of health care spending, as in any other sector, is not immune to the rules of the game and incentives. The factors that stand out most that affect the sector's dynamics are made apparent by answering the following questions:

(1) As the participants in the sector seek economic equilibrium, does income adjust to meet spending needs or vice versa?
(2) Do systems exist that incentivize those in charge of providing the care to contain costs?
(3) Do mechanisms or automatic stabilizers exist to deal with the institutions' eventual economic imbalances?

The following paragraphs present a series of stylized facts related to the existing rules and incentives in the country that could have an impact on the future evolution of health care spending.

The system places the primary responsibility for providing health care services on institutions that vertically integrate the function of insurer with that of service provider. The principal component of the income structure of these institutions is a prepayment (capitas) for each insured person. A funding mechanism based on prepayment creates an incentive to contain costs because during the period in which this value remains constant institutions can appropriate eventual cost reductions. Nonetheless, problems exist that are related to the definition of the property of the institutions that weaken this incentive. The predominating dispersion of owners weakens the incentive to minimize costs. Consequently, one of the issues that strain the relationship between firms and the regulator is the latter's proposal that efficiency factors be explicitly included in the calculation of the value of the capitas. The proposal is not to switch to a pure scheme of regulation of efficient firms, but to incorporate aspects of such a scheme that limit spending growth.

Another important component in the determination of the sectoral balances is the definition of the basket of benefits that the firms are obligated to provide in exchange for the income they receive. This definition was established and is restricted to the services listed in the Comprehensive Health Care Plan (Plan Integral de Atención a la Salud; PIAS) defined by the Ministry of Public Health (Ministerio de Salud Pública; MSP). Changes to the plan over time, at least according to the current institutional design, must be translated into changes in the value of the capitas. Thus, the dynamics of sectoral spending and funding could be affected by decisions related to the definitions of health policies, as has occurred in recent years. For example, the inclusion of mental health benefits, voluntary termination of pregnancy, and assisted reproduction.

The list of medicines that institutions that receive FONASA funds must provide was also created as a specific list. New additions to the list are generally accompanied by increased funding.

The restriction on spending on medicines that results from defining a specific list of drugs to be included can be weakened by decisions from the courts, which on some occasions have ruled in favor of patients that demand that the system provide them medicines that are not included on the list. Thus, expenditure on medicines faces soft restrictions for two reasons. First, because the list of medicines to be provided has not been clearly specified, and second, because in Uruguay the price of medicines is not regulated.

Finally, one important aspect of the institutional arrangements (or rules) for determining schemes that attempt to limit health care spending using cost-effectiveness criteria is the existence of technology evaluation agencies that advise health authorities on whether it is appropriate to incorporate or maintain specific benefits. These agencies tend to be present in developed countries and exist in countries in the region. The lack of an agency to evaluate health care technologies transforms the incorporation of new technologies into a significant threat to the sustainability of health care spending.

Epidemiology and Health Care Spending

Epidemiological characteristics are at the foundation of the determinants of health care spending, insomuch as they define the population stock and its morbimortality characteristics upon which health care services act.

It can be said that epidemiological transition in Uruguay began prematurely in comparison with other countries in the region, such that the second decade of the 20th century, between 1910 and 1920, witnessed the decline of the general mortality rate concomitant with the decline in the birth rate.

The general mortality rate was around 9 or 10 per thousand by the 1940s and has remained in this range since then. The birth rate fell more gradually, but the drop was still sustained. In the 1970s it was around 20 births per thousand inhabitants; by the end of the century it was just above 15 per thousand, and in the first eight years of the current century it fell to 14 per thousand.

Even though a gap still exists between both rates, the trend toward convergence is clear. In turn, the population grew significantly until the beginning of the 1960s, subsequently growing at a slower pace and tending to level off in the 1990s.

The infant mortality rate showed a slight downward trend during the first half of the 20th century and a pronounced decline since then at the expense of a significant fall in its postneonatal component.

This phenomenon, along with the decrease in the birth rate and the increase in life expectancy, has determined the population growth rate witnessed since then and the current demographic structure.

Life expectancy at birth also increased throughout the century and in particular increased almost five years in a span of 24 years (figure 5.2), with a slight downward trend in the gap between genders, just as has occurred in countries that have completed their transition.

Changes in the epidemiological profile accompanied these changes in the age structure, which began around the middle of the 1920s when specific mortality rates for cardiovascular diseases and cancer began to increase. By the end of the 1950s, they constituted the two leading causes of death (figure 5.3).

Since then, chronic, nontransmissible sicknesses have continued to dominate the mortality profile, but some trend changes should be kept in mind that correspond to events during the final stages of the transition period.

Figure 5.2 Life Expectancy by Gender, 1988–2012

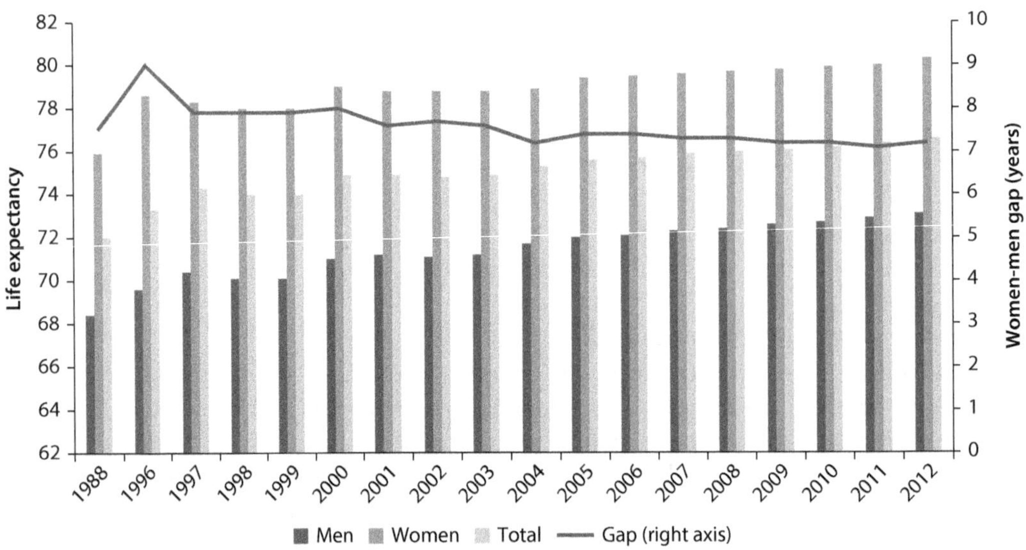

Source: Lazo 2013.

Figure 5.3 Principal Causes of Death, 1900–2002

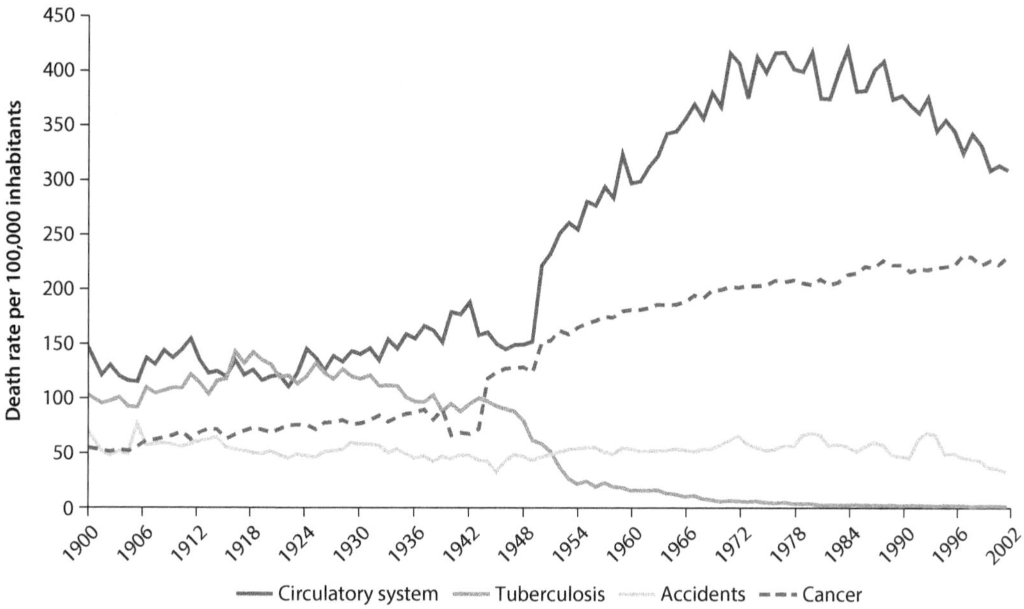

Source: National Institute of Statistics (Instituto Nacional de Estadística; INE).

Infant mortality continues to fall, but with more difficulty because of the difficulties in reducing neonatal mortality, the "hard" component of the rate.

Also, if we consider the three primary causes of mortality from 1998 to the latest year available, we observe a decline both in the number of cases as well as in the death rate from cardiovascular causes per 100,000 inhabitants and an upward trend in the gross mortality rate for cancer and respiratory diseases.

Gross mortality rates for external causes and for nervous system diseases also increased. Self-inflicted wounds and transportation accidents stand out among the primary causes, making up 45 percent of deaths from external causes in 2010, together reaching 31.9 per 100,000 inhabitants in 2010 from 30.8 in 1998.

Additionally, among nervous system diseases, the categories for "other degenerative diseases," "extrapyramidal disorders," and "demyelinating diseases" accounted for 54 percent of deaths in 1998. They increased to 60 percent in 2010, and the mortality rate rose from 12 cases per 100,000 inhabitants in 1998 to 24 in 2010.

These increases are consistent with an epidemiological pattern in which the importance of traditional chronic, nontransmissible pathologies is added to deaths caused by neurodegenerative diseases and by external causes that gradually become more important and which are responsible for a high level of morbidity.

On the other hand, the gross mortality rate for mental disorders decreased and the rates increased for metabolic and nutritional disorders and disorders related to the genitourinary system. Among the metabolic and nutritional disorders, diabetes represents 70 percent of the deaths, with mortality per 100,000 inhabitants rising from 18.7 in 1998 to 21.7 in 2010.

Among deaths from genitourinary diseases, rising mortality for kidney failure must be highlighted. It represents 57 percent of the total among this group of causes of death, growing from 9.4 deaths per 100,000 inhabitants in 1998 to 14.9 in 2010.

The significance of infectious and parasitic diseases has also increased, with a significant increase in the proportion of deaths caused by HIV/AIDS infections, accounting for 17 percent of this group in 1998 and 24 percent in 2010. Mortality from this cause grew from 3.3 cases per 100,000 inhabitants in 1998 to 5.6 in 2010.

In contrast, deaths caused by tuberculosis declined (from a mortality rate of 1.8 cases per 100,000 in 1998 to 1.2 in 2010).

Among the causes of death for cardiovascular diseases, meanwhile, the situation is not homogeneous. Although the trend is downward for the two most significant causes (ischemic heart disease and cerebrovascular diseases), the contrary trend has been witnessed in hypertensive disease.

Something similar is occurring in cancer deaths. Gross mortality rates for malignant tumors by site do not exist, but rates adjusted for age for the standard world population do. These rates moved up or down slightly during 2002–06 and 2006–10, and slightly downward among those tumors with the highest incidence.

In sum, Uruguay's epidemiological transition began prematurely, but the transition's development has been prolonged. The population is now at the end of a second phase in which epidemiological changes can be spotted that are connected to longer life expectancy. These changes translate into higher mortality from neurodegenerative and genitourinary (kidney failure) diseases and from the relative significance of pathologies related to urban lifestyles and environmental factors (increase in the mortality rates for endocrine, metabolic, and respiratory pathologies, as well as from external causes like accidents and suicides).

The evolution of health care spending and the factors that can affect it depend significantly on epidemiological characteristics. For Uruguay, the principal factors of morbidity are associated with traditional chronic, nontransmissible pathologies (cardiovascular and cancer-related), to which are added deaths from neurodegenerative diseases and from external causes. This pattern of morbidity makes it difficult to implement measures that would reduce health care spending.

Health Care Sector Expenditure and Financing

The Evolution of Total Health Care Spending

Various sources of information can be used to analyze and quantify the relative weight of health care spending in Uruguay. Two stand out: disaggregated information for the health care sector in the national accounts of the Central Bank of Uruguay (Banco Central del Uruguay; BCU) and the National Health Care Accounts in the Health Care Economy section of the MSP. The latest version of the latter covers 2009–12. The following section first analyzes expenditure considering the information provided by the Central Bank.

The Central Bank's National Accounts

From an economic perspective, the process of change begun in the health care sector in 2005 presents three important milestones. One was in August 2007 with the introduction of a new payment mechanism for individuals covered by social security, which incorporated risk adjustment and payment for care goals. A second occurred in January 2008 with the inclusion of minors under age 18 in social security coverage (FONASA). The third was the gradual inclusion of retirees and pensioners beginning in 2012. The process of incorporating this latter group is ongoing and its progress will affect the evolution of health care spending in coming years.

According to table 5.4, the ratio between the sectoral production and the economy's total production in recent years shows a similar evolution, although the former is evidence of a slight downward trend. During 2005–13, health care sector production measured at constant prices grew at an average annual rate of 4.8 percent, and total economic production grew during the same period at a rate of 5.5 percent. In other words, the set of aforementioned sectoral changes was accompanied by an increase in the health care sector's relative proportion of total economic product of 0.7 points.

Reviewing health care sector gross domestic product (GDP) at constant prices from 2005 to 2013, one can infer that health care production grew significantly. This growth is reflected in the direct analysis of available information regarding health care production during the period. Table 5.5 shows the evolution in natural units of production of services for the principal care products offered by the largest health care providers in the country.

The growth of health care GDP at constant prices during 2007–12 was 30 percent, which agrees with the evolution of the production of the principal care products and services shown in table 5.5.

Table 5.4 Health Care as a Proportion of the Economy, 2005–13

Year	*Health care GDP in constant prices (Ur$, thousands, 2005 prices)*	*GDP in constant prices (Ur$, thousands, 2005 prices)*	*Health care GDP as percent of total GDP*
2005	19,566,988	425,018,448	4.6
2006	19,838,228	442,438,158	4.5
2007	20,709,724	471,380,298	4.4
2008	22,783,946	505,207,230	4.5
2009	23,463,218	517,085,958	4.5
2010	24,465,668	560,542,314	4.4
2011	25,088,085	601,692,754	4.2
2012	26,995,625	623,813,191	4.3
2013	28,519,294	651,239,743	4.4

Source: Central Bank of Uruguay (Banco Central del Uruguay; BCU).

Table 5.5 Evolution of Health Care Production, 2007–12
index 2007 = 100.0

IAMC	*2007*	*2008*	*2009*	*2010*	*2011*	*2012*
Attention at general hospitals—consultations	100.0	116.1	123.8	127.1	131.6	139.1
Admission, moderate care	100.0	108.2	114.7	120.6	104.9	120.7
Days of admission, intensive care unit, adults	100.0	103.6	110.5	113.0	106.3	120.2
State Health Services Administration						
Consultations	100.0	99.0	118.1	116.3	126.9	137.6
Hospital releases	100.0	99.0	118.1	116.3	126.9	137.6
Surgical interventions	100.0	117.6	131.8	127.4	130.4	126.2

Sources: Elaboration based on information from the National Information System (Sistema Nacional de Información; SINADI) and the State Health Services Administration.
Note: IAMC = Collective Medical Assistance Institution (Institución de Asistencia Médica Colectiva).

Table 5.6 Evolution of Implicit Prices of Total GDP and Health Care GDP, 2005–13
index 2005 = 100.0

Year	*Total*	*Health care*
2005	100.0	100.0
2006	106.5	110.9
2007	116.6	120.0
2008	125.9	137.1
2009	132.9	157.8
2010	139.1	173.7
2011	151.6	195.4
2012	162.8	212.9
2013	175.2	234.1

Source: Central Bank of Uruguay (Banco Central del Uruguay; BCU).

Importantly, implicit prices in the health care sector grew more than implicit prices in total GDP, as tends to happen (table 5.6). During 2005–13, the implicit price index for the whole economy grew 7.3 percent at an average annual rate and health care sector prices at 11.2 percent (figure 5.4). As a result, even though at constant prices the relative proportion of health care sector GDP remains constant, at current prices it trends upward. One possible explanation of this phenomenon is that salary increases in the sector follow the trend of salary growth in other economic sectors where productivity gains are stronger.

National Health Care Accounts, 2009–12, MSP

According to the National Health Care Accounts, spending at constant prices grew during 2005–12 at an average annual rate of 7.5 percent, and GDP grew 4.7 percent. The ratio between health care spending and GDP trended upward during the period, with growth equivalent to nearly one percentage point of GDP (table 5.7).

Figure 5.4 Evolution of Total GDP and Health Care GDP at Constant Prices, 2005–13

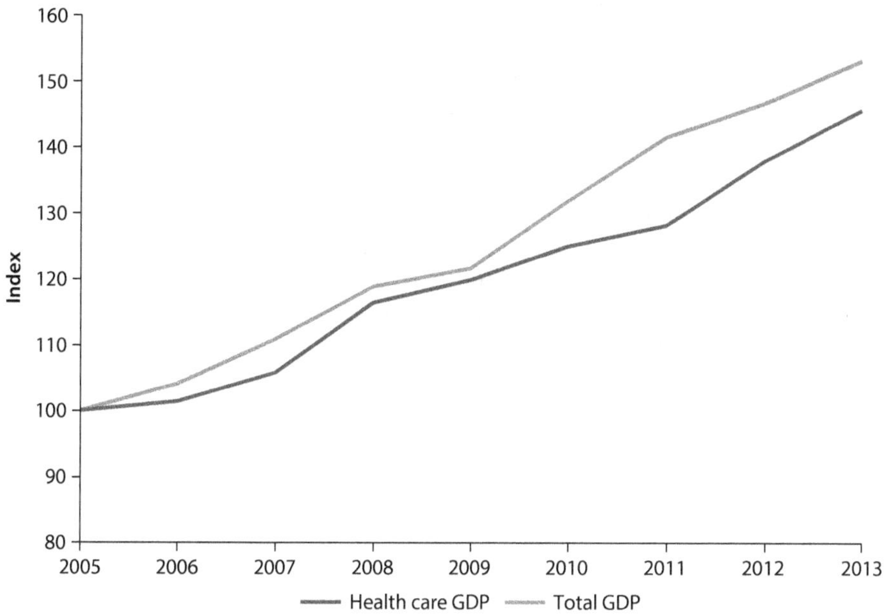

Source: Central Bank of Uruguay (Banco Central del Uruguay; BCU).
Note: 2005 = 100.

Table 5.7 Health Care Spending, 2004–12

Year	*Health care spending (constant Ur$, millions)*	*Percent of GDP*
2004	48,635	8.7
2005	47,906	8.2
2006	50,267	8.3
2007	52,612	8.0
2008	58,681	7.9
2009	67,879	9.0
2010	69,115	8.9
2011	73,669	8.6
2012	79,630	9.1

Source: National Health Care Accounts, 2009–12, Ministry of Public Health (Cuantas Nacionales de Salud, 2009–12, Ministerio de Salud Pública).

Payment of salaries constitutes the principal component of the sector's cost structure, representing around 52 percent of the total, with third-party services at 25.2 percent and medicines at 14.3 percent.

Health Care Spending by Gender and Age Group

Health care spending attributable to an individual depends on his or her morbidity (health status), which is associated with a series of variables such as the presence of chronic illnesses, lifestyle factors, gender, and age. Thus, it is possible to assign each individual an expected spending level[3] on health care (risk level) according to their characteristics.

Expected spending on health care services for an individual for each risk category can be expressed as the multiplication of the expected value of the quantity of services to be received by the expected value of the average cost of the services.

In 2007 in Uruguay a differential payment according to gender and age of the insured person was introduced for FONASA beneficiaries. The different amounts used in the per-person payments seek to reflect the expected expenditure for each risk category, understood as a specific combination of age and gender.[4] The value is equal to the expected value of spending (pure premium), but it does not include a risk premium to reimburse insurers for the predictable variability in spending.

The methodology employed to calculate the capitas assumes implicitly that the expected value of the unit cost of each service, a consultation for example, is the same for all risk categories (combinations of gender and age). This assumption could result in an underestimation of expenditure for older individuals, and therefore could underestimate the impact of population aging on the evolution of health care spending.

If one assumes that the cost of a service does not vary with gender or age, the differential value of the capitas is then defined by the differences in the intensity of use of the services of each risk profile.

In this sense, utilization rates for various health care services in Uruguay exhibit the following uniform characteristics in the variations according to gender and age:

- The evolution of utilization rates as a function of age is U-shaped, that is, higher utilization rates are observable among the younger and older populations.
- In turn, utilization rates among the elderly are higher than those among younger individuals.
- Utilization rates among women at childbearing ages are higher than those among men in the same age group.

Based on these basic truths, it is apparent that population aging will put upward pressure on an economy's health care costs. Table 5.8 presents the differences in utilization rates in the IAMC sector.

From table 5.8, one can infer which combinations of gender and age demand more services, thus explaining how the differential values of capitas are determined according to those two factors.

Impact of Health Policies

Health policies that tend to reduce the morbimortality of the population, such as those that lower tobacco use and consumption of foods high in salt, and that promote healthy lifestyles, vaccination campaigns, and procedures that can detect illnesses early, like mammograms, improve quality of life.

Table 5.8 Annual Intensity of Use Profiles for Health Care Services in the IAMC Sector, by Gender and Age, 2012

Age	*Number of consultations per person*	*Central emergency consultations per person*	*In-home consultations per person*	*Admitted days per each 1,000 persons*	*Admitted days in adult ICU per each 1,000 adults*	*Admitted days in children's ICU per each 1,000 children*
Men						
<1	13.9	2.4	1.3	1.337.1	n.a.	1,031.9
1–4	5.4	1.8	0.8	253.3	n.a.	16.9
5–14	3.3	0.8	0.3	135.3	n.a.	5.8
15–19	2.4	0.8	0.2	215.6	30.4	n.a.
20–44	2.1	0.8	0.2	226.0	25.0	n.a.
45–64	4.4	0.7	0.2	482.3	80.4	n.a.
65–74	8.4	0.8	0.4	1,119.4	207.2	n.a.
>74	9.9	1.0	1.4	1,894.4	303.4	n.a.
Women						
<1	13.9	2.2	0.7	1,188.5	n.a.	941.5
1–4	5.1	1.7	0.3	225.0	n.a.	12.4
5–14	3.3	0.8	0.3	123.4	n.a.	3.6
15–19	4.6	1.0	0.3	336.6	12.1	n.a.
20–44	5.7	1.1	0.4	497.9	17.2	n.a.
45–64	8.0	0.8	0.6	450.1	48.5	n.a.
65–74	10.6	0.7	2.3	763.3	107.0	n.a.
>74	9.3	0.8	—	1,433.7	177.8	n.a.

Source: Elaboration based on information from the National Information System (Sistema Nacional de Información; SINADI).
Note: IAMC = Collective Medical Assistance Institution (Institución de Asistencia Médica Colectiva); ICU = intensive care unit; n.a. = not applicable; — = not available.

Nonetheless, despite the dominant public discourse focusing on prevention as a mechanism to reduce health care costs, the expected impacts on spending have not been clear, a priori.

The impact of policies that tend to reduce morbimortality in the population on the health care spending trajectory depends on three factors:

1. The costs required for their implementation. For example, to carry out a vaccination campaign it is necessary to purchase vaccines and possess the human resources to supply them. In some cases the policy measure may not entail any cost, such as prohibiting smoking in public places. In some, the measure may even generate additional public resources, such as when taxes are increased on goods for which consumption is to be discouraged because they are harmful to health.
2. The reduction in health care spending associated with the decrease of the morbidity burden as a result of the policy measure. For example, reducing tobacco consumption lowers costs associated with the treatment of cardiovascular and cancer-related illnesses. When it is confirmed that the prevention policies will reduce health care spending, reference is made to this component.
3. The increase in life expectancy that the policy measure generates and the concomitant increase in health care spending associated with a longer life span.

Therefore, to be able to model the impact of health policies on the evolution of health care spending one must know: (a) the health policies that will be implemented, (b) their impact on the population's morbimortality, (c) the costs avoided as a result of the morbidity reduction that the policy aims to generate, and (d) the changes to the demographic forecasts resulting from the application of the policies.

Information available in Uruguay does not allow us to perform these types of estimates. However, evidence from other countries shows that when the evaluation is carried out over extended periods, the net impact of the measures entails an increase in health care spending. Therefore, when long-term forecasts do not include the impact of health policies, one can assume that the forecast underestimates actual expenditure.

Health Care Spending Forecasts, 2013–2100

This section presents the long-term forecasts for health care spending. First, we solely consider only demographic change in order to evaluate its impact both on total health care spending and just the portion of total spending financed with public funds.[5] Next, we incorporate scenarios associated with future changes in the funding policy for the sector. Some of the changes under consideration are already established in current regulations; thus, their probability of occurring is one. This category includes: (a) the incorporation of new groups of retirees and pensioners to the FONASA-financed system (Law No. 18,731), and (b) the gradual process described in the same law of increasing the value of the capitas for retirees and pensioners.

Other changes, which may not be formally established but have a high probability of occurring are also included in the forecasts. This category includes reducing the cost of co-payments and establishing the budget for the State Health Services Administration based on the values for the health care premiums that FONASA utilizes. Finally, we include some reflections on the impact that other, unconsidered factors in the forecasts may have on the evolution of health care spending in the long term.

Demographic Changes and Health Care Spending

Demographic changes modify morbidity of the population, affecting its need for medical care, and in turn access to this care defines health care spending.[6] In the following paragraphs, we therefore analyze how the demographic changes presented in chapter 2 will affect the evolution of health care spending.

For the analysis, it is useful to distinguish between two aspects of demographic change: the variation in the number of people while the demographic structure remains unchanged, and changes to the demographic structure while the size of the population remains constant.

The total demographic impact shows the net impact of all the changes observed in the projected demographic evolution. Some of these, such as population aging, are positively correlated with the evolution of health care spending. Others, such as the reduction in the relative proportion of women between ages

20 and 44, are negatively correlated. Therefore, the net impact of the various demographic changes is the result of a series of counteracting revisions that is interesting to explore further.

Considering the relative value of the capitas and utilizing the same assumptions related to the evolution of labor productivity and salaries, the change over time in health care spending as percentage points of GDP is defined as $g_{s,t}$ in equation 5.1:

$$g_{s,t} = \frac{\sum_i ci \cdot qit}{PBI\ t} \tag{5.1}$$

Where i represents the various combinations of gender and age, ci the values of the capitas, and qi the number of people. Figure 5.5 presents results. As a result of demographic change, total health care spending will increase from 7.8 percent of GDP in 2013 to 10.3 percent in 2100.

If we only consider the impact of the demographic changes on health care spending financed with public funds, the forecast also exhibits growth, increasing from approximately 5.2 percent of GDP in 2013 to 6.8 percent in 2100 (figure 5.6).

If we differentiate between the impact of change in the demographic structure and the impact of change in the number of people, which represent the two components of demographic change, the spending growth is explained by the former.

The impact of changes in the number of people generates a reduction in health care spending, which is reversed by the changes in the demographic structure. Figure 5.7 shows the changes over time that health care spending will experience in constant price terms after accounting for the total impact of demographic changes and the change in the number of people. The difference between these impacts is explained by the change in the demographic structure.

Figure 5.5 Evolution of Total Health Care Spending, 2013–2100

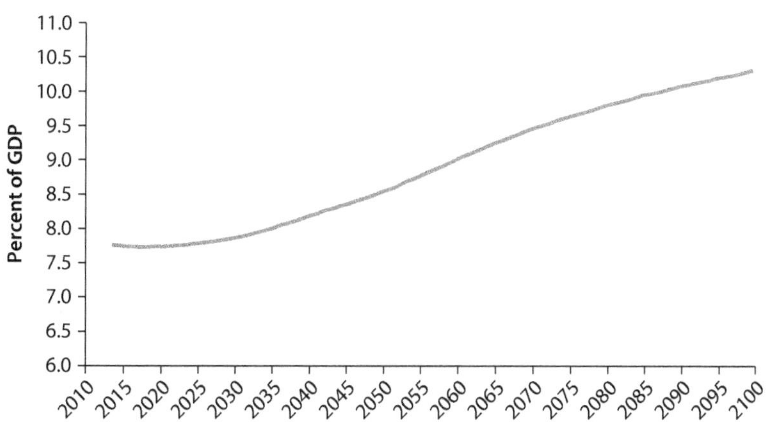

Figure 5.6 Evolution of Health Care Spending Financed with Public Funds, 2013–2100

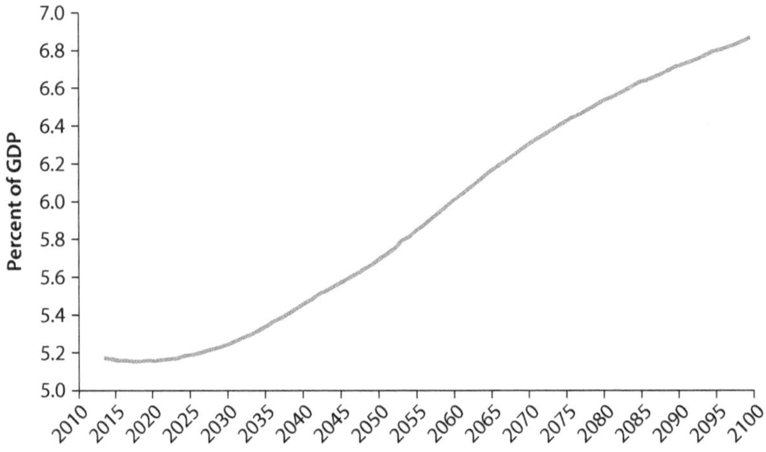

Figure 5.7 Total Impact and Impact of Change in Number of People Only, 2013–2100

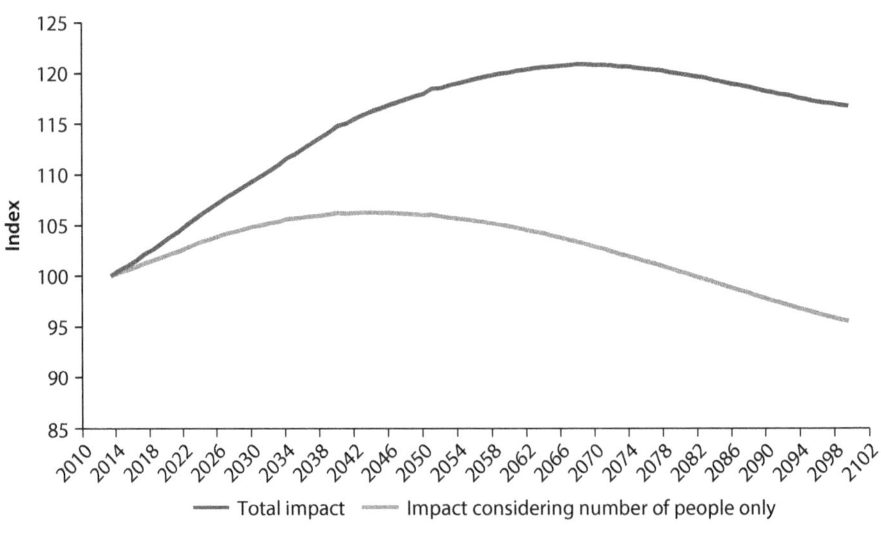

Note: 2013 = 100.

Upon analyzing the changes in the demographic structure, examining the age groups for which information on expected health care expenditure per person is available, one observes that the relative proportion of individuals under age 45 falls, while the proportion of older adults grows, particularly adults over age 74. However, the changes occur at different rates, as figures 5.8 and 5.9 show.

The size of the impact on health care spending caused by the changes in the demographic structure shown in figures 5.8 and 5.9 depends on two factors: the magnitude of the changes and the relative value of the capitas that correspond to each of the age groups.

Figure 5.8 Variation in the Relative Participation of Men by Age Group between 2013 and 2100

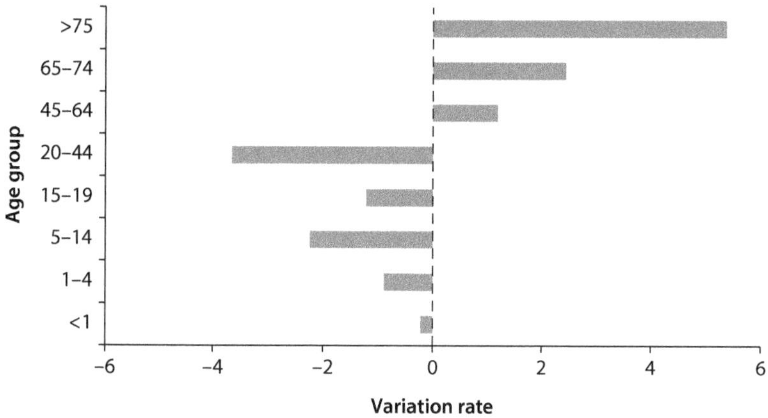

Source: Elaboration based on the demographic forecasts from chapter 2.

Figure 5.9 Variation in the Relative Participation of Women by Age Group between 2013 and 2100

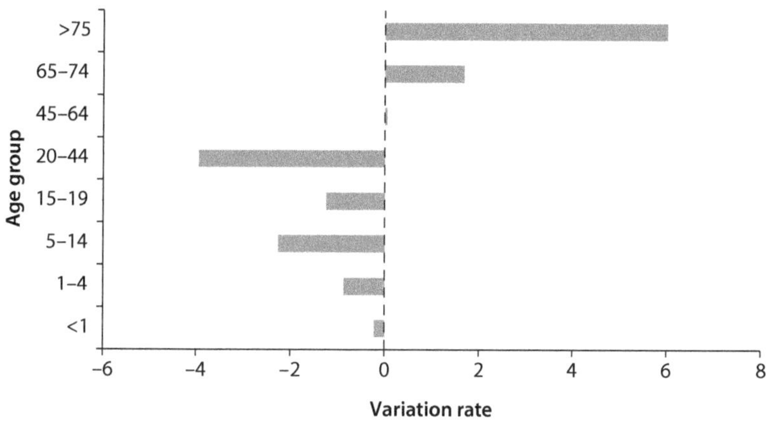

Source: Elaboration based on the demographic forecasts from chapter 2.

The effect that demographic change has over time can be estimated for each component of the risk structure (combination of gender and age) in the variability of spending as:

$$I_i = w_i \cdot g_i - 1 \tag{5.2}$$

Where I_i is the incidence of each of the combinations of gender and age in the total variation in spending caused by changes in the demographic structure while keeping the number of people constant; w_i is the proportion of spending attributable to

Figure 5.10 Incidence of Each Risk Category in the Variability of Total Spending by Age Group and Gender

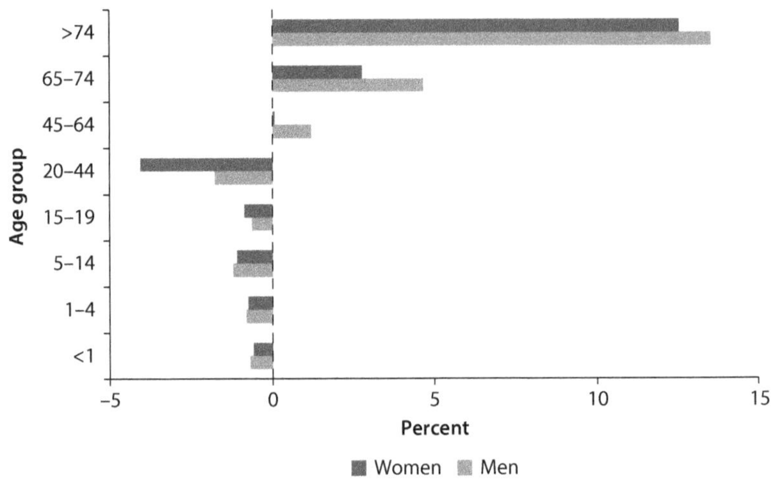

Table 5.9 Summary of the Estimate of the Demographic Changes in Health Care Spending, 2013–2100

Description	*Percent*
Change in spending considering all demographic changes	17.0
Change considering only changes in the number of people	–4.2
Change considering only changes in the demographic structure	22.2

combination *i* relative to total spending at the starting point; and g_i is the rate of variation for the spending corresponding to the age and gender profile *i*.

Figure 5.10 shows the estimate of the incidence of each risk category in the forecasts, and the counteracting forces that exist are apparent upon reviewing the overall change in the demographic structure.

Health care spending will show higher growth if we consider just the changes in the demographic structure while keeping the number of people constant. In this scenario, the health care spending growth rate would be approximately 30 percent higher than the rate if we were to consider both the effect of changes to the structure as well as the effect from changes in the number of individuals (table 5.9).

Analysis of the Changes in Sectoral Funding

Changes that will occur in health care spending will not solely be the result of the demographic changes just mentioned. It is therefore necessary to consider other factors that will affect the trajectory and eventually the relative proportion of public financing for the sector.

Among the multiple determinants of the future evolution of health care spending, the most important from the forecast perspective are those that have a high probability of occurrence and significant impact on spending. Several determinants meet these two criteria, including the inclusion of new groups of retirees in the FONASA-financed system that is planned for the coming years, the scheme to increase the value of the capitas paid for retirees, the eventual application of a health premium scheme to determine the State Health Services Administration's budget, and the possible reduction in the cost of co-payments that the IAMCs charge.

The following paragraphs estimate the impact that these changes will have, considering them in combination with the previously estimated impact of the demographic changes.

Inclusion of New Retirees in the FONASA-Financed System

Law No. 18,731 incorporates retirees and pensioners that were previously excluded from the National Health Care System into this system. The regulations establish a schedule from 2012 to 2016, gradually incorporating retirees and pensioners as a function of their age and their retirement income. Because the baseline for our forecasts is 2013, it is necessary to consider this impact along with the impact forecasted for the demographic changes.

Incorporating these retirees into the FONASA-financed system creates an increase in public financing of the sector because the individuals that are to receive FONASA coverage previously paid their premiums directly out of pocket. An increase also exists for those individuals that were previously cared for in the State Health Services Administration system because of the difference in the cost of that system and the value of the capitas that will be paid in the FONASA system.

Increase in the Value of the Capitas for Retirees and Pensioners

The law that provided for the entry of retirees and pensioners to FONASA coverage also established a schedule related to the evolution of the value of the capitas (premiums) that FONASA will pay to service providers. More precisely, the law established that the value of the health premium would increase by 20 percent of the difference that existed between an individual's premium and the value of the average premium in the first year, 40 percent in the second year, and so forth until reaching 100 percent in 2016.

The law also defined a schedule for the contributions that retirees and pensioners should pay to FONASA on a declining scale that ends in 2016, when they are fully assimilated into the general regime.

Based on information from the Continuous Household Survey, we estimate the impact of incorporating retirees and pensioners as established in the law on public health care spending. Figure 5.11 and table 5.10 present the estimated impact.

Determining the State Health Services Administration Program's Budget Based on the Value of the Health Premiums

The State Health Services Administration's income comes mostly from budgetary allocations; it only receives income from health premiums for 32.4 percent of its beneficiaries.

Figure 5.11 Public Health Care Spending: Impact of Demographic Change and the Changes Established in Law No. 18,731, 2013–2100

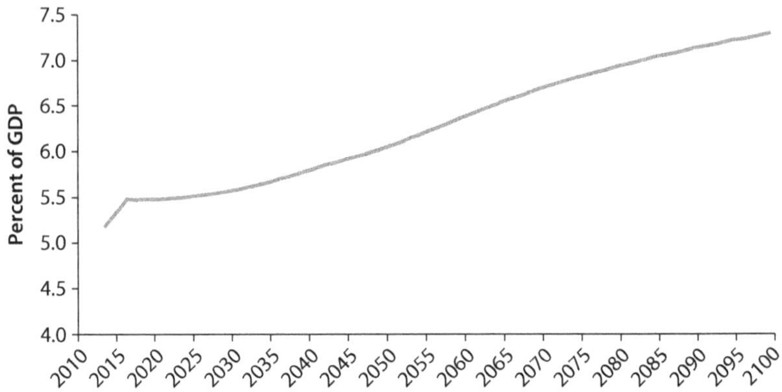

Table 5.10 Public Health Care Spending: Impact of Demographic Change and the Changes Established in Law No. 18,731, 2013 and 2100

Year	*Demographic change only (%)*	*Demographic change and law No. 18,731(%)*
2013	5.17	5.17
2100	6.87	7.30

Insofar as the State Health Services Administration is obligated to provide the same set of benefits as institutions that receive funds from FONASA, a process is already under way to standardize salaries at levels similar between public and private providers. In addition, price differences should not exist between what the State Health Services Administration pays for the rest of the resources it employs and the FONASA system. It is clear that the State Health Services Administration's budget should be set based on the value of the health premiums used in the FONASA system.

Determining the State Health Services Administration's budget based on the value of the health premiums does not necessarily mean that its beneficiaries will be incorporated into the FONASA system. Such a change would have further repercussions on spending related to beneficiaries' right to choose a provider or where to receive care. Currently, neither the State Health Services Administration nor FONASA users have these rights, and they would not necessarily acquire them based on a change in how the budget is allocated.

In summary, incorporating the State Health Services Administration as an additional service provider in the National Integrated Care System (Sistema Nacional Integrado de Salud), which would require it to offer the same benefits as the IAMCs and generally face the same rules, provides a reasonable justification that in the short or medium term the State Health Services Administration's budget would be determined based on the value of the health premiums that correspond to its beneficiary population.

Table 5.11 Impact of Setting the State Health Services Administration's Budget Based on the Value of the Health Premiums, 2013 and 2100
public health care spending as percent of GDP

Year	*Demographic change only (%)*	*Demographic change and changes in the State Health Services Administration's budget (%)*
2013	5.17	5.17
2100	6.87	7.18

Figure 5.12 Public Health Care Spending: Impact of Allocating State Health Services Administration Budget Based on Value of the Health Premiums, 2013–2100

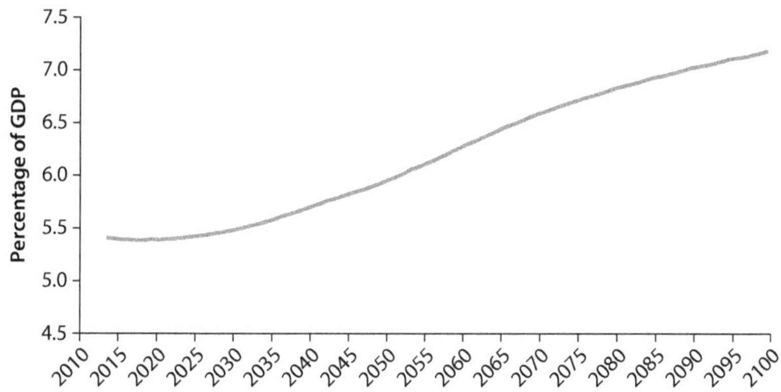

To quantify the impact understood as the gap between the resources that the State Health Services Administration has based on current criteria and the resources that it would have if its income were based on the health premiums that FONASA pays, we followed the steps outlined below.

First, income from FONASA was subtracted from the State Health Services Administration's operating costs. Next, the current capita schedule was utilized to estimate the payments that the State Health Services Administration would receive. Finally, these values were applied to the State Health Services Administration's beneficiary population that is not enrolled in FONASA to determine the budget for this group.

The increase in spending was estimated based on the difference between the cost of paying capitas, goals, and premiums corresponding to the National Fund of Resources (Fondo Nacional de Recursos) and the current budget allocation determined as described above. Table 5.11 and figure 5.12 present the impact of this measure, keeping in mind the impact of demographic change.

Reducing the Cost of Co-payments

One of the primary focuses of health policy in recent years has been facilitating access to health care services. To reach this objective, both supply and demand features were included. On the supply side, a care goal was created that awarded institutions for the number of consultations performed in certain circumstances, such as health checkups for children and pregnant women.

On the demand side, the cost of co-payments was reduced. This includes both those that are paid to go to consultations (orders) and those that apply to obtain medicines and request diagnostic tests (tickets).

It is highly probable that the process of reducing co-payments will be enhanced in coming years. Different actors, both governmental and civil society, have made clear their support for these types of measures. Specifically, at the beginning of the current administration, the incoming president included reducing the cost of co-payments as part of his commitments. Labor unions, both for doctors as well as for other officials, have suggested the need to eliminate co-payments in some cases and reduce them in others.

Reducing the cost of co-payments has two types of impacts. One direct impact is an increase in public sector financing's proportion of the total. This impact is the result of maintaining the system's sustainability, which makes it necessary to compensate the institutions for the effect that the measure has on their economic situation. The loss of income from reducing the cost of co-payments, which is a private source of financing, has up until now been accompanied in almost all cases by increases in public financing by raising the value of the capitas.

In addition, reducing the cost of co-payments would have an indirect impact; depending on the price elasticity of demand, it would have an effect on the quantity of goods and services involved and would therefore affect consumption and spending on health care. For the estimates presented below, demand for the services affected by the reduction of the cost of co-payments is considered to be inelastic because they are essential services for which there are no substitutes.

Table 5.12 shows the co-payment income received by the IAMCs[7] in the forecast baseline scenario.

Total co-payment income at the IAMCs is equivalent to approximately 6 percent of the sector's public sector financing. In other words, a 10 percent fall in the value of co-payments would increase public sector health care spending by 0.6 percent. Although a scenario in which the value of co-payments were to fall appears to be highly probable, it is not possible given available information to anticipate the magnitude of such a measure, especially over the long term.

For example, as was mentioned earlier, some important participants in the sector maintain that tickets should not exist. If the argument in favor of applying

Table 5.12 Income from Co-payments, IAMC System, 2013

	Ur$ (millions)	*Percentage of GDP*
Income from orders	617.5	0.05
Income from tickets	2,951.6	0.26
Total co-payments	**3,569.1**	**0.31**

Source: Elaboration based on information from SINADI and the BCU.
Note: BCU = Central Bank of Uruguay (Banco Central del Uruguay); IAMC = Collective Medical Assistance Institution (Institución de Asistencia Médica Colectiva); SINADI = National Information System (Sistema Nacional de Información).

Table 5.13 Public Health Care Spending: Impact of Reducing the Cost of Co-payments

	Just demographic change (%)	*Demographic change and reducing co-payments (%)*
Year		
2013	5.17	5.17
2100	n.a.	n.a.
Scenario		
1. Total elimination of tickets	6.87	7.21
2. Total elimination of orders	6.87	6.94
3. 50 percent reduction in the cost of tickets	6.87	7.04
4. 10 percent reduction in the cost of tickets	6.87	6.90
5. 50 percent reduction in the cost of orders	6.87	6.91
6. 10 percent reduction in the cost of orders	6.87	6.88

Note: n.a. = not applicable.

co-payments is to control demand based on patients' preferences, this would not apply for tickets, because they are the result of doctors' indications and not patients' spontaneous behavior.

Controlling costs in this case, for these actors, should be the result of clinical management models and not the application of barriers to access. Performing studies of medicine use and the appropriateness of prescriptions would be one way to control costs without affecting the quality of care. The development of the "salud.uy" project[8] would be one platform to carry out these types of studies.

Table 5.13 presents the estimates of the joint impact of demographic change and reducing the cost of co-payments for different scenarios defined by the assumed magnitude of the value of the reduction.

The magnitude of the impact of reducing the cost of tickets is significantly higher than for orders. For example, a 50 percent reduction would have an incremental effect of 0.17 percentage points of GDP, and for orders this effect would be 0.04.

Both the health care spending forecasts performed in this chapter and in chapter 2 are based on and critically depend on the value of the capitas included. These values are the result of an estimate that was carried out almost 10 years ago, and therefore the information is from a medical care model that differs from the current one.

Moreover, because, among other things, these values were estimated for the first time, it was necessary to make assumptions that could bias the results of the forecasts. It is worth pointing out that in the methodology used to calculate the capitas, it was assumed that the unit costs of the care products were independent of the gender and age of the patients. Thus, the capitas only capture the differences that exist in the quantity of services demanded by individuals as a function of their gender and age. This is important because it can be expected that the unit costs, such as the cost of an ambulatory consultation, would be higher for older individuals because they will surely involve more medical prescriptions, diagnostic tests, and so on. If true, then the value of these individuals' capitas should show greater difference relative to the rest of the population than for the values used in the forecasts. In other words, the estimate of the impact on the growth of health care spending caused by aging is being underestimated.

Finally, we must keep in mind that another factor exists that has not been included in the forecasts and could create health care spending increases that are higher than those estimated in the forecasts.

One commonality observed both in developed countries as well as in low-income countries is the tendency for health care spending to grow at rates above those for GDP. Multiple explanations exist for this fact, including the common explanation of aging, a factor that has been incorporated into the forecasts performed.

In addition, the technical changes in products and processes stand out as an explanatory factor in the growth of health care spending. As opposed to what happens in other sectors, technological progress in health care does not reduce costs; on the contrary, costs tend to increase.

The gap between what medicine can achieve for recovering one's health and what society is able to pay continues to grow. The process of incorporating new technology is generally one of the factors that create the greatest difficulty in achieving sustainability in the sector. The existence of technology evaluation agencies in many countries is evidence of this situation.

Although it is impossible to anticipate the product and process innovations that will appear in the future and which of these will be incorporated as benefits and will thus impact the evolution of health care spending in our country, it is certain that if the forecasts do not account for the possibility, then they will underestimate the growth of health care spending.

Finally, changes in sectoral prices can put additional pressure on spending growth. In a scenario in which productivity in other sectors of the economy grows more, services and salary increases in the sector tend to follow the general evolution of salaries in the economy, and pressures to raise prices and increase spending in the sector will exist.

Conclusions

Demographic changes in general, and population aging in particular, affect the evolution of health care spending. In Uruguay, these will increase health care spending from 7.8 percent of GDP in 2013 to 10.3 percent in 2100 and from 5.2 percent to 6.8 percent of GDP if we look only at spending financed with public funds.

This growth in the spending financed with public funds will create a significant challenge for those responsible for ensuring the sustainability of fiscal policy.

Nonetheless, not only is it to be expected that health care spending will increase, but that spending financed with public funds will especially increase due to demographic changes. A series of changes in the structure of the National Comprehensive Health Care System are already ongoing and they will create greater need for public funds in the health care sector. In addition, measures exist with a high probability of implementation, reducing the cost of co-payments for example, and these will also increase the need for public funds.

Added to this is the tension that incorporating new care products and processes can provoke. This dynamic requires appropriate coordination between the leaders in charge of regulating the sector's health aspects and those responsible for managing the economy.

The evolution that the forecasts show allows us to anticipate that health care spending will be one of the principal concerns for those responsible for achieving fiscal sustainability in the future.

Notes

1. Carlos Grau, Center for Economic Research; correspondence to cgrau@cinve.org.uy.
2. In addition to the State Health Services Administration, other organizations exist, including Military Health Care, Police Health Care, Clinical Hospital, BSE Health Services, and the health care division of the Social Security Bank.
3. To the extent that the presence or absence of an illness is a random phenomenon.
4. The system defines eight age groups, resulting in sixteen risk categories.
5. Relying on the forecasts in chapter 2.
6. More precisely, spending to recover one's health. Spending on prevention may be determined by other factors.
7. Co-payments are not charged in the State Health Services Administration system.
8. This project is part of the Electronic Government and Information Society Agency, which depends on the Office of the President.

References

Central Bank of Uruguay (Banco Central del Uruguay [BCU]). http://www.bcu.gub.uy/Estadisticas-e-Indicadores/Paginas/Cou_Base2005.aspx.

Lazo, A. 2013. "La Esperanza de Vida en Uruguaya lo largo de los Siglos XIX, XX y XXI y sus Probables Valores Futuros." Draft. http://www.bps.gub.uy/bps/file/6826/1/07_esperanza_vida_uy_siglos_xix_xx_xxi.pdf.

National Institute of Statistics (Instituto Nacional de Estadística). http://www.ine.gub.uy/.

SINADI (National Information System [Sistema Nacional de Información]). http://www.msp.gub.uy/publicaciones/direccipercentC3percentB3n-general-del-sistema-nacional-integrado-de-salud/econom percentC3 percentADa-de-la-salud/sistema.

State Health Services Administration (Administración de los Servicios de Salud del Estado). http://www.asse.com.uy.

CHAPTER 6

Demographic Change and the Education System

Cecilia Llambí and Maren Vairo[1]

Introduction

Pressure on the Uruguayan public purse to fund education has been relieved by the recent fall in the school-age compared to the economically active population, whose efforts indirectly fund the education system. This demographic trend opens a window of opportunity to free up resources for education; for example, to allocate spending to areas where funding is currently in deficit and to invest more per student.

This chapter focuses on the choices for the education system presented by Uruguay's demographic profile, which, as we saw in chapter 2, is characterized by low fertility and a moderate increase in life expectancy. It estimates in particular the potential savings for public spending on education from the demographic dividend and examines how the goals of ensuring universal coverage for education and increasing per-student investment can be achieved, even with no change in spending.

The examination of the challenges and opportunities for policy makers starts with a description of the recent evolution of the Uruguayan education system, in coverage, educational trajectories, and grade completion. The subsequent section describes the recent evolution of public spending across different levels of education and puts this in international context. To propose some long-term goals for investment per enrolled student, three basic indicators that determine the main cost component of education, salary costs per student are compared. These indicators—the student-to-teacher ratio, teaching time, and teacher salaries—help identify where the most significant deficits are likely to emerge, and to propose some long-term goals for investments per enrolled student. The fourth section presents exercises simulating public spending on education as a percentage of gross domestic product (GDP) under different policy objectives, keeping in mind Uruguay's predicted demographic evolution. Finally, we share considerations based on the analysis.

Coverage and Completion

The formal education system in Uruguay comprises five levels. The first level is early childhood education (*educación inicial*). This is aimed at children from ages three to five[2] and is compulsory for ages four and five. Primary school takes children from age six. It is structured across six grades and is compulsory. Middle school encompasses two levels: basic and upper secondary education. Basic secondary education comprises three grades and is provided through general education in public and private schools, and the exclusively public technological education and basic rural systems. Upper secondary education also consists of three grades, where students choose specialist subjects and the service is provided by public and private schools, as well as professional technical and technological education, which is almost entirely in the public sector.

Basic secondary education has been compulsory since 1973, while upper secondary education was made compulsory in the 2008 education law. In this way, compulsory education was expanded to 14 years, starting at age 4 until completion of the final grade at upper secondary (which a student usually completes around age 17 or 18). Finally, tertiary education is either non-university tertiary, teacher training, or university education, and is provided by the public and private sectors.

In 2013, about 900,000 people were in the formal education system in Uruguay. Total enrollment has changed significantly since 1990 to the present day. Primary education has remained the most stable, and has offered universal coverage since the middle of the 20th century; however, it has seen enrollment drop systematically, with enrollment falling 11.2 percent between 2005 and 2013 (from 355,000 students to 315,000[3]), almost entirely due to the demographic changes featured in figure 6.1.[4] At all other levels, enrollment expanded significantly from the 1990s to the present day. That is especially so for early childhood education, where enrollment grew strongly from the mid-1990s after a reform that expanded the supply of public education to reach universal coverage for ages 4 and 5.

The educational enrollment indicators collect changes that are separate from access to education, changes that are associated with demographic transition, such as enrollment indicators related to the size of the school-age population. Figure 6.2 shows the coverage for the different levels of education, via net enrollment ratios (NERs).[5] In this respect, primary education stands out for its stable and universal attendance rates around 95 percent of eligible children during the entire period under analysis. Early childhood education in contrast has shown consistent, significant growth in enrollment in recent decades—51 percent of children from ages 3–5 attended early childhood education in 1991 and this rose to 84 percent by 2013.

In secondary education, attendance at the basic level was more modest, growing from 66 percent in 1991 to 76 percent in 2013, while the enrollment rate in upper secondary education fell from 44 percent in 1991 to 41 percent in 2000 and reversed between 2001 and 2005, with the NER increasing (reaching its

Figure 6.1 Total Enrolled Students by Education Level, 1990–2013

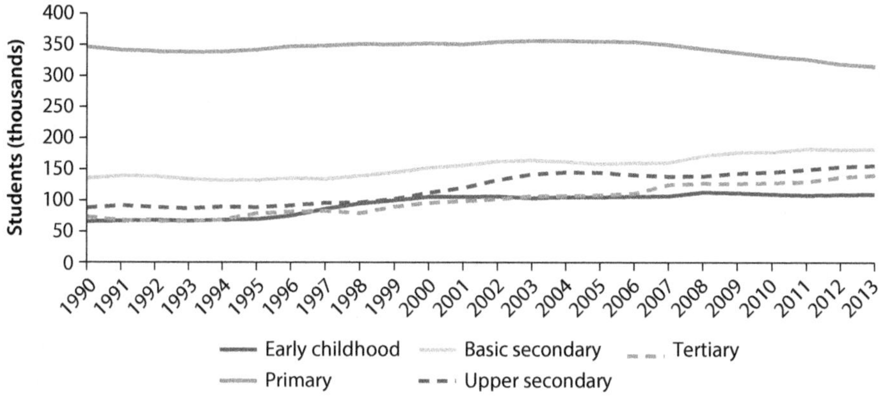

Sources: Elaboration based on data from the Education Observatory at the National Administration of Public Education (Administración Nacional de Educación Pública; ANEP) (http://www3.anep.edu.uy/observatorio/) and the *Statistical Yearbook for Education* from the Ministry of Education and Culture (Ministerio de Educación y Cultura; MEC) from 1990–2013 (http://www.mec.gub.uy/innovaportal/v/11078/5/mecweb/publicaciones_?3colid=927).
Note: Enrollment in early childhood education refers to the system within the ANEP's sphere. Primary education does not include special primary education.

Figure 6.2 Net Enrollment Ratios by Education Level, 1991–2013

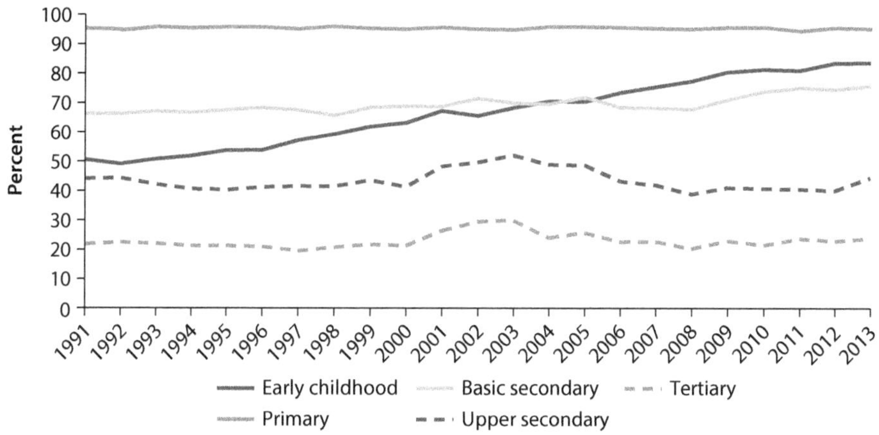

Source: Elaboration based on data from the Education Observatory at the National Administration of Public Education (Administración Nacional de Educación Pública; ANEP) (http://www3.anep.edu.uy/observatorio/).
Note: The enrollment ratios are calculated based on the percentage of the population: ages 3–5 attending early childhood education; from ages 6–11 attending primary education; from ages 12–14 at basic secondary education; from ages 15–17 at upper secondary education; and ages 18–22 attending the tertiary level. The data refer exclusively to urban localities with more than 5,000 residents.

highest level in 2003 with an attendance rate of 52 percent). This phenomenon was possibly associated with the recession and economic crisis in Uruguay at that time, which reduced the size of the labor market, thus lowering the opportunity cost of remaining in the education system for young people of ages 15–17. A similar pattern is seen in the enrollment rate in tertiary education, but the dynamic is absent at other educational levels, given that youth and children are not yet part of the working-age population.[6] Once economic recovery began in 2005 the NERs for upper secondary and tertiary education declined and then leveled off.

Rates are low in secondary education, particularly in upper secondary, even as attendance is compulsory. This demonstrates that the setting of attendance requirements is not always accompanied by increases in coverage. In this sense, early childhood education exemplifies a case where establishing attendance requirements, accompanied by significant effort to expand supply, succeeded in bringing more children into the system; while for secondary education compliance with attendance requirements is far from complete.[7]

In early childhood education, the NER is universal at age 5 (99 percent in 2013). At the same time, enrollment at age 4 grew from 53 percent in 1991 to 91 percent in 2013, associated with the significant effort to build more public schools in 1996 (figure 6.3). Age 3 was not explicitly prioritized by policy measures in the period in the analysis, so NER growth was less pronounced until recent years, with the NER growing from 41 percent in 2009 to 65 percent in 2013. In conclusion, at this level a small coverage gap persists at the compulsory age 4 and the gap is more significant at age 3. Closing the gap at age 3 is currently a priority target in a government program begun in March 2015.

In addition to school attendance, the outcomes children and young people can achieve are important, especially their likelihood of advancing through the education system. In this sense, to the extent that moving to a higher level requires

Figure 6.3 Net Enrollment Ratios for Early Childhood Education, 1991–2013

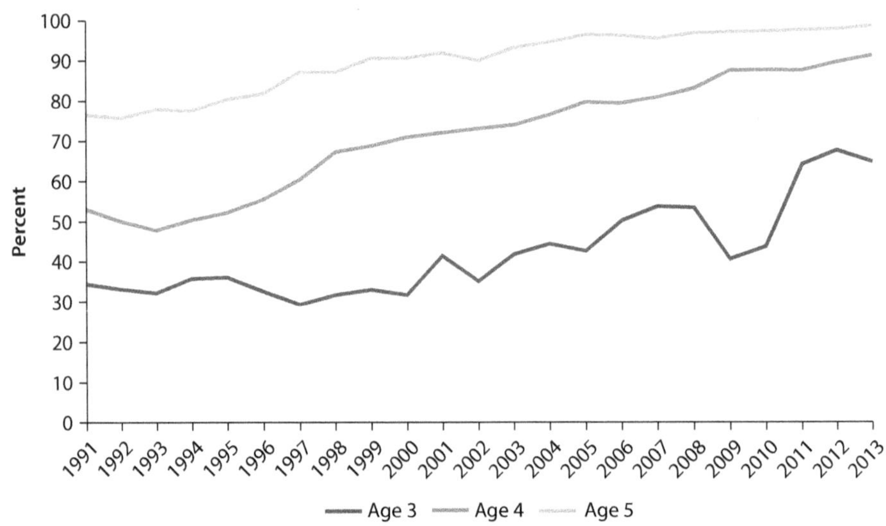

Source: Created based on the Continuous Household Survey database from the National Institute of Statistics (Instituto Nacional de Estadística; INE).
Note: The data refer exclusively to urban localities with more than 5,000 residents.

passing an earlier level, a low completion rate at a given level will have implications for coverage at higher levels.

As with our observations regarding attendance, significant differences in completion rates are apparent. Nearly the entire population between ages 15–17 have completed primary education, and that is observed in the high rates of attendance at that level throughout the period under analysis. The difficulties begin to manifest during secondary education where, despite the high proportion of students that complete primary education, about 70 percent of students complete the basic secondary level (figure 6.4), and this low completion rate translates into a 40 percent completion rate in upper secondary. These trends have remained stable over the last two decades, with no signs of any reversal. Accordingly, both in coverage and completion, secondary education constitutes the principal challenge for the Uruguayan education system.

To include considerations about efficiency in the challenges for the Uruguayan education system, figure 6.5 shows the evolution of the over-age enrollment ratio—the ratio between the total number of students in a level and the number of students in the age group fitting for that level—for the basic secondary level. The lag in educational trajectories has implications on efficiency, insofar as it requires investment of greater economic resources to help a student complete the level. At the same time, staying at the same level

Figure 6.4 Completion Rates by Education Level, 1991–2013

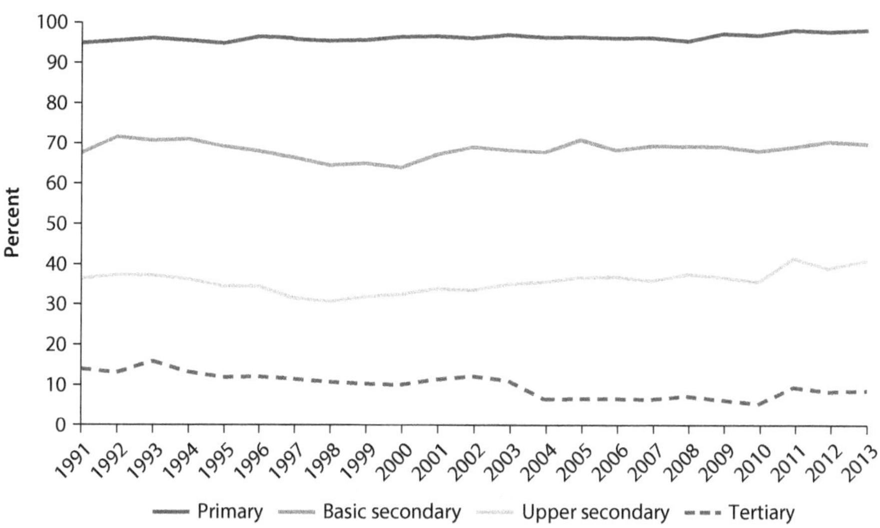

Source: Created based on data from the Education Observatory at the National Administration of Public Education (Administración Nacional de Educación Pública, ANEP; http://www3.anep.edu.uy/observatorio/) and the Continuous Household Survey from the National Institute of Statistics (Instituto Nacional de Estadística; INE).
Note: We consider individuals from 15 to 17 years old for primary completion, from 18 to 20 years old for basic secondary, and from 21 to 23 for upper secondary (*bachillerato*). The data refer exclusively to urban localities with more than 5,000 residents.

Figure 6.5 Over-Age Enrollment Ratio by Education Level, 1991–2013

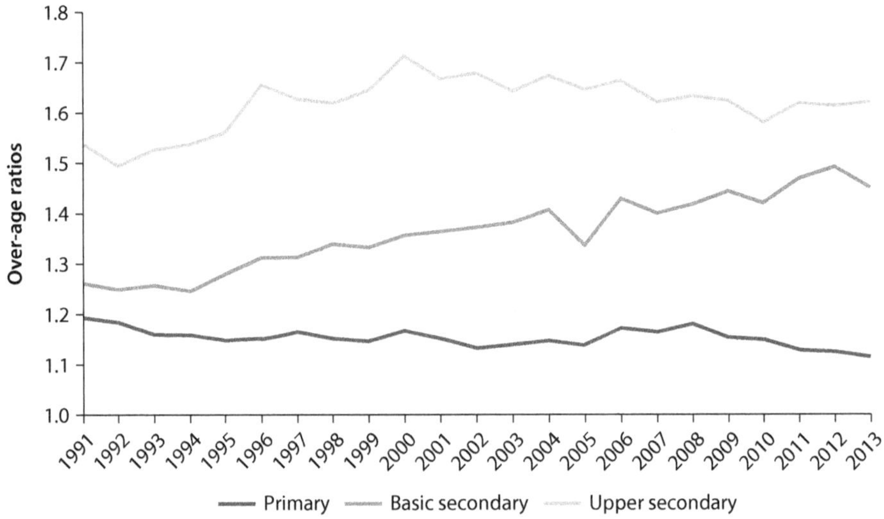

Source: Created based on data from the Education Observatory at the National Administration of Public Education (Administración Nacional de Educación Pública, ANEP; http://www3.anep.edu.uy/observatorio/).
Note: The over-age enrollment ratio is obtained as the ratio between total enrollment and the enrollment level that comprises just students from the age group that should be studying at that level (ages 6–11 in primary, ages 12–14 in basic secondary, and ages 15–17 in upper secondary). The over-age ratio at the upper secondary level refers exclusively to secondary education. The data refer exclusively to urban localities with more than 5,000 residents.

for too long may leave young people feeling discouraged, and result in them disconnecting from the system.

Figure 6.5 shows different realities for different education levels. The over-age enrollment ratio for primary education was around 1.2 in 2008. That means enrollment was approximately 20 percent higher with over-age students than what it would have been without them. As a consequence of the drop in repetition rates in public primary education, it has dropped to 10 percent. However, at the basic secondary level the over-age enrollment ratio is noticeably higher, at 1.43 in 2013. This feeds through to upper secondary, where the over-age ratio reaches nearly 1.6 in 2013. In turn, it is possible to argue that various problems identified at the secondary level are closely linked: as the lag in moving on to age-appropriate grades results in desertion, this will reinforce the low coverage and persistent completion problems.

The actual General Law of Education conceives of education as a means for reducing socioeconomic inequalities, which, to the extent that factors associated with this are exogenous to children and youth, may be classified as unjust. In this sense, the law proposes equal opportunities as a guiding principal for government-led public education, according to which "the State will provide necessary specific support to those individuals and sectors in special situations of vulnerability, and will act in such a way as to include individuals and sectors that have been discriminated against culturally, economically, and/or socially, such that they achieve a true equality of opportunities in terms of access, continuity, and attainment of learning" (General Law of Education, Ch. IV, Art. 18). Within this framework, equality in educational opportunities would require equal access to the education system, in attendance and completion of different levels, for children and youth from different socioeconomic backgrounds.

Figure 6.6 shows the net enrollment rates for children and youth from households with different incomes. At the primary level, characterized by universal coverage, disparities in access according to socioeconomic background are not observed, but rather approximately 100 percent of the population in the first and last income quintiles has access to this level. The significant access gaps in early childhood education at the beginning of the 1990s have nearly disappeared with the expansion of public education and subsequent increase in attendance, although coverage continues to be greater for children from better-off socioeconomic backgrounds.[8]

On the other hand, considerable inequalities can be seen in access to secondary education. At the basic secondary level, the NER in 2013 for the richest income quintile was 24 percentage points higher than the lowest income quintile (89 percent and 65 percent, respectively). This gap remained relatively constant throughout the period under consideration. The disparities are even greater in upper secondary education, where the NER for the highest income quintile is about four times higher than for the lowest income quintile (78 percent and 21 percent, respectively). In turn, for 1991–2013, this trend has been exacerbated as the richest quintile's NER has grown.

In turn, inequalities at later levels manifest as disparities in completion rates. So, while completion of primary education is nearly universal and equal, inequalities intensify as one moves up the educational scale (figure 6.7). In basic secondary education, the completion rate of the richest quintile is more than double

Figure 6.6 Net Enrollment Ratios by Education Level and Household Income Quintile, 1991–2013

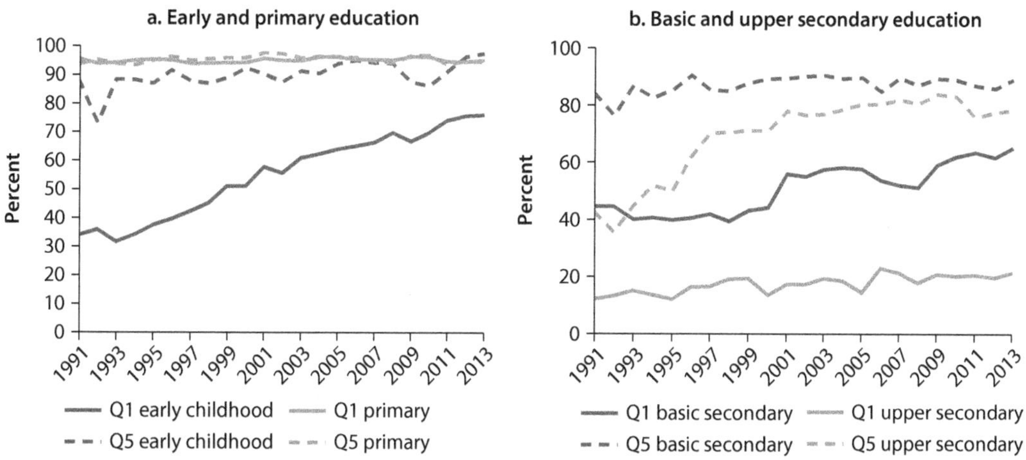

Source: Elaboration based on the Continuous Household Survey database from the National Institute of Statistics (Instituto Nacional de Estadística; INE).
Note: The data refer exclusively to urban localities with more than 5,000 residents. Q = income quintile.

Figure 6.7 Completion Rates by Education Level and Household Income Quintile, 1991–2013

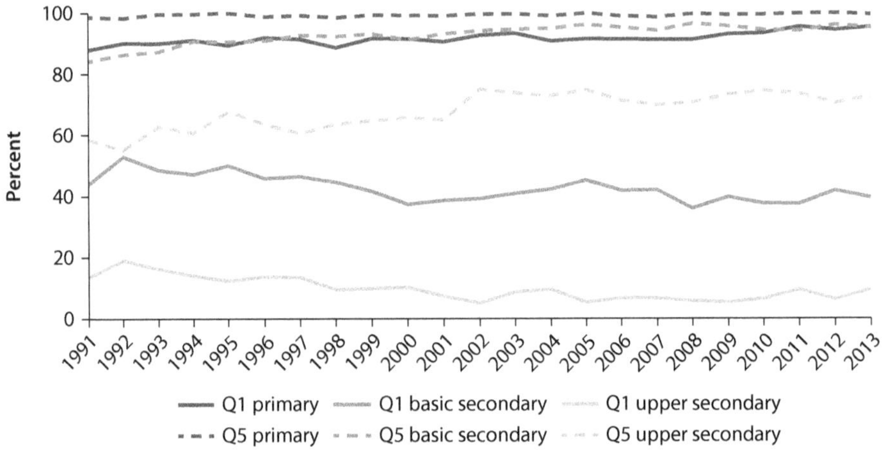

Source: Created based on the Continuous Household Survey database from the National Institute of Statistics (Instituto Nacional de Estadística; INE).
Note: We consider individuals from 15 to 17 years old for primary completion, from 18 to 20 years old for basic secondary education, and 21–23 for upper secondary. The data refer exclusively to urban localities with more than 5,000 residents. Q = income quintile.

that of the poorest (95 percent and 40 percent, respectively). In upper secondary education the gaps are even starker, as the percentage of youth in the highest quintile that complete this level is more than seven times that of youth from the first quintile (completion rates of 73 percent and 10 percent, respectively). In all cases, the trends have remained stable in the last two decades. It is worth noting that inequality in education has implications for inequality during one's adult life, to the extent that it undermines the ability of young people from vulnerable backgrounds to join the workforce and the problem becomes a transmission vector for intergenerational income inequality.

In the case of upper secondary education, considerable completion gaps exist among young people from households in the highest income quintile, which reflects problems inherent to the education system that are not exclusively the product of the attendance difficulties within vulnerable populations.

In conclusion, the most significant challenges for coverage and completion in the Uruguayan education system are at the secondary level, particularly upper secondary. The high over-age enrollment ratio and a low completion rate in secondary education are very significant challenges. Additionally, in early childhood education a coverage challenge exists for age 3. Although at this age attendance is not compulsory, it is a priority on the Uruguayan education agenda.[9] Finally, coverage and completion challenges at various levels are closely linked to reducing disparities between students from different socioeconomic backgrounds, although some problems in secondary education have a different origin.

Education Spending

Principal Education Spending Trends in Uruguay and Latin America Relative to Developed Countries

One feature of the Uruguayan education system is the significant participation of the public sector. Figure 6.8 shows the dominance of public provision throughout the compulsory system, with an especially significant share of secondary education. In 2013, public secondary education served 88 percent of the students at this level. Public funds paid for 73 percent of children in early childhood education and 83 percent of the children attending primary schools in the same year.

In Uruguay, the largest portion of public spending on formal education is directed by the National Administration of Public Education (Administración Nacional de Educación Pública; ANEP) and the University of the Republic (Universidad de la República; UdelaR).[10] While ANEP supplies public early childhood, primary, secondary, and some tertiary education (tertiary through teacher-training and technical tertiary education), UdelaR encompasses almost all public university education.[11] As figure 6.9 shows (panel a), the proportion of the GDP of the Uruguayan economy directed to public funding of formal education has grown significantly since 2008, when the country set the goal of directing 4.5 percent of GDP to public education.[12]

With reference to figure 6.9, panel b enables us to analyze the evolution of public education spending relative to enrollment sizes. We find that, although spending by the UdelaR and the ANEP on teacher training[13] has grown during the periods under consideration, the per-student resources for tertiary education relative to the economic capacity per inhabitant (relative to GDP per capita) fell markedly between the mid-1990s and 2008, at which point it rebounded. Even so, the tertiary sector spends the most resources per student (23 percent of per

Figure 6.8 Public Sector Proportion of Total Enrollment by Education Level, Selected Years

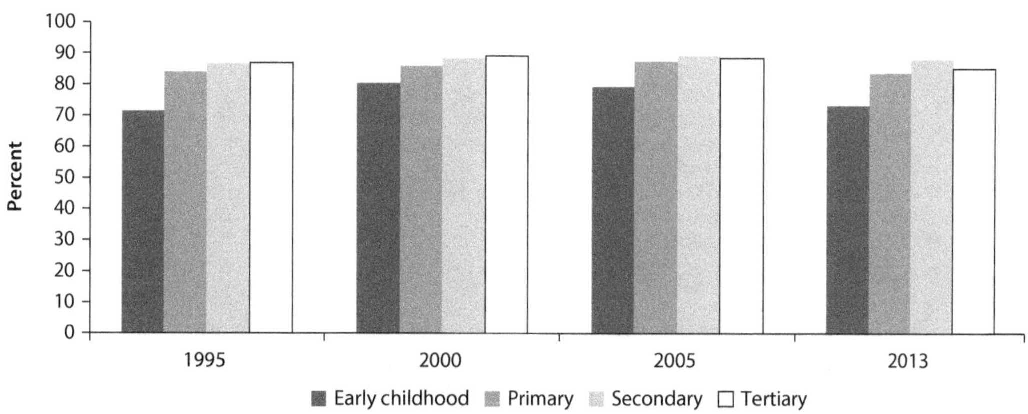

Source: Elaboration based on the Education Observatory database at the National Administration of Public Education (Administración Nacional de Educación Pública, ANEP; http://www3.anep.edu.uy/observatorio/).

Figure 6.9 Public Spending on Education in Uruguay

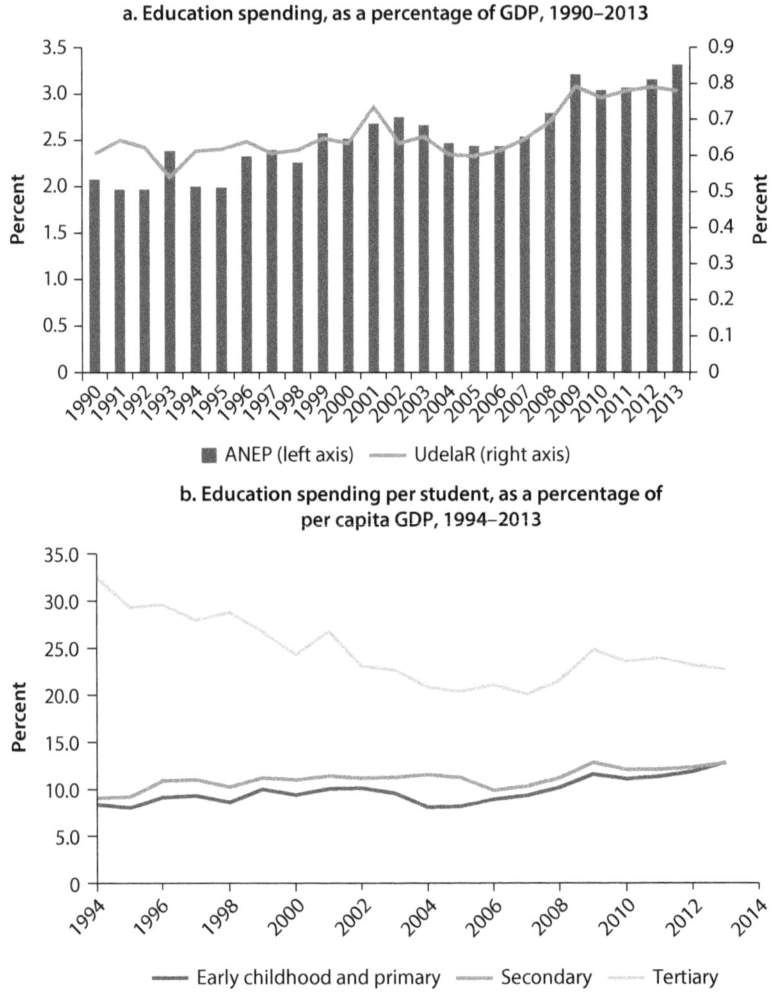

Source: Statistical Yearbook for Education from the Ministry of Education and Culture 1990–2013 (http://www.mec.gub.uy/innovaportal/v/11078/5/mecweb/publicaciones_?3colid=927) based on data from the Ministry of Economy and Finances, and the Education Observatory at the National Administration of Public Education (Administración Nacional de Educación Pública, ANEP; http://www3.anep.edu.uy/observatorio/).
Note: In panel a, ANEP spending includes early childhood, primary, secondary (basic and upper), technical/professional education, and teacher training. In panel b, the tertiary level comprises spending on university education executed by the University of the Republic and spending on teacher training executed by the ANEP. To calculate spending per student for the ANEP included here (early childhood, primary, and secondary) each level was assigned the corresponding portion of the Central Administrative Council (Consejo Directivo Central; CODICEN) spending, which is the product of each level's proportion of the ANEP's total spending.

capita GDP in 2013, according to the most recent data). In addition, early childhood, primary, and secondary education show similar changes. Historically, spending per secondary student was slightly higher than for primary students, but this difference disappeared in 2013, when both subsystems spent the equivalent of 13 percent of per capita GDP.

Comparative data for public spending on basic education in Uruguay and other countries (figure 6.10) show that in 2013, Uruguay directed 3 percent of GDP to fund basic public education, below the Latin American average (3.4 percent). Argentina, Brazil, and Bolivia stand out for greater efforts to fund public education relative to their economic capacity, insofar as they all allocate around 5 percent of GDP for this purpose. In addition, countries that are more developed are generally characterized by spending a higher share of GDP on public education compared to Latin America (on average, Organisation for Economic Co-operation and Development [OECD] countries allocated 4.2 percent of GDP to basic public education in 2011). The international comparison reveals that even though in recent years Uruguay has increased its funding for education, it is still lower than in other Latin American countries and the average spend of relatively more developed countries. There is still room for progress in Uruguay in funding and the quality of spending to reach goals such as greater coverage and higher completion rates throughout the educational levels.

Figure 6.11 shows comparative data for spending by other countries on basic education relative to the number of enrolled students. The illustration entails incorporating dimensions related to the age structure of the population (insofar as the number of school-age youth has a clear relationship with the size of enrollment) and a system's coverage rate. Upon consideration of these dimensions,

Figure 6.10 Public Spending on Basic Education in Latin America and OECD Countries

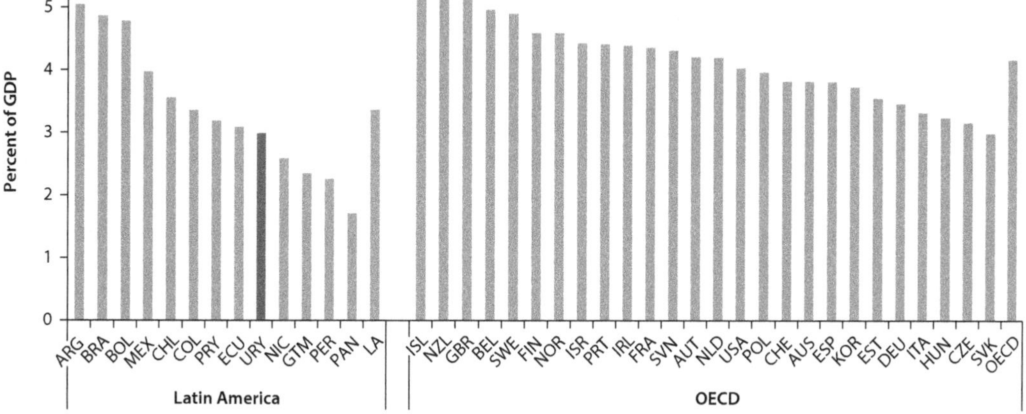

Sources: UNESCO Institute of Statistics (http://data.uis.unesco.org) and the 2013 *Statistical Yearbook for Education* (Ministry of Education and Culture, MEC; http://www.mec.gub.uy/innovaportal/v/11078/5/mecweb/publicaciones_?3colid=927).
Note: The "LA" (Latin America) and "OECD" (Organisation for Economic Co-operation and Development) bars refer to the average for the countries from each group included in the figure. Public spending on early childhood, primary, and secondary education is included. The data refer to the most recent year available: 2010 for Brazil, Iceland, Germany, Norway, Poland, Portugal, Spain, Sweden, the United Kingdom, and the United States; 2012 for Chile, Colombia, Ecuador, the Netherlands, New Zealand, Peru, and Switzerland; 2013 for Uruguay; and 2011 for the remaining countries. **Latin America:** ARG = Argentina; BOL = Bolivia; BRA = Brazil; CHL = Chile; COL = Colombia; ECU = Ecuador; GTM = Guatemala; MEX = Mexico; NIC = Nicaragua; PAN = Panama; PER = Peru; PRY = Paraguay; URY = Uruguay. **OECD:** AUS = Australia; AUT = Austria; BEL = Belgium; CHE = Switzerland; CZE = Czech Republic; DEU = Germany; ESP = Spain; EST = Estonia; FIN = Finland; FRA = France; GBR = United Kingdom; HUN = Hungary; IRL = Ireland; ISL = Iceland; ISR = Israel; ITA = Italy; KOR = Korea, Rep.; NLD = Netherlands; NOR = Norway; NZL = New Zealand; POL = Poland; PRT = Portugal; SVK = Slovak Republic; SVN = Slovenia; SWE = Sweden; USA = United States.

Figure 6.11 Public Spending on Basic Education per Student in Latin America and OECD Countries

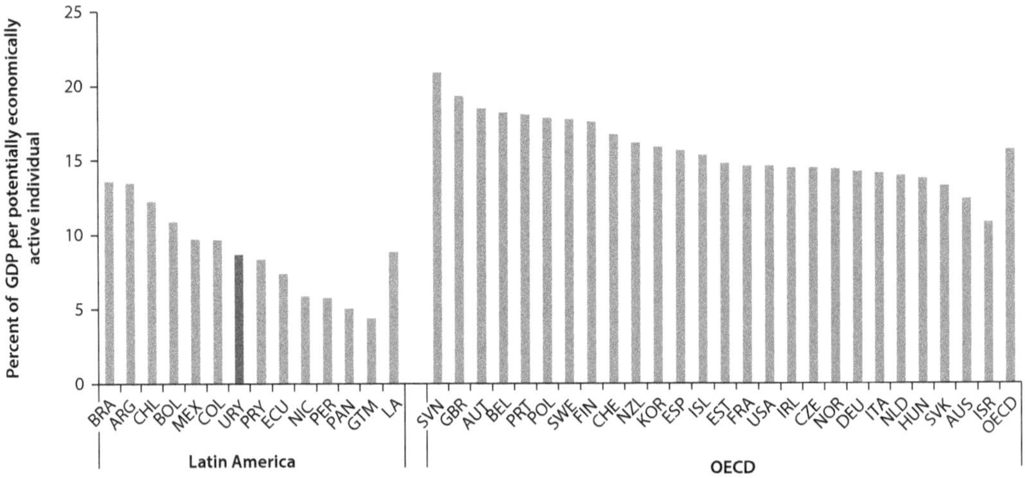

Sources: UNESCO Institute of Statistics (http://data.uis.unesco.org) and the 2013 *Statistical Yearbook for Education* (Ministry of Education and Culture, MEC; http://www.mec.gub.uy/innovaportal/v/11078/5/mecweb/publicaciones_?3colid=927).

Note: The "LA" (Latin America) and "OECD" (Organisation for Economic Co-operation and Development) bars refer to the average for the countries from each group included in the figure, respectively. Public spending on early childhood, primary, and secondary education is included. The data refer to the most recent year available: 2010 for Brazil, Germany, Iceland, Norway, Poland, Portugal, Spain, Sweden, United Kingdom, and United States; 2012 for Chile, Colombia, Ecuador, the Netherlands, New Zealand, Peru, and Switzerland; 2013 for Uruguay; and 2011 for the remaining countries. **Latin America:** ARG = Argentina; BOL = Bolivia; BRA = Brazil; CHL = Chile; COL = Colombia; ECU = Ecuador; GTM = Guatemala; MEX = Mexico; NIC = Nicaragua; PAN = Panama; PER = Peru; PRY = Paraguay; URY = Uruguay. **OECD:** AUS = Australia; AUT = Austria; BEL = Belgium; CHE = Switzerland; CZE = Czech Republic; DEU = Germany; ESP = Spain; EST = Estonia; FIN = Finland; FRA = France; GBR = United Kingdom; HUN = Hungary; IRL = Ireland; ISL = Iceland; ISR = Israel; ITA = Italy; KOR = Korea, Rep.; NLD = Netherlands; NOR = Norway; NZL = New Zealand; POL = Poland; PRT = Portugal; SVK = Slovak Republic; SVN = Slovenia; SWE = Sweden; USA = United States.

Uruguay improves its position, with per-student spending on basic education at the equivalent of 8.7 percent of GDP per adult in the economically active age range—although that is still lower than the regional average. Uruguay takes seventh place among Latin American countries according to this spending indicator. Compared to OECD countries, per-student spending in Uruguay and the Latin American region is noticeably lower; with average spending among OECD countries at 15.7 percent of GDP per adult in the economically active age range.

The analysis presented here provides evidence of the significant effort that more developed countries are making in education, particularly as it relates to funding per student. However, even though the goal of increasing spending per student could be beneficial in and of itself, it is interesting to investigate the components of that spending, insofar as the relationship between per-student spending and students' ability to benefit from actual improvements in learning is not always direct. It is important to also be aware of how the most significant categories of spending are organized, since they determine the resources per student. With this purpose in mind, we turn to those aspects of the education system that provide an idea of how resources are allocated.

When one analyzes spending per student at each level of education, the results again indicate a wide gap between Uruguay and OECD countries, although the size of the gap depends on the level (table 6.1).[14] The greatest shortfalls can

Table 6.1 Public Spending per Student by Education Level in Uruguay and the OECD as a Percentage of GDP per Economically Active Person

	Per-student spending/ GDP per worker	*Percent of difference compared to the OECD*
Uruguay		
Early childhood	7.2	85
Primary	8.5	75
Basic secondary	8.9	87
Upper secondary	10.4	60
Tertiary	14.5	72
OECD average		
Early childhood	13.3	n.a.
Primary	14.9	n.a.
Basic secondary	16.6	n.a.
Upper secondary	16.6	n.a.
Tertiary	25.0	n.a.

Sources: OECD 2014 and 2013 *Statistical Yearbook for Education* (Ministry of Education and Culture, MEC; http://www.mec.gub.uy/innovaportal/v/11078/5/mecweb/publicaciones_?3colid=927).
Note: The data for Uruguay are from 2013, while OECD data are from 2011. OECD = Organisation for Economic Co-operation and Development; n.a. = not applicable.

be seen in early childhood and basic secondary education, insofar as it would be necessary to increase current per-student spending by approximately 85 percent in both levels to reach a per-student benefit similar to that seen in developed countries in terms of GDP per economically active person. The challenge is also large for basic secondary and tertiary education, where an approximately 75 percent increase in spending would be necessary, while in upper secondary education a necessary 60 percent increase in spending would be lower, although still entail considerable fiscal effort.

The cost of salaries per student is the largest component when we analyze per-student spending. Three factors determine the salary cost per student: (a) instruction time (the number of classroom hours per year); (b) the student-teacher ratio and class size; and (c) teacher salaries. In the following paragraphs we analyze some indicators of these characteristics in Uruguay, taking a comparative perspective.

With regard to the student-teacher ratio (figure 6.12), it is clear that secondary education in Uruguay is well positioned internationally, with a ratio of 11 students per teacher, placing it below the average for Latin American countries and at a level close to the OECD average. However, it is important to keep in mind the coverage problems that affect secondary education in Uruguay and, therefore, the potential deterioration of this indicator if the country were to improve low attendance rates at this level. The case of primary education is different; the Uruguayan education system is able to serve the entire school-age population and enjoy a level of teachers per student close to that in the OECD (14 students per teacher in both cases). Primary education exhibits universality and student-teacher ratios similar to those of developed countries. However, Uruguay appears to lag behind on early childhood education, with a ratio of 26 students

Figure 6.12 Students per Teacher in Latin America and OECD Countries

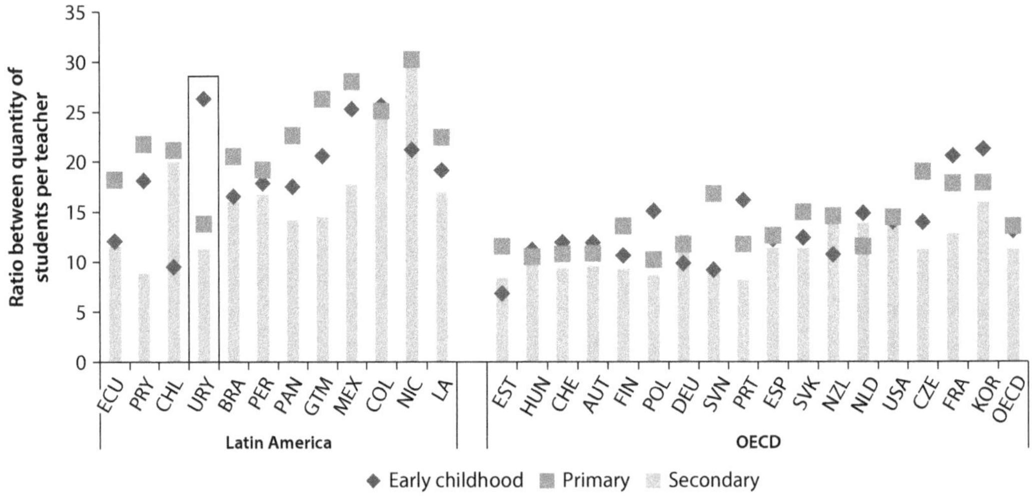

Source: UNESCO Institute of Statistics (http://data.uis.unesco.org).
Note: The "LA" (Latin America) and "OECD" (Organisation for Economic Co-operation and Development) bars refer to the average for the countries from each group included in the figure. The data refer to the most recent year available: 2010 for Nicaragua and Uruguay; 2011 for Chile, Colombia, Guatemala, Republic of Korea, and Paraguay; and 2012 for the remaining countries.
Latin America: BRA = Brazil; CHL = Chile; COL = Colombia; ECU = Ecuador; GTM = Guatemala; MEX = Mexico; NIC = Nicaragua; PAN = Panama; PER = Peru; PRY = Paraguay; URY = Uruguay. **OECD:** AUT = Austria; CHE = Switzerland; CZE = Czech Republic; DEU = Germany; ESP = Spain; EST = Estonia; FIN = Finland; FRA = France; HUN = Hungary; KOR = Korea, Rep.; NLD = Netherlands; NZL = New Zealand; POL = Poland; PRT = Portugal; SVK = Slovak Republic; SVN = Slovenia; USA = United States.

per teacher, which is the highest among the sample of selected countries. In this regard, in early childhood education the supply of services is very disparate, especially for age 3. However, this high student-teacher ratio constitutes an education policy and funding challenge, insofar as the NER shows that a contingent of children (especially ages 3–4) still needs to enter the system. This challenge takes on special importance in the face of the current debate around the universalization of education at age 3.

Teacher salaries directly impact the attractiveness of the profession as a career. Under certain circumstances, it may also reflect or drive increases in teacher quality or productivity. A preponderance of low teacher salaries in the labor market affects the quality of the education system, to the extent that it may constitute a disincentive to become a teacher, with the result of creating a small, low-quality body of teachers. Accordingly, teacher salaries constitute an element that must be evaluated when setting the amount of spending per student.

As figure 6.13 shows, teacher salaries in Uruguay in 2013 were noticeably lower than for other professions that require a similar standard of education, insofar as a primary school teacher and a secondary school professor earned monthly salaries equivalent to 56 percent and 60 percent, respectively, of the average salary of other workers with a university education. These figures are lower than observed in OECD countries, although worldwide teacher salaries are lower than those for other professionals and specialists, with New Zealand, Portugal, Spain,

Figure 6.13 Teacher Salaries at Public Institutions in Uruguay and OECD Countries

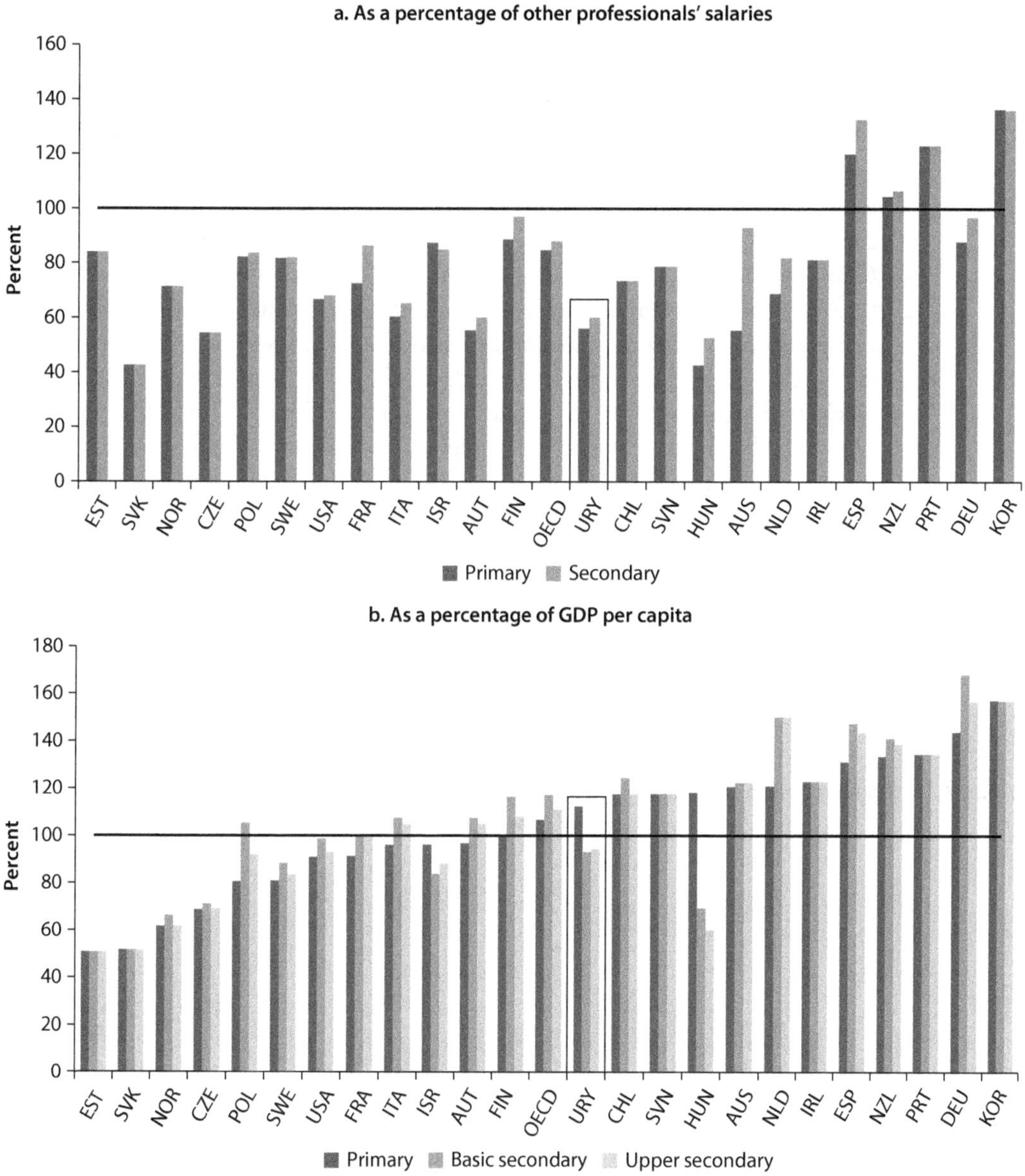

Sources: OECD 2014, Continuous Household Survey (INE), and INEEd 2014.

Note: The data refer to 2012, except for Uruguay (2013). Panel a includes full-time workers from ages 25–64 (40 hours per week or more). Panel b's data refer to the current salary in the National Administration of Public Education (Administración Nacional de Educación Pública; ANEP) for full-time teachers (in the case of primary schools) and for instructors with 30 hours of teaching per week (for basic and upper secondary education). AUS = Australia; AUT = Austria; CHL = Chile; CZE = Czech Republic; DEU = Germany; ESP = Spain; EST = Estonia; FIN = Finland; FRA = France; HUN = Hungary; IRL = Ireland; ISR = Israel; ITA = Italy; KOR = Korea, Rep.; NLD = Netherlands; NOR = Norway; NZL = New Zealand; OECD = Organisation for Economic Co-operation and Development average; POL = Poland; PRT = Portugal; SVK = Slovak Republic; SVN = Slovenia; URY = Uruguay; USA = United States.

and the Republic of Korea standing out as exceptions where the teaching profession is better paid than an average of other professions. In any case, Uruguay is one of the countries with the largest difference in salaries, which means that it could improve teacher salaries to make them more competitive, increasing the profession's attractiveness to create an appropriately sized teaching body.

When we compare teacher salaries with GDP per capita, Uruguay falls near the international average. In turn, when we compare between levels of education, while Uruguayan full-time primary school teachers receive a salary above per capita GDP, secondary school instructors are paid 93 percent to 94 percent of GDP per capita. Moreover, to obtain data comparable with that from the OECD, the figure represents staff with higher workloads. This means that the comparison would be less favorable considering primary school teachers who do not work full-time or those in secondary schools working less than 30 hours a week, which is common in public education in Uruguay, with 57 percent of primary school teachers and 50 percent of secondary school teachers, respectively, with workweeks of less than 30 hours, according to data from the Continuous Household Survey performed by the National Institute of Statistics (Instituto Nacional de Estadística [INE]) in 2013.

Finally, comparison of class time (figure 6.14) highlights that in the international context Uruguay is behind, although considerable disparity exists in instruction times that OECD countries dedicate to basic education. The largest gap is seen at upper secondary, where teaching time per year is 37 percent

Figure 6.14 Teaching Time in Uruguay and OECD Countries

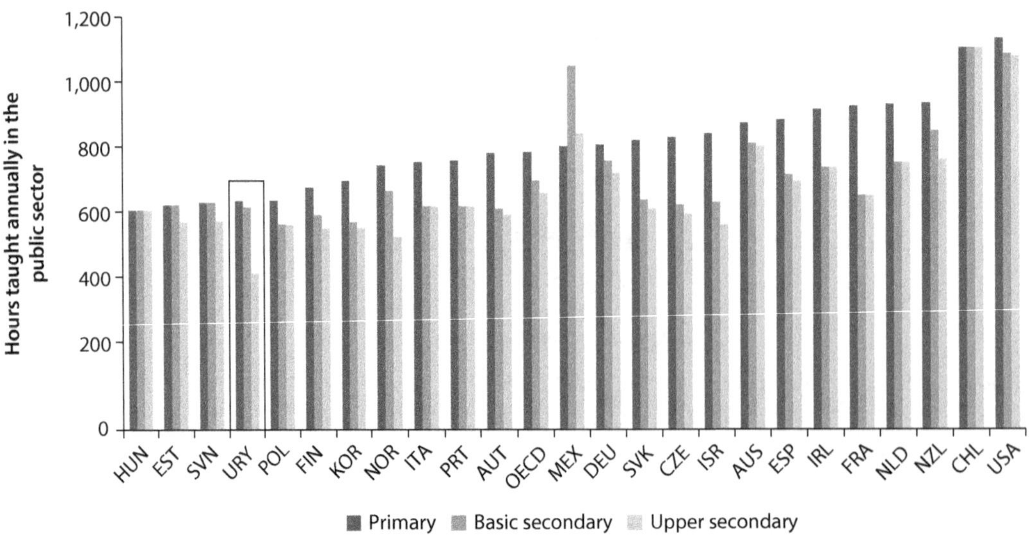

Sources: OECD 2014 and INEEd 2014.
Note: The data refer to 2012, except for Uruguay (2010). AUS = Australia; AUT = Austria; CHL = Chile; CZE = Czech Republic; DEU = Germany; ESP = Spain; EST = Estonia; FIN = Finland; FRA = France; HUN = Hungary; IRL = Ireland; ISR = Israel; ITA = Italy; KOR = Korea, Rep.; MEX = Mexico; NLD = Netherlands; NOR = Norway; NZL = New Zealand; OECD = Organisation for Economic Co-operation and Development average; POL = Poland; PRT = Portugal; SVK = Slovak Republic; SVN = Slovenia; URY = Uruguay; USA = United States.

below the OECD average. In primary and basic secondary education, annual teaching times are 19 percent and 12 percent, respectively, below that.

In summary, basic per-student spending indicators show that Uruguay is still behind the international norm. Per-student spending relative to GDP per capita is little more than half that of the OECD average. Uruguay is also behind in instruction time and moderately behind on teacher salaries. Both of these characteristics are partially linked since part of the difference in relative teacher salaries results from the difference in the hours of instruction between various countries. However, the number of hours that teachers are employed in more developed countries do not entirely correspond with greater instruction time, but reflect full-time workdays in an educational institution, with teaching hours and other time dedicated to teaching-related tasks (coordination, working on institutional projects, pedagogical leadership, and work with families, among others). This is notably different from Uruguay, where remuneration is almost entirely linked to classroom hours, often in more than one educational institution, particularly at secondary schools (INEEd 2014).

In conclusion, part of the relative gap in per-student spending for Uruguay is explained by less teaching time, less than full-time schedules for teachers (which means they work as teachers and have other jobs), and a moderate gap in teacher salaries compared with other countries.

Spending Breakdown

Although educational spending as a percentage of GDP constitutes an important indicator for understanding the amount of effort an economy allocates to funding education, it is important to incorporate other considerations, such as spending relative to the number of students in the system, its coverage level, and the age structure of the population. In this section, we explore these points by breaking down education spending in a number of exercises using the methodology devised by Marchionni and Alejo (2014).

To break down education spending as a proportion of GDP during year t, we use the following arithmetic identity:

$$\frac{B_t}{Y_t} = \frac{B_t/E_t}{Y_t/P_{15-64,t}} x \frac{E_t}{P_{e,t}} x \frac{P_{e,t}}{P_{15-64,t}} \tag{6.1}$$

where spending on basic education (B_t) as a proportion of GDP (Y_t) is the product of three factors: per-student spending (B_t/E_t) as a proportion of GDP per potentially economically active individual ($Y_t/P_{15-64,t}$); the gross enrollment ratio (GER) in the education system $\left(\frac{E_t}{P_{e,t}}\right)$ and the school-age dependency ratio (SDR) $\left(\frac{P_{e,t}}{P_{15-64,t}}\right)$, which reflects the size of the school-age population (that is, potential beneficiaries of education spending) relative to the population in the economically active age range (the potential funders of education spending). These three components enable us to identify the effects of demographic and economic factors that underlie per-student spending, for a given level of total spending, relative to GDP. In turn, this breakdown highlights some of the trade-offs that exist between the different objectives of education policy; for example, it is not possible to increase coverage $\left(\frac{E_t}{P_{e,t}}\right)$ without in some way reducing per-student benefits $\left(\frac{B_t/E_t}{Y_t/P_{15-64,t}}\right)$, for a given population age structure $\left(\frac{P_{e,t}}{P_{15-64,t}}\right)$ and aggregate spending level on education $\left(\frac{B_t}{Y_t}\right)$.

Table 6.2 shows the results of the breakdown of education spending for the different levels of basic education in Uruguay. At first glance, one feature the data show is that spending allocated per student grows throughout a student's education cycle, with per-student spending in secondary education (8.9 percent and 10.4 percent of GDP per potential worker at the basic and upper secondary levels, respectively) higher than for basic education (8.7 percent). In addition, as we saw in the previous section, it stands out that in early childhood education, and particularly in upper secondary, considerable room exists to improve coverage. Therefore, it would be advisable to increase aggregate spending on education (as a percentage of GDP) so that per-student spending does not suffer. Nonetheless, population forecasts show a persistent downward trend in the SDR for each of the age groups in basic education, indicating that it is possible to expand coverage without sacrificing spending per student.

Table 6.2 Breakdown of Public Spending on Basic Education by Education Level, with the Gross Enrollment Rate, 2013

Level	*(1) Education spending (% of GDP)*	*(2) Spending per student (% of GDP/worker)*	*(3) Gross enrollment ratio*	*(4) School-age dependency ratio*
Early childhood	0.4	7.2	88.1	6.7
Primary	1.2	8.5	105.6	13.7
Basic secondary	0.7	8.9	118.7	7.0
Upper secondary	0.6	10.4	78.6	7.2
Total	**3.0**	**8.7**	**99.3**	**34.6**

Sources: (1) and (2) General Accounting Office of the Nation (CGN) and Central Bank of Uruguay; (3) and (4) Education Observatory at the National Administration of Public Education (Administración Nacional de Educación Pública, ANEP; http://www3.anep.edu.uy/observatorio), CGN, and population forecasts from chapter 2.

Note: In order to break down total spending from the Early Childhood and Primary Education Council (Consejo de Educación Inicial y Primaria, CEIP) into the early childhood and primary education components, we took the proportion of the level in question of total CEIP enrollment. This entails assuming that per-student spending is the same in early childhood and primary education. In turn, early childhood education spending also includes INAU (Instituto del Niño y Adolescente del Uruguay–Institute of Children and Youth of Uruguay) spending in this category. The same criteria were used to break down spending by the Secondary Education Council (Consejo de Educación Secundaria, CES) and the Technical Professional Education Council (Consejo de Educación Técnica Profesional, CETP) on basic and upper secondary education. In order to calculate spending for the ANEP on the levels under consideration, each level was assigned the corresponding portion of spending on central services (CODICEN) that arose from that level's proportion of total ANEP spending. Spending on central services by the Ministry of Education and Culture was also distributed among these levels based on their proportion of the education system's total spending. The calculations for primary education do not include enrollment in special primary education, while the calculations for upper secondary education include the CES and the Technological Secondary Education component of the CETP.

In the cases of primary and basic secondary education, where the GERs exceed 100 percent, the potential improvements in per-student spending (because of the fall in school-age dependency and/or an eventual political effort aimed explicitly at increasing funding per student) could translate into improvements in the quality of services provided.

On the other hand, table 6.3 breaks down education spending by Latin American countries and the OECD average. As was previously outlined, spending on basic education as a percentage of GDP in Uruguay is lower than the regional level, although the situation improves slightly for per-student spending data. This contrast comes about because Uruguay has one of the lowest SDRs in the region (is exceeded only by Chile and is 9 percentage points below the regional average), despite high enrollment rates relative to the regional average, which would put pressure on the low per-student spending at any given level of education spending. Therefore, Uruguay's demographic transition has enabled it to allocate per-student funding equal to the average for Latin America on spending that takes a relatively lower percentage of GDP (below the regional average).

However, even when the demographic panorama is favorable for the per-student spending and GER objectives, comparison with the experience of OECD countries shows that it will not be sufficient to simply let the demographic transition run its course. Forecasts for Uruguay place the SDR at a minimum of 27.2 percent by the mid-2060s. Given this demographic structure, allocating 3 percent of GDP to basic education, and at current GERs, Uruguay will reach

Table 6.3 Breakdown of Public Spending on Basic Education in Latin America and the OECD

	(1) Education spending (% of GDP)	*(2) Spending per student (% of GDP/worker)*	*(3) Gross enrollment ratio (%)*	*(4) School-age dependency ratio*
Argentina	5.0	13.5	98.5	38.0
Bolivia	4.8	10.9	80.9	54.4
Chile	3.6	12.2	97.4	29.9
Colombia	3.4	9.7	88.3	39.4
Ecuador	3.1	7.3	104.5	40.2
Guatemala	2.4	4.4	88.2	60.9
Mexico	4.0	9.7	94.9	43.1
Nicaragua	2.6	5.8	86.3	51.8
Panama	1.7	5.0	89.0	38.4
Paraguay	3.2	8.3	72.6	52.9
Peru	2.3	5.7	91.2	43.3
Uruguay	**3.0**	**8.7**	**99.5**	**34.6**
Latin America	3.2	8.4	90.9	43.9
OECD	4.2	15.7	101.6	25.9

Sources: (1) and (3) UNESCO Institute of Statistics (http://data.uis.unesco.org/), General Accounting Office of the Nation (CGN), and the Central Bank of Uruguay (BCU); (2) UNESCO Institute of Statistics, CGN, BCU, and population forecasts from chapter 2; (4) is computed residually as a function of equation 6.1.

Note: Public spending on early childhood, primary, and secondary education is included. The data refer to the most recent year available: 2012 for Chile, Colombia, Ecuador, and Peru; 2013 for Uruguay; and 2011 for the remaining countries.
OECD = Organisation for Economic Co-operation and Development.

per-student spending per potential worker of 11.6 percent of GDP in the mid-2060s, much less than the current OECD average. With the present demographic structure, an SDR of 34.6 percent, and current GER, Uruguay would have to increase public spending on basic education to 5.4 percent of GDP (that is, increase public spending by 2.4 points of GDP) to reach per-student spending of 15.7 percent of GDP per potential worker, the present OECD average.

In conclusion, to reach per-student spending comparable to the OECD average, Uruguay must make substantially greater effort than these countries (1.2 points of GDP more in basic education spending) because its demographic structure is fundamentally different (the average SDR in the OECD is almost 9 percentage points lower than in Uruguay). In other words, if Uruguay were to spend the same on basic education relative to GDP as the OECD average (4.2 percent), per-student spending relative to GDP per potential worker would be 12.1 percent, or 3.6 percentage points lower than in these countries, and that would be due principally to the difference in the SDRs.

Additionally, a high GER, although indicative of good coverage, may also hide the reality of over-age enrollment, to the extent that a high proportion of enrollment for a given level could be made up in large part by individuals older than the age group for that level. This would result in increased investment becoming necessary for delayed students to complete their grades. In order to incorporate these considerations, a second alternative for breaking down education spending is presented as:

$$\frac{B_t}{Y_t} = \frac{B_t/E_t}{Y_t/P_{15-64,t}} x \frac{E_{e,t}}{P_{e,t}} x \frac{E_t}{E_{e,t}} x \frac{P_{e,t}}{P_{15-64,t}} \quad (6.2)$$

where $\left(\frac{E_{e,t}}{P_{e,t}}\right)$ represents the proportion of school-age youth in a given education level (which therefore represents the NER), and $\left(\frac{E_t}{E_{e,t}}\right)$ is the ratio between the level's total enrollment and enrollment corresponding to the theoretical age group (the over-age enrollment ratio). Thus, this equation differs from the first in that it breaks down GER into two subcomponents: the NER and the over-age enrollment ratio. This breakdown enables us to identify and distinguish between issues linked to coverage (via the NER) and efficiency (through the over-age enrollment ratio).

This type of analysis enables us to propose goals associated with both dimensions, as well as understand how education policies aimed at coverage and efficiency affect the per-student benefit at any amount of aggregate spending. This is the case insofar as improvement in the NER (for a given population age structure) increases enrollment and, therefore, results in a decline in the per-student benefit. In contrast, improvements in efficiency through reductions in the over-age enrollment ratio would improve the per-student benefit, all else remaining constant.

As table 6.4 shows, the breakdown of the GER (columns 3 and 4) in Uruguay reflects a situation with significant incidence of over-age enrollment at the secondary level. Significant room exists at that level to make simultaneous

Table 6.4 Breakdown of Public Spending on Basic Education by Education Level, with Net Enrollment Ratio and Over-Age Enrollment Ratio, 2013

Level	*(1) Education spending (% of GDP)*	*(2) Spending per student (% of GDP/worker)*	*(3) Net enrollment ratio (%)*	*(4) Over-age enrollment ratio*	*(5) School-age dependency ratio*
Early childhood	0.4	7.2	85.2	1.03	6.7
Primary	1.2	8.5	97.2	1.09	13.7
Basic secondary	0.7	8.9	80.3	1.48	7.0
Upper secondary	0.6	10.4	49.4	1.59	7.2
Total	**3.0**	**8.7**	**80.9**	**1.23**	**34.6**

Sources: (1) and (2) General Accounting Office of the Nation (CGN) and Central Bank of Uruguay (BCU); (3), (4), and (5) Education Observatory at the National Administration of Public Education (ANEP; http://www3.anep.edu.uy/observatorio) and the population forecasts from chapter 2.
Note: In order to break down total spending from the Early Childhood and Primary Education Council (CEIP) into the early childhood and primary education components, we took the proportion of the level in question of total CEIP enrollment. This entails assuming that per-student spending is the same in early childhood and primary education. In turn, early childhood education spending also includes Institute of Children and Youth of Uruguay (INAU) spending in this category. The same criteria were used to break down spending by the Secondary Education Council (CES) and the Technical Professional Education Council (CETP) on basic and upper secondary education. In order to calculate spending for the ANEP on the levels under consideration, each level was assigned the corresponding portion of spending on central services (CODICEN) that arose from that level's proportion of total ANEP spending. Spending on central services by the Ministry of Education and Culture (MEC) was also distributed among these levels based on their proportion of the education system's total spending. The calculations for primary education do not include enrollment in special primary education, while the calculations for upper secondary education include the CES and the Technological Secondary Education component of the CETP. Given that the age of the students that attend the different levels is unknown, we calculate based on data from the ECH (Encuesta Continua de Hogares; Continuous Household Survey). Based on the net enrollment ratio (NER), we take data from the gross enrollment ratio presented in table 6.2 to calculate the over-age enrollment ratio. Insofar as the NERs reported here refer to the total for the country, they do not necessarily coincide with the NERs reported in figure 6.2 (just urban areas) and, therefore, with the over-age enrollment ratios presented in figure 6.5.

progress in two objectives: increasing coverage (from just 80 percent and 49 percent of the population in the theoretical age groups that attend basic and upper secondary education, respectively) and reducing over-age enrollment (32 percent of those who attend basic education and 37 percent of those in upper secondary are in grades behind in their age group). Both goals must be targeted at the same time as striving to achieve universal completion at each level of education. In this framework, there is a unique, dual objective: ensure that young people attend secondary education and at the same time that they complete the different grades that make up each level. In early childhood and primary education, over-age enrollment is not a significant problem, so the conclusions about coverage extracted for both levels from the first breakdown remain valid; that is, a coverage challenge in early childhood education, while primary education had achieved universality and faced a slight challenge in reducing over-age enrollment.

The Uruguayan Demographic Transition: Implications for Education Policy

The following section analyzes the process of demographic transition described in chapter 2, with emphasis on the implications that changes in population age structure may have on achieving some education goals (such as increasing coverage and per-student benefits, and reducing over-age enrollment) and the funding needs associated with those goals.

Figure 6.15 presents two dependency indicators that can be deduced from the age structure of the population, providing the context of the demographic situation in this analysis. The indicators are the total dependency ratio (TDR), which is the ratio between the dependent population (younger than age 15 and older

Figure 6.15 Total and School-Age Dependency Ratios, Forecasted 2010–2100

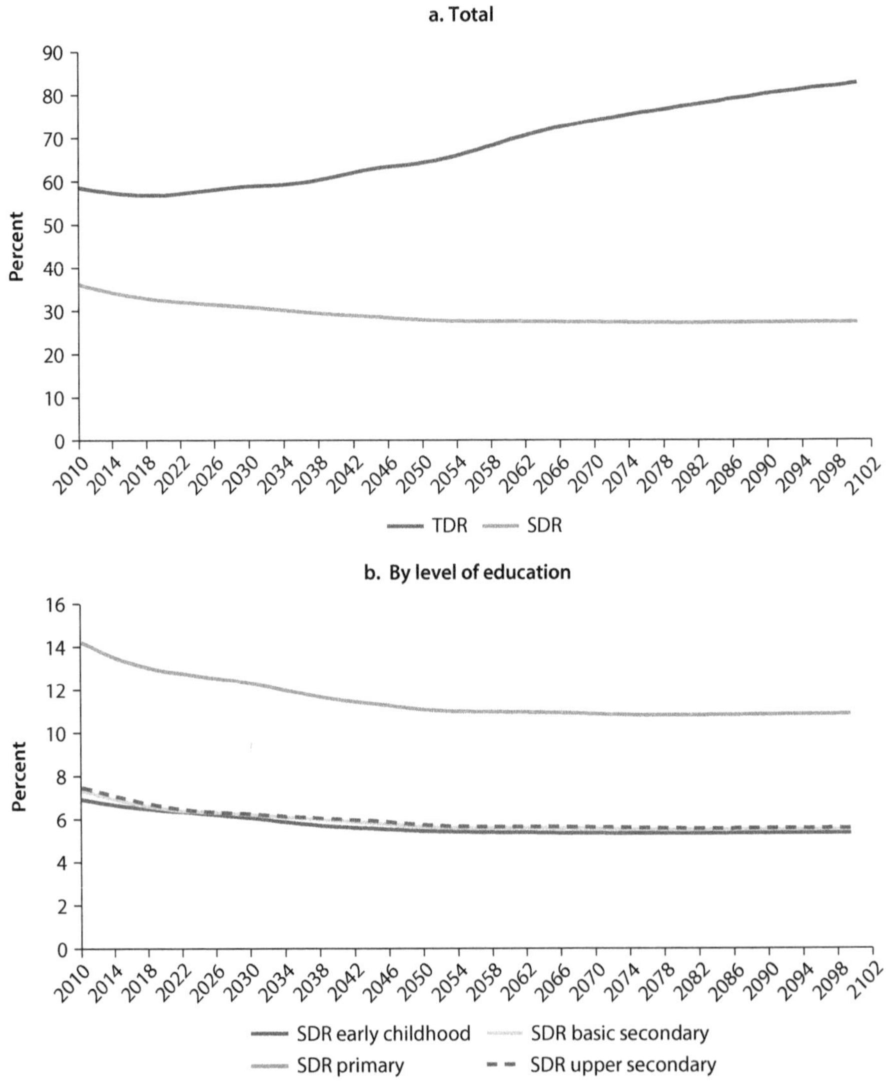

Source: Elaboration based on the forecasts from chapter 2.

Note: The total dependency ratio (TDR) is calculated as the ratio between the population younger than age 15 or older than 64 years old and the population from 15 to 64 years old. The school-age dependency ratios (SDRs) have the same denominator as the TDR, while the numerator is: the population from 3 to 17 years old for the total TDR, from 3 to 5 years old for the early childhood level, from 6 to 11 years old for primary, from 12 to 14 years old for basic secondary, and from 15 to 17 years old for upper secondary education.

than age 64) and the population in the economically active age range (ages 15–64), and the SDR, the ratio between the school-age population (ages 3–17) and the population in the economically active age range. In both cases, the ratio reflects the size of the population that requires public services, relative to the size of the population that could potentially fund provision of these services, primarily through their labor income.

In this regard, the population forecasts show a persistent rise in the TDR. In particular, growth of the population over age 64 will increase the dependent population (even as the population younger than age 15 is falling) and will be accompanied by a fall in the population of economically active age. Both trends lead to a greater dependency ratio, which will increase from 58 percent in the 2013 status quo to 83 percent by 2100. The phase of the demographic transition marked by lower levels of dependency, the demographic dividend, constitutes a window of opportunity for economic growth and funding state spending. If we use a reference value for the TDR of less than 60 percent (6 dependent individuals for every 10 potential workers), then the period of demographic dividend in Uruguay will extend until 2035.

In terms of education policy, a high SDR gives rise to a large school-age population and a relatively scarce group of workers to fund spending associated with this demand. In the Uruguayan case, demographic transition will result in a decline in the SDR, due principally to a persistent drop in the school-age population. In the status quo, with a total SDR of 35 percent, there are 3.5 school-age youth for every 10 people in the economically active age range, while by the end of the demographic dividend (2035) the SDR will be 30 percent. This fall will enable Uruguay to save around 13 percent of public spending on education (all else remaining constant).

Within this framework, the demographic dividend and the expected fall in school-age dependency create an opportunity to achieve educational goals with less funding. The SDR analysis by education level offers similar conclusions: in 2013 the SDR was 14 percent in primary education and 7 percent for each other level. The expected fall in the SDR at each level will result in a potential savings of 13–15 percent for each, which can be reinvested to meet the coverage, efficiency, and per-student benefit goals mentioned earlier in this chapter. It is worth clarifying that the demographic forecasts indicate the SDR will continue to fall even after 2035, and will reach a low of 27.6 percent around the mid-2060s.

Spending on Basic Education, per-Student Resources, and Demographic Prospects: Simulation Exercises

This section analyzes to what extent the opportunity offered by the demographic dividend enables Uruguay to generate resources to achieve some coverage and efficiency goals in basic education. To do this, we begin with the current situation (2013) in Uruguay and simulate spending trajectories relative to GDP as well as per-student spending relative to GDP per potential worker, based on various scenarios that are presented in sequential steps.

So far, we have analyzed public spending on education using Uruguay's budget data (as with countries in the international comparison), which include current and investment spending. The analysis in this section considers only the (current) consumption spending that was presented in chapter 3, in line with all other chapters. In any case, consumption expenditure represents 90 percent of spending on basic education.[15] Total spending on basic education relative to GDP was around 3 percent in 2013; while including just current expenses produces a figure around 2.7 percent of GDP.

The scenarios simulated for basic education are described in the following paragraphs.

First, we define a "base case" that forecasts per-student expenditure relative to GDP considering just projected demographic changes, and leaving per-student spending relative to potential GDP as fixed. This scenario serves to quantify the "savings" that the demographic transition will produce all else remaining equal. Second, we specify goals for coverage and reducing over-age enrollment, leaving the per-student spending relative to GDP per potential worker as fixed. The first scenario (Scenario 1) just sets coverage goals, leaving the over-age enrollment ratio constant at current levels. Scenario 2 sets coverage and over-age enrollment reduction goals simultaneously, setting the goal for the latter at near the average for OECD countries. In both scenarios, we alternately set the per-student spending level while leaving the aggregate fiscal spending level endogenous (public spending on education relative to GDP), or setting total spending, while per-student spending is determined endogenously.

Scenario 1 provides information about what spending level would be necessary to achieve universality of coverage for basic education without sacrificing per-student spending; or, alternatively, what sacrifice in terms of per-student spending would be necessary to reach universal coverage without increasing aggregate spending.

Scenario 2 tells us how much should be spent on education relative to GDP so as to achieve universal coverage while also reducing over-age enrollment, with the current per-student spending levels. Or, alternatively, once the investment per student is chosen, the scenario informs us if universal coverage will be achieved and if over-age enrollment will be reduced to levels near the OECD average, leaving the overall spending level constant.

The design of Scenario 2 requires further explanation. Clearly, reducing over-age enrollment must have some associated cost, unless it is achieved in a purely administrative manner by, for example, abolishing grade repetition without any compensating measures. However, since grade repetition is a strategy utilized to deal with students' poor performance, reducing repetition will entail substituting this strategy with alternative measures to improve student performance, which will probably require additional investment (for example, hiring more learning support staff, increasing instruction time, or improving teacher quality). Assuming a drastic reduction in over-age enrollment while per-student spending remains constant does not appear to be realistic given these considerations.

However, the design of Scenario 2 fulfills a function, which is to provide information about the cost of over-age enrollment (or, alternatively, the potential "savings" that would result from reducing inefficiencies in educational trajectories), which emerges from comparing Scenario 2 with Scenario 1. It cannot be inferred that such "savings" will constitute resources truly freed up for other uses. Part (or all) of these savings should be redirected to strategies that are distinct from mere grade repetition, to enable the system to reduce repetition by improving student performance.

Nonetheless, it is not clear how much money will need to be invested per student to improve learning, and thereby educational trajectories throughout the basic education system. Although various strategies have been tried in other countries, information is still limited regarding the cost and impact of each one. Uruguay has employed strategies that have involved the use of teaching support staff to provide extra assistance to students experiencing difficulties, in addition to other strategies such as extending the school day, especially in primary education.[16] However, estimates of impacts and costs are not available for each, except in the case of full-time schools (Cerdan Infantes and Vermeesch 2007; Llambí 2014).

As a result, in these simulation exercises we chose not to assign any additional cost to the reduction of over-age enrollment, and instead analyze how much money could be freed up if over-age enrollment were reduced to near the OECD average. These newly freed resources should be understood as money that would be available to be reinvested in policies to improve learning and reduce over-age enrollment.

Here we should point out why we focus on reducing grade repetition and over-age enrollment. One could take the view that repetition is a valid way of dealing with poor student performance, and a necessary cost to help students to actually achieve the standards required by the system. However, empirical evidence tends to show that repetition is a costly and ineffective way to improve student performance, since it achieves minimal and short-term academic benefits. Grade repetition entails not just allocating more direct resources to provide an additional year of education, but an opportunity cost is associated with the delay in entering the labor market. Additionally, repetition increases students' likelihood of disconnecting from the education system and affects significantly more students from more unfavorable socioeconomic backgrounds, which increases the performance gap (Manacorda 2012; OECD 2011, 2013).

In addition to the scenarios describing increases in coverage and reductions of over-age enrollment, we simulated a third scenario (Scenario 3) that considers Uruguay's deficit relative to the average for developed countries in investment in education per student, relative to GDP per potential worker. Thus, Scenario 3 simulates the trajectory of funding relative to GDP, simultaneously considering changes in coverage rates, the reduction of over-age enrollment, and increases in per-student benefit relative to the potential GDP currently observed for the average of OECD countries. Table 6.5 presents the description of the scenarios simulated for pretertiary education.

Table 6.5 Description of Scenarios Simulated for Basic Education

	Status quo Uruguay 2013	*Scenario 1*	*Scenario 2*	*Scenario 3*
Public spending on basic education/GDP	2.7%	Endogenous/constant	Endogenous/constant	Endogenous
Per-student spending/GDP per potential worker				
Early childhood	6.4%	Constant/endogenous	Constant/endogenous	11.8%
Primary	7.9%	Constant/endogenous	Constant/endogenous	13.7%
Basic secondary	8.0%	Constant/endogenous	Constant/endogenous	14.9%
Upper secondary	9.4%	Constant/endogenous	Constant/endogenous	15.0%
School-age dependency ratio	34.6%	Forecast	Forecast	Forecast
Net enrollment ratio				
Early childhood	85%	100%	100%	100%
Primary	97%	100%	100%	100%
Basic secondary	80%	100%	100%	100%
Upper secondary	49%	100%	100%	100%
Over-age enrollment ratio				
Early childhood	1.05	Constant	Constant	Constant
Primary	1.09	Constant	1.06	1.06
Basic secondary	1.48	Constant	1.12	1.12
Upper secondary	1.59	Constant	1.12	1.12
Period for completion				
Early childhood	n.a.	2025	2025	2025
Primary	n.a.	2025	2025	2025
Basic secondary	n.a.	2025	2025	2025
Upper secondary	n.a.	Endogenous	Endogenous	Endogenous

Sources: Elaboration based on data from the ANEP Education Observatory (http://www3.anep.edu.uy/observatorio), population forecasts from chapter 2, and consumption estimates from chapter 3.
Note: n.a. = not applicable.

Scenario 1 lays out just goals associated with coverage expansion (NER), without changing the over-age enrollment ratio and assuming that the current spending per student is maintained across all levels. For early childhood, primary, and basic secondary education, we propose an NER goal of 100 percent, with a completion deadline of 2025.[17] Once universal coverage is achieved, we forecasted enrollment until 2100 using the school-age population multiplied by the over-age enrollment ratio. For the three levels we assumed convergence on a uniform rate toward the goal.[18]

In the case of upper secondary education, we forecasted the NER by assuming that it would, after a delay of three years, mimic the growth in coverage for basic secondary education. Once universal coverage in basic secondary has been achieved, we assume growth at an equal rate in the NER at upper secondary until every young person of the correct age to attend this level is covered. In this way, we forecast reaching 100 percent coverage in upper secondary (compulsory level), but the time necessary to reach the goal is determined endogenously, based on the assumptions made. Once universal coverage is reached at the upper secondary level (NER = 100 percent), we obtain enrollment projected to 2100 as the population at the age to attend multiplied by the current over-age enrollment ratio.

Scenario 2 adds goals associated with over-age enrollment to the coverage goals expressed in Scenario 1. In the case of early childhood education, we do not set over-age enrollment goals, leaving the current ratio constant (5 percent).[19] At this level, the forecasts are identical to those that emerged from Scenario 1. For primary and basic secondary education, we set a goal for over-age enrollment equivalent to the OECD average. The procedure is similar to that used in Scenario 1: we assume uniform convergence until meeting the goal in 2025, although in this scenario the situation converges simultaneously toward the goals of reducing over-age enrollment and increasing the NER.

For upper secondary education, we also assume an over-age enrollment goal based on the average value among OECD countries, but we set a completion deadline equivalent to the date that was obtained endogenously for meeting the coverage goal in Scenario 1. After 2017, enrollment grows as the NER for basic secondary education grew three years earlier, while we project that over-age enrollment will drop starting in 2017. At all levels, once the over-age enrollment and coverage goals are reached, enrollment through 2100 is obtained by multiplying the population at the correct age to attend by the over-age enrollment ratio goal.

Scenario 3 addresses the coverage and efficiency objectives proposed in the previous scenarios and introduces a factor related to education quality, by proposing goals for increasing per-student spending as a percentage of GDP per potential worker. Although the empirical evidence is ambiguous regarding the relationship between funding and results (see Glewwe et al. 2011; Hanushek 2002), some indications show that below a certain development threshold an increase in resources is positively correlated with an improvement of educational results (OECD 2013). Additionally, research based on experimental data, or that also analyzes some aspect of the quality of resources, has generally provided evidence of a positive relationship between funding and results (Card and Krueger 1996; Card and Payne 2000).

The per-student spending goals were defined using as a reference value the current values observed for the OECD average at each education level.[20] In this context, the levels for which we forecast greater proportional growth in per-student spending relative to the status quo are for early childhood and basic secondary education, in both of which an increase around 85 percent is proposed. As has been pointed out, the student-teacher ratio in early childhood education falls significantly below other countries, meaning that part of the increase in spending could be utilized to reduce class sizes. In turn, at the secondary level we found a lot of room for improvement in classroom hours and teacher salaries and working conditions. Moreover, an improvement in per-student benefits at this level could help achieve the goals related to reducing over-age enrollment that were set out in Scenario 2. We also identified deficits in classroom hours and teacher salaries at the primary level, meaning that the increase in spending proposed for this level (in the order of 75 percent) could also lead to improvement in the salary expense component per student.

The deficits shown in instruction time, teacher hours, and teacher salaries are indicative of the possible ways any increase in per-student resources in Uruguay could be executed. Allocating resources between various components may vary the effectiveness of the results, although addressing these options is outside the objectives of this study.

Scenario 3 does not make any enrollment forecasts, insofar as enrollment in this scenario coincides with enrollment from Scenario 2 during the entire period. It does change aggregate spending on education as a percentage of GDP with respect to the earlier scenarios, which is used to forecast the aggregate funding needed to take per-student spending to the reference levels, reach the 2025 efficiency and coverage goals set out in Scenario 2, and maintain these achievements until 2100.

The following figures show the enrollment forecasts for each level of pre-tertiary education, under the base case and the first two scenarios.

For the early childhood level, we only simulate Scenario 1 (in addition to the base case), because this level has no over-age enrollment reduction goals. Achieving universal coverage at this level, given the predicted demographic changes, will entail reaching peak enrollment at around 150,000 students in 2025 (the year the goal is reached). However, subsequently a systematic reduction will occur that at the beginning of the 2040s will return early childhood enrollment to its current level; subsequently, it will continue to fall (figure 6.16).

In primary school, simulated trajectories for the various scenarios are very similar (figure 6.17), given that net enrollment at this level is nearly 100 percent.

Figure 6.16 Enrollment in Early Childhood Education (Ages 3–5) by Scenario, 2010–2100

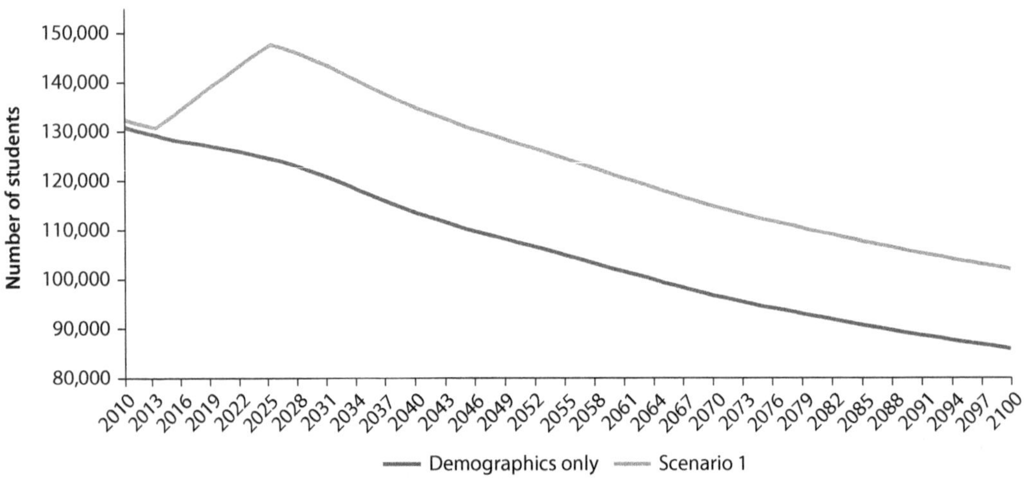

Source: Elaboration based on the forecasts from chapter 2 and the assumptions specified in table 6.5.

Figure 6.17 Enrollment in Primary Education by Scenario, 2010–2100

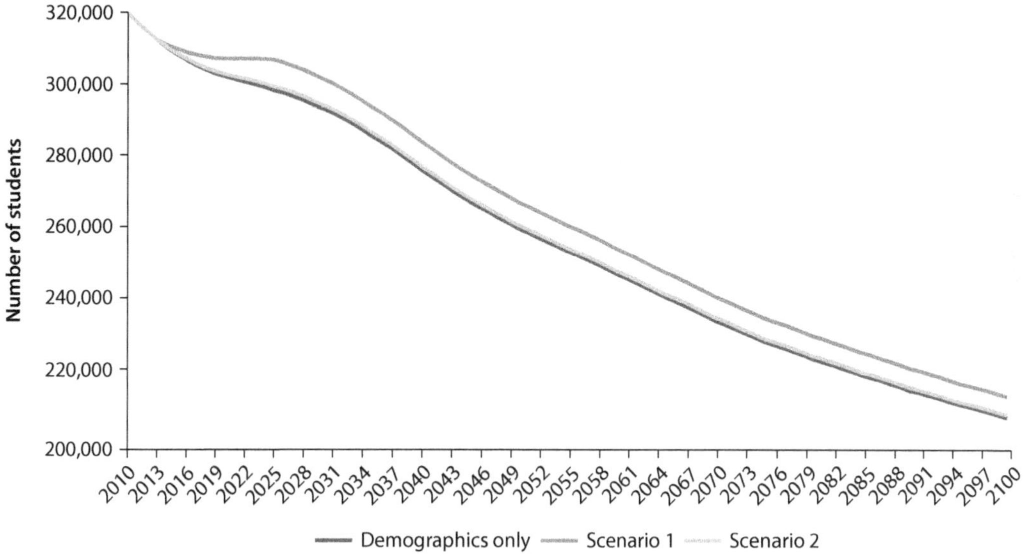

Source: Elaboration based on the forecasts from chapter 2 and the assumptions specified in table 6.5.

When the over-age reduction goal is added, the evolution of enrollment is very similar to that seen when we only consider demographic changes. Accordingly, at the primary level a systematic reduction in enrollment can be expected throughout the period, which would free considerable resources to increase per-student spending across all levels.

In basic secondary education, under Scenario 1, peak enrollment will reach 212,000 students the year the coverage goal is achieved; by around 2050 demographic changes will again place students at the current number, which will subsequently continue falling (figure 6.18). However, if over-age enrollment in basic secondary is reduced, total enrollment will grow below that indicated by demographic forecasts. In other words, reducing over-age enrollment to levels similar to those in OECD countries will more than offset the increase in enrollment caused by including young people who currently do not attend basic secondary; which also means that the coverage deficit could be filled through the current public supply.

Some trade-offs arise from this outcome. Uruguay must consider them in defining concrete policies to achieve universal coverage in basic secondary education. For example, the present supply of infrastructure is clearly insufficient if the country would like to include all the young people outside the secondary education system (Filardo and Mancebo 2012). However, a policy to increase educational trajectory efficiency could free up resources in such a way that the need for additional infrastructure would be significantly reduced (at the limit including reducing them to zero, in the current conditions of students per classroom), in addition to reducing recurrent spending.

Figure 6.18 Enrollment in Basic Secondary Education by Scenario, 2010–2100

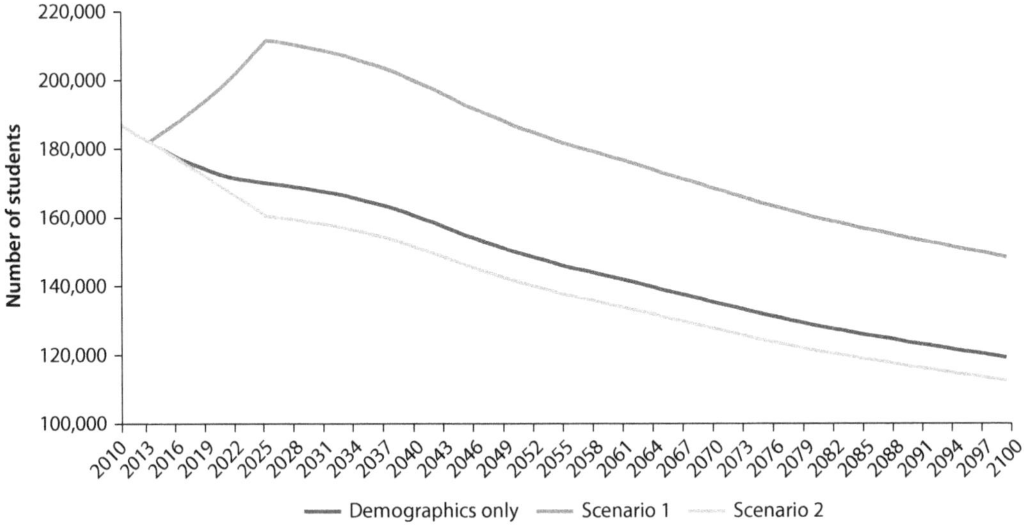

Source: Elaboration based on the forecasts from chapter 2 and the assumptions specified in table 6.5.

Figure 6.19 Enrollment in Upper Secondary Education by Scenario, 2010–2100

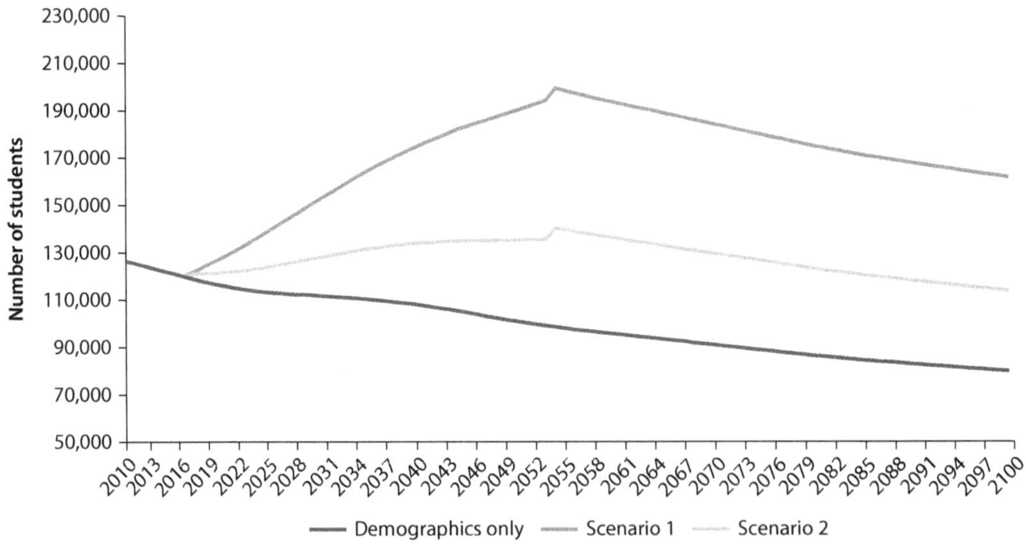

Source: Elaboration based on the forecasts from chapter 2 and the assumptions specified in table 6.5.

The situation in upper secondary education is different from basic secondary because the coverage gap is considerably higher. Even reducing over-age enrollment drastically, the enrollment forecast to achieve universal coverage at this level indicates that enrollment will increase steadily until around 2050, under the assumptions used (figure 6.19). Based on the demographic changes predicted, peak enrollment in 2054 (the year that the attendance rate reaches 100 percent) will reach some 140,000 students. If policies are not implemented to improve educational trajectories (that is, if over-age enrollment remains at its current high rate), the enrollment peak will reach some 200,000 students.

At the aggregate level, and considering all of basic education, a universal coverage scenario with a drastic reduction in over-age enrollment will result in a decline in total enrollment in pretertiary education throughout the period under analysis, although this would happen at a slower rate than when we consider demographic projections alone. In other words, the demographic opportunity means that the "size" of the entire basic education system (in number of students) will not have to increase—and should even decrease consistently—if the country is able to reduce over-age enrollment to the OECD average, even as it also accommodates those who do not currently attend. If policies designed to reduce over-age enrollment are not defined and the ratio remains at current levels, then the total number of students in basic education will reach a peak of 800,000 students around 2030 (figure 6.20).

Figure 6.21 presents the simulated trajectory of per-student spending under the assumption that fiscal funding for basic education remains constant at the current level. In the base case, where only the demographic structure changes, maintaining that spending relative to GDP fuels a considerable increase in per-student spending relative to potential GDP, reaching 10 percent by the end of the period.

Figure 6.20 Total Enrollment in Basic Education by Scenario, 2010–2100

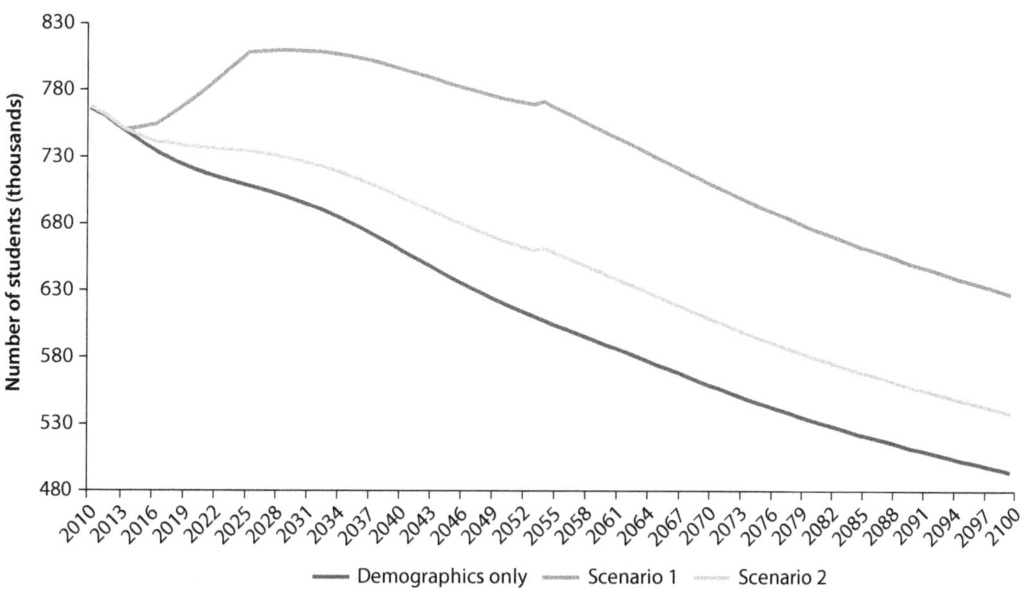

Source: Elaboration based on the forecasts from chapter 2 and the assumptions specified in table 6.5.

Figure 6.21 Per-Student Spending Relative to GDP per Potential Worker Assuming Constant Funding by Scenario, Total for Basic Education, 2010–2100

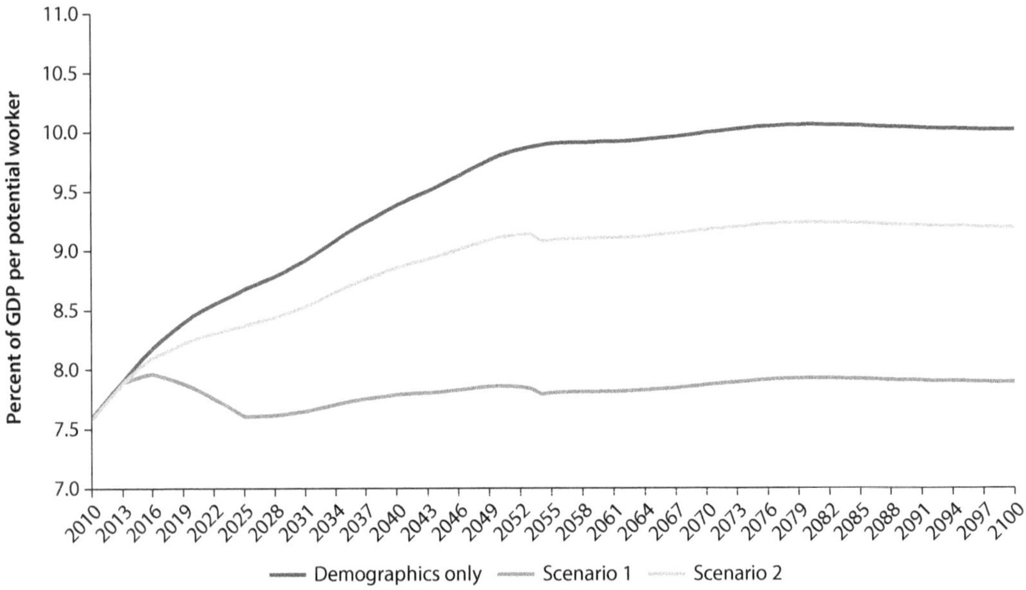

Source: Elaboration based on the forecasts from chapter 2 and the assumptions specified in table 6.5.

The situation changes when the coverage expansion and over-age enrollment reduction goals are considered. In Scenario 1, where universal coverage is reached at all levels while the current over-age enrollment ratio is maintained, keeping funding at the same level relative to GDP would result in a slight reduction of resources per student relative to potential GDP, during the coverage expansion years and also beyond. In conclusion, expanding the number of students under a scenario where funding remained constant would have a short-term cost equivalent to as much as 0.3 percentage points of the GDP per potential worker with respect to the starting point (per-student spending would fall from 7.9 percent to 7.6 percent of GDP per potential worker between 2013 and 2025 and following years, when universal coverage in basic secondary education was established). However, in the long term the fall in SDR would free up sufficient resources to achieve universal coverage at all education levels while per-student spending remained the same, without any need for additional funding. Essentially, under universal coverage and current internal efficiency conditions, per-student spending in all of basic education would be at the same starting level (7.9 percent of GDP per potential worker) if the current level of funding was maintained. However, this scenario would require reallocating resources from primary to secondary education to keep per-student spending constant for each level.

In Scenario 2, where universal coverage is achieved for all education levels while over-age enrollment is also reduced to the OECD average, per-student spending could even be increased without changing aggregate funding (per-student spending relative to GDP per potential worker would increase from 7.9 percent to 9.2 percent by the end of the period). In other words, given the high over-age enrollment ratio in secondary education, just reducing over-age enrollment would be more than enough to "free up" resources to help the system achieve universal coverage and increase per-student spending, for a given aggregate funding. In particular, reducing over-age enrollment would enable Uruguay to increase per-student spending up to 1.3 points of the GDP per potential worker, at a constant level of fiscal funding (the difference between the forecasts for Scenarios 1 and 2). This increase should be interpreted as resources that will remain available for policies to improve learning and reduce over-age enrollment. However, it is not clear from this analysis if these resources will be sufficient to achieve this goal.

In fact, this level of spending per student is significantly below the average for more developed countries.

Figure 6.22 presents per-student spending forecasts relative to GDP per potential worker and disaggregated by education level for Scenario 2, the situation where coverage and efficiency objectives are reached throughout the education system and funding relative to GDP remains constant at the current amount. Under these assumptions, demographic changes and improvements in the

Figure 6.22 Per-Student Spending Relative to GDP per Potential Worker (Scenario 2), 2010–2100

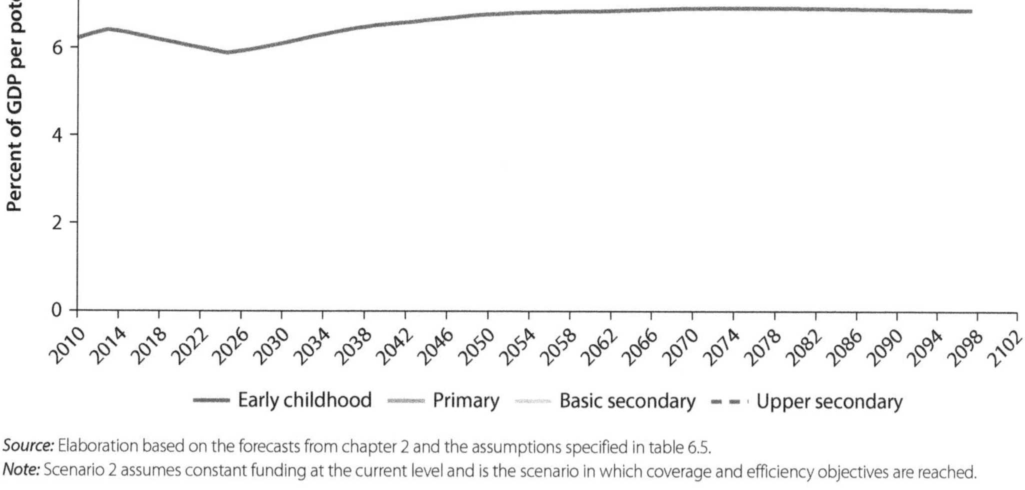

Source: Elaboration based on the forecasts from chapter 2 and the assumptions specified in table 6.5.
Note: Scenario 2 assumes constant funding at the current level and is the scenario in which coverage and efficiency objectives are reached.

efficiency of educational trajectories would enable the per-student benefit to increase for all but upper secondary education. Essentially, per-student spending in the medium term would reach 6.9 percent of GDP per potential worker for early childhood, 9.9 percent for primary, and 10.8 percent for basic secondary education. In contrast, for upper secondary, the substantial increase in coverage required would entail cutting per-student spending if aggregate funding remained the same, even allowing for the effects of the demographic dividend and a substantial improvement in efficiency. In this case, the estimated per-student spending relative to potential GDP would be around 8.5 percent, which is lower than the projection for primary education.

In all of the cases, per-student spending relative to GDP per potential worker would be very different from that in relatively more developed countries (see table 6.1). If we compare the long-term per-student spending that emerges from Scenario 2 with the current OECD average, the differences vary from 3.8 percentage points of GDP per worker (primary) to 6.5 percentage points of GDP per worker (upper secondary).

The following figures illustrate how much funding should rise relative to GDP to achieve per-student spending goals equal to the OECD average for each education level. We compare these numbers with those produced by incorporating the coverage and efficiency goals, while keeping per-student spending constant.

In the case of early childhood education, if the per-student benefit were to remain at the current level, the fall in the school-age dependency index would more than offset the increase in coverage, which would translate into a slight reduction in the required funding, from 0.4 percent of GDP to 0.36 percent of GDP in 2100 (figure 6.23). However, incorporating a goal of increasing per-student spending to the relative level of the OECD average would increase the required funding by approximately 0.3 percent of GDP (the difference between the blue line and the orange line). The financing needs would increase noticeably until the coverage goal was reached (in 2025 under the proposed scenario), and fall moderately later. The maximum funding in this scenario would be 0.77 percent of GDP in 2025.

In primary education, where coverage is already practically universal, the fall in the SDR while per-student spending remains constant would translate into a reduced need for financing from 1.2 percent to 0.9 percent of GDP by 2050, and remain stable thereafter. Incorporating the goal of reducing over-age enrollment produces practically the same conclusion. In a more ambitious goal of increasing per-student spending to the OECD average, 0.7 percent more of GDP would be needed to fund it. The increased funding requirements would present themselves in 2025, the year it is assumed that the efficiency and per-student spending objectives for primary education would be reached, and would grow to as much as 1.8 percent of GDP, falling to 1.6 percent of GDP in the long term (figure 6.24).

In the case of basic secondary education, if per-student spending were to remain constant, funding needs would remain practically the same under the universal coverage objective, or would fall by 0.2 percent of GDP under the

Figure 6.23 Current Spending on Early Childhood Education Relative to GDP, Assuming a Goal of Universal Coverage, Per-Student Spending, 2010–2100

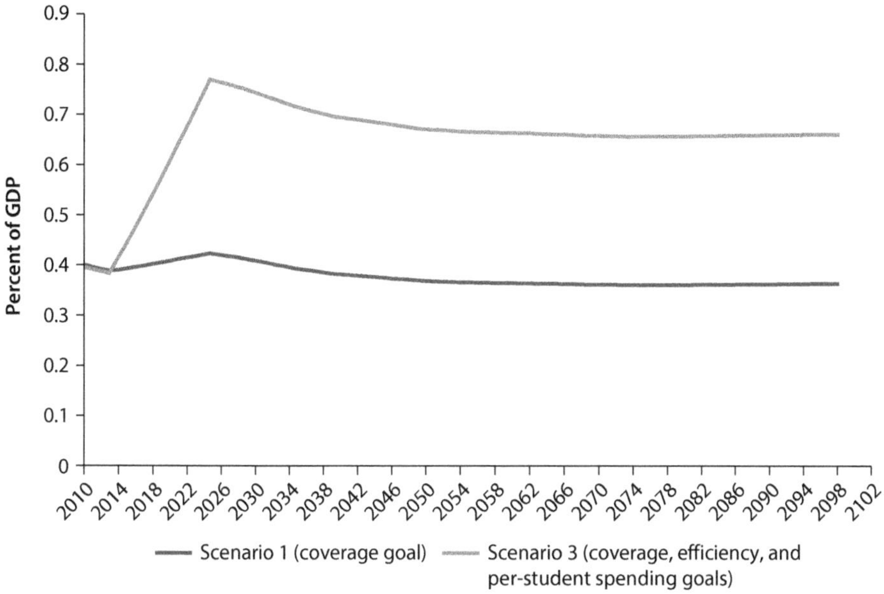

Source: Elaboration based on the forecasts from chapter 2 and the assumptions specified in table 6.5.
Note: Scenario 1 proposes increasing the net attendance rate to 100 percent, while Scenario 3 proposes both increasing the attendance rate as well as increasing per-student spending.

Figure 6.24 Current Spending on Primary Education Relative to GDP under Alternative Scenarios, 2010–2100

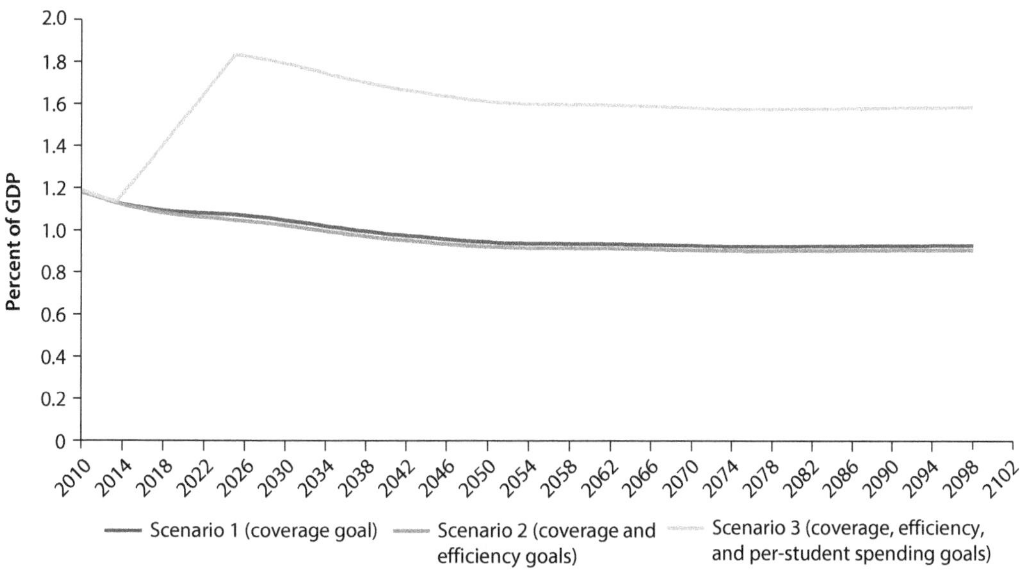

Source: Elaboration based on the forecasts from chapter 2 and the assumptions specified in table 6.5.
Note: Scenario 1 proposes increasing the net attendance rate to 100 percent, Scenario 2 proposes a net attendance rate of 100 percent and reducing over-age enrollment, and Scenario 3 proposes increasing the attendance rate as well as per-student spending and reducing over-age enrollment.

Figure 6.25 Current Spending on Basic Secondary Education Relative to GDP under Alternative Scenarios, 2010–2100

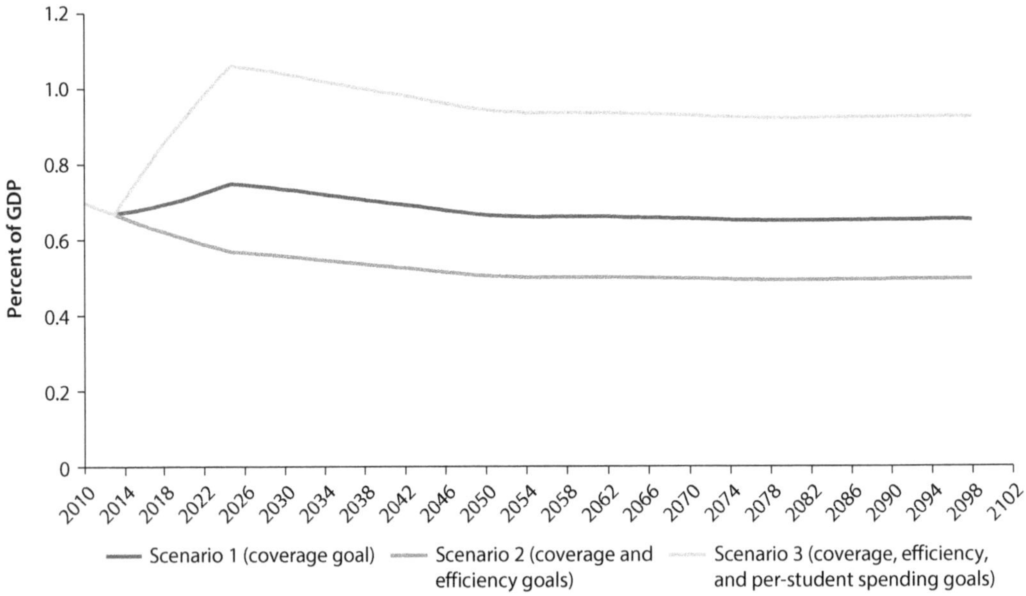

Source: Elaboration based on the forecasts from chapter 2 and the assumptions specified in table 6.5.
Note: Scenario 1 proposes increasing the net attendance rate to 100 percent, Scenario 2 proposes a net attendance rate of 100 percent and reducing over-age enrollment, and Scenario 3 proposes increasing the attendance rate as well as per-student spending and reducing over-age enrollment.

increased efficiency scenario (figure 6.25). However, the goal of increasing per-student spending would raise funding requirements by 0.2 percent of GDP in the long term, as long as it were to bring an increase in efficiency that would reduce over-age enrollment to a ratio similar to the average for more developed countries. In this case, the financing needs would be around 0.9 percent of GDP in the long term, after peaking at 1.1 percent in 2025, the year the proposed goals would be achieved.

Finally, given the high coverage deficit, resources freed up by demographic changes will not be sufficient to reach the universal coverage goal for upper secondary education, even assuming a drastic reduction in the over-age enrollment ratio. In an extreme scenario of universal coverage and a substantial improvement in efficiency, maintaining spending per student at the current level would increase funding needs slightly, from 0.53 percent to 0.58 percent of GDP in the long term (figure 6.26). The goal of increasing per-student spending would require more funding requirements, rising to 0.93 percent of GDP in the long term. Note that the scenario of universal coverage without changes in the over-age enrollment ratio would entail funding of 0.82 percent of GDP for the *current* per-student spending level. In other words, reducing the over-age enrollment ratio in upper secondary would enable the system to free up resources such that the goal of increasing per-student spending to the OECD average would be

Figure 6.26 Current Spending on Upper Secondary Education Relative to GDP under Alternative Efficiency and Per-Student Spending Scenarios, 2010–2100

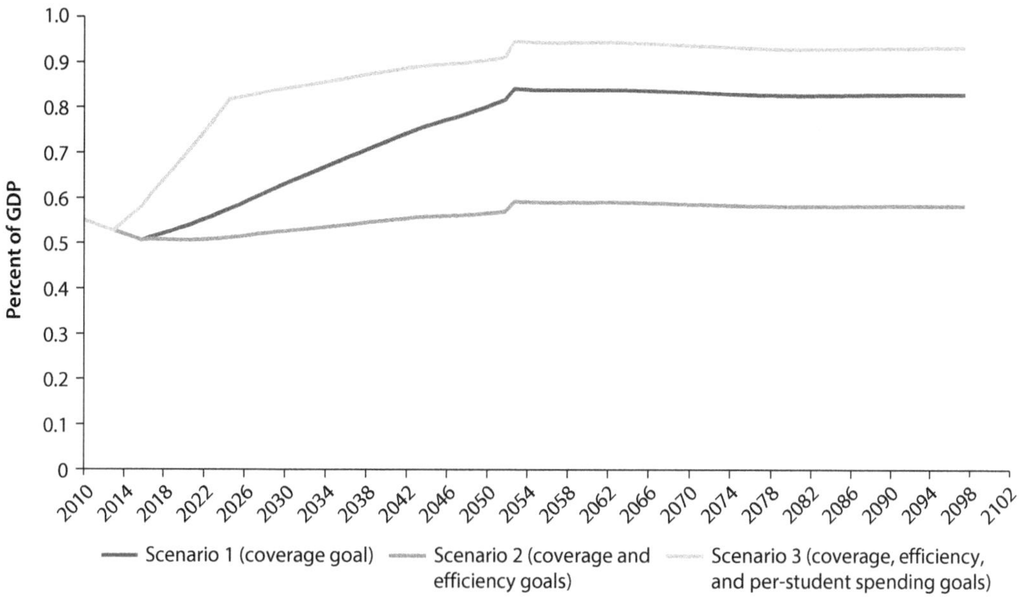

Source: Elaboration based on the forecasts from chapter 2 and the assumptions specified in table 6.5.
Note: Scenario 1 proposes increasing the net attendance rate to 100 percent, Scenario 2 proposes a net attendance rate of 100 percent and reducing over-age enrollment, and Scenario 3 proposes increasing the attendance rate as well as per-student spending and reducing over-age enrollment.

achieved by only adding 0.11 percent of GDP to the estimated resources needed to reach universal coverage.

Finally, as mentioned previously, if resources per student in the entire basic education system remained at the current level (7.9 percent of GDP per potential worker), in the long term demographic changes would lead to sufficient resources being freed up to achieve universal coverage at all education levels, with very little additional aggregate funding needed to maintain current per-student spending (see forecasts for Scenario 1 in figure 6.27). However, note that maintaining per-student spending during the coverage expansion phase would require a slight increase in funding, from 2.7 percent to 2.8 percent of GDP until the coverage goal was reached for basic secondary education. Moreover, this would require a transfer of resources from early childhood, primary, and basic secondary education to upper secondary education (at different times) to avoid cutting per-student spending where coverage deficits exist.

However, the effort to simultaneously fund the coverage and efficiency goals at the same time as increasing per-student spending for the entire pretertiary education system would require current spending equivalent to 4.5 percent of GDP at the highest point (2025), from 2.7 percent of GDP at present, which would subsequently fall to about 4 percent of GDP in the long term.

Figure 6.27 Current Spending on Pretertiary Education Relative to GDP under Alternative Efficiency and Per-Student Spending Scenarios, 2010–2100

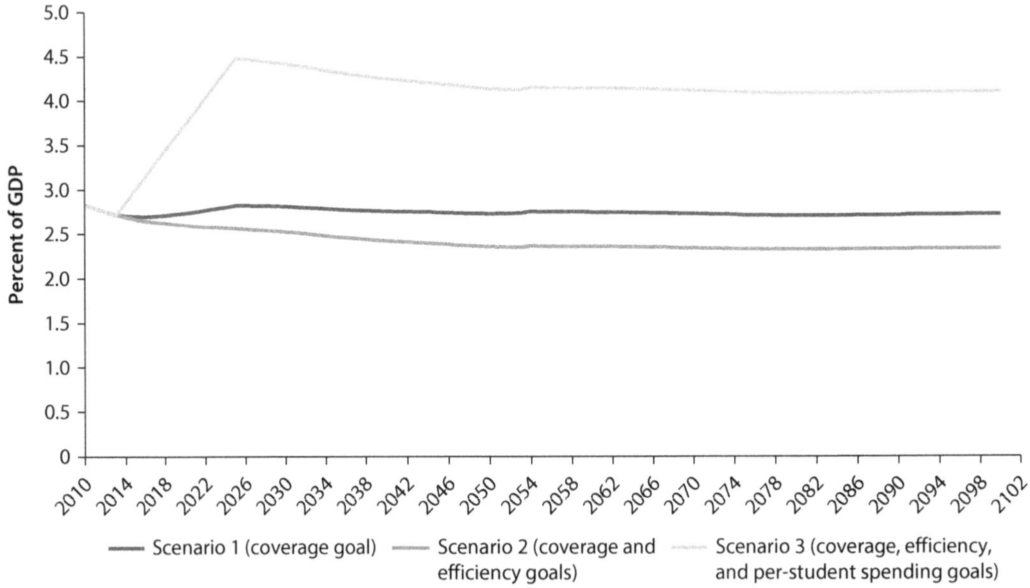

Source: Elaboration based on the forecasts from chapter 2 and the assumptions specified in table 6.7.
Note: Scenario 1 proposes increasing the net attendance rate to 100 percent, Scenario 2 proposes a net attendance rate of 100 percent and reducing over-age enrollment, and Scenario 3 proposes increasing the attendance rate as well as per-student spending and reducing over-age enrollment.

In conclusion, in order to reach relative per-student spending levels similar to the OECD average, the resources freed up as a result of the demographic dividend and eventual improvements in efficiency will not be sufficient. A goal of this type requires an increase in funding relative to GDP of 1.3 percentage points for pretertiary education in the long term.[21]

Spending on Tertiary Education

In the long term, as Uruguay moves toward achieving universal basic education, demand for tertiary education will increase. Coverage and completion rates at the tertiary level are well below regional and international peers, which creates the need to set out goals for improvement.

It is assumed that the reference population for calculating the school-age dependency ratio and enrollment rates comprises ages 18–23, although we recognized this is a tentative range due to heterogeneity in the duration of tertiary studies. Although in table 6.6 we present gross and net enrollment ratios, and the over-age enrollment ratio, these are just estimates and no simulations are carried out on the latter.

For tertiary education we first performed simulations for the entire enrolled population under various scenarios. Second, we performed specific scenarios for teacher training. Teacher training goals should contemplate the short-term additional requirements that the increase in coverage and quality of basic

Table 6.6 Gross and Net Enrollment Ratios and the Over-Age Enrollment Ratio for Tertiary Education, 2013

Level	*(1) Gross enrollment ratio (%)*	*(2) Net enrollment ratio (%)*	*(3) Over-age enrollment ratio*
Other tertiary	34.0	20.2	1.7
Teacher training	7.7	2.3	3.3
Total tertiary	41.7	22.5	1.9

Sources: Elaboration based on data from the 2013 Continuous Household Survey and the 2013 *Statistical Yearbook for Education* from the Ministry of Education and Culture (http://educacion.mec.gub.uy/innovaportal/v/11078/5/mecweb/publicaciones?3colid=927&breadid=1794).
Note: The school-age population used here is from 18 to 23 years old.

Table 6.7 Description of Scenarios Simulated in Tertiary Education

	Status quo Uruguay 2013 (%)	*Scenario 1*	*Scenario 2*	*Scenario 3*
Public spending on tertiary education/GDP	0.7	Endogenous	Endogenous	Endogenous
Per-student spending/GDP per potential worker	12.1	Constant	Constant	20.9%
School-age dependency ratio	14.4	Forecast	Forecast	Forecast
Gross enrollment ratio	41.7	Endogenous	Endogenous	Endogenous
Graduation rate	5.3	Constant	15.0%	15.0%
Period for completion	n.a.	Endogenous	2100	2100

Sources: Elaboration based on the 2013 *Statistical Yearbook for Education* from the Ministry of Education and Culture (http://educacion.mec.gub.uy/innovaportal/v/11078/5/mecweb/publicaciones?3colid=927&breadid=1794), the population forecasts from chapter2, and the consumption estimates from chapter 3.
Note: The graduation rate is defined as the ratio of individuals that graduate to the total tertiary enrollment for the year in question. n.a. = not applicable.

education will demand, principally the challenge of increasing training capacity and, possibly, quality. Thus, simulations for funding teacher-training goals may be understood as part of the requirements for achieving goals related to basic education.

Table 6.7 shows the scenarios related to coverage in the tertiary education system. In addition to the base case, where enrollment projections are based on predicted demographic changes, Scenario 1 forecasts the estimated evolution of enrollment in tertiary studies, assuming that they will mimic the increase in upper secondary enrollment with a three-year delay. We assume that tertiary enrollment increases until reaching universal coverage in upper secondary, from which point on no additional "carryover" effect is seen. The reason for not establishing a concrete coverage goal for tertiary education is that just the effect of increasing secondary attendance, if accompanied by actual completion of the cycle and, subsequently, by increased demand for higher education, will lead to a gross enrollment rate of 80 percent in tertiary education by 2057 (3 years after upper secondary education achieves universal coverage). This rate is slightly higher than currently observed for OECD countries (76 percent in 2012, according to data from UNESCO), which would mean that just the "carryover" effect from secondary education would enable Uruguay to achieve the reasonable long-term goal of increasing tertiary education coverage. It should be noted that this figure refers to gross enrollment; that is, it includes students at ages above the reference range.

Second, we present Scenario 2 for the tertiary level, which incorporates efficiency targets. As for Scenario 1, we chose not to consider over-age enrollment, because it is difficult to establish a single theoretical age range for attendance. Therefore, in Scenario 2, in addition to the coverage improvement forecasted in Scenario 1, we create a goal for improving the graduation rate: to reach a graduation rate of 15 percent of total enrollment per year by 2100.[22] For the same increased coverage, the increased efficiency of completion of studies results in a fall in enrollment (and therefore in the gross enrollment rate) compared to Scenario 1.

Finally, following the same criteria as in basic education, Scenario 3 incorporates goals for improving per-student spending to reach the OECD average. In this scenario, the spending projections for tertiary education as a proportion of GDP assume the simultaneous achievement of the coverage and efficiency goals proposed in Scenario 2, along with an increase in per-student spending relative to GDP per potential worker on the order of 73 percent, to reach a per-student benefit of 21 percent of GDP per potential worker by 2100.

Figure 6.28 illustrates the evolution of tertiary education enrollment in the scenario that only considers demographic changes, and in the scenarios where only coverage varies (Scenario 1) and coverage and efficiency change simultaneously (Scenario 2). A scenario without changes in coverage would translate into a steady reduction of enrollment in tertiary education in the period under analysis. In contrast, if one assumes a delayed carryover effect from the increase in secondary education enrollment until universal coverage is reached, this would mean that the gross enrollment rate in tertiary education would reach 80.2 percent in 2057. Enrollment in tertiary education would rise considerably, peaking at a little more than 200,000 students around that year.

Finally, forecasts for Scenario 2 show enrollment slightly below enrollments in Scenario 1, although the trajectories are very similar. Thus, in Scenario 2, a continual increase in tertiary enrollment will occur as secondary education becomes universal, reaching a peak of 195,000 students (with a 78 percent GER) in 2057. After that, a more pronounced fall in enrollment than in Scenario 1 will be observed as improvement in graduation versus enrollment is consolidated. Under the assumptions adopted for improvements in efficiency and coverage, the GER would be around 73 percent in 2100.

Figure 6.29 illustrates the forecast of current spending relative to GDP for the different scenarios considered here. If changes in coverage do not take place, the demographic opportunity will translate into a reduction in funding

Figure 6.28 Tertiary Education Enrollment, by Scenario, 2010–2100

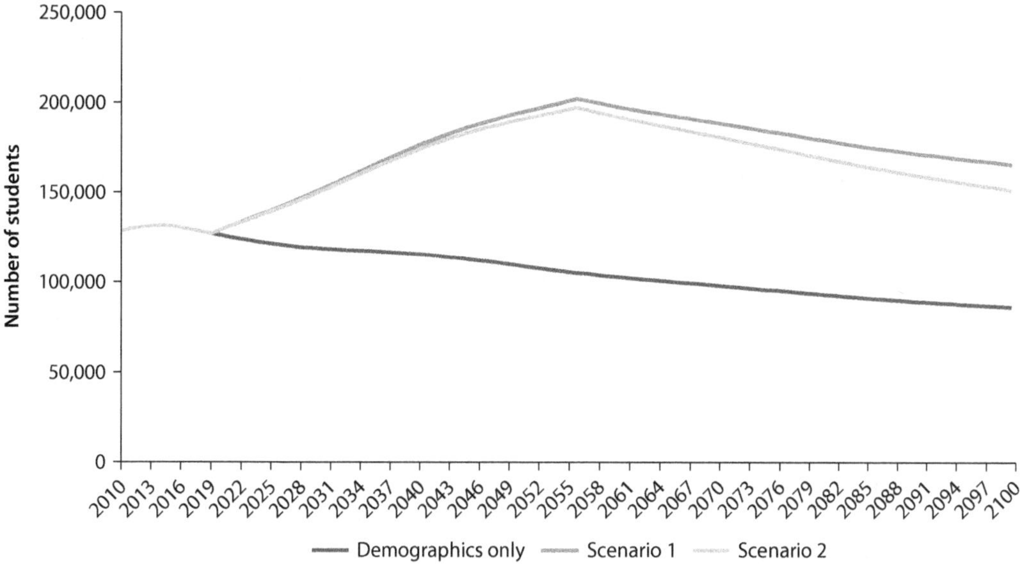

Sources: Elaboration based on the forecasts in chapter 2 and the assumptions specified in table 6.7.
Note: Scenario 1 proposes increasing the net attendance rate to 100 percent, while Scenario 2 proposes both a net attendance rate of 100 percent and an increase in the graduation rate.

Figure 6.29 Current Spending on Tertiary Education Relative to GDP, under Alternative Coverage, Efficiency, and Per-Student Spending Scenarios, 2010–2100

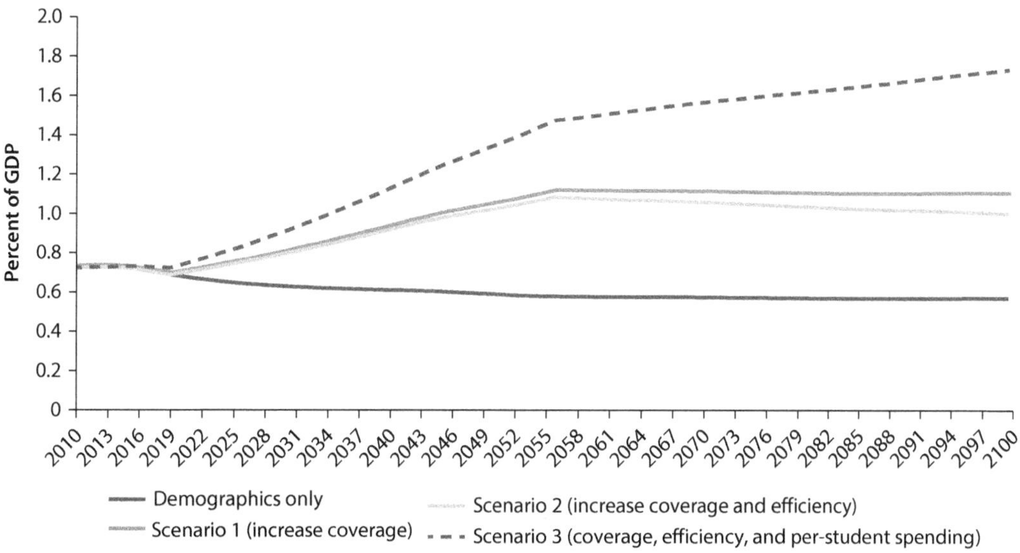

Sources: Elaboration based on the forecasts in chapter 2 and the assumptions specified in table 6.7.
Note: Scenario 1 proposes increasing the net attendance rate to 100 percent, Scenario 2 proposes both a net attendance rate of 100 percent and an increase in the graduation rate, while Scenario 3 proposes increasing the attendance rate, the graduation rate, and per-student spending.

relative to GDP of around 0.15 percent in the long term, without sacrificing per-student spending (the solid blue line). If demand for tertiary education grows, and coverage is expanded for secondary education (notwithstanding any assumed improvements to efficiency), the demographic dividend will be more than offset by the extra funding needed to maintain per-student spending due to increased enrollment. Under these assumptions, current spending per student directed to tertiary education would grow from 0.7 percent of GDP to 1.1 percent of GDP in Scenario 1 or 1 percent of GDP in Scenario 2 (the orange line and the green line, respectively, in figure 6.29). Finally, incorporating a per-student spending goal comparable to the current OECD average would require a substantial funding effort, even accounting for a substantial improvement in the efficiency of educational trajectories. Incorporation of this goal would put the tertiary education spending requirement relative to GDP at 1.7 percent at the end of the period.

Finally, we present the scenarios simulated for enrollment in teacher training. In this case, we do not propose specific goals, but rather we simulate enrollment consistent with the scenarios proposed for basic education, such that the current student-teacher ratio remains constant. This means that the scenarios for this level (see table 6.8) coincide with the enrollment scenarios for basic education. First, we obtain the number of teachers necessary to accompany the evolution of enrollment in primary and secondary education

Table 6.8 Description of the Scenarios Forecasted for Teacher Training

	Status quo Uruguay 2013 (%)	*Demographics only*	*Scenario 1*	*Scenario 2*
Teacher training				
Public spending on teacher training/GDP	0.1	Endogenous	Endogenous	Endogenous
Per-student spending/GDP per potential worker	12.6	Constant	Constant	Constant
School-age dependency ratio	14.4	Forecast	Forecast	Forecast
Gross enrollment ratio	7.7	Endogenous	Endogenous	Endogenous
Graduation rate	5.3	Constant	Constant	Constant
Primary education				
Net enrollment ratio	97.2	Constant	100%	100%
Over-age enrollment ratio	1.09	Constant	Constant	1.06
Student-teacher ratio	13.8	Constant	Constant	Constant
Secondary education (basic/upper)				
Net enrollment ratio	80.3/49.4	Constant	100%	100%
Over-age enrollment ratio	1.48/1.59	Constant	Constant	1.12
Student-teacher ratio	11.3	Constant	Constant	Constant

Sources: Elaboration based on the 2013 Continuous Household Survey, the 2013 *Statistical Yearbook for Education* from the Ministry of Education and Culture (http://educacion.mec.gub.uy/innovaportal/v/11078/5/mecweb/publicaciones?3colid=927&breadid=1794), the population forecasts from chapter 2, and the consumption estimates from chapter 3.
Note: The graduation rate is defined as the ratio of individuals that graduate to the total tertiary enrollment for the year in question.

for the scenario in which enrollment only follows demographic patterns, then repeat for Scenario 1, where a 100 percent attendance target is proposed, and for Scenario 2, in which the over-age enrollment reduction goal is added. To obtain the enrollment in teacher training needed to reach the projected requirement for teachers we make two assumptions: first, that the graduation rate remains constant at its current level (5.3 percent); and second, that 4.5 percent of teachers will leave the profession each year (through retirement, changing professions, and so on). Once these two assumptions have been made, it is possible to forecast enrollment and aggregate spending on teacher training needed to achieve the goals set out for basic education, without sacrificing the student-teacher ratio.

Figure 6.30 illustrates the evolution of enrollment in teacher training programs for the base case and the two proposed scenarios. If we only allow changes to basic education enrollment due to demographic changes, then the need for teacher training will decline in the medium and long term (blue line). However, in a scenario where coverage in basic education increases without changes in efficiency a considerable initial increase in enrollment (and graduation) in teacher training programs will be required, in the order of 27 percent more trainees at the highest point (2024, one year before reaching the goal for early childhood, primary, and basic secondary education) than are currently enrolled. Alternatively, improvement in the efficiency of educational trajectories in basic education (Scenario 1) could considerably reduce the number of teachers necessary to keep the student-teacher ratio unchanged, although at

Figure 6.30 Enrollment in Teacher Training under Simulated Scenarios, 2010–2100

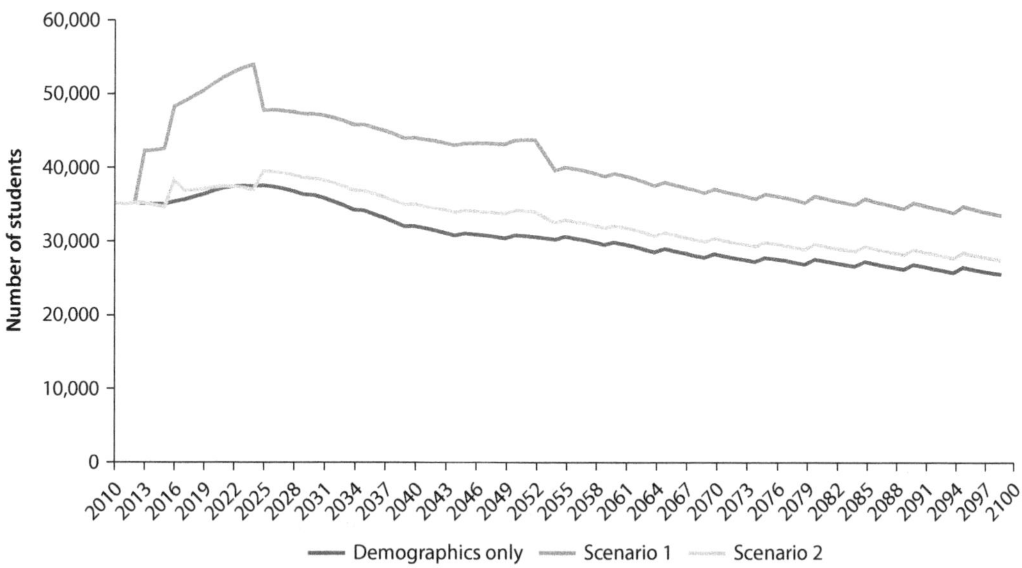

Source: Elaboration based on the forecasts in chapter 2 and the assumptions specified in table 6.8.

Figure 6.31 Current Spending on Teacher Training Relative to GDP under Alternative Coverage and Efficiency Scenarios in Basic Education, 2010–2100

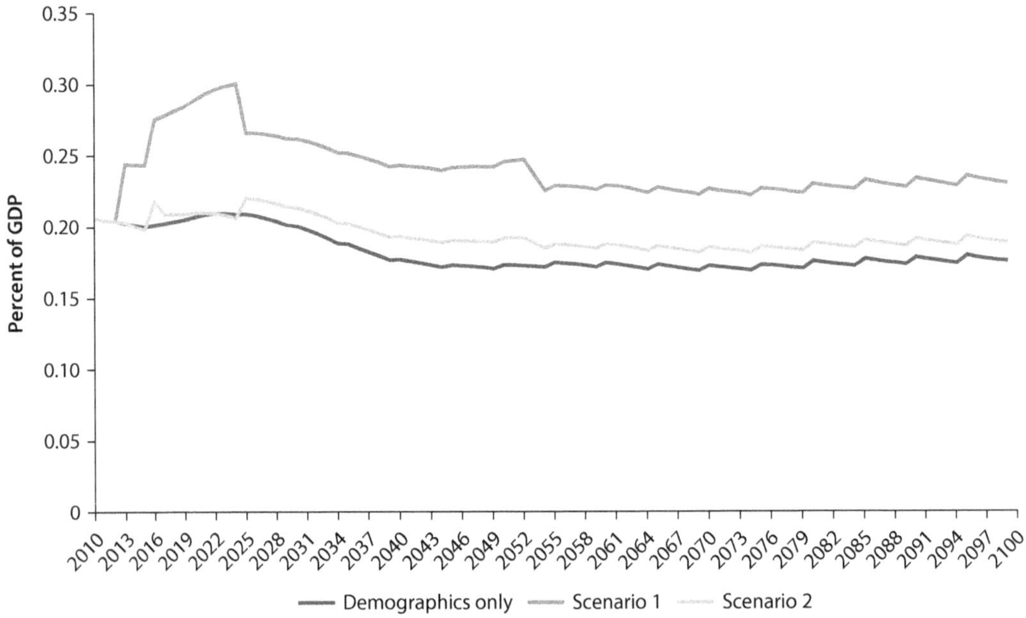

Source: Elaboration based on the forecasts in chapter 2 and the assumptions specified in table 6.8.

the beginning it would require enrollment in teacher training programs to be increased. Moreover, the improvement in educational efficiency could require that the student-teacher ratio be raised, which could increase the need for teacher training relative to the situation that arises from Scenario 2. In conclusion, the scenarios that propose universal coverage goals for basic education will require teacher training to be increased significantly at the beginning, even assuming that substantial improvements in efficiency of basic education will occur.[23]

Similar considerations are taken into account to analyze the current per-student spending for trainee teachers that emerges in the proposed scenarios (see figure 6.31). The coverage goals in basic education could increase the need for current spending on teacher training up to 0.3 percent of GDP at its highest point, starting from 0.21 percent now, if per-student spending in teacher training programs were to remain constant.

Finally, figure 6.32 illustrates the trajectory of current spending in basic and tertiary education relative to GDP, under the different scenarios. Note that simultaneously reaching the objectives proposed for basic education, the "carryover" simulated for tertiary education, and the goal of raising per-student spending at all levels to the OECD average, would entail an increase in financing needs of some 2.3 percentage points of GDP in the long term (the difference between the current level of 3.5 percent and 5.8 percent at the end of the period).

Figure 6.32 Current Spending on Education (Basic and Tertiary) Relative to GDP under Alternative Efficiency and Per-Student Spending Scenarios, 2010–2100

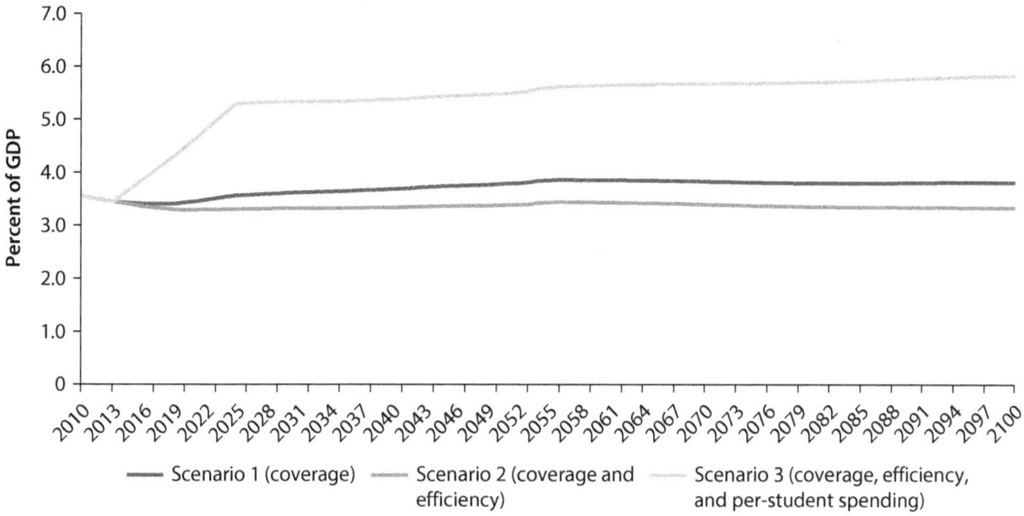

Source: Elaboration based on the forecasts from chapter 2 and the assumptions specified in tables 6.5 and 6.7.

Final Considerations

This chapter has quantified the impact of demographic changes on public expenditure required to finance basic and tertiary education. Simulation exercises incorporated predicted demographic changes as well as policy goals related to coverage, efficiency, and the per-student benefit.

The demographic opportunity foreseen for Uruguay allows for considerable freeing up of resources for education in the medium and long terms. If spending allocated to basic education is maintained at the current level relative to GDP, resources freed up due to the demographic opportunity would be sufficient to achieve universal coverage goals at all education levels almost without any reduction in per-student spending, as a result of the proposed sequence of achieving the goals.

For early childhood and basic secondary education, demographic changes would offset the greater coverage requirements in the medium and long terms. During the initial years after the goal was met it would be necessary to commit slightly more fiscal resources to avoid diminishing per-student spending. In upper secondary education, the bigger coverage deficit means that the demographic dividend would be insufficient to offset the cost of required expansion in enrollment.

All of the above translates into the following: at the level of the basic education system, reaching universal coverage under current funding relative to GDP would translate into a slight reduction in spending per student of approximately 0.3 percentage points of GDP per potential worker.

The conclusions change drastically when, in addition to universal coverage, the goal is to substantially improve the efficiency of educational trajectories. In these conditions, the universal coverage goal could be achieved across the entire basic education system while simultaneously increasing spending per student with no change in aggregate spending, although this would entail significantly redirecting resources to upper secondary education. Under this scenario, per-student spending relative to GDP per potential worker would increase from 7.9 percent in 2013 to 9.2 percent in 2100 on average by the end of the period.

Nonetheless, this increase in per-student expenditure would still place Uruguay well below the average OECD spending in GDP per potential worker. If a comparable per-student benefit is established as a goal (in relative economic capacity) to approximate levels allocated in more developed countries, Uruguay would have to increase its funding for basic education. According to the exercises shown in this chapter, current spending would have to reach 4.5 percent of GDP at the peak of coverage expansion and improvement of efficiency in educational trajectories, then subsequently would fall to 4 percent of GDP in the long term (1.3 percentage points of GDP more than the current situation). The expansion of basic education in turn would put pressure on teacher training, possibly requiring an increase of around 0.1 percent of GDP in the initial years, to at least maintain per-student spending in teacher training programs at the current level.

If we also consider a potential expansion of tertiary education as expansion and efficiency goals in secondary education are achieved, and we incorporate a per-student spending goal for secondary education that is comparable to the most developed countries, then the financing needs could increase by 1 percentage point of GDP in the long term, directed to tertiary education.

The importance of increasing the benefit per student at the same time as improving efficiency should be highlighted. Uruguay exhibits elevated rates of over-age enrollment in secondary education and low completion rates in the compulsory cycle, even in the regional comparison. These rates are not just associated with caring for the populations from unfavorable backgrounds, or with an allocation of resources per student that is lower than the average for countries in Latin America. They are indicative of problems with resource allocation and/or utilization that affect the quality of education and therefore the final educational outcomes. In this context, an increase in the per-student benefits should be directed to achieving the transformations in organization and curriculums necessary for effectively translating increased resources per student into improved performance and enhanced educational trajectories.

Finally, the proposed goals entail a substantial increase in the average education level of the economically active population, which will be addressed in chapter 7. If better education leads to the greater acquisition of abilities and knowledge, this will enable improved adaptation to the needs of the labor market and will allow workers to complete tasks more efficiently, in addition to contributing to the creation and uptake of new technologies (Barro 2001). According to growth theories, the improvement in worker formation would translate into increases in productivity and therefore contribute to higher economic growth.

In the framework of the prospects of long-term population aging, an increase in productivity is essential to ensuring economic sustainability, which means that the goals set for education in Uruguay are more than relevant. Nonetheless, the quantitative goals for coverage and completion of educational cycles should be accompanied by improvements in educational quality so that they actually translate into increased human capital and contribute to the necessary improvements in productivity.

Notes

1. Cecilia Llambí and Maren Vairo, CINVE—Center for Economic Research. Correspondence to cllambi@cinve.org.uy, mvairo@cinve.org.uy.
2. Early infancy, which comprises 0 to age 2, is excluded from the analysis because it is not a formal part of the education system (see the 2013 *Statistical Yearbook for Education* from the Ministry of Education and Culture, MEC).
3. These figures do not include enrollment in special primary education.
4. During this period, the population between ages 6–11, the typical age group that attends primary school, fell by 11 percent. Also during this period, repetition rates in public primary schools fell moderately, which also contributed to the reduction in total enrollment.
5. The NER is defined as the ratio between the total number of enrolled students for the theoretical age group for each level and the total population in the said age group.
6. In Uruguay, the minimum working age is 14.
7. Although upper secondary education is compulsory according to Law No. 18,437 of 2008, supervision is not yet regulated, which means the requirement does not constitute a real obligation (2013 *Statistical Yearbook for Education* from the MEC, http://educacion.mec.gub.uy/innovaportal/v/11078/5/mecweb/publicaciones?3colid=927&breadid=1794).
8. The differences according to socioeconomic level are mainly observed at age 3, and to a lesser extent among children of age 4.
9. Coverage among children of age 3 has been established as a priority in the education system and in the care system.
10. In 2012, these two institutions' proportion of total public education spending reached 85 percent (2012 *Statistical Yearbook for Education* from the MEC, http://educacion.mec.gub.uy/innovaportal/v/11078/5/mecweb/publicaciones?3colid=927&breadid=1794).
11. The UdelaR was the only public university institution until 2013. Beginning in 2014, with the opening of the Technological University, the public university system now has two institutions.
12. The figure refers to all public spending on education, including recurring expenses and investment. In addition to the spending by ANEP, UdelaR, and the MEC, it also includes funds executed by the "Plan Ceibal," spending related to education programs from the Ministry of Social Development, spending on military and police education, the student ticket subsidy, and other lesser expenses.
13. Spending on tertiary-level training provided by the ANEP via the Technical Professional Education Council (Consejo de Educación Técnica Profesional; CETP) is

not included because said component's share of the council's total spending is unknown.

14. In all cases, we consider public spending per student. In addition, public funding of education for the average OECD country is equivalent to 84 percent of total funding, which means that public spending per student is a good approximation of total spending per student in these countries.
15. During the last decade, education spending directed by the ANEP was allocated approximately 80 percent to salaries, 10 percent to other current spending, and 10 percent to investment expenses.
16. The strategies for providing additional support to students experiencing difficulties include, for example, the Community Teachers program at the primary level, Teacher + Teacher at the primary level, and Tutoring at the basic secondary level. The Community Teachers program consists of assigning additional teachers to primary schools classified in quintiles 1 and 2 according to the sociocultural situation index created by the ANEP's Directorate of Research and Statistics. These teachers work with children with low educational performance, attendance problems, grade repetition, and integration problems, in addition to working with families. The Teacher + Teacher program is directed at students in the first and second years of primary school who show low educational performance, via two modalities: in some schools the school day is extended and children work during their "nonschool hours" with a teacher who coordinates activities with their classroom teacher, while in other schools the program is organized such that two teachers work together with the same group of students simultaneously. The Tutoring program was set up in secondary schools that recorded the highest repetition rates and is organized based on tutoring to students with poor performance. Examples of extending the school day include full-time schools (seven-and-a-half-hour school days, with full-time teachers); extended schedule schools (seven-hour school days with expression workshops run by workshop professors).
17. We considered the statements of goals proposed in the platform of the incoming administration in Uruguay. Some goals refer to 2020, others to 2030, and others do not have a fixed timeline. We carried out this exercise, tentatively setting 2025 as the deadline to meet the goals for early childhood and basic secondary education.
18. In primary education, the NER is 97 percent, meaning that there were virtually no changes simulated at this level.
19. In early childhood education, repetition does not exist as a strategy, so the over-age enrollment ratio seen here may be due in part to the way it is calculated based on ECH (Encuesta Continua de Hogares) records. To reduce this problem, we calculated the NERs with data just from the first semester of the year, but a slight overestimation of over-age enrollment could have persisted at all levels.
20. To the extent that international data reports per-student spending (and not consumption) carried out in said countries, we impute growth of per-student consumption observed in 2013 equal to that which should be verified in per-student spending in order to reach the developed countries' spending levels.
21. Note that if the additional funding effort is assumed by the public sector, this would entail a relative fall in private sector participation, both in coverage of students and in the proportion of funding. Currently, private financing represents around 28 percent of total funding in pretertiary education. If all of the additional funding effort is assumed by the public sector (and the private sector follows the per-student spending

trend), the proportion of private financing would be around 20 percent. As a reference, private financing is around 16 percent for the average of OECD countries (see INEEd 2014).

22. If we consider that the average duration of university studies is currently 5 years, a reasonable goal with 100 percent total efficiency in completion of tertiary studies would entail reaching graduation rates of 20 percent.
23. An alternative to increased teacher training would be that the current teachers be willing to increase their work hours in order to deal with the additional enrollment. However, teachers' workday is not on average less than that for other occupations if one takes into account the number of hours worked at home. When this factor is considered, on average teachers work an amount similar to other professionals and specialists (see INEEd 2014). The fact that teachers dedicate part of their time working at home is related to current working conditions, in which time spent in the classroom is the predominant activity while at educational institutions.

References

Barro, R. 2001. "Human Capital and Growth." *American Economic Review* 91 (2): 12–17.

Card, D., and A. Krueger. 1996. "School Resources and Student Outcomes: An Overview of the Literature and New Evidence from North and South Carolina." NBER Working Paper 5708, National Bureau of Economic Research, Cambridge, MA.

Card, D., and A. Payne. 2000. "School Finance Reform, the Distribution of School Spending and the Distribution of Student Test Scores." *Journal of Public Economics* 83 (2002): 49–82.

Cerdan Infantes, P., and C. Vermeesch. 2007. "More Time Is Better: An Evaluation of the Full Time School Program in Uruguay." Policy Research Working Paper 4167, World Bank, Washington, DC.

Continuous Household Survey from the National Institute of Statistics (Encuesta Continua de Hogares del Instituto Nacional de Estadística [INE]). http://www.ine.gub.uy/microdatos/microdatosnew2008.asp#ech.

Education Observatory at the National Public Education Administration (Observatorio de la Educación de la Administración Nacional de Educación Pública [ANEP]). http://www3.anep.edu.uy/observatorio/.

Filardo, V., and M. E. Mancebo. 2012. "Universalizar la Educación Media en Uruguay: Ausencias, Tensiones y Desafíos." Edición Art. 2, Comisión Sectorial de Investigación Científica, Universidad de la República, Montevideo.

Glewwe, P., E. Hanushek, S. Humpage, and R. Ravina. 2011. "School Resources and Educational Outcomes in Developing Countries: A Review of the Literature from 1990 to 2010." NBER Working Paper 17554, National Bureau of Economic Research, Cambridge, MA. http://www.nber.org/papers/w17554.

Government of Uruguay. 2008. Law No. 18,437: General Law of Education. http://www.parlamento.gub.uy/leyes/ley18437.htm.

Hanushek, E. 2002. "The Failure of Input-Based Schooling Policies." NBER Working Paper 9040, National Bureau of Economic Research, Cambridge, MA. http://www.nber.org/papers/w9040.

INEEd (Instituto de Evaluación Educativa). 2014. *Informe Sobre el Estado de la Educación en Uruguay 2014*. INEEd, Montevideo.

Llambí, C. 2014. "La Política de Tiempo Completo y los Resultados Educativos en la Enseñanza Media." *Revista de Economía, Segunda Época* 21 (1): 101–52.

Manacorda, M. 2012. "The Cost of Grade Retention." *Review of Economics and Statistics* 94 (2): 596–606.

Marchionni, M., and J. Alejo. 2014. "El Financiamiento de la Educación Básica a lo largo de la Transición Demográfica en Argentina." In *Los Años No Vienen Solos: Oportunidades y Desafíos Económicos de la Transición Demográfica en Argentina*, edited by M. Gragnolati, R. Rofman, I. Apella, S. Troiano, 253–90. Buenos Aires: World Bank.

Ministry of Education and Culture. Various years. *Statistical Yearbook for Education*. http://www.mec.gub.uy/innovaportal/v/11078/5/mecweb/publicaciones_?3colid=927.

OECD (Organisation for Economic Co-operation and Development). 2011. *When Students Repeat Grades or Are Transferred Out of School: What Does It Mean for Education Systems?* PISA in Focus, 6. Paris: OECD Publishing.

———. 2013. *PISA 2012 Results: What Makes Schools Successful? Resources, Policies and Practices*. Vol. 6, PISA. Paris: OECD Publishing.

———. 2014. "Education at a Glance." OECD, Paris. http://stats.oecd.org/.

CHAPTER 7

Labor Market and Productivity

Verónica Amarante and Maira Colacce[1]

Introduction

The expected changes in demographic structure of the Uruguayan population in coming decades, analyzed in depth in chapter 2, will have significant repercussions on the labor market. Demographic transformations, particularly population aging, will determine the number of workers and the composition of the population by age and gender. We can also expect other factors to affect choices in the labor market. Some of these factors are linked to demographic features like the number of children and when parents have them, others to cultural factors that affect women's labor participation, and still more to the increase in the population's accumulation of education, which tends to delay labor market entry.

The changes in Uruguay are marked by the early start of the demographic transition. For example, its older population, compared with other countries in the region, creates an economic challenge for the active population to support the substantial inactive population. As chapter 2 discussed, the ratio of the potentially dependent population (younger than 15 and older than 65) to the potentially income-generating population (15–65), now equivalent to 57 percent, will grow significantly and quickly from 2025, driven by the increase in the number of the elderly. And forecasts signal that this figure will rise to 63 percent in 2050 and above 80 percent by 2100.

A similar view emerges when we analyze the ratio of the population growth rate to the population with surplus income, that is, individuals consuming less than their labor income. According to criteria discussed in chapter 3, in Uruguay the surplus population corresponds to those individuals ages 28–57. As figure 7.1 illustrates, the country's prospects are not very encouraging, because the growth rate of the population with surplus income is not just negative after 2033, but it is also lower than the growth rate for the entire population. This means that, if no other changes occur, the country's economic growth will tend to decrease simply as an effect of the demographic changes. However, this pessimistic perspective does not necessarily

Figure 7.1 Population Growth Rate Compared to Total Population and the Surplus-Generating Population, Five-Year Moving Averages, 1953–2098

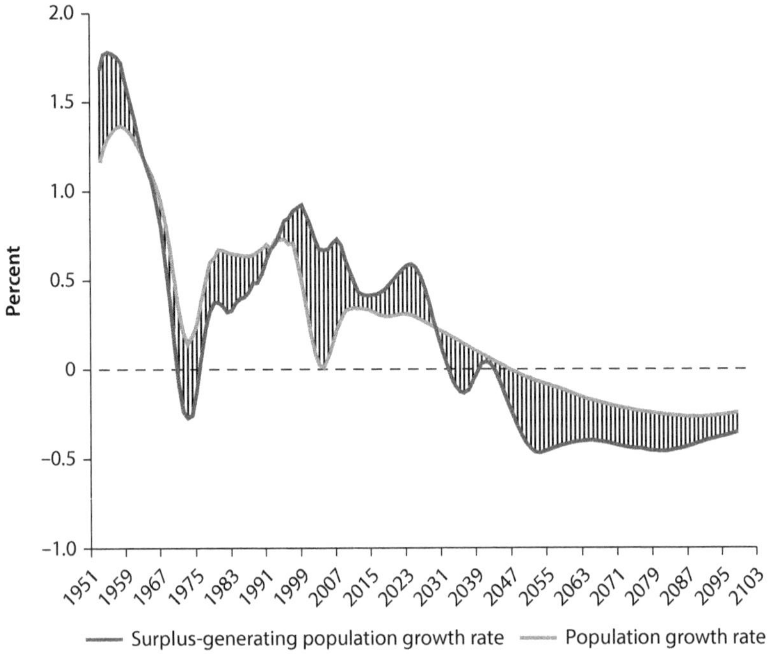

Source: United Nations 2014.

have to become a reality because, among other things, changes in the underlying parameters are probable—for example, in the ages at which individuals are considered surplus-generating or dependent. In addition, a window of opportunity exists until 2033 to generate the savings and investment to increase the productivity of the labor force and avoid the slowing or reduction of economic activity.

Even so, we must recognize that Uruguay's demographic and fiscal dividends are modest in the international context. And the country cannot expect to receive large economic and fiscal impacts from its demographic changes (González and Bucheli 2014).

Measuring how all these changes will affect the labor market long term is, without doubt, very ambitious. Without pretense of providing accurate predictions, however, it is possible to outline scenarios and analyze the potential long-term trajectories of the principal variables of the labor market.

That is this chapter's objective. The chapter analyzes the future evolution of two key variables: the economic activity rate and labor productivity. To do this, it first analyzes the recent evolution of both variables, disaggregating along three key dimensions: age, gender, and education level ("Labor Participation and Productivity: Recent Evolution" section).

Next, we design various scenarios that allow us to evaluate the impact that population aging will have on the levels of labor activity, productivity, and total and per capita product until the end of the century. On one hand, we do this purely considering the effect of this demographic process, and, on the other, considering the effect that it would have in combination with changes in women's participation and productivity as well as the population's education level ("What Can We Expect from the Evolution of Labor Force Participation?" section). To clearly identify the impact these changes could have, the analysis in this section is developed under the assumption that it will not produce any technological innovation, additional accumulation of capital, institutional changes, or other processes that could affect workers' productivity in a manner exogenous to demographics.

Finally, in the section that follows we consider the combined effect of the changes discussed previously and a process of independent growth in productivity, utilizing as an assumption the growth that has been observed during recent decades ("The Effects of Changes in Worker Productivity" section). The chapter closes with "Final Comments."

Labor Participation and Productivity: Recent Evolution (1981–2013)

The analysis is based on information from the Continuous Household Surveys carried out by the National Institute of Statistics covering 1981–2013. To ensure comparability among the surveys, the analysis is restricted to the urban population (localities with 5,000 or more residents), given that only beginning in 2006 did the surveys begin to represent the entire population.[2]

Labor Participation

One feature of the labor market during the last 30 years is the increase in the labor force participation rate, or the economic activity rate—63.8 percent in 2013 from 52.7 percent in 1981—measured as the number of individuals that work or seek to work relative to the working-age population (14 years old and above). As figure 7.2 shows, the economic activity rate follows movements in gross domestic product (GDP), although more smoothly.

Labor force participation exhibits differences throughout individuals' lives. In general terms, it can be expected that individuals will slowly join the labor market during their youth as they finish their formal education, participate in large numbers during middle age, and reduce their participation as they near retirement age, exhibiting very low rates at the end of their lives. This evolution, which is associated with the traditional life cycle, is reflected in figure 7.3, which illustrates significant changes during the period considered. Two movements are distinguishable: a rightward shift in the curve, reflecting an increase in the entry and retirement ages in the labor market; and an upward movement, which reflects the increase in labor force participation at all ages over age 20. This latter movement is essentially the result of women's entry into the labor market, as we will see later.

Figure 7.2 Evolution of the Economic Activity Rate and the GDP Index, 1981–2013

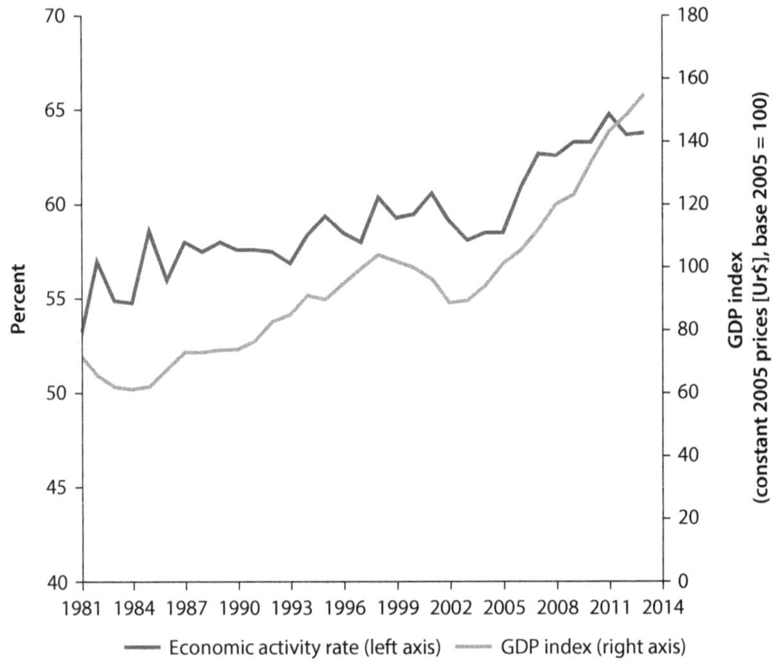

Sources: Central Bank of Uruguay, Instituto Nacional de Estadística (National Institute of Statistics) Continuous Household Surveys 1981–2013.
Note: The data for 1982, 1983, and 1985 refer exclusively to Montevideo.

To analyze the increase in the entry and retirement ages for the labor market (rightward shift in the curve) in greater detail, the evolution of youth (figure 7.4) and older adult (figure 7.6) labor force participation is presented.

With regard to labor market entry, labor force participation among the youngest group (ages 14–19) fell from 37.6 percent in 1981 to 26.3 percent in 2013. However, among youth ages 20–24, the rate was steady around 77 percent, and the rate increased about 7 percentage points for those ages 25–29. These movements are due to opposing forces: the increase in labor force participation among women (analyzed later) and the extension of years spent studying, which is accompanied by the postponement of entry to the labor market (Bucheli 2007). As figure 7.5 shows, attendance at educational institutions is growing among all youth age groups, which is consistent with reduced labor market participation.

We can expect that both forces will act on all age groups, and the resulting evolution of the economic activity rate will depend on how these movements counteract each other. When the evolution presented in figure 7.4 is broken down (see figure 7A.1 in annex 7A), distinct patterns are evident. The fall in the economic activity rate among adolescents is evident in males and females,

Figure 7.3 Economic Activity Rate by Single-Year Age Group, Urban Population, 1981 and 2013

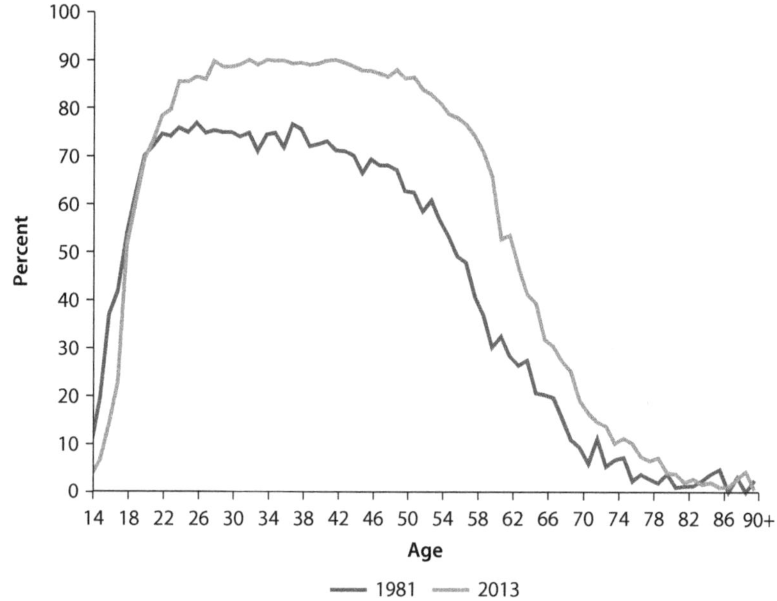

Source: Instituto Nacional de Estadística (National Institute of Statistics) Continuous Household Surveys 1981 and 2013.
Note: The data are from urban centers with 5,000 or more residents.

Figure 7.4 Evolution of the Economic Activity Rate among Youth by Age Group, Urban Population, 1981–2013

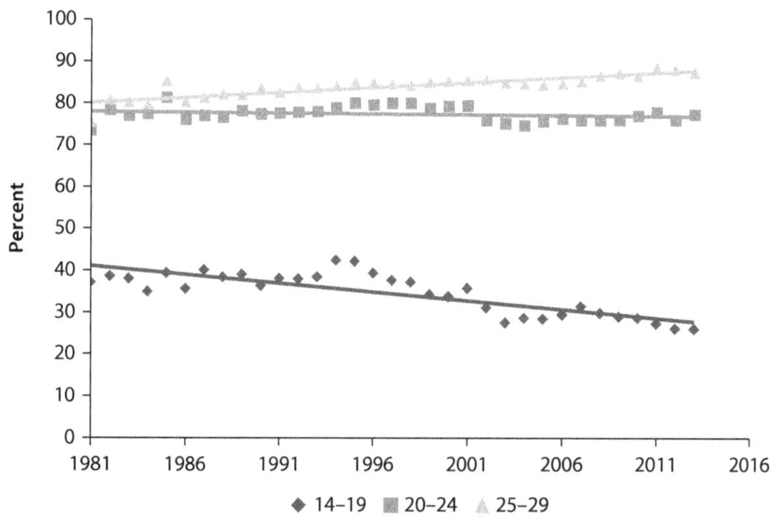

Source: Instituto Nacional de Estadística (National Institute of Statistics) Continuous Household Surveys 1981–2013.
Note: The data for 1982, 1983, and 1985 refer exclusively to Montevideo. The data are from urban centers with 5,000 or more residents.

Figure 7.5 Evolution of Educational Institution Attendance by Age Group, Urban Population, 1981–2013

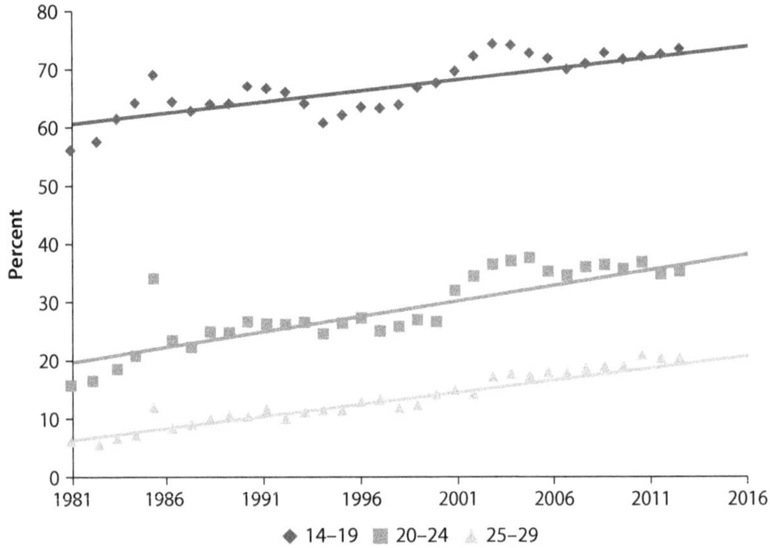

Source: Instituto Nacional de Estadística (National Institute of Statistics) Continuous Household Surveys 1981–2013.
Note: The data for 1985 refer exclusively to Montevideo.

although it is more pronounced among the former. Stability also exists in both genders in the middle age group. The greatest gender difference is among people ages 25–29: among men the economic activity rate fell during the period under analysis, and increased significantly among women (from more than 60 percent to more than 80 percent).

As Bucheli (2007) pointed out, understanding the determinants of labor force participation among youth has become more complex. Historically, men joined the labor market once they had completed their studies and remained active until their retirement, and women either dedicated themselves to household work after completing studies or entered the labor market with a series of interruptions in their participation that corresponded to marriage and having children.

Currently, the transition from the education system to the labor market is no longer linear, but rather intermittent labor attachments occur, along with high unemployment rates, temporary school abandonment, and periods of simultaneous study and work. And the differences between the genders, although they remain, are no longer as noticeable. In Filardo (2010), on labor market entry calendars among youth and detachment from the education system among the genders (based on the 2008 National Youth Survey), although men leave the education system and enter the labor market at nearly the same time, the proportion of women leaving the education system is always higher than the proportion entering the labor market.

Among the older population labor force participation increases among all subgroups considered, marking a trend of postponing retirement from the labor market (figure 7.6). In any case, this trend is also influenced by the massive incorporation of women into the labor market. Previous studies observed this same trend, showing that the retirement age among men was stable from 1985 to 2007, and increased significantly among women (Álvarez et al. 2009).

Various factors are behind changes in the retirement age. Among them—as Riedel and Hofer (2013) point out—are pension system characteristics (minimum retirement age, benefit generosity, and income replacement rate inside and outside the labor market) and individual and household characteristics (health, education, marital status). Also included are determinants associated with work (labor conditions, firm characteristics, work hours, salary) and the macroeconomy (unemployment, economic performance, labor legislation).

The passage of Law No. 16,713 in 1995, discussed in chapter 4, significantly changed the Uruguayan pension system, standardizing the minimum retirement age for men and women at age 60. Previously, the minimum retirement age for women had been age 56. Studies indicate that this reform increased "permanence" in the labor market (Álvarez et al. 2010; Durán, Poplavski, and Vernengo 2003; Espino and Leites 2008). And following the reform, the economic activity rate among women accelerated and the retirement age began to peak at the minimum retirement ages (Álvarez et al. 2009).

Figure 7.6 Evolution of the Economic Activity Rate among Urban Adults by Age Group, 1981–2013

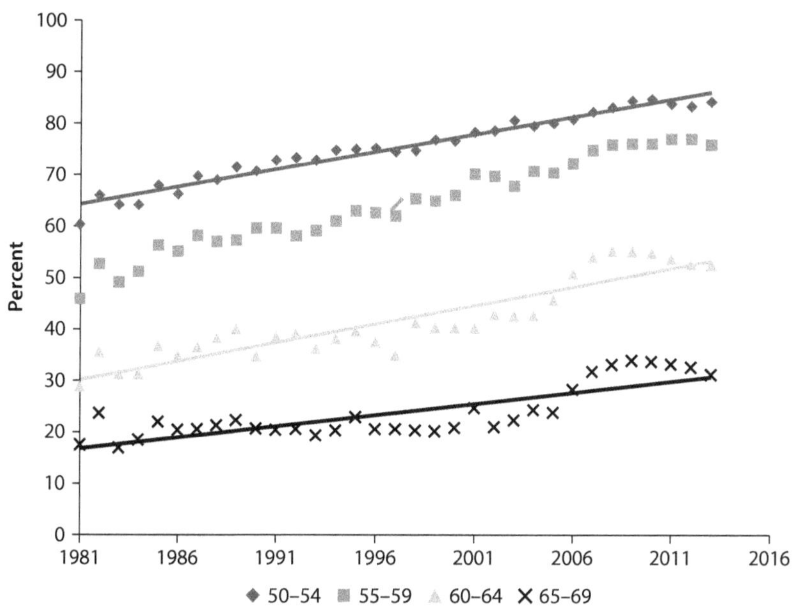

Source: Instituto Nacional de Estadística (National Institute of Statistics) Continuous Household Surveys 1981–2013.
Note: The data for 1982, 1983, and 1985 refer exclusively to Montevideo. The data are from urban centers with 5,000 or more residents.

Gender is another relevant variable for analyzing labor force activity. The legacy of the once predominant gender-based division of labor, with the man working for pay outside the household and the woman dedicated to homemaking and care, has meant that women participate in the labor market much less than men. Thus, while men's participation is essentially determined by their potential salary in the labor market, women's participation depends on a larger set of factors, including if they have children, how many, and their ages; the presence of other adults in the household; their responsibilities in domestic tasks; and cultural factors that either promote or limit women's labor force participation outside the home (ECLAC 2014a).

In this environment, it is important to observe that in Uruguay, as in much of the world, the increase in the economic activity rate in the last 30 years was generated mostly by the increase in women's labor force participation. As figure 7.7 shows, the male economic activity rate remained practically unchanged during the period, but rose almost 20 percentage points among women. Yet, women's labor force participation remains significantly below men's: in 2013, 73.4 percent of working-age men participated in the labor market, while just 55.3 percent of women did.

Comparing economic activity rates in 1981 to those in 2013, disaggregating by gender and single-year age groups, male participation changes, but only slightly compared to women. At the same time, figure 7.8 shows an increase in

Figure 7.7 Evolution of the Economic Activity Rate, Urban Areas, 1981–2013

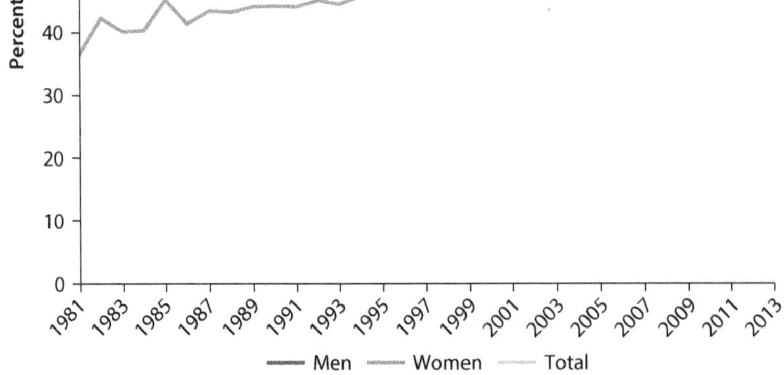

Source: Instituto Nacional de Estadística (National Institute of Statistics) Continuous Household Surveys 1981–2013.

Note: Data for 1982, 1983, and 1985 refer exclusively to Montevideo. The data are from urban centers with 5,000 or more residents.

Figure 7.8 Economic Activity Rate by Single-Year Age Group and Gender, Urban Population, 1981 and 2013

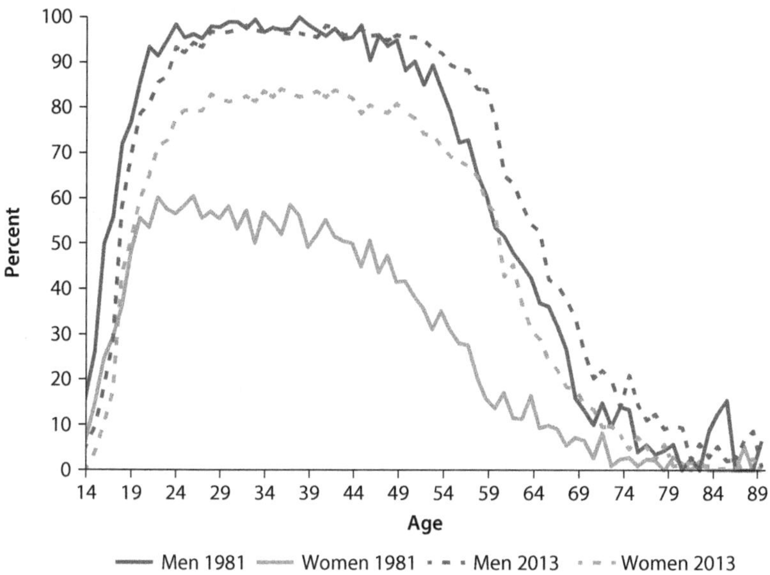

Source: Instituto Nacional de Estadística (National Institute of Statistics) Continuous Household Surveys 1981 and 2013.
Note: The data are from urban centers with 5,000 or more residents.

the labor market entry and retirement ages among men, evident in a rightward shift in the participation curve. Importantly, among men ages 21 and 49 in 1981 and 24 and 56 in 2013, participation rates are equal to or greater than 90 percent, that is, practically full.

Stated differently, the movements in the male labor force participation rate between 1981 and 2013 show that overall the economic activity rate among men was stable as movements at the two age extremes offset each other. An increase at older ages (from 71.3 percent to 83.3 percent among ages 50–64 and from 22 percent to 32.4 percent among ages 65–74) offsets a decline in the economic activity rate among youth below age 25 (from 67.5 percent to 55 percent). Among middle-aged men the rates remained practically unchanged (96.7 percent in 1981 and 96.2 percent in 2013).

Movements among women are very significant and therefore more difficult to isolate. An increase in labor force participation among women is observed among all but the youngest age groups. Espino and Leites (2008) analyze the evolution of the participation gaps between 1981 and 2006 by constructing pseudo-panels and find a strong cohort effect. While among the generations from 1927 to 1931 the male economic activity rate among different age groups was on average 60 percent higher than the female rate, in the 1967–71 generation this dropped to 26 percent. They also observed an increase in the age up to which women are willing to work, as a potential response to the changes put in place with the reform of the social security system, which increased minimum retirement age among women.

Several works have analyzed the expansion of the supply of female labor in Uruguay and possible explanations (Espino and Leites 2008; Espino, Leites, and Machado 2009; Sanroman 2006). The principal factors usually include the reallocation of resources from the manufacturing industry to the tertiary sector, which increases demand for women, as well as the reduction of the salary gaps between women and men, which would affect the allocation of tasks inside and outside the home. The effect of the increase of women's education level should be considered, as well as the increase of returns to education beginning in the 1990s. Other factors have to do with cultural and institutional trends that have contributed to the reduction in discrimination against women in the labor market. In addition, factors linked to marriage trends, the increase in divorces, and the reduction in fertility have affected women's labor force participation decisions.

As a result of all of these factors, women's and men's labor force participation profiles become increasingly similar, just as in the rest of the world (Blau and Kahn 2005; Blundell and MaCurdy 1999; Goldin 1990). This translates into a reduction of the economic activity gap between genders. While in 1981 women's participation was only 50 percent of men's, by 2013 it was 75 percent (figure 7.9).

Although the gender gap in labor force participation declined strongly during the period under analysis, significant room remains to increase women's participation in the labor market (figure 7.9). This fact is fundamental for forecasts later in this chapter.

Changing education levels have also been important in recent decades. As discussed, labor force participation is closely linked to education decisions. Individuals with higher education have higher expected salaries, raising the

Figure 7.9 Ratio between the Female and Male Economic Activity Rates, Urban Population, 1981–2013

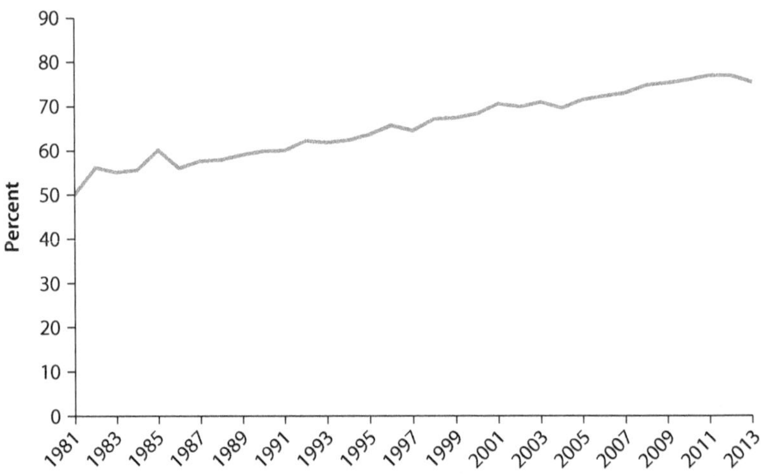

Source: Instituto Nacional de Estadística (National Institute of Statistics) Continuous Household Surveys 1981–2013.

Note: The data for 1982, 1983, and 1985 refer exclusively to Montevideo. The data are from urban centers with 5,000 or more residents.

opportunity cost of not working. Yet to obtain higher education it is necessary to postpone labor market entry (at least full-time entry) and sacrifice income during the period. The expected higher income will then allow recovery of this lost income. All of this means that individuals with higher education levels participate more actively in the labor market.

Looking at labor force participation by education level and gender, the differences are significant (figure 7.10). First, men vary little by education level, with much lower differences between the two years considered. Only less educated men exhibit a significant change between 1981 and 2013, with a shift toward older ages at entry to and retirement from the labor market.

By contrast, the changes among women by education level are more substantial. As education level increases, so does labor force participation among women, reaching levels that are practically equal to men's levels at the tertiary level. In contrast, less educated women exhibit very low economic activity rates, although they increased during the period under analysis. Female participation also increases with age, which indicates its strong relationship with the reproductive

Figure 7.10 Economic Activity Rate by Single-Year Age Group, Gender, and Education Level, Urban Population, 1981 and 2013

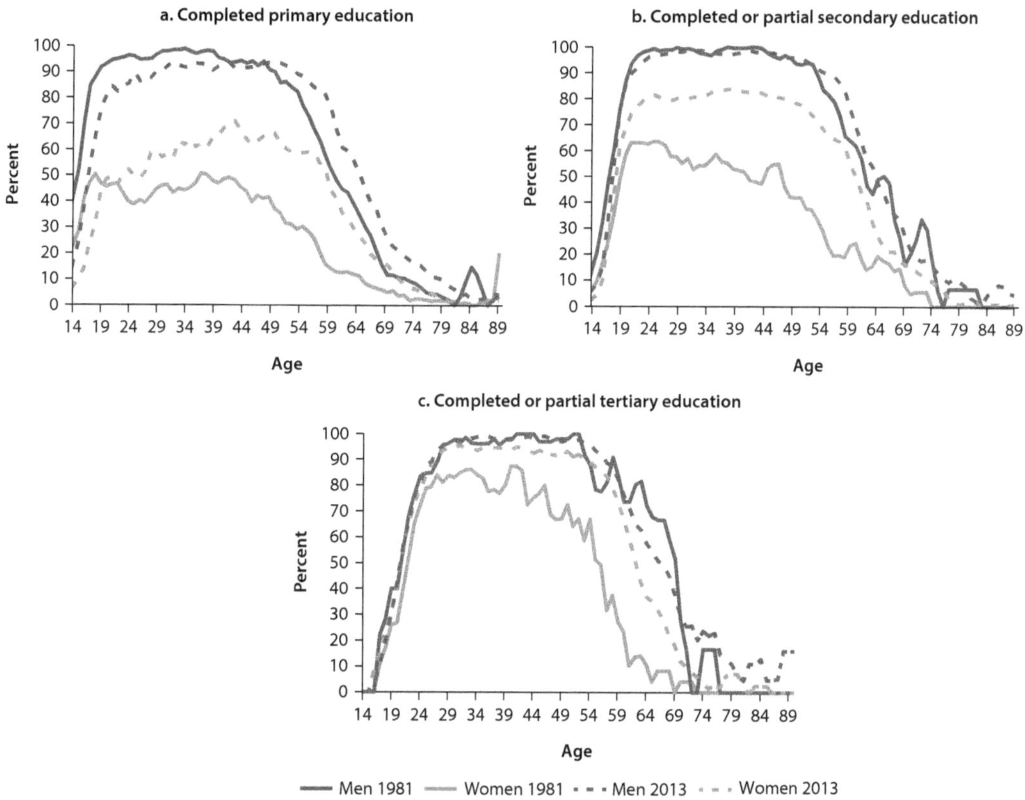

Source: Instituto Nacional de Estadística (National Institute of Statistics) Continuous Household Surveys 1981 and 2013.
Note: The data are from urban centers with 5,000 or more residents.

period. The largest increase in labor force participation between 1981 and 2013 was observed among women with an intermediate education level.

Because the difference in participation by education level is so significant, one must ask how education has evolved during the last 30 years. The available information reflects an increase in attendance at educational institutions among all youth age groups, although levels remain low, especially among those over age 20 (figure 7.5).[3]

The sustained increase in attendance has raised the population's number of years of education. Figure 7.11 shows growth in the average years of education among all age groups. It is most noticeable in the over-18 age group, with an increase of 2.8 years on average, and a maximum increase of 4 years of education among people age 52. Importantly, the curve does not just move upward, but rather years of education accumulate more in the middle-aged population, which participates most in the labor market. And women in 2013 accumulated more education than men, a gap which was not significant in 1981.

Nonetheless, Uruguayan education levels are low: they do not exceed an average of 12 years of education among any age group.

Figure 7.11 Years of Education by Single-Year Age Group and Gender, Urban Population, 1981 and 2013

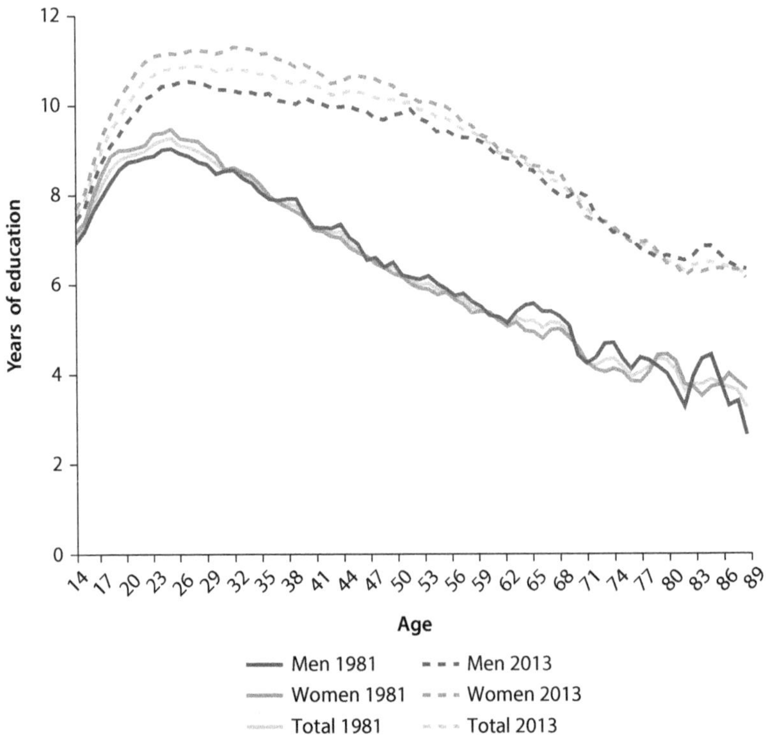

Source: Instituto Nacional de Estadística (National Institute of Statistics) Continuous Household Surveys 1981 and 2013.
Note: The data are from urban centers with 5,000 or more residents.

Labor force participation changes in the last 30 years were very significant: the population's economic activity increased significantly, driven by women's participation, and the labor market entry and retirement ages increased among both genders. Years of education also increased. It is therefore reasonable to expect variations in the economic activity rate that go beyond the changes that will result from the predicted demographic changes. These variations will be driven by the female rate, both as a result of the cohort effect as well as caused by potential increases in the population's accumulated education. These elements are revisited in the design of the scenarios in the next section.

Labor Productivity

Attempts to show the efficiency of an economy, specifically increases in productivity, are necessarily limited by the measurements available. A typical productivity measure is the ratio between a measure of the volume of an economy's production and a measure of the utilization of inputs or productive factors. For labor productivity, a key variable in development both for its economic and social aspects (Kaldewei and Weller 2013), one common calculation is to divide GDP at constant prices by the number of people employed each year. This measure indicates how productively labor is used to create product, and reflects the combined influence of many elements. In effect, increases in labor productivity may occur through an increase in physical capital, through technological change, or through improvements to human capital (both in worker abilities and intensity of work) (OECD 2001).

Apparent labor productivity in Uruguay can be divided into three subperiods (figure 7.12): a growth period during 1985–97, stagnation and a subsequent

Figure 7.12 Evolution of Apparent Productivity, GDP per Worker, 1981–2013
constant 2005 prices

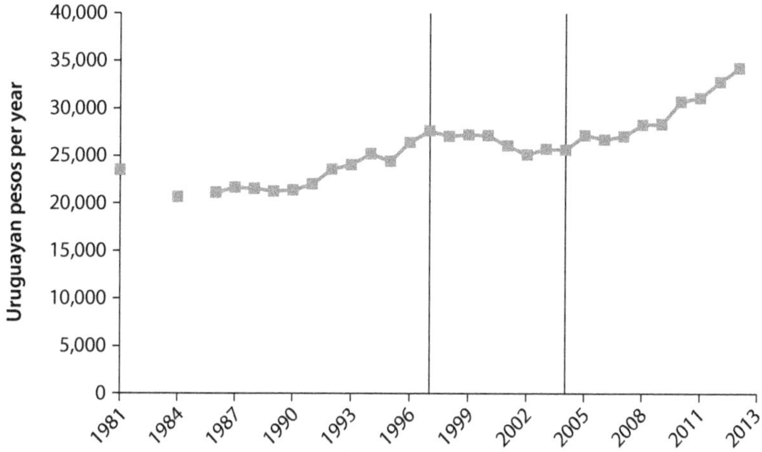

Sources: Central Bank of Uruguay, Instituto Nacional de Estadística (National Institute of Statistics) Continuous Household Surveys 1981–2013, and population forecasts.
Note: The 1982, 1983, and 1985 household surveys present problems in the identification of employed persons at the national level, so these years have been excluded.

fall that coincided with the economic crisis during 1998–2004, and a rebound during 2005–13. In the latter period of growth, Uruguay reached and widely surpassed the levels before the crisis.[4]

Uruguayan labor productivity changes are similar to those elsewhere in Latin America (Kaldewei and Weller 2013), a region where apparent labor productivity grew 1.6 percent per year between 2002 and 2012. This moderate regional advance was not sufficient to close the gap with developed countries and is considerably slower than the growth in Asian countries (ECLAC 2014b).

Neoclassical theory posits that maximizing GDP leads to a situation in which factors are paid equal to the value of their marginal product. If we assume, as is standard, a Cobb-Douglas production function, then marginal productivity is proportional to average product, because this production function assumes that productive factors' participation is constant. In the labor market this means that labor productivity (measured as the total product per worker) is equal to the salary. Thus, in theoretical terms, the salary would reflect what a worker produces, measured as the value of the product. This theoretical outcome is useful because, when it is true, it enables us to approximate the movements of labor productivity based on observations of the movements in salaries, which are more easily measurable.

However, the correlation that we would expect to see between movements in labor productivity and movements in salaries is the subject of debate in economics. Various factors could explain why both variables differ in size and do not always move together. First, total labor income should be considered, not just salaries, in order to include in-kind payments and different types of compensation that form part of payments to workers.[5] Differences may also occur due to the price indices utilized to compare productivity levels and salaries. Productivity is measured through product, and therefore uses the deflator implicit in GDP to adjust its values, while salaries are usually adjusted using other indices. Thus, any imbalance between both deflators will lead to imbalances between salaries and labor productivity. Finally, if the production function of the economy does not ensure proportionality between the marginal product and the average product, or if the economy faces other imbalances, then both variables may differ.

Figure 7.13 presents the evolution of an apparent labor productivity index and a labor income index for employed persons, both with a base of 1986 = 100. We observe that the movement of both indices is similar, but not exactly equal. Real labor income follows the movement of apparent productivity, but reacts more strongly during both growth periods as well as falls.

The relative similarity in the variation of both variables, along with the economic theory arguments, allow us to consider that the variation of labor income constitutes a reasonable approximation of the variation in productivity. We will consider the average labor income among the economically active population, instead of just the employed, in order to smooth possible short-term imbalances.[6]

The ratio between labor income and age has an inverted U shape: it increases with age as workers gain experience until reaching a peak around ages 50–55, subsequently falling as a result of the depreciation of knowledge (figure 7.14).

Figure 7.13 Evolution of the Real Labor Income Index and the Apparent Productivity Index, 1986–2013

Sources: Elaboration based on the Instituto Nacional de Estadística (National Institute of Statistics) Continuous Household Surveys 1986–2013 and Central Bank data.
Note: Base year 1986 = 100.

Figure 7.14 Labor Income of Economically Active Persons by Gender and Age Group, 2013

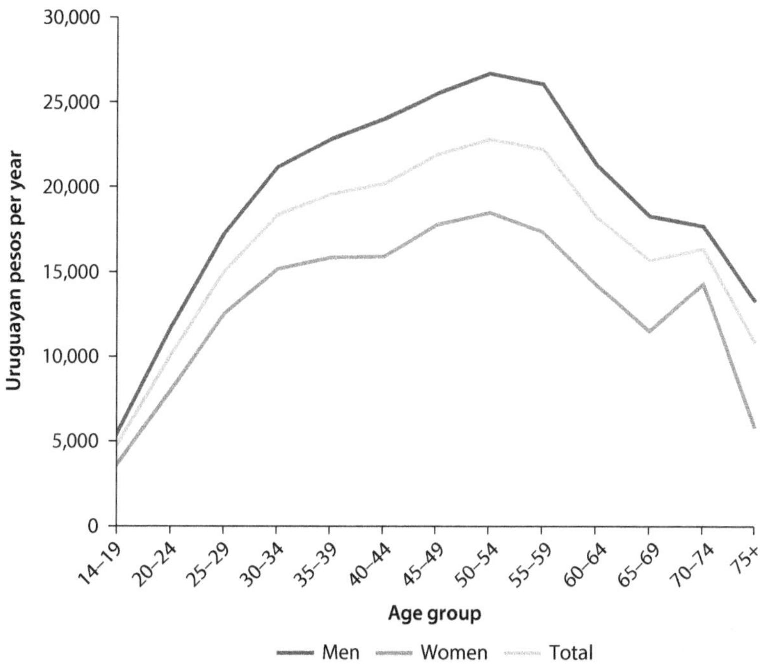

Source: Instituto Nacional de Estadística (National Institute of Statistics) Continuous Household Survey 2013.

The profiles of men and women are similar, with larger gaps around age 50. In education, we observe a skills premium that is the result of different levels of productivity (figure 7.15). Specifically, the premium for having completed higher education is particularly large, representing almost double the income of the level immediately below it (partial higher education) and more than three times the average income of those who did not complete primary education.

Table 7.1 summarizes the total and annual variations in 1981 and 2013 in the key variables analyzed previously. GDP, the modest dynamic variable, more than doubled in the period. Apparent productivity exhibits more moderate movements, nearly half of those exhibited by GDP. Movements in labor income are significantly lower and depend on the period selected for the comparison: annual variation during the 1981–2013 period is 0.1 percent, but rises to 1.4 percent if the comparison is carried out for the period since 1986. Annex 7A (figure 7A.2)

Figure 7.15 Labor Income of Economically Active Persons by Education Level, 2013

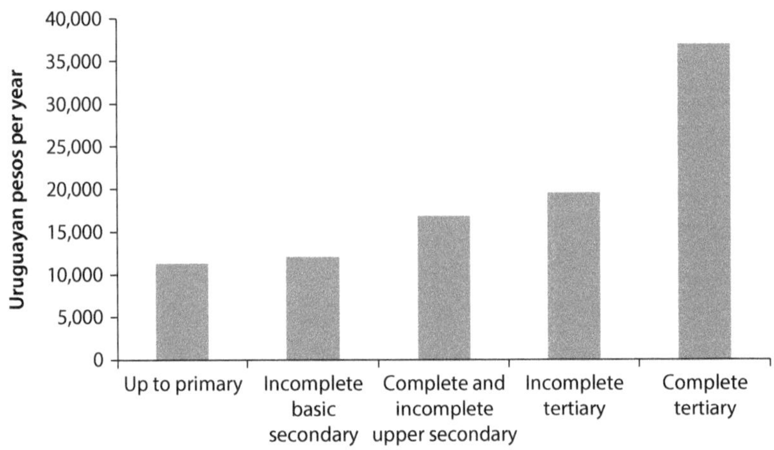

Source: Instituto Nacional de Estadística (National Institute of Statistics) Continuous Household Survey 2013.

Table 7.1 Variation of GDP, Apparent Productivity, and Real Labor Income, 1981–2013
percent

	Change	*Annual equivalent change*
	1981–2013	
GDP	113.5	2.4
Apparent productivity	45.8	1.2
Labor income, employed persons	2.5	0.1
	1986–2013	
GDP	129.1	3.1
Apparent productivity	62.2	1.8
Labor income, employed persons	44.3	1.4

Sources: Central Bank of Uruguay, Instituto Nacional de Estadística (National Institute of Statistics).

shows the evolution of real labor income during the period, allowing us to observe its strong cyclical component.

In summary, labor's contribution to GDP is influenced by the stock of human capital, which depends on the number of workers and their productivity. Because the possibilities of increasing the quantitative component are very limited for demographic reasons, as we will clearly see in the following sections, the plausible paths to maintain the levels of economic growth will fundamentally depend on the population's educational achievements and workforce training.

What Can We Expect from the Evolution of Labor Force Participation?

This section analyzes how demographic changes could affect the evolution of labor force participation, a key labor market variable. Its trajectory depends, on one hand, on the evolution of the age makeup of the population and, on the other, on shocks that are beyond the scope of demographics (changes in the education level, behavior changes that determine women's participation, technological improvements, and so on). While the former are relatively easier to predict, the latter by their nature are much more complex to predict. Creating scenarios for these types of changes is therefore difficult, although analyzing past trends may provide useful information.

With this in mind, if we estimate the evolution of the economic activity rate in 1981 and 2013 as if the only factor affecting it had been demographics—in other words if we keep the economic activity rates the same as they were in 1981 for each population segment by age and gender and we apply them to the changes in the population observed during this period, we observe that the economic activity rate would have fallen from 55 percent to 53 percent.[7] However, the evolution of labor force participation was different, increasing by almost 9 percentage points. This indicates that the increase in labor force participation observed during the period was due to changes separate from demographics, which more than offset the fall that demographic effects would have generated on their own. Table 7.2 presents the principal results of this exercise.

This exercise shows that there are significant changes in individuals' behavior in labor force participation. It would be reasonable to expect that between 2013 and 2100 we will also observe these types of changes. The scenarios we construct attempt to reflect them.

Table 7.2 Description of the Estimated Scenarios

	Women (%)	*Men (%)*	*Total (%)*
Economic activity rate 1981	36.9	74.4	55.0
Economic activity rate 2013 counterfactual	34.9	73.4	53.3
Economic activity rate 2013 observed	54.2	74.5	63.9
Variation 1981–2013 counterfactual	−5.2	−1.3	−3.1
Variation 1981–2013 observed	47.0	0.2	16.2

Sources: Elaboration based on Instituto Nacional de Estadística (National Institute of Statistics) Continuous Household Surveys 1981–2013 and population forecasts.

One must keep in mind that the three scenarios analyzed in this section assume that worker productivity for each age, gender, and education level group is fixed. By making these variables constant, this assumption enables us to evaluate the impact that comes "purely" from the effects that demographic change would have on aggregate productivity as a result of the variations in the structure of the labor force in age, gender, and education level. In other words, we do not design scenarios that assume changes in productivity as a result of factors like technological innovation, capital accumulation, or other institutional effects. Thus, in this section we estimate the "component composition" of the changes in aggregate productivity. "The Effects of Changes in Worker Productivity" section presents a scenario that includes exogenous changes in productivity.

We constructed three scenarios for labor force participation based on population forecasts. First we created a demographic scenario that only considers the expected changes in the age structure, and two scenarios that model possible external shocks: an increase in women's labor force participation and a scenario with an increase in the education level.

1. *Demographic scenario*: We applied the economic activity rates by single-year age group observed in 2013 to the population forecasts for single-year age groups presented in chapter 2. Thus, this scenario reflects the effect of the change in the population and its age structure.
2. *Female labor force participation increase scenario*: We assumed an increase in the female economic activity rate that would enable it to reach levels similar to those seen in developed countries. This scenario combines changes in the population and its age structure with the dynamics of female economic activity.
3. *Education level increase scenario*: We applied the economic activity rates by education level observed in 2013 to the population forecasts by education level from chapters 2 and 6. This scenario combines changes in the population and its demographic composition with changes in its accumulated education.

Once we obtained the changes in the economic activity rate for each of these scenarios, we calculated the productivity trajectory associated with each of them. To do so we maintained the salary structure observed in 2013, applying it to the distribution of economically active persons for each case. Thus, the scenarios deal with endogenous productivity, associated with changes in the composition of the supply of labor that result from the labor force participation assumptions we made. In the first and second scenarios we applied the 2013 labor income for women and men by age groups and in the third scenario we used income by education level. To estimate productivity for each year in each scenario, we calculated the total labor income associated with the new number and distribution of economically active persons and divided it among the total number of economically active individuals. In turn, once we knew how labor force participation and productivity had changed for each scenario, it was possible to calculate the GDP growth rate associated with these trajectories. Because we do not have information on the potential trajectories of the other

Table 7.3 Methodological Option for the Estimated Scenarios

Scenarios/forecasts	*Economically active population (assumptions)*	*Productivity (endogenous)*
1. Demographic scenario (only demographic changes)	The economic activity rates for single-year age groups in 2013 are applied to the forecasted population by age group.	Men's and women's labor income for each age group in 2013 are applied to the forecasted economically active population.
2. Increasing female labor force participation scenario	Increases in female labor force participation until reaching a participation rate among women that is similar to the current rate in Nordic countries. The male rate remains the same.	Men's and women's labor income for each age group in 2013 are applied to the forecasted economically active population.
3. Increase of the education level scenario	The economic activity rates for each education level in 2013 are applied to the forecasted population by education level.	Labor income for each education level in 2013 is applied to the forecasted economically active population.

factors that determine GDP (physical capital and technological change), these parameters are assumed to remain constant. More specifically, total labor income's proportion of GDP is assumed to be constant over time—an assumption like the one made in chapter 3—and therefore, changes in total labor income are translated into changes in GDP.

Table 7.3 summarizes the principal methodological options for each scenario.

Importantly, we analyze the supply of labor by itself, which leads to an estimation bias because the number of workers also depends on the salaries offered in the market and these are determined by the interaction between supply and demand. One could expect that the projected movements in the supply of labor would modify salaries and provoke new changes in the supply. For example, if the forecasts show a reduction in the number of workers, the relative scarcity of labor could lead to an increase in salaries, which could induce more people to participate in the labor market. However, such effects, which could affect relative salaries and education decisions, are not considered in the exercises presented below.

Scenario 1—Demographic Evolution of Economic Activity

This scenario only considers population aging. The economic activity rates for single-year age groups in 2013 are applied to the population forecasts from 2013 to 2100. Once the new numbers of economically active and inactive individuals are obtained, the total economic activity rate is calculated. In contrast with the previous section, the economic activity rates observed in 2013 for the entire country (and not just urban areas) are utilized. This is because, on one hand, the population forecasts employed refer to the entire population, and on the other hand, as has been mentioned, since 2006 the Continuous Household Survey has represented the entire country. In addition, no changes to the retirement age are considered—which could turn out to be a reasonable hypothesis based on the population aging predicted to take place (see box 7.1).

Box 7.1 Entry and Retirement Ages in the Labor Market

The evidence reviewed in the first section indicates that the ages at which individuals enter or leave the labor market change substantially over time. It was shown that these changes depend heavily on legal factors in the case of retirement age and on attendance at educational institutions in the case of entry age. At the same time, both depend on cultural and institutional factors, health, and the characteristics of the labor market.

As an approximation of the possible changes to these ages, we estimate the relationship between the economic activity rates by age and the evolution of life expectancy at birth (which turns out to be consistent with the population forecasts presented in chapter 2).

We assume that the relationship between the economic activity rates by single-year age groups and life expectancy would remain constant during the period under analysis. Thus, we apply the economic activity rate for the age which in 2013 presented the same distance to life expectancy. An example illustrates this exercise: in 2013, a person age 65 was 12 years from life expectancy (which was age 77) and the economic activity rate for this age group was 39.4 percent; in 2065 life expectancy would be age 83.8, which means that a person of age 65 would be 19 years away from this age, and thus the activity rate to be applied to this person would be that for a person of age 54 in 2013, which is 74.2 percent. The result is that the structure of labor participation by age remains unchanged, but it does shift to the right (figure B7.1.1).

Figure B7.1.1 Economic Activity Rate Forecast by Single-Year Age Groups, Selected Years

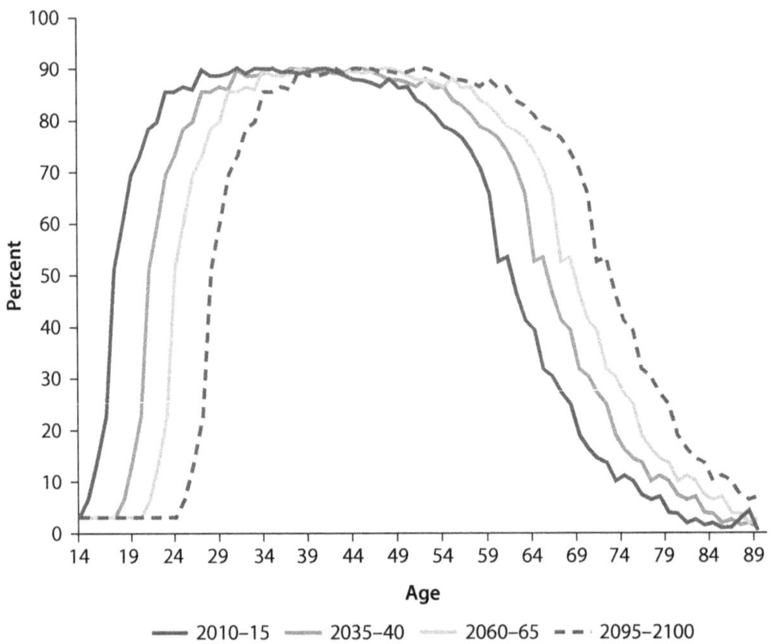

Sources: Elaboration based on the Instituto Nacional de Estadística (National Institute of Statistics) Continuous Household Survey 2013 and population forecasts.

box continues next page

Box 7.1 Entry and Retirement Ages in the Labor Market *(continued)*

Based on these economic activity rates for single-year age groups we calculate the new total economic activity rate. The results are presented in figure B7.1.2 and are very similar to those observed in the demographic scenario.

Figure B7.1.2 Economic Activity Rate Forecast, Demographic Scenario and Age Modification, 2013–2100

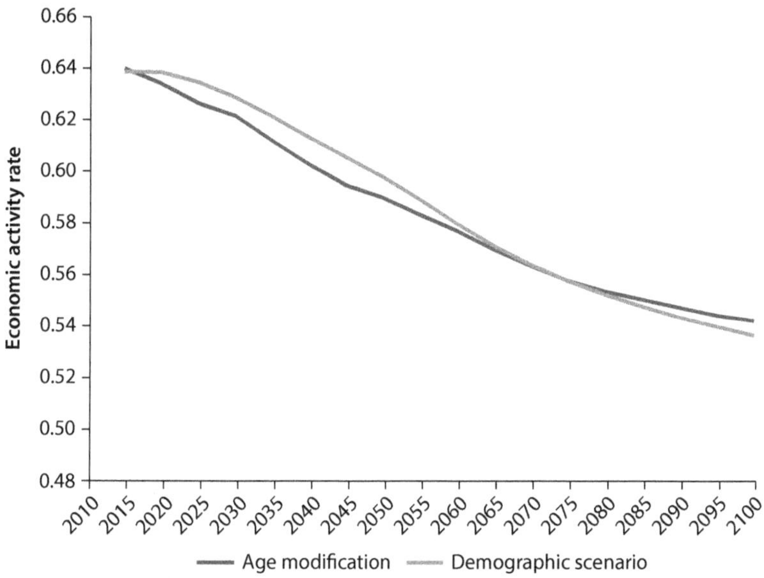

Sources: Elaboration based on the Instituto Nacional de Estadística (National Institute of Statistics) Continuous Household Survey 2013 and population forecasts.

As figure 7.16 shows, the economic activity rate would fall significantly (in this scenario) to a level at which nearly half of the population over 14 years old would not participate in the labor market in 2100. This is because population aging pushes an ever larger proportion of the total population into age groups with low labor force participation.

Not only does the population that would participate in the labor market fall, but its composition by age and gender also changes (table 7.4). In fact, the proportion of workers ages 50 to 75 increases significantly (7.3 percentage points). In any case, one must remember that the specific economic activity rates by age and gender are not modified, remaining at 2013 levels for the entire period.

Based on the forecast of the economically active population, forecasts for total labor income and productivity are created. They are the product of multiplying the number of economically active men and women by age group for each year by the corresponding labor income levels observed in 2013.[8] Figure 7.17 shows that in this scenario productivity would increase very slowly until around 2050 and subsequently stagnate. The increase results because labor income for the age

Figure 7.16 Economic Activity Rate Forecast Based on the Population Forecast, Demographic Scenario, 2013–2100

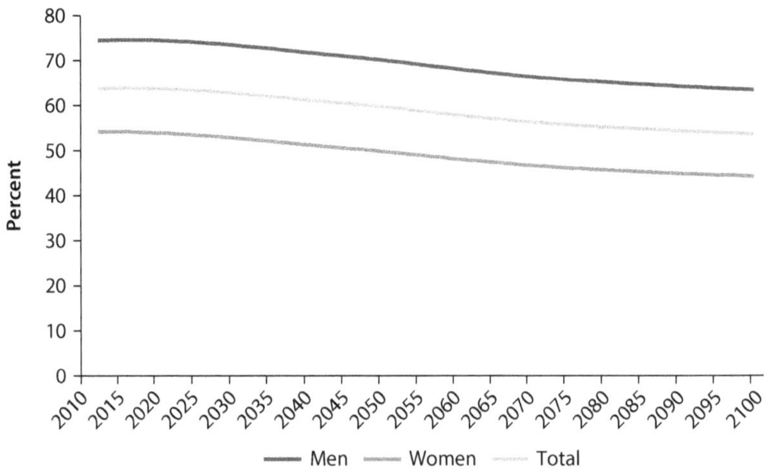

Sources: Elaboration based on the Instituto Nacional de Estadística (National Institute of Statistics) Continuous Household Survey 2013 and population forecasts.

Table 7.4 Participation of Women and Men and Age Groups in the Economically Active Population
percent

	2013	*2025*	*2050*	*2075*	*2100*	*Change between points*
14–29	28.3	26.5	23.7	22.7	22.5	−5.8
30–49	45.1	45.3	43.4	42.8	42.6	−2.5
50–75	26.0	27.6	32.0	33.2	33.3	7.3
Women	44.5	43.9	42.9	42.4	42.1	−2.4
Men	55.5	56.1	57.1	57.6	57.9	2.4
Overall economic activity rate	63.9	63.5	59.8	55.8	53.6	−10.2

Sources: Elaboration based on the Instituto Nacional de Estadística (National Institute of Statistics) Continuous Household Survey 2013 and population forecasts.

groups whose relative size increases (50–75 years old) is greater than that of the younger groups, for men and women. After 2050, the makeup of the population by age and gender of economically active individuals appears to stabilize; as does productivity. In addition, the reduction in the number of economically active individuals has two opposing effects: total labor income falls at the same time that the denominator in the productivity calculation falls.

Based on the forecasts, the evolution of per capita GDP that would result from these interactions is calculated, keeping all other determinants constant. In this demographic scenario, the abrupt reduction in the number of economically

Figure 7.17 Labor Productivity Growth Rate, Demographic Scenario, 2014–2100

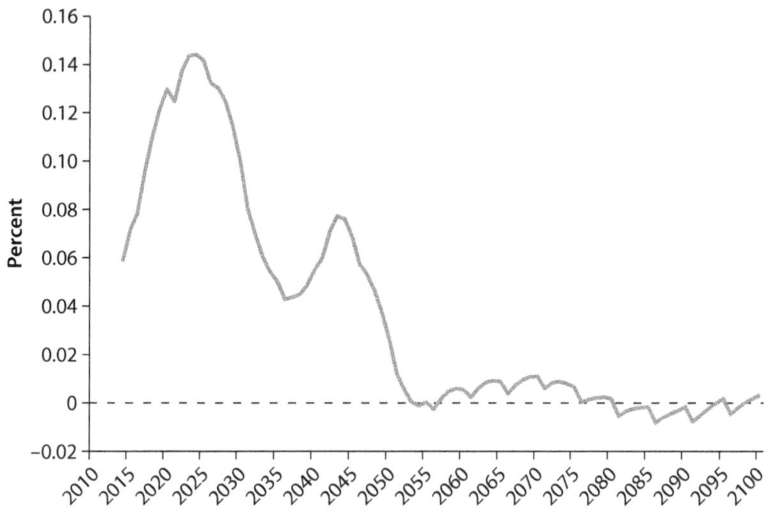

Sources: Elaboration based on the Instituto Nacional de Estadística (National Institute of Statistics) Continuous Household Survey 2013 and population forecasts.

Figure 7.18 Evolution of Per Capita GDP, Demographic Scenario, 2013–2100

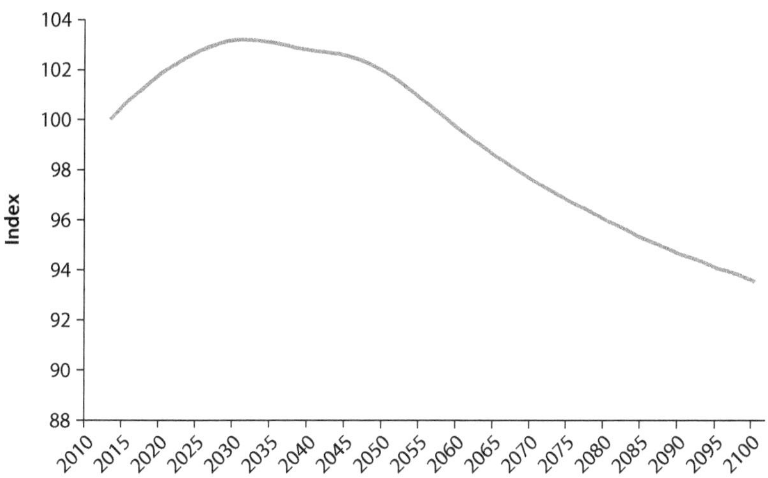

Sources: Elaboration based on the Instituto Nacional de Estadística (National Institute of Statistics) Continuous Household Survey 2013 and population forecasts.
Note: 2013 = 100.

active individuals is not offset by the increase in productivity, resulting in a fall in GDP following a few years of slight growth (figure 7.18). The abrupt fall in per capita GDP begins in 2044. This is also the year that growth of the surplus-generating population (individuals ages 28 and 57) turns negative, remaining so until the end of the period under consideration (see figure 7.1).

An interesting exercise is to measure what changes would need to occur in labor productivity, given these demographic conditions, to maintain the average GDP growth rate seen in the last 30 years (2.5 percent average annually between 1981 and 2013). Figure 7.19 shows the trajectory of the productivity growth rate corresponding to the demographic scenario, which signifies a GDP growth rate of 0.12 percent average per year during 2014–2100, as well as the rate that results from maintaining the GDP growth rate at 2.5 percent. It is evident that other factors are needed to be able to maintain the long-term growth rate. Specifically, an annual productivity growth rate of 2.66 percent would be necessary, compared to the rate that results from the demographic scenario of just 0.04 percent.

To summarize, this scenario entails a reduction in the economic activity rate of 10 percentage points, which leads to a situation in which almost half of the population over age 14 would depend on others economically. If other changes did not occur, the economy's growth rate would fall as the number of workers fell. Clearly, this scenario should be read as an illustrative simulation and not as a prediction because we should not expect such a pessimistic scenario. As has occurred during the last 100 years, it is reasonable to expect that the population's behavior will change regarding participation in the labor force, as we will explore ahead. We can also expect that other external elements will change and that they will increase labor productivity as "The Effects of Changes in Worker Productivity" section shows.

Figure 7.19 Labor Productivity Growth Rate, Demographic Scenario, 2014–2100

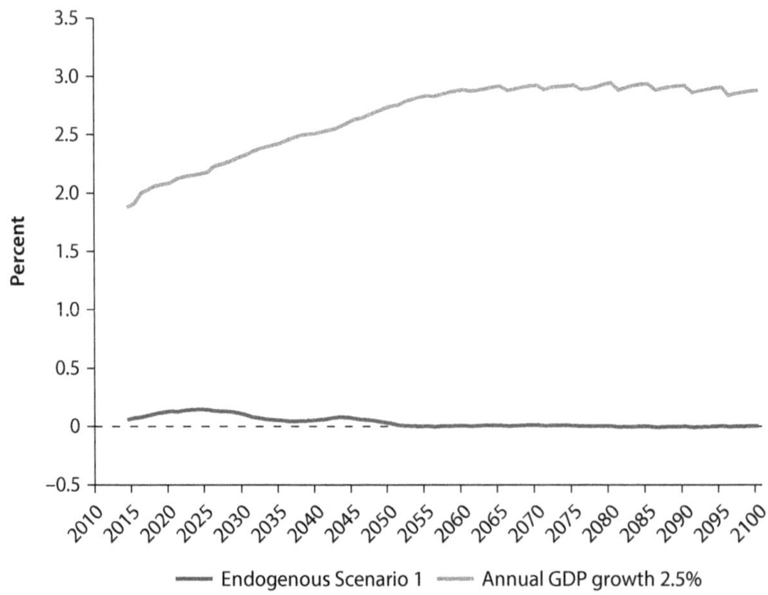

Sources: Elaboration based on the Instituto Nacional de Estadística (National Institute of Statistics) Continuous Household Survey 2013 and population forecasts.

Scenario 2—Increase in the Female Economic Activity Rate

The analysis presented in the previous section suggests that room remains to increase women's economic activity rates, which are much lower than men's rates. In fact, doing so could avoid the abrupt fall in the activity rate observed in the previous scenario: the trend from the last 30 years, which has exhibited growth in the female economic activity rate, could continue in coming years.

However, it is difficult to predict what rate Uruguayan women could achieve by 2100. One way of making an informed prediction is to consider the situation in developed countries. For example, the Nordic countries have been able to achieve levels of labor force participation that are very similar between women and men through a set of policies that promote equality in the labor market. ECLAC (2014b) describes Norway's experience with social policies that promote high levels of labor force participation among women and men. In these countries, the female economic activity rate is equivalent to between 88 percent and 93 percent of the male rate, while in Uruguay the corresponding figure was 74 percent in 2013 (figure 7.20).

Thus, this scenario is created assuming that Uruguayan women can achieve rates similar to those seen in these countries in the long term.[9] Sweden is selected as a reference point and reaching its rates is established as an objective. To respect the different patterns of entering the labor market depending on age groups, we seek to match the labor force participation rates of Uruguayan women to those for Swedish women in the same age group.[10]

Figure 7.20 Men's and Women's Economic Activity Rates, Uruguay and Selected Countries, 2013

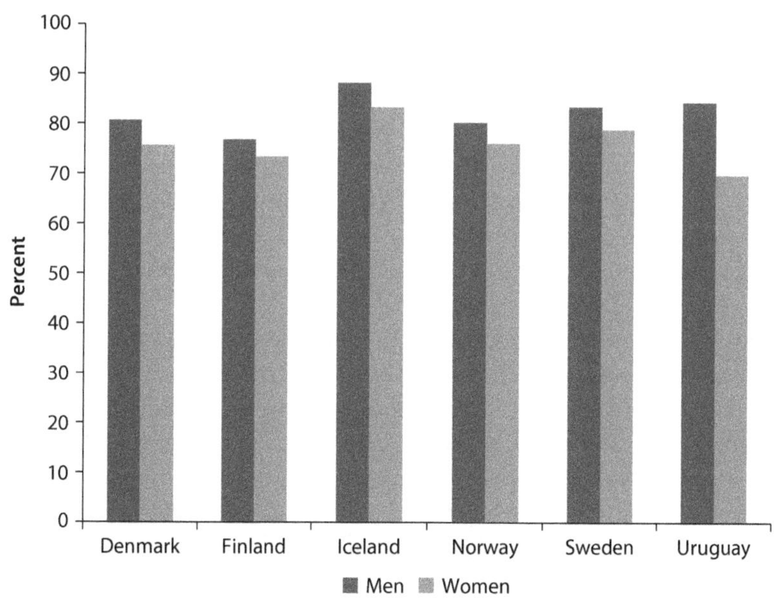

Sources: ILOSTAT and the Instituto Nacional de Estadística (National Institute of Statistics) Continuous Household Survey 2013.

Figure 7.21 Female Economic Activity Rate by Age Group, Sweden and Uruguay, 2013

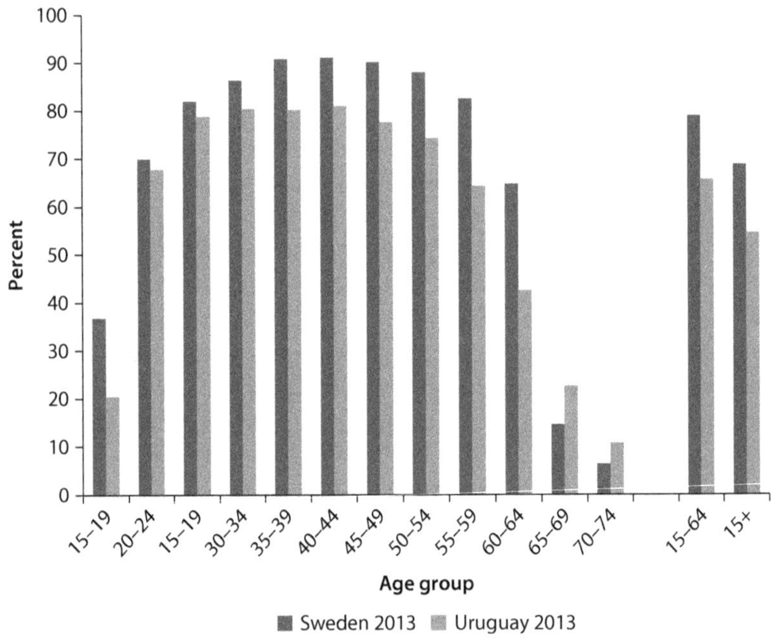

Sources: ILOSTAT and the Instituto Nacional de Estadística (National Institute of Statistics) Continuous Household Survey 2013.

As figure 7.21 shows, the Swedish economic activity rates are higher than those in Uruguay for all age groups except the last two. It is assumed that the reference country's rates will be reached, even if this would entail a reduction in the rate.

To forecast the trajectory of the female economic activity rate, we apply the average annual growth rate for the variable for 1981–2013 (1.3 percent) to the rates in 2013 to reach the target value for the age group.[11] For individuals over age 65, the economic activity rates are reduced utilizing the same annual growth rate. Once a group reaches the target value, the rate remains constant. The target rates would be reached in full in 2059, and from that point economic activity rates would not move further.

Figure 7.22 shows the projected changes in the economic activity rate when this exercise is carried out. It is important to remember that for men, the demographic forecast produced by the previous scenario is maintained. In contrast to that scenario, growth in the economic activity rate is observed, driven by the female rate, of up to 5 percentage points, subsequently returning to a downward path after 2033. This indicates that even with a significant increase in the female economic activity rate, population aging will provoke a long-term fall in the economic activity rate.

As in the previous scenario, the composition of the workforce is modified by gender and age (table 7.5).

Figure 7.22 Forecast of the Economic Activity Rate After Increasing the Female Economic Activity Rate, 2013–2100

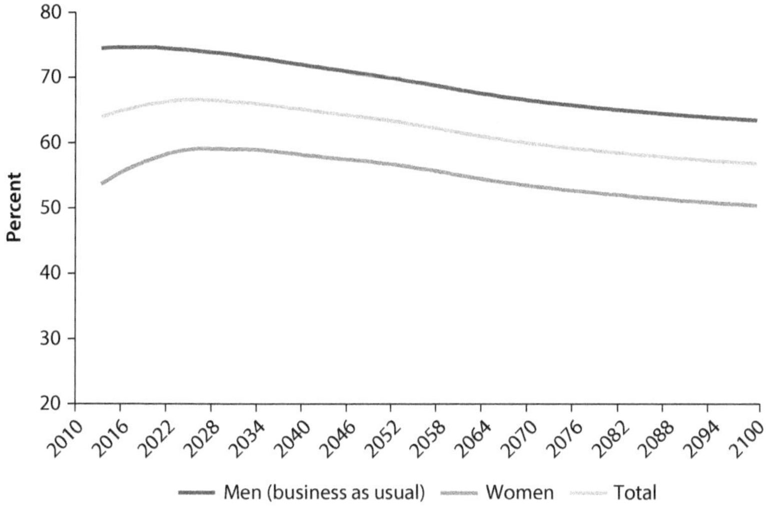

Source: Elaboration based on population forecasts.

Table 7.5 Proportion of Women and Men, and Age Groups in the Economically Active Population
percent

	2013	*2025*	*2050*	*2075*	*2100*	*Percentage point change*
14–29	28.3	25.9	23.3	22.6	22.4	−5.9
30–49	45.1	45.7	43.1	42.4	42.2	−2.8
50–75	26.1	27.8	32.7	33.7	33.8	7.8
Women	44.4	46.4	46.3	45.8	45.5	1.1
Men	55.6	53.6	53.7	54.2	54.5	−1.1
Overall economic activity rate	63.8	66.4	63.5	59.3	57.0	−6.8

Source: Elaboration based on population forecasts.

However, in contrast to the previous scenario, in this case the specific rates by age and gender are modified. Figure 7.23 shows the evolution of women's rates and presents the distribution of men's rates, which remains constant. The final values of the rates are reached in 2059, although the principal modifications occur during the first years.

The economic activity rates in 2100 are equal to or greater than those in 2013 for all age groups. However, a fall in the overall rate is observed due to demographic pressure: as the older age cohorts have more weight in the overall population, the economically active population falls because the labor force participation rates among these groups are lower. Within this framework, it is interesting to know what would happen if population aging did not exist; in

Figure 7.23 Projected Economic Activity Rate by Age Group and Gender, Selected Years

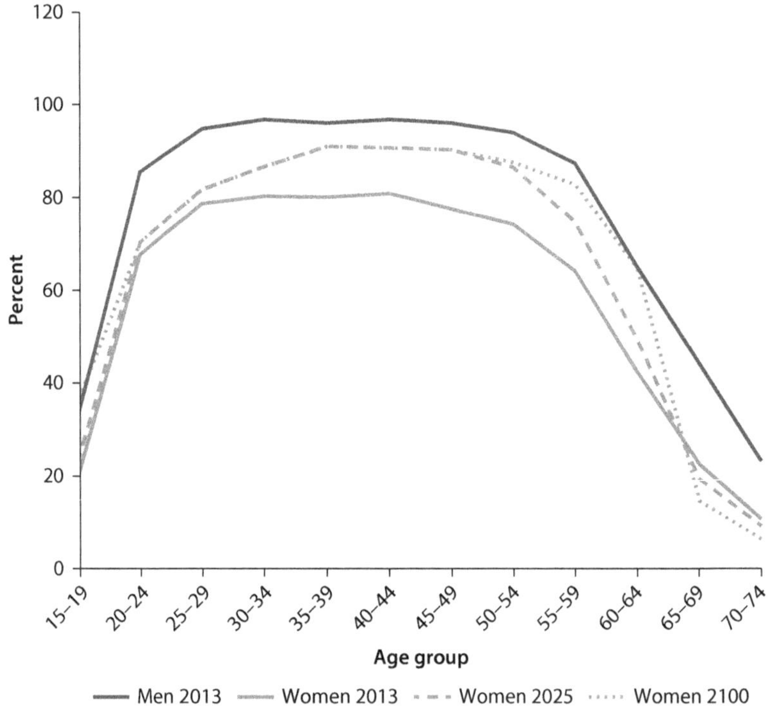

Source: Elaboration based on population forecasts.

other words, if the population remained fixed at 2013 levels. In this case, the rates would grow substantially, reaching a value of 62 percent among women and an overall rate of 68.1 percent (figure 7.24).

As in the previous scenario, it is interesting to evaluate the productivity trajectories that can be linked with these participation rates. Once again, total labor income is calculated based on the values observed for economically active individuals in 2013, differentiating by gender and age group. This total labor income is divided by the number of total economically active individuals to forecast the trajectory of labor productivity.

It should be kept in mind that our use of labor income for Uruguay from 2013 means that the income gap between men and women is not closed. In the reference countries, the differences between wages for each gender are significantly less than in Uruguay, which explains, among other things, their lower gap in labor force participation. It could be expected that the mass inclusion of women in the labor market would occur in a context of reducing the salary gaps, but this is an aspect that this chapter does not study. However, for illustrative purposes, a second alternative is presented in which the gender gaps for income are closed, as the result of the gradual increase in female incomes over a 50-year time horizon.[12] In this way, from 2063 on labor income for women and men by age group

Figure 7.24 Forecast of the Economic Activity Rate, Increasing the Female Economic Activity Rate with and without Aging, 2013–2100

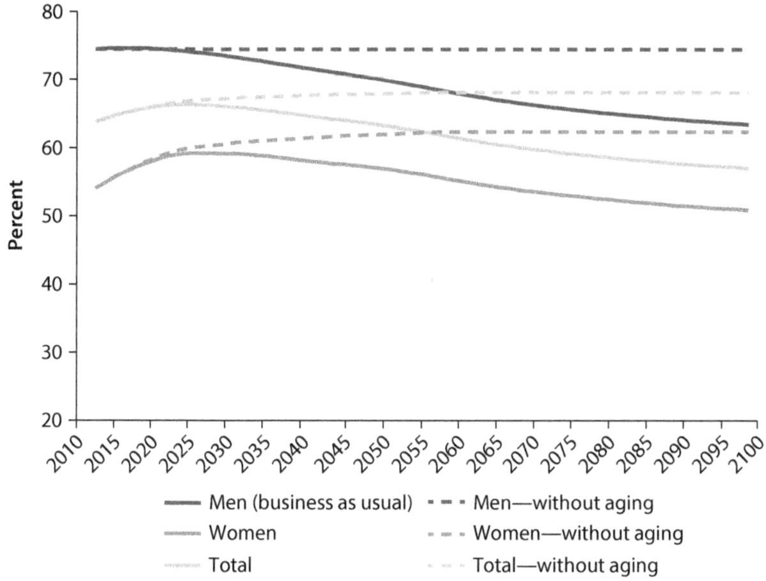

Source: Elaboration based on population forecasts.

would be the same. To calculate total labor income, the total number of economically active women is multiplied by average female income, which is obtained from this projected evolution, with the same calculation carried out for men, keeping their labor income constant at 2013 levels for each age group. This exercise is not free of problems because it is to be expected that men's salaries will fall to close the gaps, but it serves as an upper limit for the evolution of productivity.

In both exercises, productivity increases in the first half of the period under analysis and subsequently stagnates (figure 7.25). The reasons for the productivity increase are the same as in the previous scenario: the greater proportion of older individuals, whose labor income is higher than that of young people. During the period in which the income gaps are closed in Scenario 2.2, the productivity growth rate is higher because all women's salaries, both those that were already in the labor market and those that entered, increase to reach the level of men's salaries. Once the gap is closed (2064), the productivity growth rate responds to demographic factors and the projected increases in women's labor force participation rate, which causes them to match the figures observed in Scenario 2.1.

In terms of productivity levels, in the scenario in which the income gap is not closed, productivity is lower than in the exercise in which the gaps are closed and less than in the demographic scenario. This is because the women that enter the labor market will receive income lower than their male counterparts, in addition

Figure 7.25 Labor Productivity Growth Rate, Increasing Rates of Female Economic Activity Scenario, 2014–2100

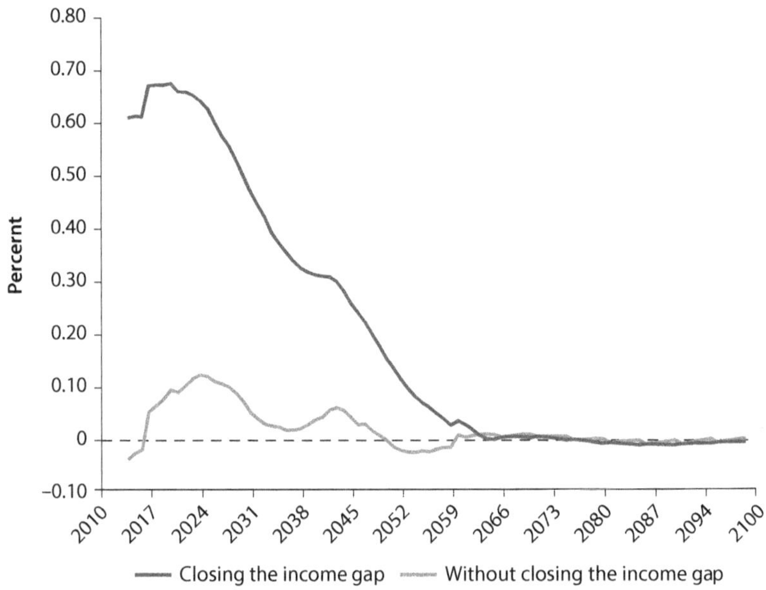

Sources: Elaboration based on the Instituto Nacional de Estadística (National Institute of Statistics) Continuous Household Survey 2013 and population forecasts.

to being below the average income in the economy. In any case, because the women that have not yet joined the labor market are less educated (see figure 7.10), and the sectors that they traditionally join are low productivity (services, domestic labor, and care services), productivity could be lower even in the context of a reduction in the salary gap between the genders for work with similar characteristics.

On the other hand, the entry of more workers into the economy creates an increase in the level of per capita GDP in comparison to the previous scenario. In any case, the dominance of the demographic factor cannot be avoided, which leads to a fall in GDP during the second half of the period under analysis in the two scenarios (figure 7.26). Closing the salary gap leads to increased GDP growth while the gap is being closed and a higher GDP for the entire period.

The average annual growth rate during the period is 0.06 percent if the income gaps are not closed and 0.05 percent if they are closed, which signifies an improvement with respect to the previous scenario, which exhibited a negative rate of 0.12 percent. However, to maintain the same growth rates that have been seen during the last 30 years, productivity would have to grow an average of 2.57 percent annually in the first alternative and 2.58 percent in the second, while the endogenous rates are 0.02 percent and 0.03 percent, respectively. This means that exogenous factors must contribute the missing 2.5 percent of the increase in productivity.

Figure 7.26 Evolution of Per Capita GDP, Increasing Rates of Female Economic Activity Scenario, 2013–2100

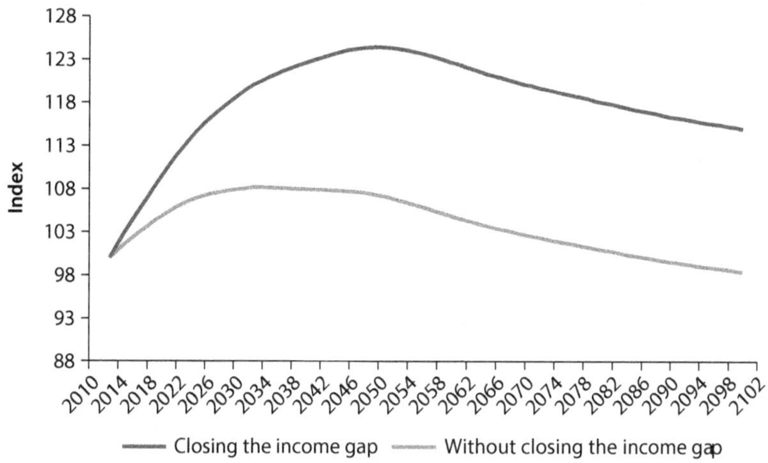

Sources: Elaboration based on the Instituto Nacional de Estadística (National Institute of Statistics) Continuous Household Survey 2013 and population forecasts.
Note: 2013 = 100.

This scenario is more encouraging than the previous one, although the increase in female labor force participation is not able to reverse the strong weight of the demographic factors. The reduction in the economic activity rate remains in the long term, even when an increase is achieved in the short term and the specific rates for each age group in 2100 are higher than those in 2013. The productivity increase is similar to that observed in the demographic scenario, but higher GDP growth rates are achieved. In any case, it is not possible to avoid that GDP begins to fall in 2045, all else remaining constant.

Scenario 3—Increase in the Education Level of the Economically Active Population

The descriptive analysis performed in the "Labor Participation and Productivity: Recent Evolution" section contributes various elements that signal the importance of the education level as a key variable for forecasting labor force participation and labor productivity. First, economic activity rates grow substantially with education level, and the same occurs with labor income. Second, the last 30 years have seen an increase in school attendance and the number of years of education, but the Uruguayan population's education level is still low compared to developed countries, and even when compared to the levels seen in other countries in the region. This indicates that it is imperative that the country increase the population's education level to drive both the increase in economic activity rates as well as productivity levels.

In the chapter dedicated to education in this volume, the authors present two scenarios with increases in enrollment at the secondary and tertiary levels, which signify substantial increases in the education level of the economically active population. Based on these inputs, a scenario is constructed that forecasts the economic activity rate and productivity associated with the enrollments presented in chapter 6. The scenario in which full coverage of basic secondary education is achieved and over-age enrollment is eliminated is used as a foundation (Scenario 2 from chapter 6). One of the methodological challenges consists of converting the enrollment forecasts (flow) to forecasts of the education level (stock) of the economically active population. Five education levels are considered, which enables us to differentiate in levels of labor force participation and income: completed primary education, incomplete basic secondary education, completed basic secondary to completed upper secondary, incomplete tertiary, and completed tertiary.

The number of individuals per education level is elaborated based on the assumptions detailed below, which are consistent with those utilized in chapter 6.

For the forecasts corresponding to secondary education:

- The working-age population includes individuals age 15 and older.
- Individuals age 15 and older who in 2013 had completed primary education or the basic cycle maintain that education level for the rest of their lives. The same occurs for those who had reached up to incomplete tertiary education or who no longer attended the education system, and for those with completed tertiary education. In these cases, the survival of these individuals is calculated by aging the cohorts based on the population forecasts.[13]
- The "incomplete basic secondary" level emerges from aggregating the individuals that belong to the working-age population (those age 15 and older in this scenario) who still attend that level. Because the theoretical age to study at this level is between 12 and 14, all of the individuals that are working age (age 15 and older) and attend the basic secondary level do so as part of the over-age enrollment. Thus, to calculate the number of potentially economically active individuals that possess an incomplete basic secondary level and attend the education system, the over-age enrollment ratio for this level is applied to its enrollment for each year. This proportion is consistent with the forecasts presented in the chapter on education.
- Finally, the "upper secondary" level is obtained as the difference.

For the tertiary level:

- We consider that faculty and teaching staff behave in the same manner as the rest of the tertiary level.
- The initial enrollment (for 2013) is calculated by applying the percentage of individuals that state they are attending tertiary education from the

Instituto Nacional de Estadística (National Institute of Statistics) 2013 Continuous Household Survey (Encuesta Continua de Hogares; ECH).

- ECH (3.68 percent) to the population forecast for that year.
- The number of graduates from tertiary education is calculated to be consistent with the forecasts presented in chapter 6. The graduates who finished this level during the previous year are added to the population with a completed university education. To age the graduates, the survival rate for 25-year-old individuals in 2013 is applied to them. Thus we obtain the stock of the economically active population with "completed tertiary" education.
- To calculate the incoming students at the tertiary level, we consider the proportion of new attendees for the year relative to the enrollment from the previous year. This rate is multiplied by the value of the previous year's enrollment. These incoming students are added to those who continue attending in order to obtain the new enrollment. The number of individuals that continue attending is obtained as the difference between the previous year's enrollment and the number of graduates.
- The number of individuals with "incomplete tertiary" education is obtained by adding the enrollment for the year to the number of individuals with a partial tertiary education that no longer attend the education system.

The enrollment forecasts signify, in the first place, that individuals with only a primary education will disappear because the entire population is able to complete this level. The same occurs for those at the incomplete basic cycle level, once full coverage is achieved and over-age enrollment is eliminated. On the other hand, the proportion of the population with completed tertiary education and with upper secondary education increases significantly. From 2050 on, less than 15 percent of the population age 15 or older would possess an incomplete basic secondary education or a lower education level. The percentage of individuals with completed or incomplete tertiary education grows from 18 percent of the population over age 14 in 2013 to 50 percent in 2100. This signifies an average growth in the population with tertiary education of 0.37 percentage points per year, which is a reasonable hypothesis given that this growth was 0.32 points per year between 1981 and 2013.

Once the population forecast by education level is obtained, the economic activity rates for each level during each year must be obtained. Because we do not have information for education levels disaggregated by age and gender, we must carry out an additional exercise to obtain economic activity rates that incorporate the expected changes in the makeup of the population by age that result from the demographic forecasts. To do this, we calculate the activity rate that the population for each year would have if all the individuals had each one of the education levels, maintaining the economic activity rates by age group and education level from 2013 (these rates are presented in table 7A.1 in annex 7A).[14] This assumes that all of the education levels have the same age structure and that they will evolve in the same way, which is a large assumption. However, this assumption enables us to isolate the effect of increasing the education level from other effects, such as the increase in the female economic activity rate and the increase in the economic activity rate among older adults.

The evolution of the economic activity rate based on the sole effect of increasing the population's education level is calculated by multiplying the rates aggregated by education level and year by the previously obtained stock of individuals per education level. The results are presented in figure 7.27. Note, to compare with the previous scenarios in this case we consider individuals age 15 and older, while previously individuals age 14 and older were considered. Because the participation of 14-year-olds (not considered in this scenario) is very low, the initial total rate in this exercise is higher than the rate in the two previous scenarios.

Sustained growth in the economic activity rate over the long term is not achieved in this scenario either; on the contrary, it falls by 8.1 percentage points during the period to a value of almost 56.5 percent in 2100. Accordingly, it is located in an intermediate position between the two previous scenarios.

As one might expect, the composition of economically active people by education level changes significantly. Figure 7.28 presents the evolution of the composition of the economically active by education level, grouping the secondary and tertiary levels. The proportion of workers with just a primary education is reduced until disappearing; in 2013, this group was nearly 30 percent of the population. At first, the number of economically active people with a secondary education (complete and incomplete) increases, but later it falls as the number of workers with a tertiary education increases (52 percent in 2013, 66 percent in

Figure 7.27 Forecast of the Economic Activity Rate with an Increase in the Education Level, 2013–2100

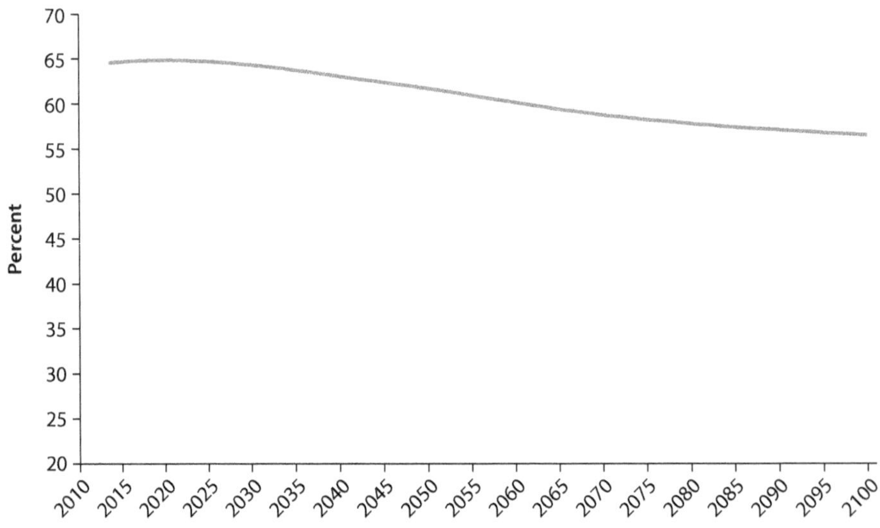

Sources: Elaboration based on the Instituto Nacional de Estadística (National Institute of Statistics) Continuous Household Survey 2013 and population forecasts.

Figure 7.28 Distribution of Economically Active Persons by Education Level, 2013–2100

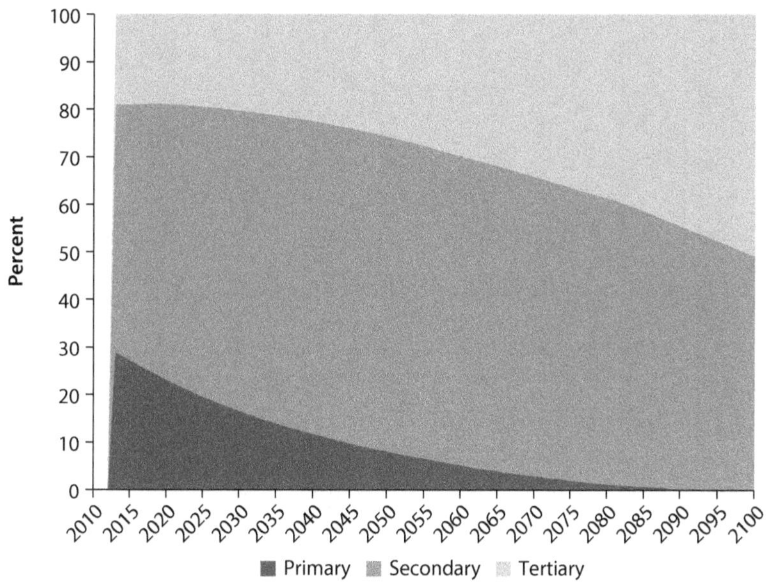

Sources: Elaboration based on the Instituto Nacional de Estadística (National Institute of Statistics) Continuous Household Survey 2013 and population forecasts.

2050, and 49 percent in 2100). The number of workers with a tertiary education increases throughout the period, both as a result of the increase in the number of individuals with a tertiary education as well as because of their high economic activity rate. In 2013, this level did not reach one-fifth of workers (19 percent), in 2050 it surpasses one-quarter of the economically active population (26 percent), and by 2070 it is more than one-third (34 percent). At the end of the period under analysis, more than half of the economically active population has some level of tertiary education (complete or incomplete) (51 percent).

To obtain the evolution of productivity, the level of labor income observed in 2013 for each education group is multiplied by the number of active workers in said group.[15] The results presented in figure 7.29 show that, in contrast to the previous scenarios, the productivity growth rate does not converge to zero, even when its growth stops around 2050, in the same way that occurred in the other cases. That productivity keeps growing is the result of the high income differential that increased education levels exhibit and the strong growth of these levels in this scenario. It should be kept in mind that we do not estimate general equilibrium effects, and the labor income differentials observed in 2013 are maintained throughout the period, which is a very simplistic assumption. These differentials show the different levels of productivity for each education level, but they are also the result of the relative numbers of workers in each level. One can expect that as the population's average education level increases, the skills premium will fall. In fact, in recent years a reduction in returns to education has

Figure 7.29 Labor Productivity Growth Rate, Increasing Education Level Scenario, 2014–2100

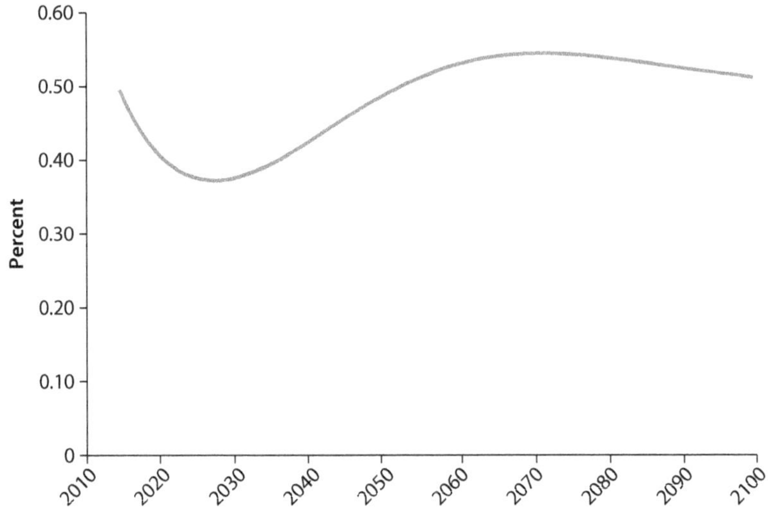

Sources: Elaboration based on the Instituto Nacional de Estadística (National Institute of Statistics) Continuous Household Survey 2013 and population forecasts.

been observed in the region, caused at least in part by an increase in the population's accumulated education level (Gasparini and Lustig 2011; López-Calva and Lustig 2010; Paes de Barros, de Carvalho, and Franco 2007).

In contrast with the two previous scenarios, in Scenario 3 per capita GDP's growth does not cease during the period under analysis (figure 7.30). The average growth rate during the period is positive and reaches 0.39 percent per year. However, this is still far from the average rate recorded during 1981–2013, which means that even in this more optimistic scenario additional factors are needed to maintain the growth levels observed in previous decades.

As in the previous scenarios, we calculate what the productivity growth rate would need to be to maintain that average GDP growth rate. Productivity should grow at an average of 2.60 percent per year during the period, but the scenario's figure is 0.48 percent. The distance to the goal is shorter compared to the rates calculated in the demographic scenario and the increasing female economic activity rate scenario because the productivity of the economically active population is higher than that recorded in the two previous scenarios.

This scenario is able to reverse the fall in GDP that the two previous scenarios exhibited thanks to the significant increase in the level of higher education and the existence of large productivity differentials between education levels. In this case, the forecast's limitation in estimating general equilibrium effects becomes evident: one must ask if these differentials will remain once upper secondary and tertiary education become more generalized and lower education levels tend to disappear. Nonetheless, the increase in the education level is not sufficient on its

Figure 7.30 Evolution of Per Capita GDP, Increasing Education Level Scenario, 2013–2100

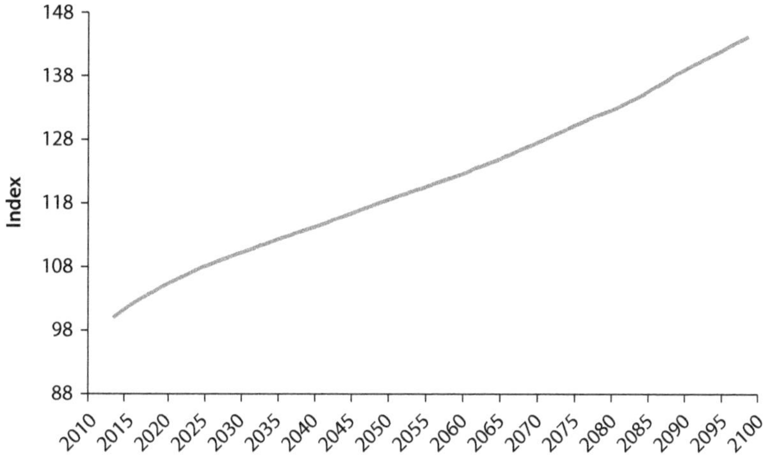

Sources: Elaboration based on the Instituto Nacional de Estadística (National Institute of Statistics) Continuous Household Survey 2013 and population forecasts.
Note: 2013 = 100.

own to maintain the economy's current activity rates, nor is it enough to reach the average GDP growth rates needed to maintain the growth rates of recent decades.

Comparison of the Scenarios

In the following section we present the principal results of the three proposed scenarios. The demographic scenario (Scenario 1) exhibits the lowest economic activity rates because the only effects come from demographics (figure 7.31). The aging of the population means that the proportion of older age groups grows, and these groups exhibit lower economic activity rates than younger groups. The second scenario seeks to alleviate this fall by increasing the economic activity rate among women, because room exists for them to enter the labor market. By matching the economic activity rates for women seen in Sweden, we achieve the highest economic activity rates seen in the three scenarios. However, the scenario is not able to reverse the aforementioned effect, and the rate falls in the long term after growing during the early years. The final scenario, with an increase in the education level that emerges from the enrollment forecast carried out in the chapter on education, lands in the middle, increasing the distance between it and the demographic scenario as the population's education levels increase over time.

The first two scenarios do not manage to maintain positive productivity growth rates in the long term, exhibiting null or negative rates after 2050 (figure 7.32). The productivity increase observed is the result of the growth of the number of older workers, and these workers' average productivity is higher than that of younger groups whose relative proportion of the labor force decreases.

Figure 7.31 Evolution of the Economic Activity Rate for Each Scenario, 2013–2100

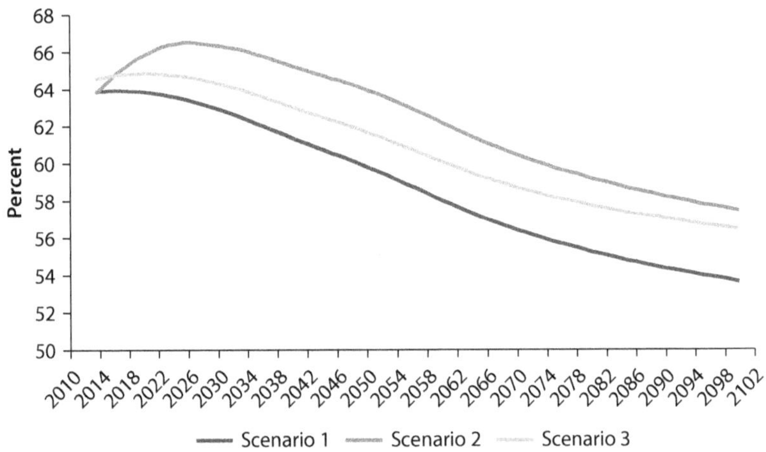

Figure 7.32 Evolution of the Productivity Growth Rate for Each Scenario, 2013–2100

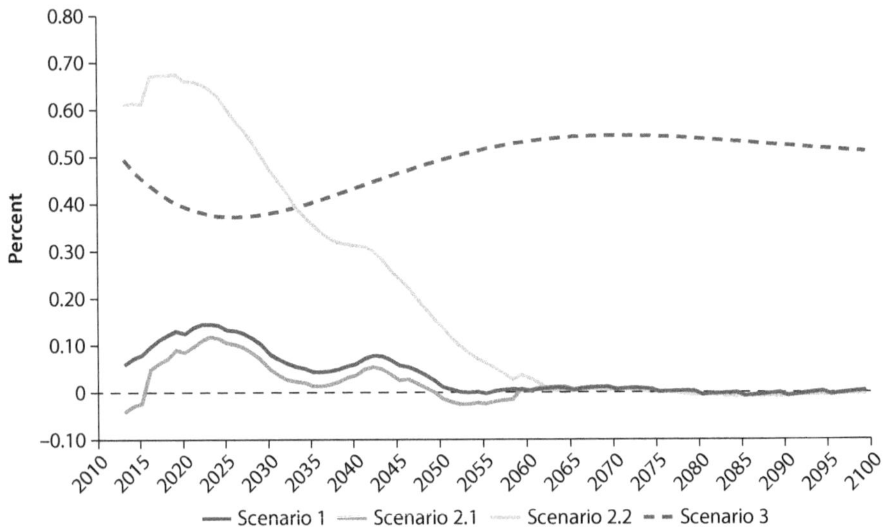

In Scenario 2.1, we observe the lowest levels of productivity that result from the previous effect and because women that join the labor market have lower productivity than both men and the average for the economy, which causes average productivity to fall. This effect is reversed in Scenario 2.2 because salaries for all female workers are increased to reach the salary observed for men in 2063. Therefore, the productivity growth rate records high values until this point and subsequently matches the rate estimated for the scenario without closing the salary gap. In the first two cases, productivity's average growth rate is located in values close to zero: 0.04 percent and 0.02 percent average per year for Scenario 1 and Scenario 2.1, respectively, and reaches 0.2 percent in Scenario 2.2 due to the high values obtained at the beginning of the period.

The third scenario is the only one that is able to increase productivity and avoid the stagnant state that the other two scenarios exhibit; however, after 2050 the growth level stabilizes, just as occurred in the previous scenarios. This is principally the result of the existence of a skills premium and the significant increase of higher education levels. The average productivity growth rate that emerges from this scenario is 0.48 percent per year. However, this growth rests on a very strong simplistic assumption that the income differentials between education levels will remain the same. In any case, on its own it is not able to reach the productivity growth rate needed to maintain the levels of GDP growth seen during the past 30 years, despite being the scenario that contributes the highest growth.

The demographic scenario as well as the increasing economic activity rate without closing the gaps scenario results in a decrease in per capita GDP in the long term. In the other two scenarios, the economy is able to achieve per capita GDP levels in 2100 that are higher than those observed in 2013. Only the third scenario is able to maintain constant GDP growth in the long term, while Scenario 2.1 entails a significant increase while the salary gap is closed, but demographics win out, resulting in a decrease in the second half of the period under analysis. It must be highlighted that GDP begins to fall in the first two scenarios after 2045 (figure 7.33). This point coincides with the year in which the growth rate of the surplus-generating population (those that receive more income than they consume) is negative and lower than that of the deficit-generating population.

Figure 7.33 Evolution of Per Capita GDP, Increasing Education Level Scenario, 2013–2100

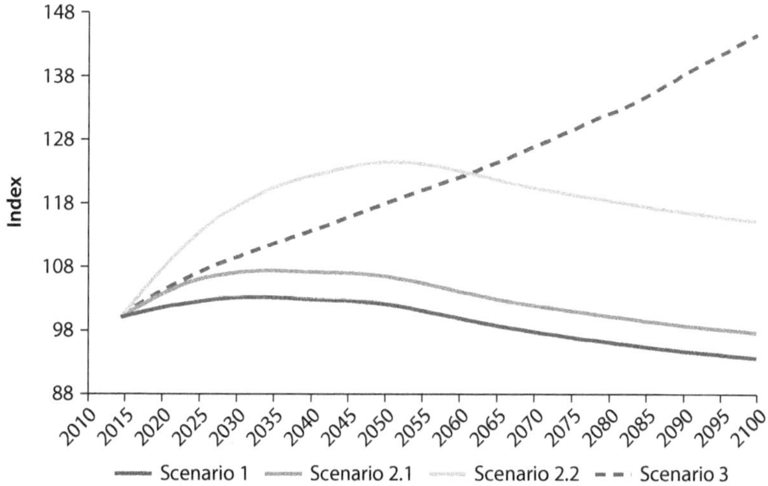

Note: 2013 = 100.

Table 7.6 Summary of the Results for Each Scenario

<table>
<tr><th></th><th>Scenario 1</th><th>Scenario 2.1</th><th>Scenario 2.2</th><th>Scenario 3</th></tr>
<tr><td>Economic activity rate in 2100 (%)</td><td>53.6</td><td colspan="2">57.0</td><td>56</td></tr>
<tr><td>Change in the economic activity rate, 2014–2100 (%)</td><td>−10.2</td><td colspan="2">−6.8</td><td>−8.1</td></tr>
<tr><td>Productivity in 2100 (2014 = 100) (%)</td><td>103</td><td>102</td><td>118</td><td>151</td></tr>
<tr><td>Average annual productivity growth (%)</td><td>0.04</td><td>0.20</td><td>0.20</td><td>0.48</td></tr>
<tr><td>Average annual implict growth of GDP (%)</td><td>−0.12</td><td>−0.06</td><td>0.12</td><td>0.39</td></tr>
<tr><td>Per capita GDP in 2100 (2014 = 100) (%)</td><td>94</td><td>98</td><td>115</td><td>144</td></tr>
<tr><td>Average annual productivity growth needed to maintain historical GDP growth rate (%)</td><td>2.66</td><td colspan="2">2.58</td><td>2.60</td></tr>
</table>

Table 7.6 summarizes the principal characteristics of the scenarios forecast in figure 7.33.

The Effects of Changes in Worker Productivity

In the previous section we constructed potential scenarios for the evolution of the economic activity rate and we analyzed what these scenarios could mean for economic growth and changes in productivity, if no other changes occurred, particularly if the productivity levels per person by gender, age, and education level remained at 2013 levels. Basically, the first scenario showed purely demographic changes, and the other two assumed the existence of exogenous changes in the economic activity rate (beyond demographics). In all of the cases, although individual productivity (by gender and education level) did not change, aggregate productivity for the economy as a whole experienced changes determined by the variations in the composition of the workforce in terms of gender and age.

In the long-term view, it is unreasonable to assume that individual productivity will not grow, although it is also difficult to create scenarios about potential exogenous variations in this parameter. However, an analysis of the available information for the central variables may provide some interesting references.

Figure 7.34 presents the evolution of per capita GDP if we perform the same exercise as in Scenario 1 backward, that is, if we apply the economic activity rates and relative income from 2013 to the population observed between 1981 and 2013. The variation in per capita GDP is very small, especially compared to that observed during the period. The total variation between 1981 and 2013 would be 4.3 percent while the variation of observed GDP is 83.9 percent. This suggests that the principal source of GDP variation is not a component of the makeup of the workforce, but rather factors that are exogenous to demographics, such as technological change, innovation, and institutional changes, among others.

Regarding the evolution of apparent productivity, in table 7.1 we can observe annual growth of 1.2 percent between 1981 and 2013. Along the same lines, the estimates created by the Economic History Department of the Institute of Economics[16] indicate that per capita GDP grew by 1 percent annually during 1906–2006.

Figure 7.34 Per Capita GDP Index, as Observed and Assuming Just the Effects of Composition of the Labor Force, 1981–2013

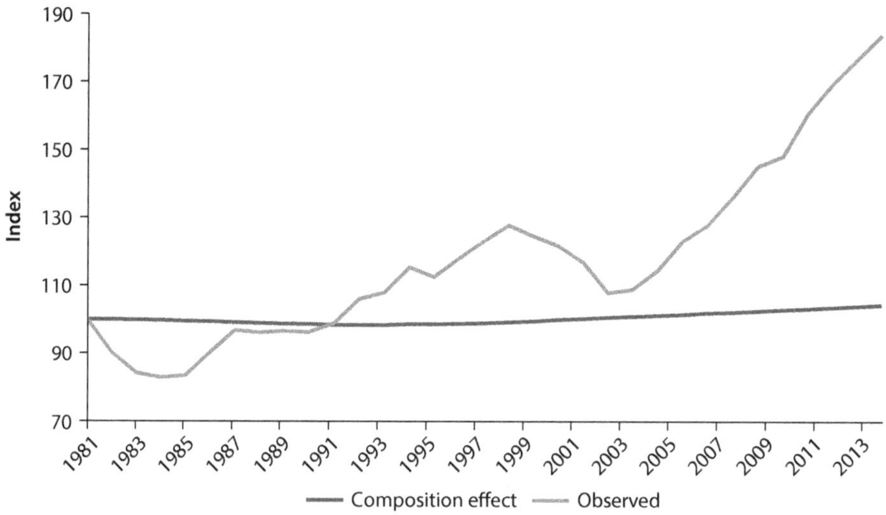

Source: Elaboration based on the Instituto Nacional de Estadística (National Institute of Statistics) Continuous Household Surveys 1981–2013.
Note: 1981 = 100.

When we analyze individuals' labor income, changes are highly dependent on the economic cycle, with small changes in the long term, which vary depending on the reference period. As table 7.1 illustrated, labor income exhibited an annual variation of 0.1 percent from 1981 to 2013, but if we consider 1986–2013, the annual variation increases to 1.4 percent. At the same time, it varies by age group, gender, and education level, as table 7.7 shows.

Below, we add to the three previously analyzed scenarios, combining them with exogenous variations in productivity levels. The magnitude of these variations emerges from historical series of productivity and income data analyzed in previous paragraphs.

Exogenous Productivity Growth of 1.2 Percent per Year

First, we incorporate a business-as-usual growth rate for productivity (and therefore for its proxy, labor income), using the rate observed for annual apparent productivity growth from 1986 to 2013 (1.2 percent). Because we do not have information on disaggregated apparent productivity, we apply the same growth rate to all of the age, gender, and education level groups, which means that the trajectories presented signify an increase in the forecast rates for each scenario of 1.2 percent, which is applied as a trend. The average growth rate for productivity during the period would be 1.24 percent in Scenario 1, 1.22 percent and 1.40 percent in Scenarios 2.1 and 2.2, respectively, and 1.69 percent in Scenario 3.

Table 7.7 Labor Income Growth Rates among the Economically Active Population
constant 2006 Ur$ (%)

	Observed growth rate, 1986–2013		
Age group and education level	*Total*	*Women*	*Men*
14–19	1.1	1.2	1.1
20–24	1.0	1.3	0.9
25–29	1.0	1.4	0.7
30–34	1.2	1.9	0.8
35–39	1.3	2.3	0.9
40–44	1.0	1.8	0.8
45–49	1.4	2.4	1.1
50–54	1.8	2.9	1.6
55–59	1.6	2.9	1.5
60–64	1.3	2.5	1.3
65–69	2.1	2.7	2.1
70–74	2.3	4.2	1.9
75+	0.8	1.4	0.9
Total	**1.4**	**2.3**	**1.2**
Up to primary		0.6	
Incomplete basic cycle		0.7	
Complete and incomplete upper		0.8	
Incomplete tertiary		1.0	
Complete tertiary		1.5	

Source: Elaboration based on the Instituto Nacional de Estadística (National Institute of Statistics) Continuous Household Surveys 1986 and 2013.

Figure 7.35 presents the trajectory that per capita GDP would exhibit if we incorporated the trend. All of the scenarios show an increase in per capita GDP, in response to the trend we introduced. As in the exercises carried out earlier, the highest GDP is obtained in the education level improvement scenario.

Growth of Estimated Productivity Based on Labor Income by Gender, Age, and Education Level, 1986–2013

In this exercise we opt to assume an exogenous productivity growth trend equivalent to the change observed in labor income during 1986–2013 for each of the age and gender groups (Scenarios 1 and 2) as well as education level groups (Scenario 3). The corresponding growth rate is applied to each group (see table 7.7). For example, for women ages 50–54 a 2.9 percent per year trend is applied, while a rate of 0.7 percent is applied to men ages 25–29.

In this case, we achieve significantly higher growth rates than those observed in the previous scenarios, particularly compared to Scenarios 1 and 2 (figure 7.36). This is because the growth rates applied are higher for the older age groups, which are the groups that make up a larger proportion of the total population during the period under analysis. Accordingly, demographics work in favor of productivity increases.

Figure 7.35 Evolution of Per Capita GDP for Each Scenario, with 1.2 Percent Annual Trend, 2013–2100

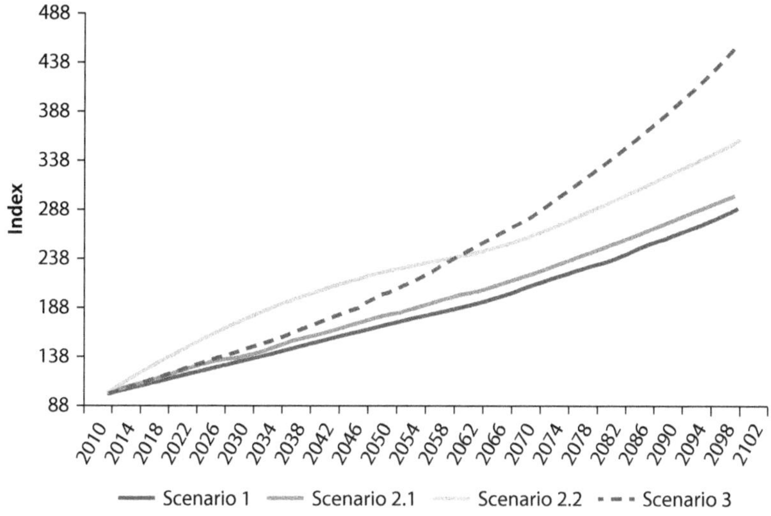

Note: 2013 = 100.

Figure 7.36 Evolution of Per Capita GDP for Each Scenario, with Trend for Characteristics, 2013–2100

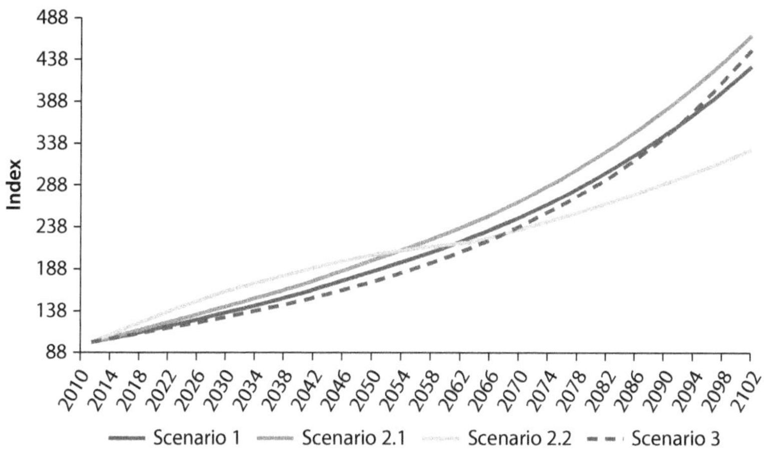

Note: 2013 = 100.

This difference in the growth rates of labor income between men and women also explains why Scenario 2.2 lags behind. Because the growth rates for female incomes are higher than those for men, on average women's incomes exceed those of men from 2046 forward. In Scenario 2.2, men's income levels are applied to all workers once the gap is closed (2063), which in this case means that the incomes that are applied are lower than in Scenarios 1 and 2.1 from 2046 forward.

Sustained growth is achieved in all of the scenarios. In contrast with previous exercises, the worst result is obtained from Scenario 2.2 for reasons that have already been covered.

Final Comments

The demographic changes that Uruguay will face in the coming decades will entail important changes in the labor market. Research in this chapter presents exercises that enable us to delineate the future trajectories of economic participation and its consequences for economic growth. The simulation exercise enables us to observe that, without any other changes, population aging would lead to a significant fall in the economic activity rate, and although the associated labor productivity would increase during the initial years, it would later begin a significant process of decline. The combination of the trajectory of both variables would suggest significant decreases in overall economic activity, and a slight fall in per capita GDP.

The expected increase in female labor force participation could help ease this effect, but it would not have significant impacts in the long term, meaning that the economic activity rate would eventually fall. Changes in demographics and female labor behaviors are not sufficient so that associated labor productivity would be at a level to allow for sustained economic growth, and per capita GDP would remain practically stable at the 2013 level. The situation would be slightly better if the salary gaps between men and women were closed, and even though the economy would not exhibit an aggregate growth trend, per capita GDP could increase slightly during the next 40 years and subsequently decrease slowly, settling slightly above 2013 levels in 2100. Moreover, it must be pointed out that in order for more women to be incorporated into the labor market, very significant changes in the division of paid and unpaid tasks within households would be necessary, as well as strengthening public policies to support care services. This means that the second scenario involves very important challenges in terms of public policies. On the other hand, if the salary penalty that women experience in the labor market were eliminated, the economy would reach higher levels of productivity associated with the second scenario. This outcome alerts us to another important area of intervention for public policies. Additionally, it is necessary to think about where the women that would enter the workforce in such large numbers would work. In the context of the aging process that motivates the reflections in this book, it is possible to think about a reconfiguration of the care system and in the incorporation of women to paid care systems. Questions arise related to the productivity of these jobs as well as issues related to re-creating the traditional roles of men and women, this time within the labor market, and perpetuating gender segregation in the labor market.

Finally, the third scenario proposes an optimistic situation in terms of very important growth of tertiary education, which again requires specific public policies for it to become a reality. In this scenario, the economy would achieve increases in associated productivity without any exogenous changes in productivity. These changes are strictly the result of changing the composition of the supply of labor and increasing the number of highly educated workers. It must be kept in mind that the strong expansion of tertiary education could entail very significant reconfigurations in the profile of the supply of labor, depending on the options and fields of study that are prioritized. However, this scenario is also unable to reverse the fall in the overall activity rate in the economy, nor avoid the stagnation of productivity growth, although it does remain above zero in contrast to the previous scenarios. In this final scenario it is reasonable to expect a significant change in the salary premium associated with higher education, an aspect that was not dealt with in the present chapter.

The outcomes observed in the simulations discussed here clearly show that the changes in the composition of the labor force would not, in any case, be able to promote increases in labor productivity that would enable the economy to maintain the levels of growth observed during the last three decades. In effect, all of these exercises assume that individual productivity does not change, and the changes that would occur in the trajectory of overall productivity are a response to the demographic and labor force participation assumptions that are applied to it (demographic change, increase in female economic activity, increase in the education level). These productivity changes that emerge as a result of the changes in the composition of the labor supply are insufficient to maintain a sustained growth trajectory. Thus, such a path will have to emerge from other channels, such as changes to physical capital, technological change, changes in productive structures, and changes to institutions, among others.

As a result, we proposed additional simulations in which a trend in individual labor incomes was applied to reflect exogenous changes in labor productivity. In the first case the observed growth trend in productivity from 1986 to 2013 (1.2 percent) was applied, and in the second the average growth rate for labor income for each of the age, gender, and education level groups was applied in the same period. Both exercises achieved sustained growth in per capita GDP.

Thus, it is clear that the effect of the composition of the supply of labor resulting from demographic changes, or even behavior changes like the increase in female labor force participation, would generate a period of growth in productivity, and therefore GDP, but it would be exhausted before the middle of the century. Therefore, the driver of longer-term growth rests in the hands of external forces that provoke increases in individual and overall productivity.

Annex 7A: Some Key Labor Indicators

Figure 7A.1 Evolution of the Economic Activity Rate among Youth by Age Group and Gender, Urban Population, 1981–2013

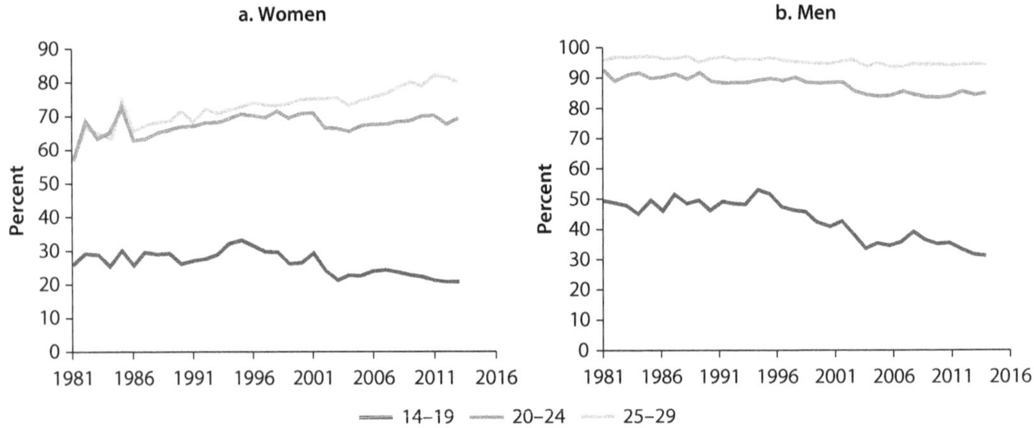

Source: Instituto Nacional de Estadística (National Institute of Statistics) Continuous Household Surveys 1981–2013.
Note: Urban localities have 5,000 or more residents.

Figure 7A.2 Evolution of the Real Labor Income Index for Employed Persons, 1981–2013

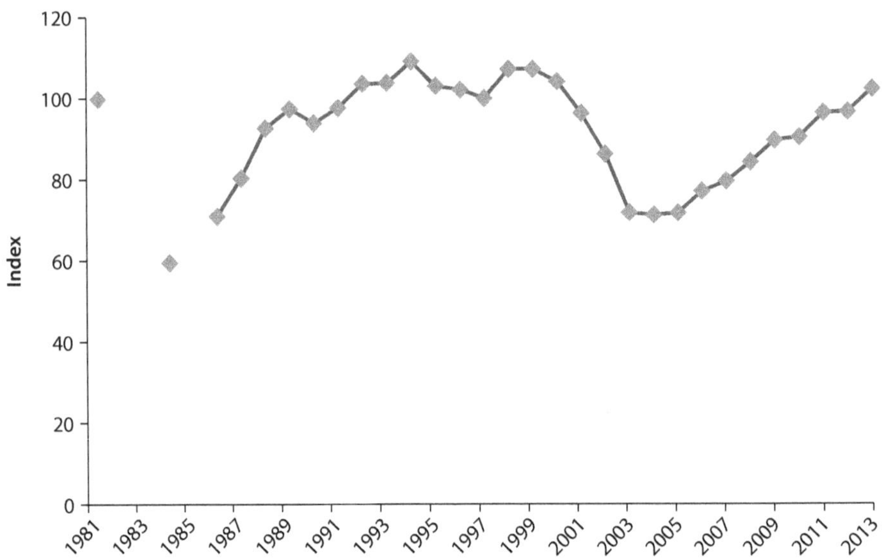

Source: Elaboration based on the Instituto Nacional de Estadística (National Institute of Statistics) Continuous Household Surveys 1981–2013.
Note: 1981 = 100; constant 2006 prices (Ur$).

Table 7A.1 Economic Activity Rate by Education Level and Age Group, Entire Country, 2013
percent

Age group	*Primary*	*Incomplete basic secondary*	*Upper secondary*	*Incomplete tertiary*	*Complete tertiary*
14–19	44.3	32.9	29.0	23.5	0.0
20–24	72.6	81.1	84.8	60.7	91.8
25–29	73.6	83.7	89.6	86.0	97.8
30–34	76.8	84.4	90.6	92.6	97.8
35–39	78.6	87.6	90.6	93.1	97.6
40–44	79.8	87.5	91.2	92.9	96.9
45–49	78.2	85.0	89.2	91.5	96.2
50–54	76.2	81.4	85.7	89.6	95.0
55–59	70.7	72.3	76.7	83.2	85.7
60–64	49.4	51.7	55.3	56.4	58.9
65–69	32.2	33.5	30.4	35.2	37.6
70–74	15.5	16.0	17.4	16.1	13.2
75–79	9.0	8.8	8.8	9.7	10.9
80–84	2.9	1.6	4.0	3.8	4.5
85–89	2.1	3.3	2.2	5.3	3.8
90+	1.1	0.0	1.4	0.0	0.0

Source: Instituto Nacional de Estadística (National Institute of Statistics) Continuous Household Survey 2013.

Notes

1. Verónica Amarante (veronica.amarante@cepal.org) and Maira Colacce (maira.colacce@cepal.org), Economic Commission for Latin America and the Caribbean (ECLAC) Montevideo office. We would like to thank Rodrigo Arim, Rafael Rofman, Ignacio Apella, and the rest of the authors of this book for their comments.
2. Urban localities of 5,000 or more residents make up approximately 85 percent of the Uruguayan population.
3. For more detail on the evolution of the educational dimension of the Uruguayan population see the chapter on education.
4. The fall observed during the crisis may reflect certain rigidities in the labor markets that mean that during times of crisis, the drop in GDP is not mirrored by a similar fall in the number of workers, although the effects of the crisis could be seen in the number of hours worked. The fall in employed persons between 1999 and 2003 was 9 percent, while the reduction in GDP was almost 14 percent.
5. Throughout this chapter we utilize total liquid labor income, which includes other cash and in-kind payments.
6. It should be kept in mind that in this chapter we utilize labor income figures that come from the Continuous Household Survey (Encuesta Continua de Hogares; ECH) instead of utilizing labor income figures from the National Transfer Accounts that were calculated in chapter 3. This is due to the fact that we require a level of disaggregation (by gender and education level) that is not currently available for the National Transfer Accounts.

7. The economic activity rates that we use as references in this exercise refer to the rates for localities with 5,000 or more residents because we do not have information for the entire country for 1981. At the same time, the population forecasts available for the 1981–90 period present the age 80+ population aggregated in a single category. In order to calculate the rates observed in 2013, we follow the same method so that the figures are comparable: The rates by gender and age observed for localities with 5,000 or more residents are applied to the 2013 population by single-year age groups, utilizing the open group of 80+ year-olds. This means that the rates we obtain differ from the rates presented in the previous sections of this chapter.
8. Labor income is considered in constant pesos from December 2006, and includes all income from individuals' labor, except for the National Health Care Fund (Fondo Nacional de Salud; FONASA). They represent liquid income. We consider five-year age groups from 14 to 74 years old, while the final age group is open-ended and includes all individuals age 75 and older. As has been previously mentioned, the income figures used come from the ECH and do not match the data presented in chapter 3.
9. Only the specific rates for age groups are modified in order to reach those observed in these countries. No assumption is made regarding postponing entry into the labor market as a result of remaining in the education system.
10. The statistics for these countries consider that the working-age population begins at 15 years old, while in Uruguay this limit is set at 14 years old. For the estimates, individuals age 14 are considered in the same manner as those age 15.
11. Alternatively, the forecast was carried out considering the growth rates for each age group, but this option was discarded because in the 15- to 19-year-old age group the target rate was not reached by 2100.
12. The trajectory of women's labor income is modeled using a quadratic function.
13. An example is offered to illustrate. The percentages of the individuals who have completed up to primary education by single-year age groups as reported by the 2013 household survey are applied to the population forecasts for this year by single-year age groups. Thus the total number of individuals with up to a primary education is obtained for 2013. Those same percentages of individuals with up to a primary education are applied to the population forecasts for the years that follow, but the ages are advanced by one year. In other words, we apply the percentage of 28-year-old individuals with up to a primary education from 2013 to the forecasts of 29-year-old individuals in 2014, and so forth until the cohorts disappear. Due to the differences observed between the genders, the process is carried out separately for women and men.
14. For example, in order to calculate the economic activity rate of the up to primary education level in 2030, we work as if the entire population was at this education level (up to primary education completed): the economic activity rates are applied for each age group of those who had this level in 2013 to the total number of persons in these age groups in 2030, according to the population forecasts. Thus, we obtain the total number of economically active persons as if all of these individuals' education level was having completed up to primary education, while maintaining the economic activity rates by education level and age group from 2013. The total economic activity rate for this level in 2030 is calculated, which will be utilized to obtain the estimate of the economically active individuals with that education level in 2030.
15. As in the case of the economic activity rates, by keeping the labor income from 2013 constant we operate as if the age structure of economically active persons did not

change in this respect. An additional exercise was carried out, assuming that the structure did change, just as was performed with the economic activity rates, and the results did not change substantially. Therefore, in an attempt to simplify the model, we decided to keep labor income constant from 2013.

16. School of Economic and Management Science of the University of the Republic.

References

Álvarez, I., N. Da Silva, A. Forteza, and I. Rossi. 2009. "El Retiro de los Trabajadores Uruguayos y la Seguridad Social." *Revista de Economía* 16 (2): 147–84.

———. 2010. "Qué Incentivos al Retiro Genera la Seguridad Social? El Caso Uruguayo." *Cuadernos de Economía* 47 (136): 217–48.

Blau, F. D., and L. M. Kahn. 2005. "Changes in the Labor Supply Behavior of Married Women: 1980–2000." NBER Working Paper Series 11230, National Bureau of Economic Research, Cambridge, MA.

Blundell, R., and T. MaCurdy. 1999. "Labor Supply: A Review of Alternative Approaches." *Handbook of Labor Economics* 3: 1559–695.

Bucheli, M. 2007. "Mercado de Trabajo Juvenil: Situación y Políticas." Serie Estudios y Perspectiva, Número 6, ECLAC, Montevideo.

Durán, V., G. Poplavski, and A. Vernengo. 2003. "Impacto de la Reforma de la Seguridad Social en la Edad de Retiro y la Evasión." Trabajo Monográfico de la Facultad de Ciencias Económicas y de Administración, Universidad de la República, Montevideo.

ECLAC (Economic Commission for Latin America and the Caribbean). 2014a. *Pactos para la Igualdad: Hacia un Futuro Sostenible*. Santiago de Chile: United Nations.

———. 2014b. *Panorama Social de América Latina 2014*. Santiago de Chile: United Nations.

Espino, A., and M. Leites. 2008. "Oferta Laboral Femenina en Uruguay: Evolución e Implicancias 1981–2006." Serie Documentos de Trabajo 07/08, Instituto de Economía, Universidad de la República, Montevideo.

Espino, A., M. Leites, and A. Machado. 2009. "Cambios en la Conducta de la Oferta Laboral Femenina: El Incremento de la Actividad de las Mujeres Casadas. Diagnóstico e Implicancias. Uruguay: 1981–2006." Serie Documentos de Trabajo 03/09, Instituto de Economía, Universidad de la República, Montevideo.

Filardo, V. 2010. "Transiciones a la Adultez y Educación." Cuadernos del UNFPA 4 (5), Montevideo.

González, L., and N. Lustig. 2011. *The Rise and Fall of Income Inequality in Latin America*. New York: Oxford University Press.

Goldin, C. 1990. *The Gender Gap: An Economic History of American Women*. New York: Cambridge University Press.

González, C., and M. Bucheli. 2014. "Bono Demográfico y Envejecimiento en Uruguay." Documento de Trabajo 10/14, Departamento de Economía, Universidad de la República, Montevideo.

INE (Instituto Nacional de Estadística [National Institute of Statistics]). 1981–2013. Continuous Household Survey. Montevideo.

Kaldewei, C., and J. Weller. 2013. "Empleo, Crecimiento Sostenible e Igualdad." Serie Macroeconomía del Desarrollo 145, ECLAC, Santiago de Chile.

López-Calva, L., and N. Lustig. 2010. *Declining Inequality in Latin America: A Decade of Progress?* Washington, DC: Brookings Institution Press.

OECD (Organisation for Economic Co-operation and Development). 2001. *Measuring Productivity: Measurement of Aggregate and Industry-Level Productivity Growth: OECD Manual.* Paris: OECD.

Paes de Barros, R., M. de Carvalho, and S. Franco. 2007. "O Papel das Transferencias Públicas na Queda Recente da Desigualdade de Renda Brasileira." *Desigualdade de Renda No Brasil: Uma Análise da Queda Recente* 2: 41– 86.

Riedel, M., and H. Hofer. 2013. *Determinants of the Transition from Work into Retirement.* Austrian Center for Labor Economics and the Analysis of the Welfare State, Johannes Kepler University, Linz, Austria.

Sanroman, G. 2006. "Returns to Schooling in Uruguay." *Revista de Economía* 13 (2): 171–200.

United Nations. 2014. *World Population Prospects: The 2012 Revision.* New York: United Nations.

CHAPTER 8

Demographic Transition in the International Context

Rafael Rofman and Ignacio Apella[1]

Introduction

Uruguay is currently in a very advanced stage of its first demographic transition as the oldest population in Latin America with fertility, mortality, and migration rates similar to those of some European countries. This chapter aims to place Uruguay in context with other countries to identify and quantify similarities and differences, and thus provide policy makers with guidance.

The chapter first describes Uruguay's demographic context compared with the rest of the world, in particular neighboring countries in the region, member countries of the Organisation for Economic Co-operation and Development (OECD), and selected Asian countries, including China, the Republic of Korea, and Japan. It then moves on to a comparative analysis of consumption and income profiles, and the life-cycle deficit. The fourth section discusses the generosity of public social spending, especially spending directed to finance education, pensions, and health care. To conclude, we offer some final reflections.

The Demographic Transition and the Demographic Dividend

As a consequence of the fall in fertility and mortality rates presented in chapter 2, people over age 65 are making up an ever-increasing proportion of the Uruguayan population. This phenomenon, which is slow and steady, is no different from what is happening in the rest of the world. Figure 8.1 presents the evolution of the population over age 65.

The population over age 65 will represent 22 percent of Uruguay's total population in 2050, and 30 percent in 2100, maintaining a profile similar to that of the group of OECD countries in this analysis. In effect, not just the starting point, but also the trend coincide significantly between Uruguay and those countries.

Comparison of Uruguay with other Latin American countries shows that in the long term the characteristics of all population profiles converge, but we

Figure 8.1 Percentage of the Population over Age 65, Uruguay and Selected Countries, 1950–2100

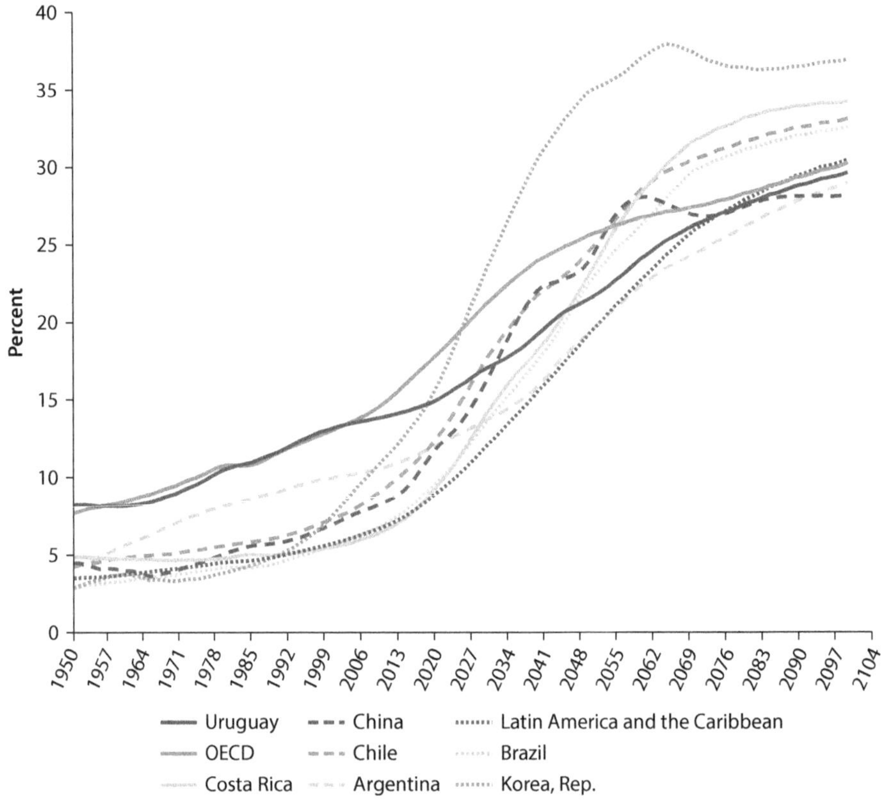

Source: United Nations, Population Division.
Note: OECD = Organisation for Economic Co-operation and Development.

identify significant differences in the numbers aged over 65. In effect, the pace of population aging in Latin America and the Caribbean will increase until reaching convergence in 2100. Based on these results, it can be suggested that Uruguay is now in a very advanced phase of its first demographic transition. The aging population is principally the product of a significant decline in fertility and to a lesser extent the fall in mortality. Figure 8.2 presents the historical evolution of fertility and a forecast for the rate and life expectancy at birth in Uruguay and selected countries.

As we can appreciate from the results in panel a, Uruguay's fertility rate maintains a historical trend and forecast similar to that seen in neighboring Argentina, at below three children per woman since 1955. Significant differences emerge when comparing Uruguay with countries like Brazil, China, the Republic of Korea, and with the aggregate for Latin America, which in 1955 exhibited significantly higher fertility. For example, as a whole, Latin America fell from a total fertility rate of 5.89 in 1955 to 2.27 in 2010, while in Uruguay it fell from 2.83 to 2.12 in the same period. In part, this explains the society's advanced aging process relative to most other countries in the region.

Figure 8.2 Total Fertility and Life Expectancy at Birth, Uruguay and Selected Countries, 1955–2100

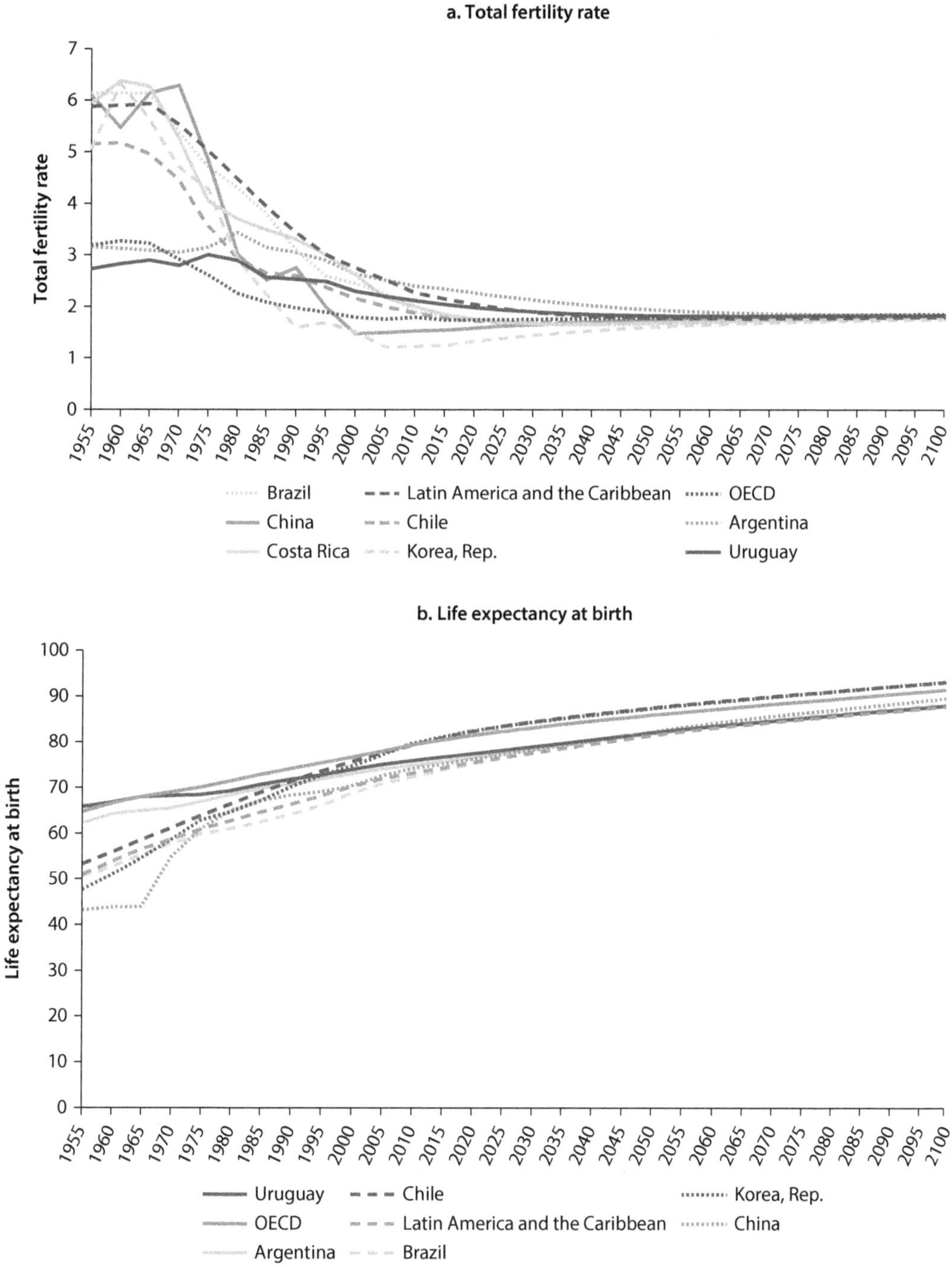

Source: United Nations, Population Division.
Note: OECD = Organisation for Economic Co-operation and Development.

However, the forecasts estimate a convergence in the total fertility rate around the middle of this century.

In terms of mortality, Uruguay has always been characterized as in a better situation than the other countries in the region, as well as better off than China and the Republic of Korea. Specifically, Uruguay's life expectancy at birth during the second half of the last century was nearly 70 years, the same as in Argentina and the average for OECD countries. The forecasts suggest that the countries would converge on the same value for this indicator around 2030, while the Republic of Korea and OECD countries will converge at a higher level.

The process of change of the population's age structure is important from a social and economic point of view, insofar as it brings an increase in the relative weight of the age groups that belong to the potentially inactive population relative to age groups considered as potentially active or economically productive.

At the beginning of the demographic transition, the dependency ratio is high because of the high percentage of children. The subsequent fall in fertility leads to a phase (which can last several decades) in which the proportion of middle-aged individuals increases, which is the demographic dividend or "window of opportunity" because the proportion of the population dependent on the income of third parties falls to a low point and therefore an opportunity exists to generate a surplus or overall savings.

In order to determine the length of the demographic dividend phase, we look to the total demographic dependency ratio,[2] which measures the ratio of children/adolescents and the elderly (under age 15 and over age 65) relative to the working-age population (ages 15–64). Figure 8.3 presents the ratios between the inactive and active populations for Uruguay and for a group of selected countries.

The Uruguayan dependency ratio was 55.6 percent in 2015 and will fall to a low of 55.3 percent in 2020. Subsequently, it will begin a sustained rise to more than 60 percent in 2040. Uruguay's dependency ratio is much higher than the Latin America and Caribbean average and is even higher than that of OECD countries. However, by 2050 the regional average is set to converge.

The results show that, in contrast with what is happening in other countries in the region and even in the OECD, Uruguay finds itself in the middle of its demographic window of opportunity, which will continue until the beginning of the 2040s. This demographic dividend not only has a shorter duration than for the other countries in the region but also is less intense, even compared to the dividend in OECD countries.

This period is especially favorable for development, due to the greater viability of increasing savings and the opportunity for investing in economic growth, at the same time as the pressure for resources for basic education is reduced (as was seen in chapter 6). This is directly related to the pattern of consumption and income, which defines the total surplus (savings) in the life cycle of a society.

Figure 8.3 Demographic Dependency Ratio, Uruguay and Selected Countries, 1950–2100

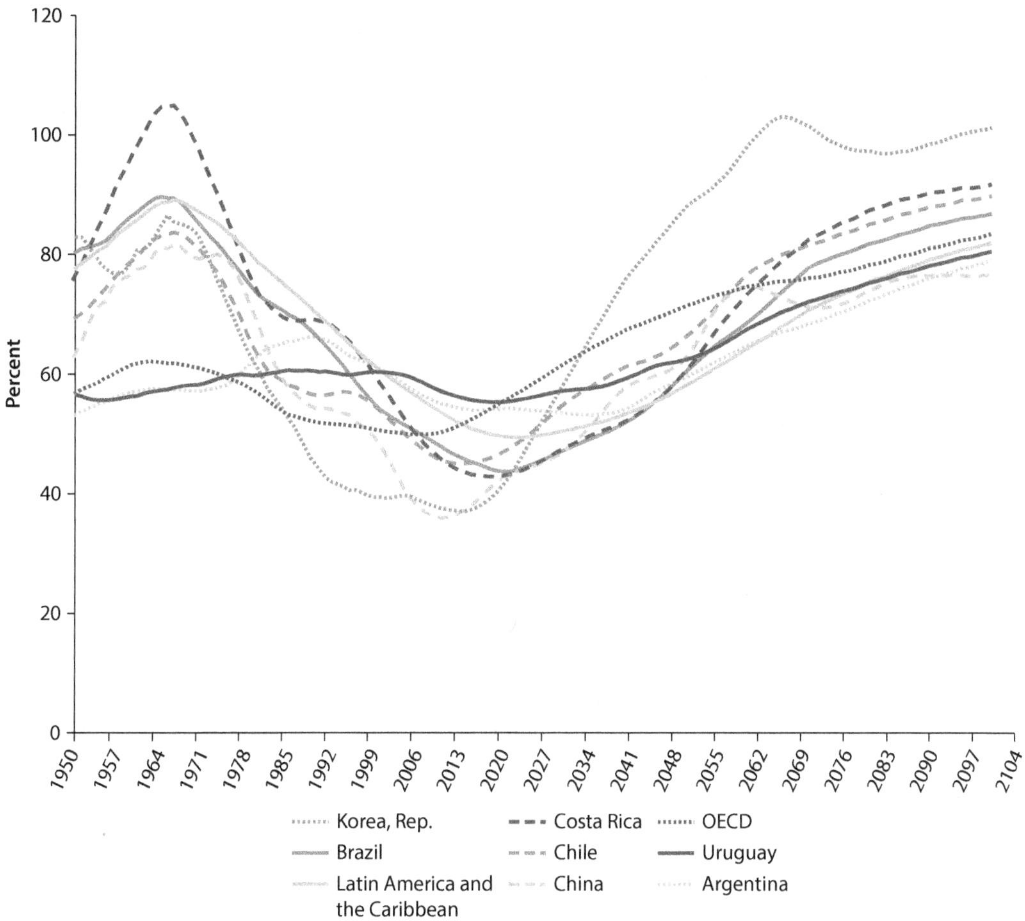

Source: Elaboration based on United Nations, Population Division.
Note: OECD = Organisation for Economic Co-operation and Development.

The Life-Cycle Deficit and Sustaining Consumption

To understand the impact of demographic transition on economic growth, as well as on requirements for fiscal financing, it is necessary to consider the consumption behavior and income of cohorts in estimates provided by the National Transfer Accounts, which enables definition of the life-cycle deficit.

Not only are the size and composition of the population important aspects, but so is the change in the age structure, since patterns of consumption and labor income are modified throughout the life cycle. Accordingly, economic participation and consumption, income, and savings, among other relevant socioeconomic phenomena, exhibit characteristic profiles that mean that decreasing a change in the relative size of a specific group will have consequences on the aggregate of the phenomenon in question. For example, population aging could signify, all things being equal, a reduction in the relative size of the labor force (or an increase in economic dependency) and therefore a lower number of individuals capable of saving.

As was discussed in chapter 3, throughout individuals' life cycles consumption and production are not constant. In two clearly defined phases in life—childhood and old age—consumption exceeds production and the opposite occurs in the economically active period. As a whole, the outcome of these deficit and surplus phases is known as the life-cycle deficit.

To better understand the structure of the population according to phases of the life cycle and how Uruguay compares with other countries, figure 8.4 presents the profile of per capita income and consumption (expressed by average income for ages 30–49) for Uruguay and some participant countries in the National Transfer Accounts project.

Similar profiles are seen across all countries, and in less developed countries more resources are generated during the youngest and oldest years (Mason and Lee 2011). In general, three clearly differentiated phases are identified according to whether income is less than or greater than consumption: zero income during childhood, growing income after a certain age during youth, and decreasing income at some point during old age. Meanwhile, consumption presents a relatively constant behavior pattern for each age, with a slight increase at older ages in some countries, associated with higher spending on health care.[3]

As was discussed in chapter 3, in the Uruguayan case the period in which labor income is higher than the level of consumption is ages 28–57. This 30-year span represents the period in which individuals have the capacity to generate savings, and is known as the period of life-cycle surplus.

In contrast, Argentina and the Republic of Korea have somewhat longer periods with potential surpluses: 33 and 34 years, respectively. Lifestyle surpluses in Uruguay's neighbors that participate in the National Transfer Accounts project, Brazil and Chile, are not as prolonged, at 23 and 29 years, respectively. Finally, China deserves special mention because, according to the per capita consumption and income profiles, the number of years during which an average individual's income exceeds consumption reaches 38 years, that is, ages 22–59.

Uruguay's surplus period, as in its Latin American neighbors, is significantly less than the surplus period in selected high-growth Asian countries. During these periods, the difference between labor income and consumption for China, Japan, and the Republic of Korea is much higher than in Uruguay, Argentina, Brazil, and Chile. This evidence, according to Fanelli (2014), indicates that primary savers in Uruguay have less propensity to forego consumption (with the same happening in Argentina, Brazil, and Chile). The weakness in savings does not suggest these countries are able to take great advantage of the window of opportunity.

With the goal of expanding these profiles to the country's total values, figure 8.5 presents the income and consumption profile in aggregate terms (normalized). That is, in addition to reflecting the individual patterns from figure 8.4, it also shows the specific age structure of the population in each country. These values are obtained by multiplying the average for each age group

Figure 8.4 Profile of Normalized Per Capita Consumption and Income (Relative to Average Income between Ages 30–49), Uruguay and Selected Countries, 2000s

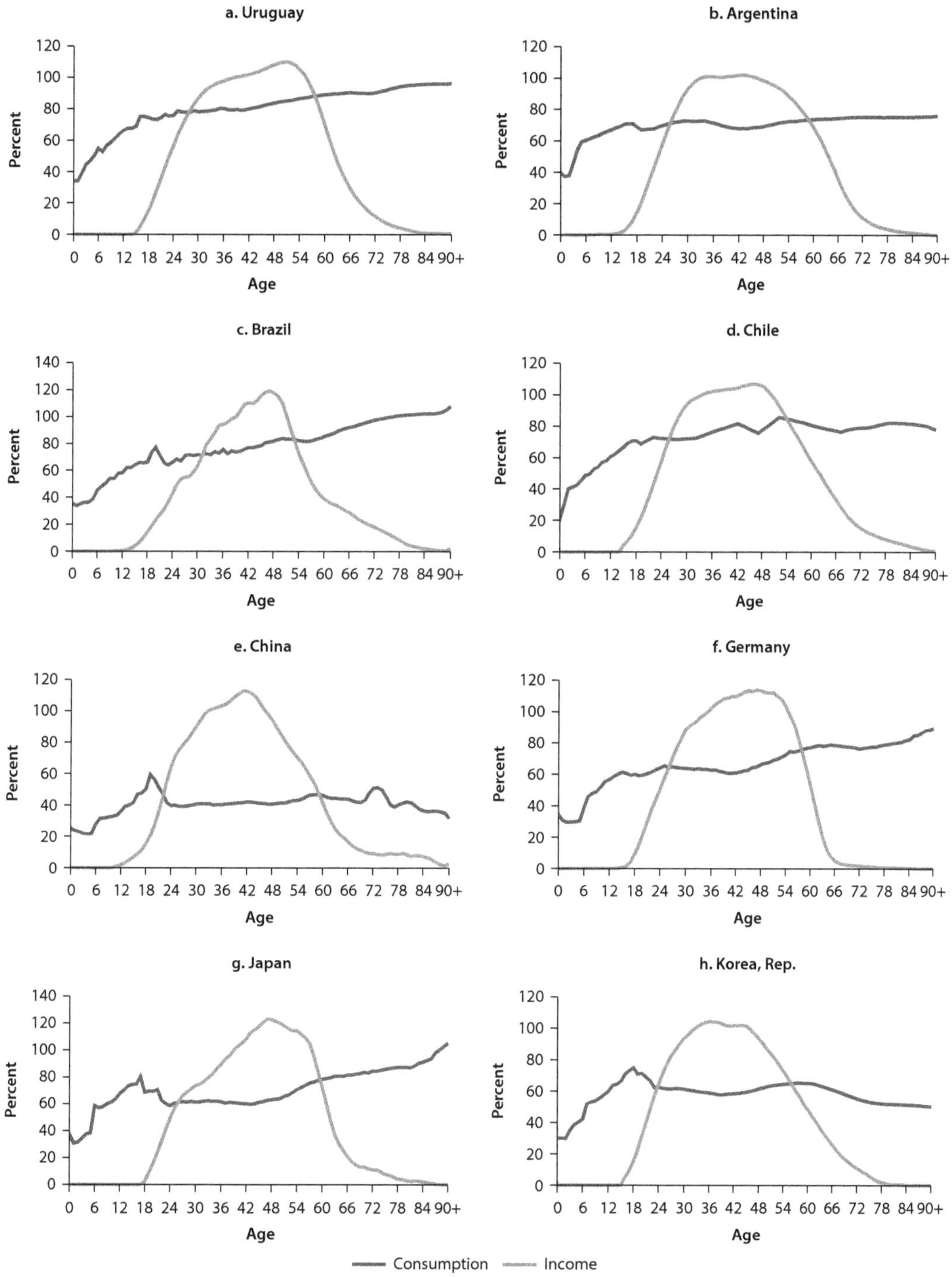

Sources: Uruguay: chapter 3; Argentina: Comelatto 2014; rest of the countries: National Transfer Accounts project, http://ntaccounts.org.

Figure 8.5 Normalized Aggregate Profile of Consumption and Income (Relative to Average Income between Ages 30–49), Uruguay and Selected Countries, 2000s

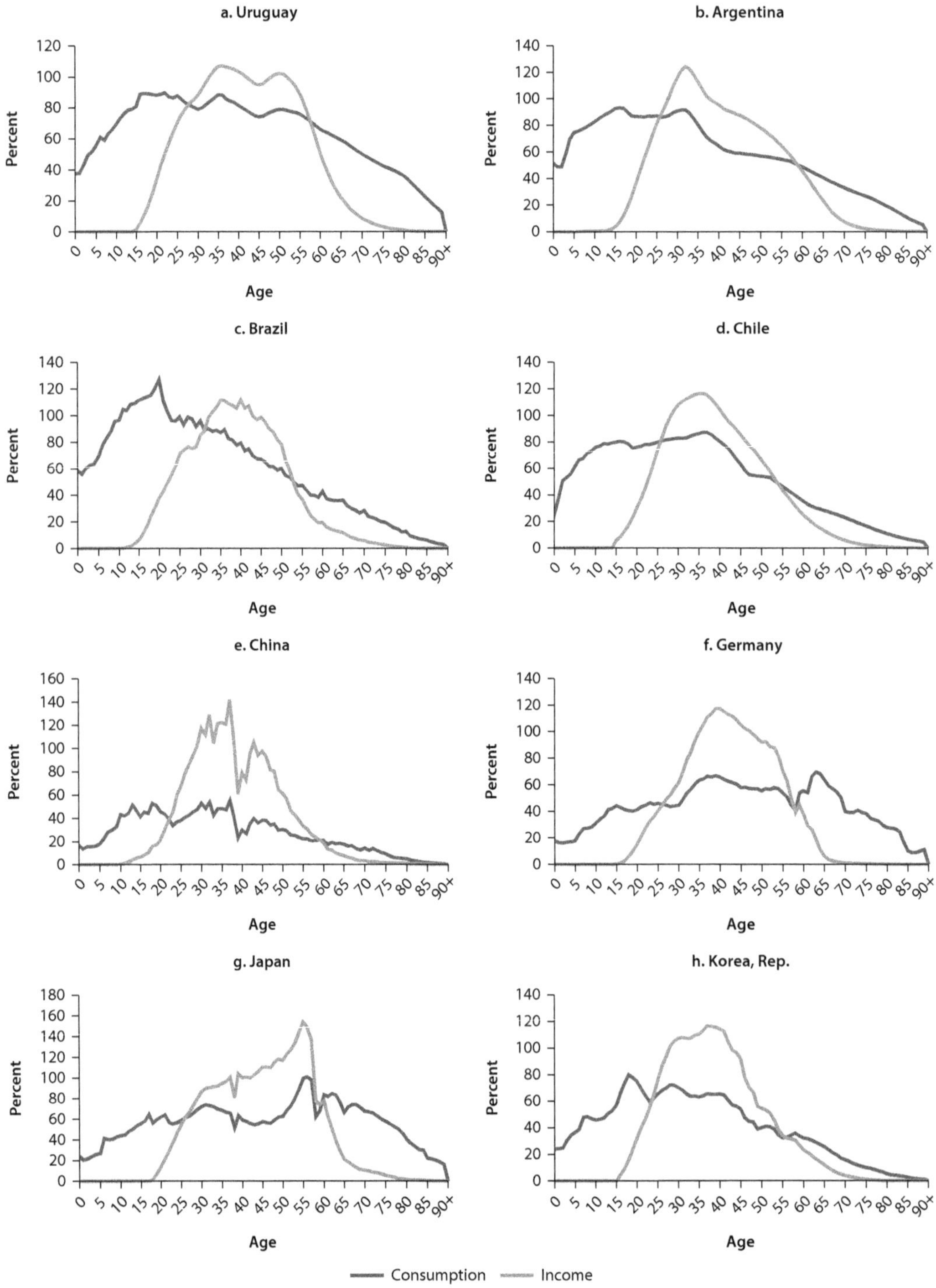

Sources: Uruguay: chapter 3; Argentina: Comelatto 2014; rest of the countries: National Transfer Accounts project, http://ntaccounts.org.

by the population in each age group, in such a way that the sum of these values represents the country's labor income and consumption.

Figure 8.5 enables us to observe how the population's age structure combines with individual profiles to create a completely different panorama from the point of view of the aggregate financing needs of the deficit age groups.

In relative terms, Uruguay has the highest combined deficit for children and older adults, equivalent to 64.8 percent of aggregate labor income. In turn, the deficit for children is 1.5 times larger than that of older adults. Argentina's combined deficit is 57.3 percent, followed by Japan (54.7 percent), Chile (54.6 percent), and Brazil (48.8 percent). For their part, China (25.5 percent) and the Republic of Korea (38 percent) have the lowest deficits combining childhood and old age.

These results are very well represented in figure 8.6, which shows the aggregate life-cycle deficit for each age group for a group of selected countries. In the figure it is possible to observe Uruguay's lower surplus than the selected countries. The higher deficit during childhood stands out, along with the rest of the countries in the region (Argentina, Brazil, and Chile).

Figure 8.6 Aggregate Life-Cycle Deficit by Age (Relative to Average Income between Ages 30–49), Uruguay and Selected Countries, 2000s

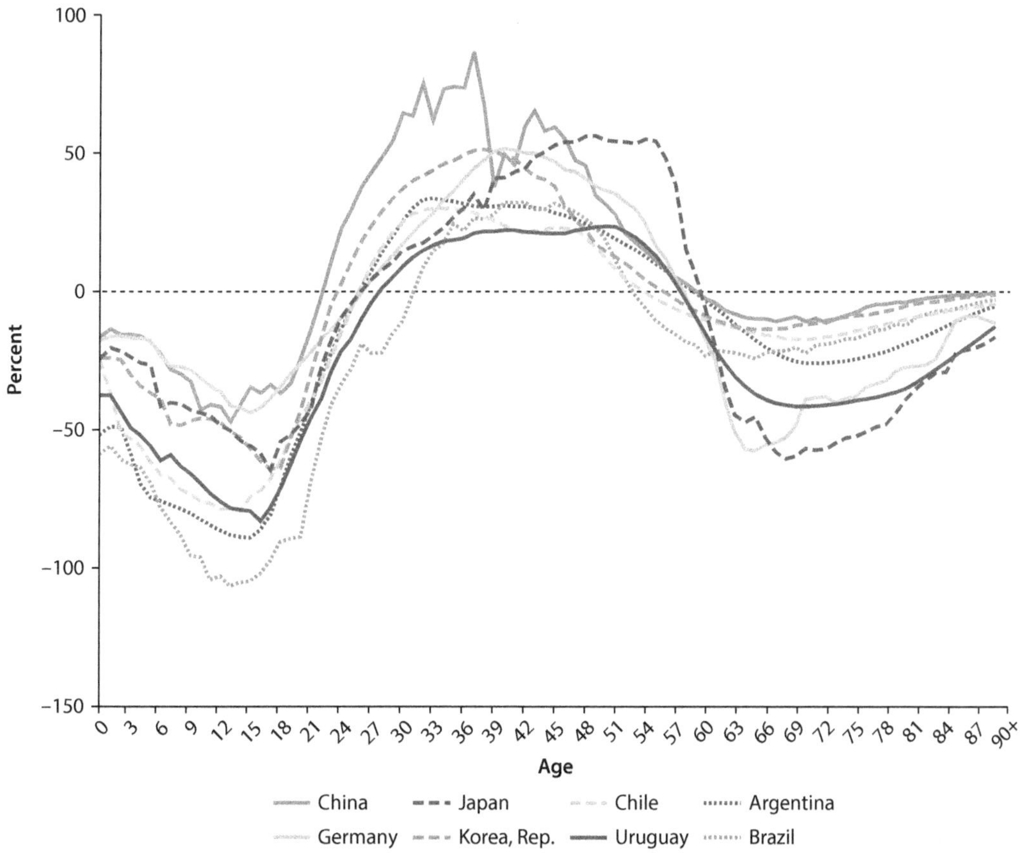

Sources: Uruguay: chapter 3; Argentina: Comelatto 2014; rest of the countries: National Transfer Accounts project, http://ntaccounts.org.

The existence of deficits during childhood and old age opens up questions about the source of financing to fund these deficits and, more specifically, the role played by public transfers. Figure 8.7 shows the percentage of the deficit financed through public transfers in a group of selected countries during childhood (panel a) and during old age (panel b). In most cases, public transfers finance a higher proportion of the deficit during old age than during childhood; in some cases, public transfers represent more than 100 percent of the deficit during old age (Sweden). We observe that in 2013 Uruguay was among the five countries with the lowest proportion of the life-cycle deficit financed by transfers, both among youth as well as older adults. Accordingly, 16 percent of the deficit during childhood and 40 percent of the deficit during old age were financed by public sector transfers in 2013.

The information presented in figure 8.7 outlines the specific effect of the public transfer programs for each deficit-generating group in each country. As a result, the small part of the Uruguayan deficit during childhood that is financed by public transfers (16 percent) stands out, placing the country in the group of the five countries with the lowest participation by public transfer programs in financing the life-cycle deficit during the first stage, along with Brazil, Chile, Costa Rica, and Mexico. At the other extreme, one finds Finland (46 percent), Hungary (52 percent), and Sweden (45 percent), the countries with the highest percentage of public transfers to children.

Figure 8.7 Proportion of the Life-Cycle Deficit Financed through Public Transfers, Uruguay and Selected Countries, Various Years

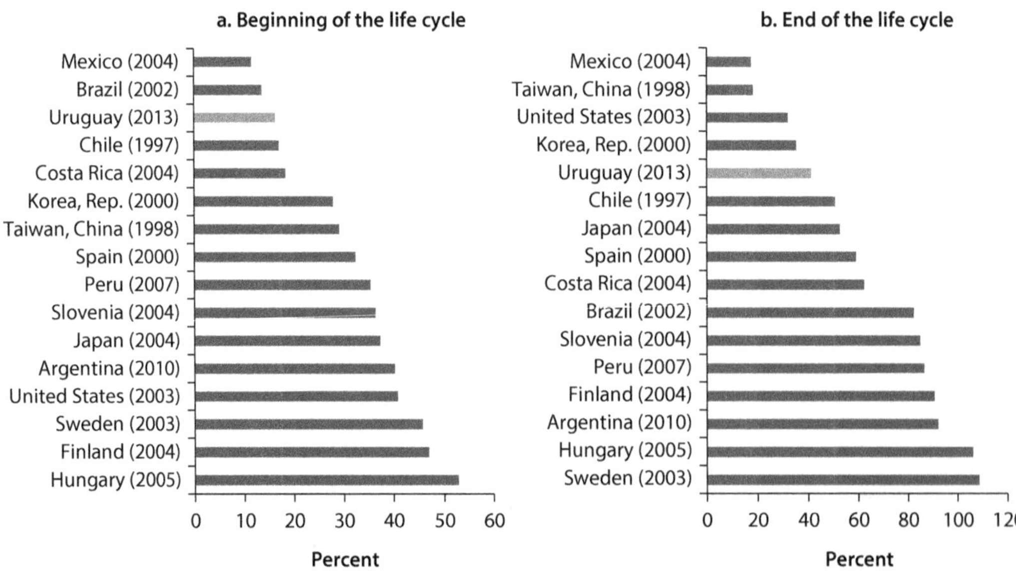

Source: Elaboration (Uruguay) and Comelatto 2014.
Note: For each country the "beginning" and "end" of the life cycle is defined as deficit-generating ages, allowing this age limit to vary from case to case.

From the point of view of the life-cycle deficit experienced during old age, we observe that Uruguay finances 40 percent of that deficit through public transfer programs. Although this funding represents more than double the proportion directed to finance the deficit during childhood, the country even so places among the countries with the lowest percentage of old-age transfers financed by the public purse, along with Chile; the Republic of Korea; Mexico; Taiwan, China; and the United States.

The smaller percentage of the old-age deficit financed by public transfers in Uruguay than other countries, especially within the region, is related to the higher life-cycle deficit in that phase of the life cycle (figure 8.6). This is a product of the higher aggregate consumption and not a lower level of income. While standardized average consumption among the elderly population in Uruguay is 0.37, in Argentina it is 0.22, and in Brazil it is 0.16.

This deficit must be financed through income sources other than labor income, including labor income from other household members, intra-family transfers, interest, rental income, and profits and dividends from businesses. According to the Continuous Household Survey, just 15.4 percent of adults over age 60 in Uruguay lived alone in 2013. In these cases, the principal source of income was from public transfers (69 percent), and this is complemented by income from the labor market (14 percent), especially profits and/or dividends from businesses in which people over age 60 do not work (7 percent), family transfers, both as food (3 percent) as well as cash (2 percent), and other types of resources not identified in the survey (5 percent).

Public transfers represent 53 percent of total income for the 32.4 percent of older adults who live in households made up of two people. Excluding labor income (35 percent), the rest of the resources come from remittances received (4 percent), profits and/or dividends from businesses (3 percent), interest earned from capital (2 percent), and other resources (6 percent).

Finally, the other half of adults over age 60 reside in households with more than three members, in general made up of young, working-age adults. From an economic point of view, the makeup of these types of households enables them to take advantage of economies of scale created by sharing common goods and services. On average, the principal source of income in this type of household comes from the labor income of the young adults (62 percent), while the proportion from public transfers is 31.3 percent.

In summary, the financing structure for the deficit during old age is made up not just of transfers like pensions, but also by a large variety of income sources that include family assistance, such as direct transfers like cohabitation with several family members, profits from businesses, interest earned on capital, and remittances from abroad, among others.

As a result of the design of these programs and the size of the respective deficit-generating groups, figure 8.8 presents the ratio between average *per capita* transfers to the older adult population (over age 65) and to children (ages 0–14). Considering the most recent available year, Uruguay finds itself among the five countries with the highest ratio, equivalent to 3.3, after Brazil (3.7), Chile (3.5),

Figure 8.8 Ratio of Net Per Capita Public Transfers between Older Adults and Children, Uruguay and Selected Countries, Various Years

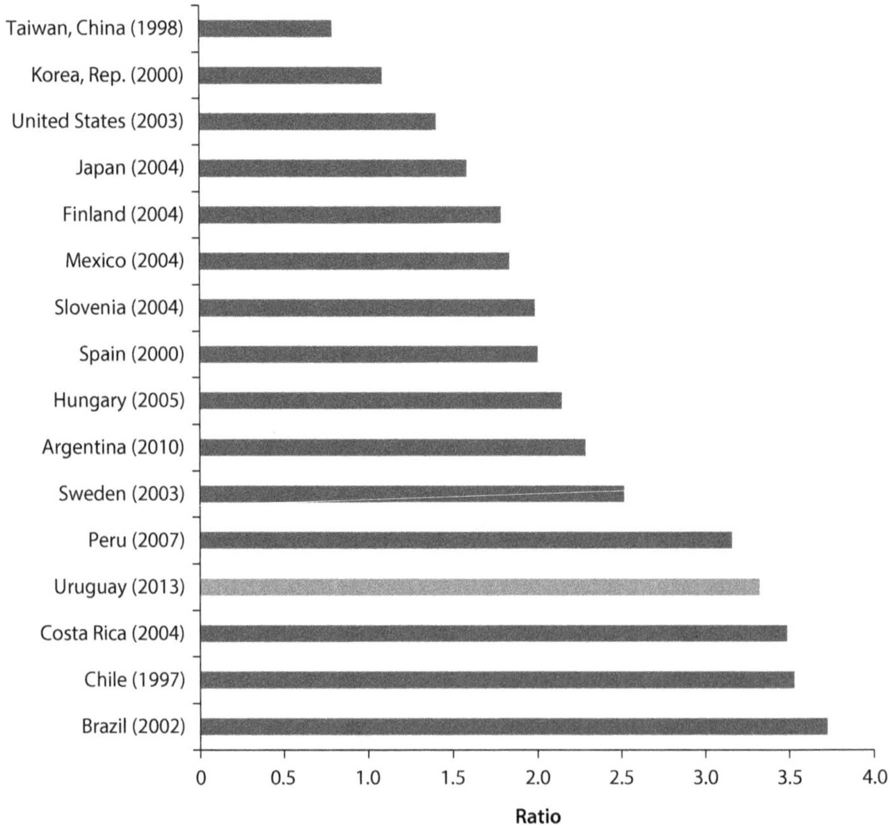

Source: Elaboration (Uruguay) and Comelatto 2014.

and Costa Rica (3.5). This is consistent with what we have observed in the previous figures.

According to the information discussed in chapter 3, net public transfers received by the population at more advanced ages are higher than those received by children and adolescents. Thus, children and adolescents make more intensive use of other channels to finance their life-cycle deficit, which can be appreciated from the gap between the life-cycle deficit curves and net public transfers.

Clearly, an older age structure raises pressure to give the older adult population greater priority for public transfers than for other population groups. However, almost all countries, except Taiwan, China, maintain a ratio that is above parity, which means that on average, per capita terms, older adults receive benefits from public transfers that are greater than those received by children.

These results give rise to a debate about the intergenerational equity of the social protection system. On one hand, considering that the pension system is the principal transfer program for older adults, it is possible to argue that this apparent inequality is not very significant. The principal arguments for this point would be that: (a) all cohorts pass through childhood and old age during the life cycle, which means that eventually everyone will benefit from this model; and (b) older adults that currently receive these benefits have made contributions, both to the social security system and through their work and payment of general taxes throughout their lives, which means that these transfers basically represent the result of their efforts during previous decades (Rofman and Apella 2014). The latter point is related to the idea that social security benefits constitute income classified as deferred salary.

A significant concern that emerges from the reality of the demographic transition refers to the ability of the working population to finance those that depend on them economically, as the age structure changes and the average age increases. The classification of people as workers or dependents according to arbitrary age limits confines this type of discussion insomuch as it does not allow reflection about the implications of the changes in socioeconomic behavior on participation in the labor market and permanence in the education system, among other things.

Additionally, a purely demographic dependency ratio assumes that the ability to generate income and the propensity to consume are homogenous within the groups of working-age individuals and dependents. However, aspects like unemployment, salary, and consumption behavior vary by age, as is reflected in the labor income and consumption estimates by age group discussed earlier.

Mason and Lee (2007) propose refining the measurement of the dependency ratio, both its numerator and its denominator. They seek that the numerator would better reflect the actual generation of resources (observed in economic terms), and not just the potential (based on demographic measurements), for which they propose adjusting the working-age population by the average income per age group. In turn, they seek that the denominator would capture the use of resources, for which they propose adjusting the population by the average consumption per age group.

Thus, in the same way that it was developed in chapter 3 for the case of Uruguay, figure 8.9 presents the support ratio[4] for a group of selected countries. The goal is to better understand the ability of the working population to finance those who depend on them economically, and place Uruguay in the context of other countries that are also passing through the demographic transition.

On one hand, Uruguay's coefficient was falling until the beginning of the window of opportunity in the mid-1990s, when the trajectory reversed and the indicator began to rise. On the other hand, we observe that the initial downward movement and subsequent increase is typical of countries that from a certain point forward experience the demographic dividend. However, the movement of Uruguay's potential support ratio—which entered the window of opportunity in 1995—is significantly smoother than the ratio observed for the other selected countries.

Figure 8.9 Support Ratio for Uruguay and Selected Countries, 1950–2100

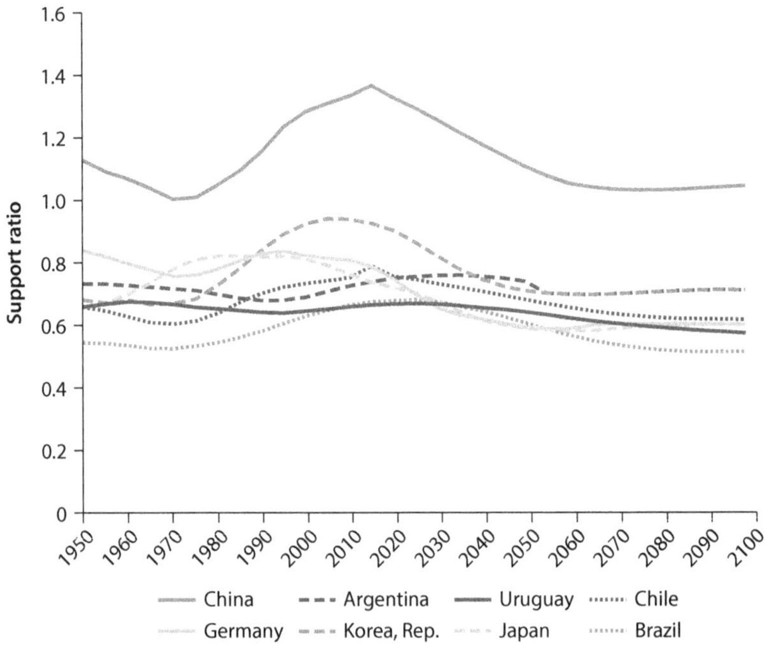

Source: Elaboration based on chapter 3 for Uruguay; Comelatto 2014 for Argentina; and the National Transfer Accounts project (http://ntaccounts.org) for the rest of the countries.

This phenomenon is related to the low intensity of the demographic dividend and to the lesser effect of the increase of total labor income due to the cohorts' greater propensity to consume, which increases the value of the actual consumers.

The same phenomenon is observed in Argentina, Brazil, and Chile, countries that save little, although not in higher-saving Asian countries. In reality, Argentina, Brazil, and Chile exhibit the lowest support ratios, all at less than one. Only China (a notable exception) reaches the level of one. Japan is included to highlight that the trajectory of the potential support ratio of an aging country is decreasing, due to the growing proportion of spending that is by retirees.

Figure 8.10 presents the evolution of gross savings as a percentage of gross domestic product (GDP) for selected countries during 1986–2013.

In relative terms, the results presented for Uruguay suggest not just a low savings rate, of around 14 percent of GDP, but also a rate that is very constant over time—the variance is just 3.7. This same situation occurs in countries such as Argentina, Brazil, and Costa Rica, although this indicator exhibits greater variability over time. In contrast, Chile maintains a savings rate equivalent to 21 percent of GDP on average, as is the case for the regional average and the OECD countries.

These results complement the findings reached earlier, relative to the elevated propensity to consume among countries in the Southern Cone and the low

Figure 8.10 Gross Savings as a Percentage of GDP, Uruguay and Selected Countries, 1986–2013

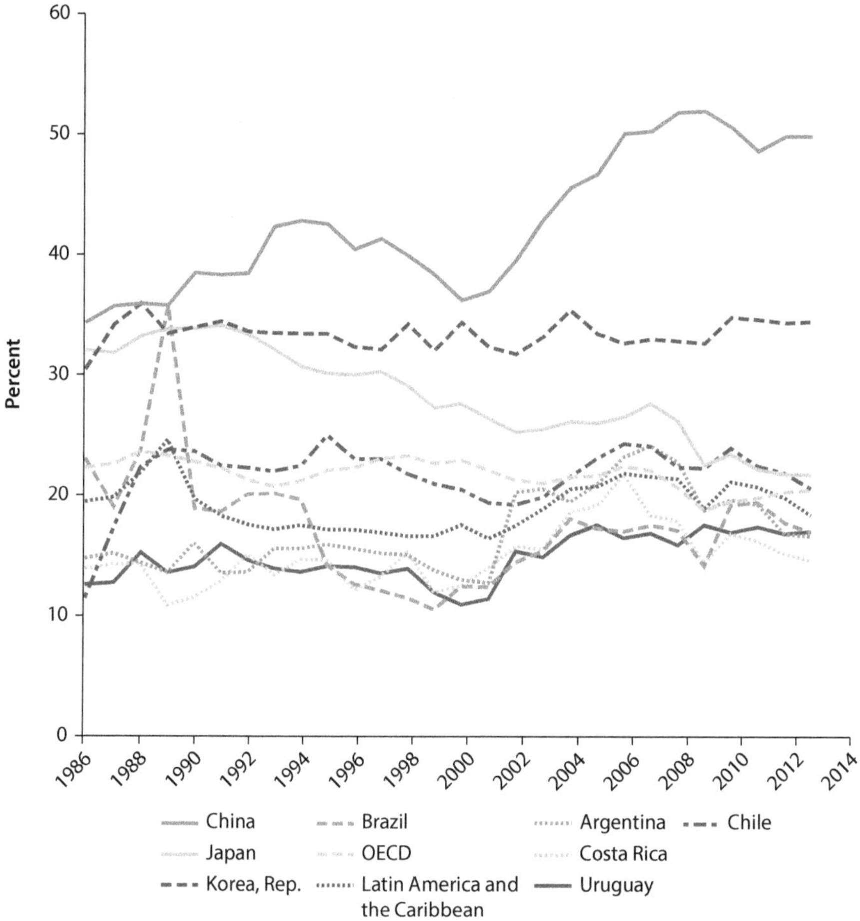

Source: World Development Indicators.
Note: OECD = Organisation for Economic Co-operation and Development.

intensity of the life-cycle surplus. In effect, the Asian countries (China, Japan, the Republic of Korea) have the highest life-cycle surpluses (figure 8.5) and this allows them, in part, to achieve their high savings rates.

In this context, it is possible to suggest that Uruguay, like its neighbors passing through the demographic transition, has encountered a great opportunity, and at the same time a great challenge. In effect, low levels of savings pose some concern related to the ability of these countries to take advantage of the demographic dividend, to accumulate capital during this period, and in this way achieve medium- and long-term productivity increases that can ease the potential effects of aging on the total productivity of the labor force. With this trend in savings rates, it is evident that society will have to make a greater effort in the remaining 25 years of the demographic dividend in order to take advantage of it.

The Generosity of Public Social Spending

As was analyzed in chapter 2, the trend toward an older society poses some concerns related to the effort that society as a whole will have to make to finance social sectors that are more sensitive to the change in the age structure, such as spending on health care, education, and pensions.

To better understand this situation for Uruguay, we compare public expenditure on education, health care, and pensions, and the degree of generosity compared to different countries, not just from the region but from the rest of the world. For this comparison, we propose that public spending on education, health care, and pensions is the product found by multiplying the per capita benefit for each age group (including in this calculation those who do not receive benefits), which we call generosity, by the number of individuals in each age group. The proportion of the product directed to public consumption of education and health care services, and the payment of pension benefits, can be divided into two multipliable components as is presented in equation 8.1.

$$\frac{B_t}{Y_t} = \frac{\frac{B_t}{PE_t}}{\frac{Y_t}{P_{20-64,t}}} \cdot \frac{PE_t}{P_{20-64,t}} \tag{8.1}$$

Where:

B_t is the total public benefit (spending) at time t for each social sector
Y_t is the GDP at time t
PE_t is the eligible population at time t for each social sector
$P_{20-64,t}$ is the working-age population.

Total public spending in a specific sector as a percentage of GDP is the product of two factors: an economic one and a demographic one. The former is represented as the average spending directed to each individual in the target population. The second is given by the size of the target population relative to the working-age population.

In equation 8.1 the economic factor is represented by the first scalar unit. According to Miller, Mason, and Holz (2009), this factor is usually known as the benefit generosity ratio, which expresses the generosity of the benefits of a specific average sector relative to per capita GDP among working-age adults. Standardizing by GDP per working-age adult is useful for making international comparisons of benefits.

The second scalar unit, $\frac{PE_t}{P_{20-64,t}}$ is called the dependency ratio and measures the size of the target population relative to the working-age population. By definition, the product of these two terms yields total spending for a given sector (education, health care, or pensions) as a share of GDP.

A higher level of benefit generosity does not necessarily indicate a more generous transfer per beneficiary. This variable captures social spending, in both monetary benefits and in coverage; that is, the real number of eligible individuals that actually access a social program or service from the government in each sector. For example, a higher benefit generosity ratio could be associated with higher spending or better coverage, or both. Equation 8.2 illustrates this decomposition. E_t represents the actual number of beneficiaries. As we can see from equation 8.2, the benefit generosity ratio is equal to the average benefit per eligible person when coverage is universal, that is, equal to one.

$$\frac{B_t}{Y_t} = \underbrace{\frac{\frac{B_t}{PE_t}}{\frac{Y_t}{P_{20-64,t}}}}_{\text{Benefit generosity ratio}} \cdot \underbrace{\frac{PE_t}{P_{20-64,t}}}_{\text{Dependency ratio}} = \underbrace{\frac{\frac{B_t}{E_t}}{\frac{Y_t}{P_{20-64,t}}}}_{\text{Average benefit per actual beneficiary (normalized by GDP per working-age adult)}} \cdot \underbrace{\frac{E_t}{PE_t}}_{\text{Coverage}} \cdot \underbrace{\frac{PE_t}{P_{20-64,t}}}_{\text{Dependency ratio}} \tag{8.2}$$

In the case of both the education and the pension systems, the eligible population group is clearly defined. While in the former this group is the school-age population from ages 5–20, in the latter the group is the population over age 65. However, in the case of the health care system, defining the dependency ratio is not so direct. Disaggregating spending in demographic and economic values is not simple. According to the decomposition method based on equation 8.1, a potential approximation emerges if we consider the population at the ages closest to death as receiving the largest portion of public health care spending.

With the goal of estimating the number of individuals in the age groups closest to death, we utilize the estimates and forecasts of the number of deaths during the next decade by cohort created by the United Nations Population Division. Basically, this group is defined through the absolute number of deaths in each cohort, which constitutes an approximation of the number of individuals with an elevated demand for health care services during the year. Studies in OECD countries have shown the greatest proportion of an individual's health care spending occurs during the final decade of life, and within that decade, during the final year (McGrail et al. 2000; Zweifel, Felder, and Meiers 1999). Therefore, health care systems usually direct a larger share of resources to curative medicine than to the provision of preventive services.

Table 8.1 presents total public expenditure in education, pensions, and health care for 2013 in Uruguay, disaggregating the dependency and generosity components. In addition, it presents information corresponding to Argentina, Brazil,

Table 8.1 Social Spending in Uruguay and Selected Countries, 2013
percent

	Uruguay	*Argentina*	*Brazil*	*Chile*	*OECD*
Public education					
Total spending (% of GDP)	3.6	5.1	6.3	4.6	5.7
Sectoral dependency ratio	36.2	38.7	38.7	34.5	23.4
Generosity ratio	10.0	13.3	16.4	13.2	24.4
Pensions					
Total spending (% of GDP)	9.4	8.5	8.5	3.6	7.8
Sectoral dependency ratio	21.6	16.4	10.4	13.5	28.5
Generosity ratio	43.7	51.8	82.0	26.3	27.4
Public health care					
Total spending (% of GDP)	5.2	4.9	4.7	3.7	7.6
Sectoral dependency ratio	14.7	12.4	10.1	9.1	15.1
Generosity ratio	35.3	39.6	46.2	40.4	50.4

Sources: Elaboration based on United Nations Population Division, UNESCO, OECD, World Health Organization, *Pensions at a Glance* (2013), and chapter 3.
Note: OECD = Organisation for Economic Co-operation and Development; UNESCO = United Nations Educational, Scientific, and Cultural Organization.

and Chile—three middle-income countries in the same region—and a group of high-income countries from the OECD.[5]

Among the three sectors considered here, Uruguay's education system is the one with significantly less public spending than in the comparator countries (between 20 percent and 40 percent). The differences in the sectoral dependency ratio are minimal compared with the other countries in the region (although it is clearly unfavorable in comparison with the OECD), but a significant difference is found in generosity: Uruguay is the country with the lowest benefit generosity ratio (at 10 percent, it is less than half the value of the OECD countries). As for the neighboring countries (Argentina, Brazil, and Chile), they maintain benefit generosity ratios that are between 30 percent and 65 percent higher than Uruguay's. These differences could be due in part to the coverage problems the education system faces among young people in the age group that would study in the final years of secondary school, but per-student spending also plays a significant role.

In its pension system, Uruguay exhibits an intermediate generosity level, with countries like Argentina and Brazil having significantly higher indicators (20 percent and 90 percent, respectively), and others like Chile and the OECD countries having lower levels. The difference with Argentina and Brazil could be generated by the broad noncontributory and semicontributory pension schemes that function in these countries, although in the opposite case (Chile) it stems from the fact that a large part of spending on pensions in Chile has been transferred to the private sector through the pension fund administrators.

Finally, for spending by the health care system, Uruguay clearly feels the pressure generated by the advanced phase of the demographic transition, which results from a smaller working-age population and therefore shows a sectoral dependency ratio similar to that seen in the OECD and higher than the ratio in its neighboring countries. This phenomenon means that even though Uruguay directs a slightly higher percentage of GDP to finance the sector than Argentina, Brazil, and Chile, its benefit generosity ratio is lower. With the goal of offsetting the effect that the higher dependency ratio has on the generosity of public spending on health care, the OECD countries direct 2.5 percentage points of GDP more than Uruguay to fund their public health care systems, which allows them to achieve a benefit generosity ratio of 50.4 percent.

Based on these results, it is evident that the degree of generosity of public social spending is not just a function of the fiscal effort that a country makes relative to GDP, but also the country's demographic structure. Accordingly, it is possible to expect that, at the same level of public spending, population aging will generate space for increasing the generosity of education spending while reducing the space to do the same in pensions and health care as a consequence of the reduction (increase) of the sectoral dependency ratios. However, this phenomenon is observed in the pension and health care systems, where benefit generosity ratios are lower than in the counterparts in neighboring countries, although not so in Uruguay's education system, which maintains a lower generosity ratio.

This poses a challenge in the medium and long run over the fiscal and economic effort that the country will direct to the sector that creates the most human capital, keeping in mind a context in which the most important factor for sustaining per capita output will not be the quantity of the labor force, but its quality.

Final Reflections

This chapter has presented a set of demographic as well as economic indicators for Uruguay, in the context of those of other countries, such as geographic neighbors, developed countries from the OECD, and some of the Asian Tiger economies. The goal is to present Uruguay's situation in a comparative manner relative to the demographic transition and its potential medium- and long-term effects. Uruguay is at a very advanced phase of its first demographic transition. The Uruguayan population is the oldest in Latin America and its dependency ratio is currently much higher than the average for Latin America and the Caribbean and is even higher that the rates observed in OECD countries. As soon as 2050, it is predicted that the regional average will converge around the same level, clearly in a state of population aging.

In contrast to the situation in other countries in the region and even in the OECD, Uruguay finds itself in the middle of its demographic window of opportunity, which will end at the beginning of the 2040s. However, in comparison with the demographic dividend that the rest of the countries in the region experience, Uruguay's window of opportunity is not only shorter in duration, but it is also less intense. For this reason, the opportunity generated during the period when the working-age population reaches its maximum proportion of the total population, is smaller than in other countries, as a result of the distinct evolution of the demographic determinants in Uruguay. In this context, the effort required of Uruguay to take advantage of the first dividend and give rise to a second dividend is much greater. In other words, the country will need to generate more savings from the economically active population with the goal of promoting increased investment and accumulation of physical and human capital to raise future productivity and maintain sustained growth in per capita output.

This does not just depend on the country's age structure and its future evolution, but also on the population's consumption and income profile, which determines the size of the population with the ability to save, commonly called primary savers. However, based on the results presented in this chapter, the expectations are not entirely favorable compared with countries like China, Japan, and the Republic of Korea, or even with Argentina. In effect, considering the consumption and income profiles described in chapter 3, the whole population has the ability to save because it generates a life-cycle surplus between ages 28–57. However, the surplus is small compared to other countries, indicating that primary savers in Uruguay have a higher propensity to consume.

All age groups in Uruguay are more likely to spend on consuming than they are to save, limiting the ability of the population in the surplus-generating phase of the life cycle to generate savings in aggregate. This weakness in savings behavior shows that Uruguay's population is not taking advantage of the window of opportunity that demographic transition affords.

Uruguay exhibits the highest life-cycle deficit (combining childhood and old age) among the countries considered here, at equivalent to 64.8 percent of aggregate labor income. This places the country 10 percentage points above Argentina, Brazil, and Chile. At the opposite extreme, we find the Asian countries, China (25.5 percent) and the Republic of Korea (38 percent) with the lowest combined deficits.

A portion of this life-cycle deficit is met through public transfers, However, based on what we have discussed in this chapter, it is possible to observe a strong age bias in these transfers because for each peso transferred to children, Uruguay transfers 3 pesos to finance the deficit during old age. Beyond the normative discussion that explains this difference, it is necessary to consider the impact of these transfer priorities in promoting human capital and economic and social development. A more significant transfer to the early phases of the life cycle could facilitate the accumulation of human capital through, for example, higher spending on education, which would result in better living conditions throughout the entire life cycle and have a greater impact on economic growth.

This is even more important when we consider that the generosity ratio of public spending on education in Uruguay is the lowest among neighboring countries and OECD members. This situation takes on even greater importance when considering the advanced phase of the demographic transition and the resulting lower school-age dependency ratio. This lower ratio enables the country to increase investment per capita in education without increasing fiscal spending.

Uruguay, as a consequence of having begun its demographic transition early, has a very low school-age dependency ratio (36.2) relative to the other countries in this study. As population aging advances, this dependency ratio will continue to fall, which would enable the country to increase investment in education per student, to reach the higher generosity ratio in OECD member countries. This constitutes a clear short-term challenge with the goal of raising the quality of the labor force and helping reverse the decline in productivity.

The fall in the dependency ratio creates an opportunity to increase the generosity of the education sector without adding fiscal pressure. Japan, the Republic of Korea, and various OECD countries direct resources freed up by the lower number of school-age individuals to improving quality. Additionally, the increased availability of resources could increase coverage, reduce over-age enrollment, and help promote inclusion of the poorest people.

In summary, Uruguay finds itself at the midpoint of its period of demographic dividend, but the opportunity this offers the economy is more limited than in other countries because the dividend will have a short duration and low intensity due to the country's demographic history. Additionally, the propensity to consume is particularly high, which means that the space to accelerate capital accumulation financed by domestic savings is limited. For this reason, the country needs a greater savings effort and accumulation of capital than required in the other countries analyzed here to be able to take advantage of the first dividend and give rise to the second demographic dividend. In other words, Uruguay's age, consumption, and income profiles limit the ability to take advantage of the first demographic dividend because doing so depends on accumulating capital to increase the productivity of the labor force and maintain a steady rate of growth of per capita output during the phase of population aging.

Notes

1. Rafael Rofman and Ignacio Apella, World Bank, Social Protection and Labor Global Practice. Correspondence to iapella@worldbank.org.
2. Although this indicator suggests three clearly differentiated stages associated with potential participation in the labor market—childhood, adulthood, and old age—this does not necessarily mean that these stages are inflexible in adapting to new scenarios. In other words, the duration of each stage (pre-labor, labor, and post-labor) may vary among individuals and is determined by not just age but also other factors. See Apella and Troiano (2014).
3. This latter point is related to the public sector's participation as a funder and provider of health care services. In countries like the Republic of Korea, where the public

supply of health care services is significant, the out-of-pocket spending requirements for households are lower.

4. The support ratio is defined as $RS_t = L_t/N_t$ where $N_t = \sum_{a=0}^{\omega} \varphi_a x_{a,t}$ and $L_t = \sum_{a=0}^{\omega} \gamma_a x_{a,t}$.
5. The high-income countries included for comparison are Austria, Finland, Germany, Japan, Spain, and Switzerland. The selection of these countries was the result of the availability of information from the National Transfer Accounts estimates. However, a comparison with official information on spending for the high-income countries from the OECD produced similar results.

References

Apella, I., and S. Troiano. 2014. "El Mercado de Trabajo Argentino en un Contexto de Transición Demográfica." In *Los Años No Vienen Solos: Oportunidades y Desafíos Económicos de la Transición Demográfica en Argentina*, edited by M. Gragnolati, R. Rofman, I. Apella, and S. Troiano, 319–50. Buenos Aires: World Bank.

Comelatto, P. 2014. "Cuentas Nacionales de Transferencias en Argentina." In *Los Años No Vienen Solos: Oportunidades y Desafíos Económicos de la Transición Demográfica en Argentina*, edited by M. Gragnolati, R. Rofman, I. Apella, and S. Troiano, 93–118. Buenos Aires: World Bank.

Fanelli, J. 2014. "Demografía y Macroeconomía: Oportunidades y Riesgos en la Argentina del Bono." In *Los Años No Vienen Solos: Oportunidades y Desafíos Económicos de la Transición Demográfica en Argentina*, edited by M. Gragnolati, R. Rofman, I. Apella, and S. Troiano, 373–411. Buenos Aires: World Bank.

Mason, A., and R. Lee. 2007. "Transfers, Capital, and Consumption over the Demographic Transition." In *Population Aging, Intergenerational Transfers and the Macroeconomy*, edited by R. Clark, A. Mason, and N. Ogawa, 128–62. Cheltenham, UK: Elgar Press.

———. 2011. "Population Aging and the Generational Economy: Key Findings." In *Population Aging and the Generational Economy: A Global Perspective*, edited by R. Lee and A. Mason, 434–45. Cheltenham, UK: Edward Elgar Publishing.

McGrail, K., B. Green, M. L. Barer, R. Evans, C. Hertzman, and C. Normand. 2000. "Age, Costs of Acute and Long-Term Care and Proximity to Death: Evidence for 1987–88 and 1994–95 in British Columbia." *Age and Aging* 29 (3): 249–53.

Miller, T., C. Mason, and M. Holz. 2009. "The Fiscal Impact of Demographic Change in Ten Latin American Countries: Projecting Public Expenditures in Education, Health, and Pensions." Paper presented at the Workshop on Demographic Change and Social Policy, World Bank, Washington, DC, July 14–15.

OECD (Organisation for Economic Co-operation and Development). 2013. *Pensions at a Glance 2013: OECD and G20 Indicators*. Paris: OECD Publishing. doi:http://dx.doi.org/10.1787/pension_glance-2013-en.

Rofman, R., and I. Apella. 2014. "El Sistema de Protección Social Argentino en un Contexto de Transición Demográfica." In *Los Años No Vienen Solos: Oportunidades y Desafíos Económicos de la Transición Demográfica en Argentina*, edited by M. Gragnolati, R. Rofman, I. Apella, and S. Troiano, 143–68. Buenos Aires: World Bank.

United Nations, Department of Economic and Social Affairs, Population Division. 2015. *World Population Prospects: The 2015 Revision*. DVD edition. http://esa.un.org/unpd/wpp/.

Zweifel, P., S. Felder, and M. Meiers. 1999. "Ageing of Population and Health Care Expenditure: A Red Herring?" *Health Economics* 8 (6): 485–96.

CHAPTER 9

Macroeconomic Effects of Demographic Change: Contributions from a Long-Term Perspective

Fernando Lorenzo and Gonzalo Zunino[1]

Introduction

Demographic transition is a structural phenomenon, yet it indisputably impacts economic actors and a broad range of government-funded public policies. Economic theory has contributed abundant and solid arguments on the multiple ways that changes in population and the availability of human capital influence growth, and as a result the study of the influence of demographic factors takes on special meaning when we analyze the long-term trends of modern economies such as Uruguay.

The aging of Uruguay's population has significant influence on the behavior of households as consumers, and on the availability of the internal savings needed to finance the accumulation of capital. Demographic trends not only influence aggregate consumption behavior, but also they are felt when determining how public and private money is spent.

This chapter seeks to quantify the potential macroeconomic impacts of the demographic transition, analyzing the principal implications of population aging, and identifying its effect on the long-term dynamics of the Uruguayan economy. It briefly introduces the literature on the macroeconomic effects of demographic change, then highlights the importance that demographic topics have on the behavior of the Uruguayan economy. The fourth section analyzes how demographic change transforms economic growth: based on the analysis of simulation exercises, we draw conclusions about the implications of population aging for the long-term growth of the economy. The fifth section considers the tensions that population aging generates on consumption and explains the economic significance of the intergenerational transfers that this process could provoke. The sixth section considers the effects of the demographic transition on public finances, while the final section presents some reflections that conclude our analysis.

Macroeconomic Impacts of Demographic Transition

Demographic transitions occur in three major phases. The first is the early transition, the second—as we have seen in previous chapters—is usually identified as the demographic dividend, and the third is known as the population aging phase.

During the demographic dividend phase, the overall proportion of the working-age population increases, while an increase is seen in segments that do not participate in the labor market and do not generate income from participation in productive activities (children and the elderly). As the demographic transition reaches the population aging phase, this trend is reversed and the dependent sectors increase in their relative shares of total population. During this phase, the growth of the dependent population occurs exclusively through the increasing share of the elderly in the population because during the aging phase we normally observe a reduction in the relative share of young people.

According to the analysis developed by Mason and Lee (2006), the effects of the demographic transition on economic growth are related to what they call the first and second "growth dividends." According to these authors, during the demographic dividend phase, a window of opportunity is created, characterized by favorable conditions for increasing economic growth. These "growth dividends" are the most notable manifestations of the changes that demographic transition brings to growth in economic activity.

The first growth dividend refers to the increase of the relative share of the working-age population during the window of opportunity. The effect of this change in the age structure is to increase per capita output. This first growth dividend disappears, and even reverses, when the population enters the aging phase and the dependent segments as a share of the total population begin to grow again.

The second growth dividend during the window of opportunity is attributable to the increase of the share of the population that can be considered to include "net savers" (their disposable income exceeds their consumption expenditure) during the demographic dividend. This situation, which favors an increase in the savings rate, can be seized upon to raise investment and increase the accumulation of physical capital. In the population aging phase, net savers begin to decline as a proportion of the total population. However, the effects of the second dividend need not be temporary. In effect, if quality investments are made during this phase, for example developing infrastructure which raises productivity, it is possible to achieve a sustained increase in productivity, extending the effects of the second dividend over time, at least during the first part of the population aging phase.

One can appreciate that the demographic transition is far from a neutral process with respect to the dynamics of economic growth. Lack of neutrality relates, specifically, to the two growth dividends. The first dividend makes labor more available, generating favorable conditions for economic expansion during the demographic dividend phase. In contrast, the population aging phase reverses the effect of the first dividend and begins to slow down economic growth. In turn, the second growth dividend acts on the conditions for saving in the economy, indirectly reducing the ability to finance investment projects, and therefore to accumulate physical capital. Although the second dividend directly helps in the accumulation of physical capital, because the dynamics of total factor productivity are closely linked to physical capital accumulation and improvements in the population's level of education, this second dividend can be expected to have an additional impact through total factor productivity, because it increases.

Beyond aspects linked to economic growth, demographic change impacts the dynamics of the economy in other spheres. A fundamental feature of population aging is that it modifies consumption patterns, skewing spending patterns toward an increased share of spending on goods and services consumed by elderly people. This change in the composition of aggregate consumption means that during the population aging phase Uruguay can expect to see a significant increase in spending on health care, and at the same time it is reasonable to expect a decrease in the proportion of aggregate spending dedicated to education.

Similarly, demographic transition can be expected to transform the patterns of intergenerational income transfers. In this context, social security spending will increase, while transfers needed to protect the youngest sectors of the population should decrease.

Demographics and the Uruguayan Economy

Uruguay was one of the first countries in Latin America to enter the demographic transition, characterized by the consolidation of low birth rates and a steady increasing trend in life expectancy at birth. It is perhaps as a result of this that population dynamics have played such a significant role in discussions about the long-term behavior of the Uruguayan economy.

The significance of migratory flows throughout the country's history has contributed to the central role of demographics in distinctive features of Uruguayan society and economy. The quantitative and qualitative importance of migratory flows during the final part of the 19th century, which further increased during the first half of the 20th century, has been highlighted in many studies analyzing the influence of demographics on the functioning of the economy and on the dynamics of long-term growth. The economic implications again gained importance during the period of emigration that began in Uruguay at the end of the 1960s and extended through the first years of the current century.

Demographic factors have been linked consistently to difficulties the Uruguayan economy has exhibited in sustaining growth at rates comparable to those of other countries in the region. Recurring discussions take place on the need to increase the birth rate and the expediency of implementing initiatives to attract Uruguayans living abroad to return. Proposals have not been lacking to implement policies to draw in immigrants who could contribute to overcoming limits that poor population growth places on economic expansion, particularly in the context of high employment rates and low rates of unemployment and underemployment in the context of the capacity of the economy during the last decade to absorb new workers.

As discussed in chapter 2, Uruguay's demographic evolution indicates that the dependency ratio—between the working-age population and the dependent population—has not changed significantly since the middle of the last century. The behavior observed suggests that the demographic dividend phase has manifested up to now in a very understated manner. The explanation for this may be related to the intense migration into the country since the final decades of the 20th century. It must be highlighted that emigrants who left the country during that period belonged to segments of the working-age population with higher skills than the average worker, which meant that the economic effect of this process may have been even more significant and may have hurt the economy's productivity.

Demographic forecasts indicate that Uruguay will record a slight reduction in the dependency ratio between 2000 and 2020, in accordance with the distinctive features of the demographic dividend. Consequently, Uruguay is very close to finishing the demographic dividend phase and entering the population aging phase, in contrast with what has been observed in other countries in Latin America.[2]

Demographic transition, against a backdrop of long-term economic growth at higher rates than the average in the second half of the 20th century, will predictably change intergenerational transfer schemes. As in other countries, it is probable that Uruguay will progressively undergo a process characterized by substantial increases in social security spending and reductions in spending on public programs whose objective is to protect individuals during childhood and adolescence (as is the case with the family allowances program).

Since the state is responsible for most education, health care, and social security transfers, one can expect that demographic change will have impacts on public finances and that these transformations may involve changes in fiscal policy.

The Demographic Transition and Economic Growth

This section presents the methodological framework and results from simulation exercises that provide information about the predictable impact of demographic changes on economic growth during this century.

The principal objective is to put the tensions that we predict will accompany population aging into perspective, comparing estimates of the expected effects over the coming decades with the contribution that population dynamics have made to economic performance during recent years.

Growth Accounting

The methodological focus in this chapter relies on a traditional process of factor decomposition of gross domestic product (GDP) growth. This tool enables us to estimate, on one hand, the contribution to growth from the accumulation of primary productive factors, and, on the other, the contribution of total factor productivity (TFP). The contribution from purely demographic factors, as well as the predicted closing of education and gender gaps in the economically active population, will enable us to evaluate the importance of the window of opportunity offered by Uruguay's demographic transition.

The growth accounting exercise in this work follows guidelines from the pioneering work of Solow (1956). This methodology is based on a neoclassical production function, in which the endowments of physical capital and labor, including human capital, are considered to be the factors of production. These productive factors are combined based on a technology of constant returns to scale.

Specifically, to perform the factor decomposition of growth we use a Cobb-Douglas production function (equation 9.1):

$$Y_t = e^{z_t} K_t^{\alpha} L_t^{\beta}, \tag{9.1}$$

where Y_t represents the economy's real GDP during period t, K_t is the stock of physical capital, L_t is the labor force, including the stock of human capital, and z_t is a stochastic process that controls technological change.

As is standard in this type of literature, the parameters α and β are fixed such that they correspond to the shares of total national income directed to compensate each factor of production. This approximation rests on the implicit assumption that the factors' compensation is equal to the values of their marginal productivity. Specifically, under these assumptions, the coefficients of a Cobb-Douglas production function are equivalent to the share of the compensation that each factor receives from total national income.

The functional distribution of income used to estimate the parameters α and β corresponds to the measurement from the 2005 National Accounts. This is the base year in the current National Accounts System used by the Central Bank of Uruguay, in addition to representing the last year for which an official measurement of the functional distribution of income is available.

Based on this information, the parameter α was allocated a value of 0.45[3] and the parameter β 0.55. The sum of both parameters is equal to 1 because we are working with a production function with constant returns to scale.

Once the production function has been calibrated, using logarithmic differences we obtain the following decomposition of economic growth:

$$\Delta y = \Delta z + \alpha \Delta k + \beta \Delta l, \tag{9.2}$$

where the lowercase letters represent the logarithmic transformations of the variables. The expression Δz is commonly known as the Solow residual and is usually interpreted as an approximation of TFP.

In short, equation 9.2 shows that GDP growth during a specific period can be decomposed as the sum of the variations of the accumulation of physical capital and labor (including human capital), weighted by the parameters α and β, respectively, plus the variation of TFP.

Based on this decomposition it is possible to describe the contribution of the primary factors of production and TFP to the economy's performance during the last 10 years. The results of this exercise will be utilized as the reference framework to evaluate the effects of demographic change over the coming decades.

Implementing the decomposition proposed in equation 9.2 required us to construct a time series of physical capital and human capital. To this end, we utilized the database created by Lanzilotta and Llambí (2005), which was updated using the same methodology employed by the authors. The same methodology was utilized in subsequent works by Carbajal et al. (2007) and Domínguez et al. (2014).

The Starting Point

During the last decade Uruguay has experienced a strong economic growth, with real GDP growth averaging 5.2 percent annually between 2005 and 2014 (figure 9.1). If we set aside the influence of cyclical fluctuations and focus our attention on the GDP growth trend, we observe that the economy's average annual growth rate over those years was 5 percent.[4]

The period under analysis was characterized by significant accumulation of productive factors, including both labor and capital. The expansion of capital accumulation occurred while productive investment was accelerating significantly. At the same time, many more people than before joined the labor force.

Figure 9.2 illustrates the increase observed in investment, expressed as a percentage of GDP. The trajectory of gross fixed capital formation observed during the last decade represented a real structural break from the historical dynamics of capital accumulation in the Uruguayan economy. By the end of the period, the investment rate was consistently above 20 percent of GDP. This contrasts with

Figure 9.1 Seasonally Adjusted GDP and Trend GDP, 1997–2014

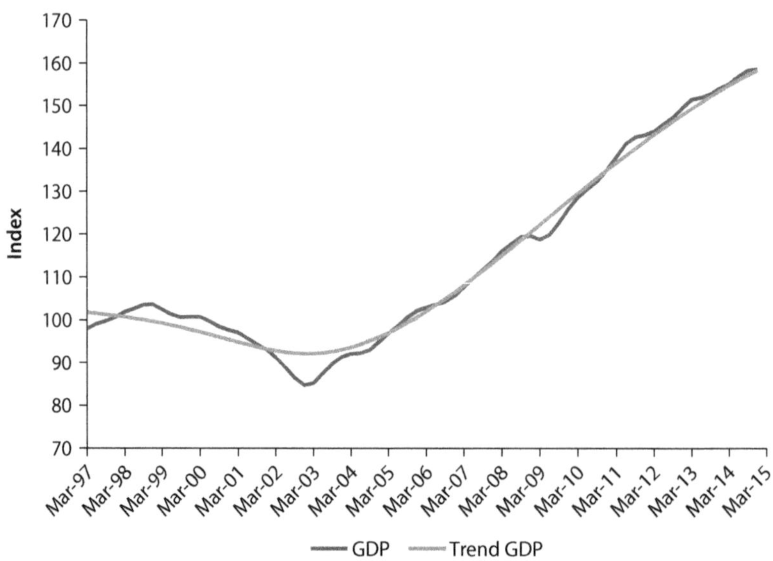

Source: Estimates based on Central Bank of Uruguay (Banco Central del Uruguay; BCU) data.
Note: Base 2005 = 100.

Figure 9.2 Gross Fixed Capital Formation, 1990–2014

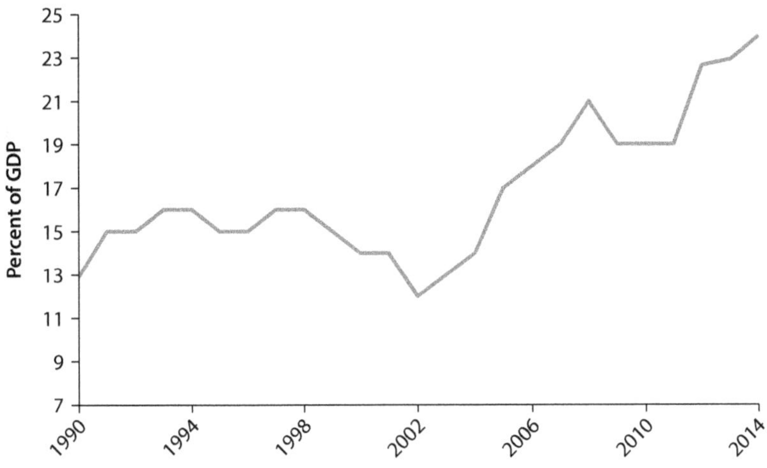

Source: Constructed based on Central Bank of Uruguay (Banco Central del Uruguay; BCU) data.

Figure 9.3 Stock of Physical Capital, 1997–2014

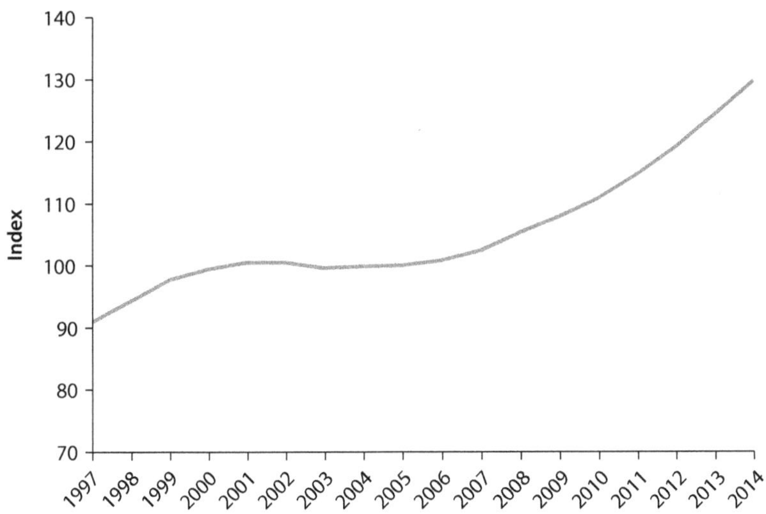

Source: Estimates based on Central Bank of Uruguay (Banco Central del Uruguay; BCU) data.
Note: Base 2005 = 100.

this variable's average value during the preceding 50 years, when investments in Uruguay were consistently the lowest in the region.

Figure 9.3 allows us to appreciate how the dynamism of investment contributed to significant growth in the stock of physical capital, at an average annual rate of 2.9 percent from 2005 to 2014.

During the last decade the labor force has grown strongly. Figure 9.4 shows that the economic activity rate increased by about 7 percentage points between 2004 and 2014. This growth is explained by structural phenomena, such as the

Figure 9.4 Economic Activity Rate and Unemployment Rate, 1997–2014

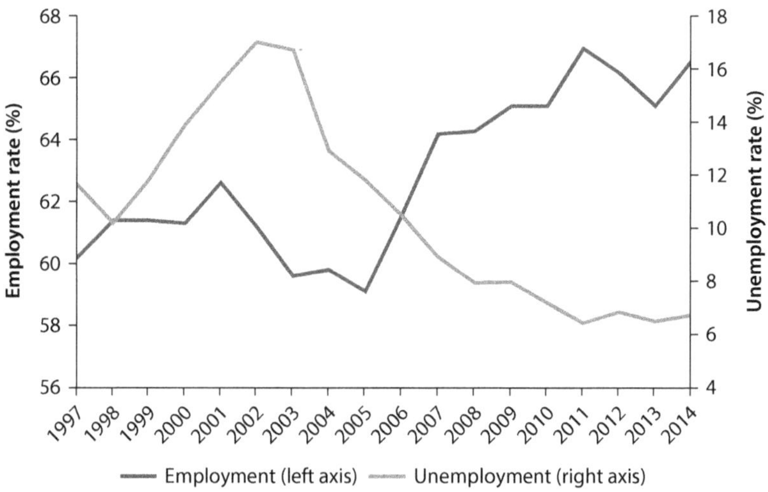

Source: National Institute of Statistics (Instituto Nacional de Estadística; INE).

persistent decrease in the economic activity gap by gender, as well as by the economic dynamism that stimulated more people to join the labor market.

Structural unemployment consolidated at a new low. Both factors contributed simultaneously to growth in the employment rate of 9 percentage points during 2004–14.

In an attempt to obtain an estimate that would allow us to approximate the contribution of human capital to GDP growth, we adjusted the number of employed workers, while considering their productivity. To estimate productivity, we used estimates from chapter 7 of salary returns for each education level.

The methodology employed to construct the human capital index has two stages. In the first, we estimated the Mincer earnings functions of the salary returns linked to education, categorizing individuals by the highest level of education reached. In the second stage, the estimated salary returns were used to approximate workers' productivity differentials. That is, we constructed the human capital index by aggregating the number of employed persons at each education level, weighting them according to the returns to education.

By combining the number of employed individuals and their productivity into a single variable, we created the human capital index presented in figure 9.5, showing that human capital accumulation has accelerated significantly during the last decade. The estimates show that during the period under analysis total human capital stock in Uruguay increased by approximately 26 percent.

Keeping in mind the strong expansion in labor and capital endowments, the results of the growth decomposition exercise performed here indicate that a significant portion of the economic growth in the last decade cannot be explained by the accumulation of primary factors of production (table 9.1). In effect, according to the estimates here, the accumulation of factors would explain 53.5 percent of GDP growth during the period, or 2.8 percentage points of the

Figure 9.5 Human Capital Index, 1997–2014

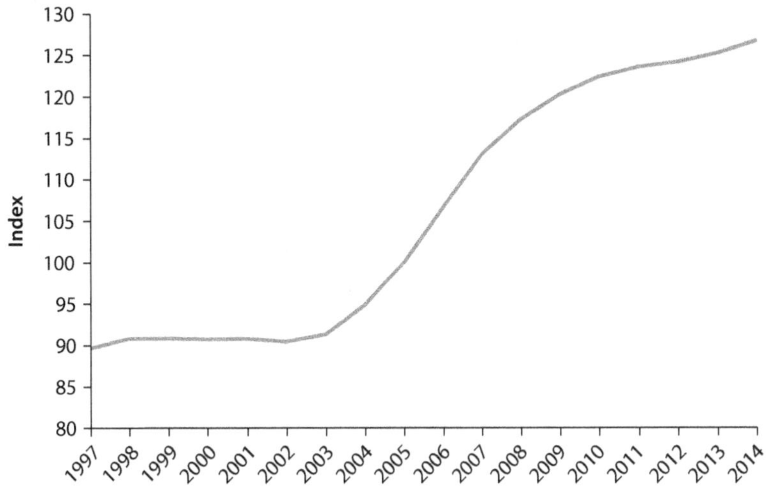

Source: Estimates based on National Institute of Statistics (Instituto Nacional de Estadística; INE) data.
Note: Base 2005 = 100.

Table 9.1 Factor Decomposition of Growth
percent

	K	*Contribution L (human capital)*	*TFP*	*Total*
GDP	1.3	1.5	2.4	5.2
GDP (in total)	24.3	29.5	46.5	
Trend GDP	1.3	1.5	2.2	5.0
Trend GDP (in total)	25.3	30.7	44.0	

Note: K = physical capital; *L* = labor; TFP = total factor productivity.

(5.2 percent) average growth rate. The results of this growth accounting exercise show that the contribution of TFP would account for the remaining 46.5 percent (2.4 percentage points of annual average GDP growth).[5]

Table 9.1 shows that the contribution of labor, including human capital, explained 29.5 percent of economic growth during the period, while physical capital contributed 24.3 percent.

If we perform the growth decomposition exercise on the trend component of GDP, we obtain results that are essentially the same: the accumulation of primary factors of production explains 56 percent of the expansion of economic activity recorded during the period, while TFP is responsible for the rest.

The exercise performed on the trend component of GDP provides more interesting information, to the extent that it allows us to obtain estimates related to long-term growth.

The First Growth Dividend: Direct Contribution of Labor

Using the results from the exercise carried out with data from the last decade as a frame of reference, we can evaluate the effects of the demographic transition on projected growth of GDP during 2015 to 2100. The analysis is based on the three scenarios considered in chapter 7 of this study, related to the evolution of the labor force during the rest of the 21st century.

Scenario 1, called the "trend/business as usual" considers the evolution of the human capital stock only incorporating predicted changes in the economic activity rate as a consequence of demographic change. Scenario 2 considers the case if rising female labor force participation reaches a rate similar to those currently observed in developed countries. Scenario 3 assumes that the gap in female labor force participation is closed and workers are educated to higher levels, which would improve workers' productivity.[6]

If we compare the results of the simulation exercises in this work with the last decade, they signal a reduction of human capital's contribution to economic growth during this century. The decrease in the contribution from labor occurs in all the scenarios considered, although the reduction is obviously less in the third scenario.

These results offer predictive information about how demographic trends will reduce long-term growth in the Uruguayan economy. The demographic transition, and especially the gradual aging of the population, will diminish the potential for economic growth. In the case of the "business-as-usual" scenario, labor's reduced contribution to growth during 2015–40 would be somewhat more than 1.2 percentage points per year compared to the contribution made by human capital during the past decade. Closing the gender gap and improving the labor force's productivity reduces the impact of the demographic trends, but they are not enough to keep economic growth from falling by at least half a percentage point in any case.

The reduction of labor's contribution to long-term economic growth shown in the different simulation exercises was, to a certain extent, a predictable outcome of at least two factors. First, the increase in labor market participation during the last decade is very much higher than observed in historical data, and an extrapolation of the future labor environment based on the past decade cannot be considered a reasonable result. We can confirm that the growth rates recorded for the economically active population and the expansion of employment during recent times cannot be maintained in the long term. Uruguay has had low population growth for several decades and a historical analysis of the labor market shows that unique and unrepeatable characteristics were created in the past decade. Second, as mentioned in previous chapters, the demographic trends predicted for Uruguay will reduce the effect of human capital's contribution to economic growth because we expect the working-age population's growth rate to slow and subsequently this population itself will begin to shrink.

The impact of demographic trends on growth in output intensifies as we extend the reference time. By the end of 2015–2100, the period contemplated in the simulations, the reduction of the contribution from labor will reach at least one percentage point of growth per year. Table 9.2 shows that the least negative result is from Scenario 3, in which human capital's contribution in 2100 is forecast to be equivalent to 0.4 percentage points of annual economic growth. In the case

Table 9.2 Human Capital's Contribution to Economic Growth
percent

	Average 2015–2040	*Average 2015–2100*	*2100*
Scenario 1	0.30	−0.12	−0.40
Scenario 2	0.70	0.12	−0.40
Scenario 3	0.70	0.40	0.10

Source: Created based on data from chapter 7.

of the business-as-usual scenario, identified as Scenario 1 in table 9.2, human capital's contribution would actually shrink, falling to around −0.4 percent by the end of the period.

In summary, the scenarios considered here predict that human capital will reduce its contribution to average annual economic growth during 2015–2100 by between 1.1 and 1.6 percentage points as compared to the past decade. By 2100, human capital's contribution will fall by between 1.4 and 1.9 percentage points.

The downward trend in the contribution of human capital means that during the next quarter-century the negative impact of demographic trends on economic growth will be moderate. If we consider the forecasts for 2015–40, the period preceding Uruguay's definitive entry into the population aging phase, human the capital's contribution will be between 0.3 and 0.7 percentage points, shrinking from the past decade's 0.8 to 1.2 percentage points of annual growth.

The Second Growth Dividend: Effects on Capital Accumulation

As we have pointed out, the demographic transition's effects on economic growth are not only the product of its impact on the labor force. The second growth dividend suggests that changes in the population will raise savings and improve the capital accumulation process.

In effect, the evolution of savings is fundamental for analyzing the long-term dynamics of productive investment because savings constitute the principal source of financing for such investment. For example, during 2009–13 gross capital formation averaged 21.5 percent of Uruguayan GDP. External savings during recent years represented a little more than 3 percent of GDP a year, while foreign direct investment reached an annual average of 5.3 percent of GDP in the same period. Consequently, even during a period characterized by elevated external savings and significant capture of foreign direct investment flows, internal savings continued to be the principal source of financing for investment, providing the resources for approximately three-fourths of the total gross fixed capital formation in the Uruguayan economy.

Analysis of the demographic transition's effects on the accumulation of capital is supported by the forecasts of the economic support ratio presented in chapter 3 of this book. This indicator is based on the ratio between actual consumers and actual workers for each year based on the income and consumption structure (and therefore also considering savings) of the population by age groups.[7] In this way, as the demographic transition affects the population's age structure, changes are seen in expected internal savings.

The economic support ratio expresses the ratio between consumption and labor income, which means that if we maintain the assumption from the growth accounting exercise that the factor distribution of income remains constant, then it is possible to extrapolate the value of the ratio between consumption and total income, keeping in mind that labor income in the Uruguayan economy represents approximately 55 percent of total income.

Based on the information provided by this ratio, which may be interpreted as a ratio between actual consumption and labor income, it is possible to obtain the marginal propensity to consume in the economy (and, therefore, the marginal propensity to save). The propensity to consume is the proportion of aggregate income that is used for consumption. However, the forecasts of the economic support ratio provided in chapter 3 give a projection for the ratio between actual consumption and labor income while only accounting for the changes in the demographic structure, which could produce biased results about the trajectory of consumption.

This work presents corrected estimates for consumption that consider, in turn, potential changes to the marginal propensity to consume as aggregate income changes. A negative ratio between the marginal propensity to consume and incomes can be expected from a theoretical standpoint, assuming that the marginal utility of consumption is decreasing, in addition to being empirically consistent with observations from data across countries. Figure 9A.1 in annex 9A presents information that supports the hypothesis in this work that the marginal propensity to consume declines as aggregate income increases.

Consequently, the marginal propensity to consume will be determined by two opposing trends in this century. On one hand, following a limited period for the window of opportunity, population aging will increase the marginal propensity to consume (and decrease the propensity to save) just as we see from the trajectory of the economic support ratio. On the other hand, economic growth will decrease the economy's marginal propensity to consume as a consequence of the increase in the population's income. The contraposition of these two forces may produce very different trajectories for internal savings, depending on the growth rates seen in the Uruguayan economy through the period under analysis.

Figure 9.6 shows three scenarios related to the evolution of the marginal propensity to consume. The first proposes a trajectory without economic growth, which therefore only considers the effect on the propensity to consume that results from population aging. The second scenario outlines a situation in which per capita GDP grows by 1 percent per year, while the third scenario contemplates per capita GDP growth of 3 percent per year. These scenarios enable us to estimate the effects of population aging on capital accumulation under the assumption that the proportion of external savings in total investment financing does not change.

One can appreciate that in the absence of economic growth, the propensity to consume exhibits different behavior. In this scenario we observe that until the

Figure 9.6 Marginal Propensity to Consume (Consumption/GDP), 2015–2100

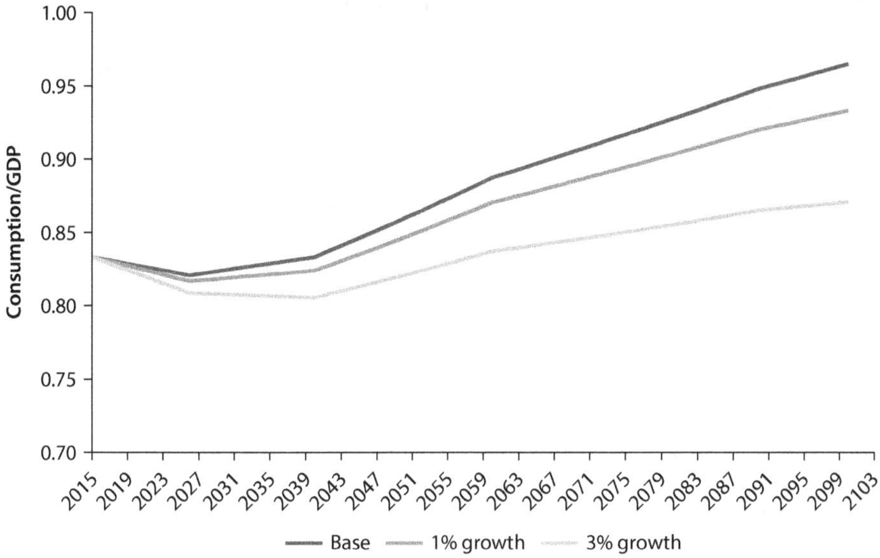

beginning of the 2040s the propensity to consume will trend lower, which basically results from the increase in the proportion of "net savers." After this time, the propensity to consume will begin to grow slowly but steadily, as a consequence of the progressive advance in population aging.

Analysis of the other scenarios shows that if Uruguay is able to maintain steady growth during the coming decades, the wealth effect could offset a significant portion of the effect of population aging on internal saving that is associated with the reversal of the second growth dividend. In these circumstances, internal savings could remain high and continue to sustain the same gross fixed capital formation observed in recent years. In this way, Uruguay would be able to mitigate the reduction in economic growth caused by the slower pace of human capital accumulation.

However, if Uruguay were not able to grow significantly during the coming decades, the "wealth effect" would be insufficient to neutralize the effects of population aging and the demographic change would begin to decrease the economy's internal savings rate, particularly during the second half of the century. In this context, maintaining high investment would only be possible through increasing attraction for foreign savings, which would have to reach amounts that do not appear to be very plausible. Keep in mind that the marginal propensity to consume would increase by approximately 10 percentage points of 2015 GDP in a scenario in which per capita GDP would grow at a rate of 1 percent per year between 2015 and 2100. In this case, maintaining investment relative to GDP at current rates would assume attracting 10 additional points of GDP in external savings.

Effects on Long-Term Economic Growth

The demographic transition's repercussions for long-term economic growth are the result of the direct effects of this on the evolution of the economically active population relative to the dependent population (first dividend) and the indirect effect of the process on the marginal propensity to save, keeping in mind the impact of internal savings on capital accumulation (the second dividend).

In the previous section, we argued that the effect of the reversal of the second dividend could be neutralized, at least partially, if the economy grew significantly strongly during the rest of the demographic window of opportunity. Keeping in mind the expected changes in both factors of production (human capital and physical capital), as well as progress in TFP, we proceed to evaluate the total impact of demographic change on Uruguay's economic growth during the 21st century. We base our conclusions from consideration of four scenarios that arise from making different assumptions about human capital's contribution and the evolution of TFP, to the extent that physical capital's contribution is endogenous and depends on the trajectory of internal savings and the availability of external savings.

The first two scenarios contemplate changes in human capital guided solely by the predicted evolution of people in employment, the case we call "business-as-usual" in chapter 7, and they are differentiated by their assumptions about the behavior of TFP. In the literature on the topic, changes in TFP are usually linked to advances in technology and improvements in worker productivity resulting from better education. In this context, it appears reasonable to link changes in TFP with the accumulation of the primary factors of production.

Accordingly, in the first scenario we assume that TFP's contribution is proportional to the accumulation of factors of production. Specifically, in the simulation exercise we assume that accumulation explains one-third of economic growth. This proportion is lower than in the last decade, when TFP explained 44 percent of growth, but it is in line with TFP's contribution over the last 30 years.

In the second scenario, we assume an exogenous contribution from TFP that is somewhat lower than that observed in recent years. In this case, TFP would result in average annual GDP growth of 1.5 percent.

In the third and fourth scenarios we assume that human capital will evolve according to the dynamics predicted in the third hypothesis considered in chapter 7. In this case, the trajectory of human capital not only includes predicted changes in the number of people in work, but also assumes a growing proportion of women in the labor force and a closing education gap that would enable Uruguay to increase average productivity in the labor force. In the third scenario, we assume that TFP changes are linked to the accumulation of primary factors of production, which is similar to the assumption made in the first scenario. In the fourth scenario, we assume that TFP's contribution is exogenous, as we did for the second scenario.

The results of the simulation exercises as they relate to GDP growth are presented in figure 9.7. Physical capital's contribution is presented in figure 9.8,

Figure 9.7 Index of the Physical Size of GDP, 2015–2100

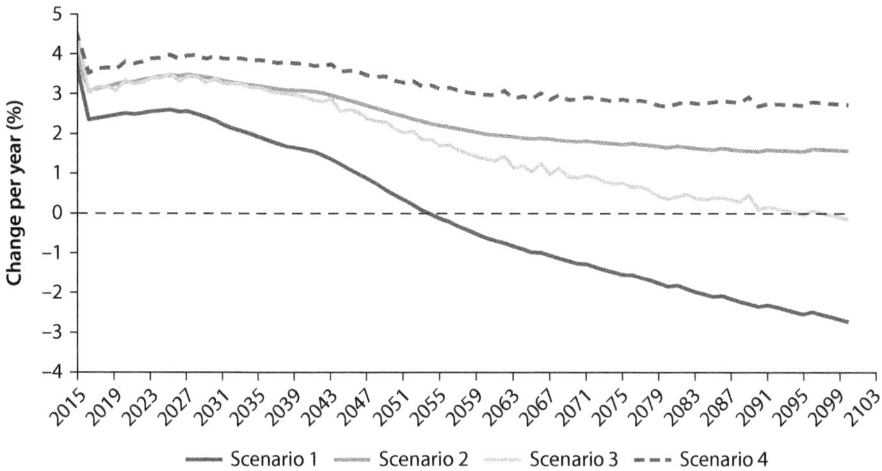

Figure 9.8 Physical Capital's Contribution to Growth, 2015–2100

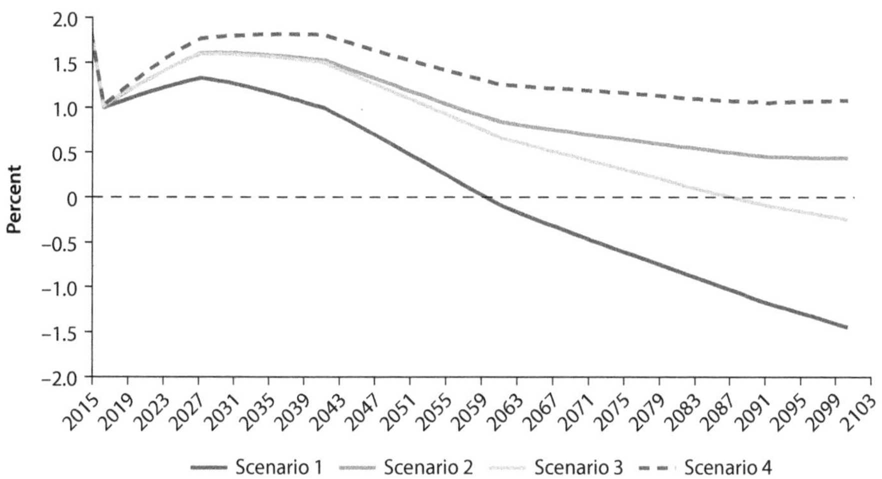

while that of human capital is shown in figure 9.9. Figure 9.10 includes the contribution from TFP. In each case, we considered trajectories corresponding to all four scenarios.

Analysis of the results of the simulations reveals, first, that appreciable differences exist between the trajectories for each of the four scenarios. This means that the effects of the demographic transition on Uruguay's long-term economic growth largely depend on the behavior of factors that are independent of demographics. The sensitivity of the results of the hypotheses with respect to TFP's contribution and the closing of the gender and education gaps among the economically active population demonstrate the difficulty of evaluating the effects of demographic trends independently of the influence of other

Figure 9.9 Human Capital's Contribution to Growth, 2015–2100

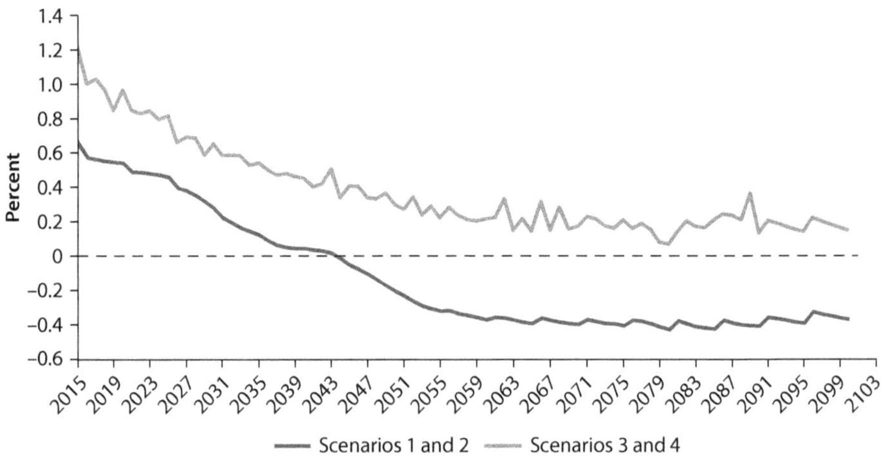

Figure 9.10 Total Factor Productivity's Contribution to Growth, 2015–2100

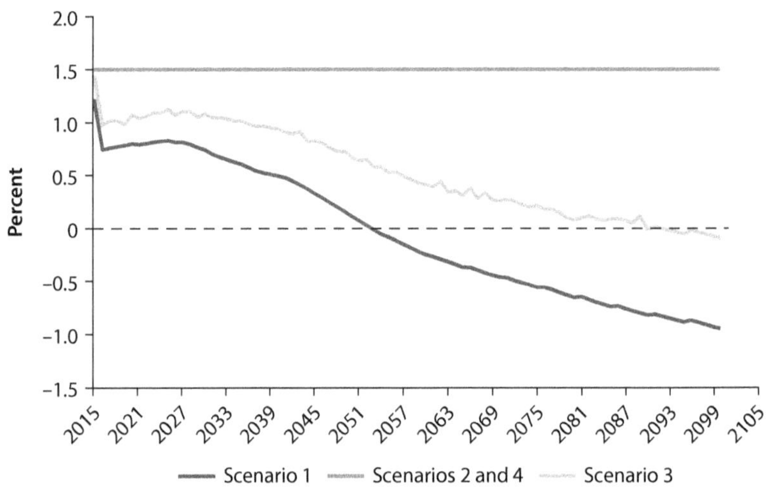

factors such as the contribution from public policies that affect consumption and investment decisions.

Second, the results indicate that, beyond the differences in the magnitude of predicted growth, in all the cases GDP exhibits two distinct phases. In the first phase, which ranges from 12 to 21 years depending on the scenario, demographic changes accelerate the pace of economic growth. The trajectory in this first phase is a clear example of the length of the window of opportunity for the Uruguayan economy. The second phase is characterized by a steady deceleration in GDP growth, which is compatible with the progressive aging of the population.

During the period of decelerated growth, we can see the scenarios produce differing results. In the first and third scenarios—in which we assume that the evolution of TFP is linked to the accumulation of primary factors of production—we observe a permanent decline in GDP growth, as over time the contributions from declining human and physical capital are consolidated. Growth in human capital falls over time principally as a result of the reduction in the economically active population in absolute terms. In turn, the decrease in the contribution of physical capital is explained by the decline in the marginal propensity to save, which is created by population aging. According to the results of the simulations, the influence of this factor, which reduces the ability to accumulate capital, is not offset by the wealth effect created by economic growth. The simulation exercises show that the effect of the weakening potential to accumulate physical capital would be accentuated during the second half of the 21st century, as the predicted deceleration in economic growth reduces the wealth effect and therefore produces a more pronounced drop in the internal savings rate.

In addition to the effect of these factors, in both scenarios we expect the contribution of TFP to decrease because of the assumption that links this variable with the accumulation of factors of production.

On the other hand, in the scenarios where we assume a constant TFP contribution, GDP growth would tend to stabilize around the rate achieved in last two decades of the 21st century. In effect, in the second and fourth scenarios, the exogenous contribution from TFP "guarantees" a minimum growth rate that enables the wealth effect to offset the effect of population aging, thus avoiding an important shrinkage of physical capital. In these cases, the deceleration of long-term economic growth appears to be associated almost directly with the decrease in the contribution from human capital.

To analyze the impact of population aging on social well-being, it is more informative to look at changes in per capita output than aggregate output. With this in mind, figures 9.11 and 9.12 show per capita GDP in each of the scenarios constructed.

Figure 9.11 Per Capita GDP, 2015–2100

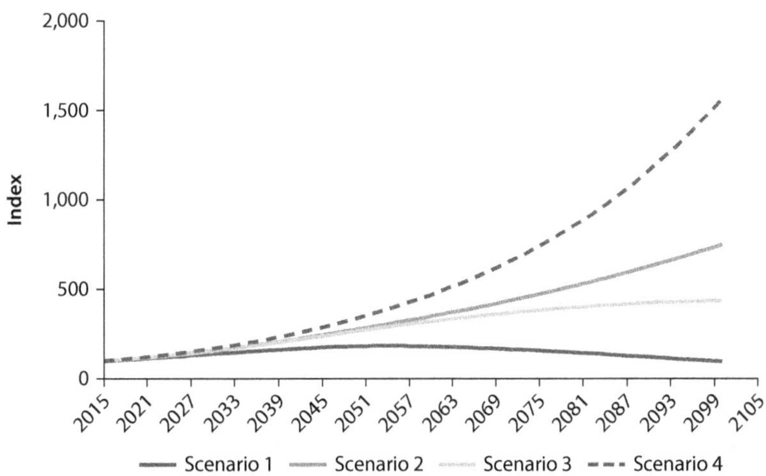

Note: Base 2015 = 100.

Figure 9.12 Annual Change in Per Capita GDP, 2015–2100

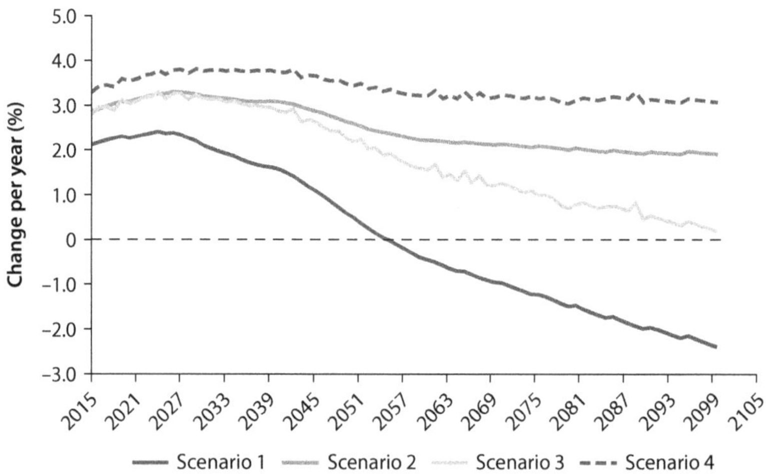

As can be observed from figure 9.12, the predicted, very moderate, change in national population means that practically no differences exist between the growth trajectories for the aggregate GDP growth rate and per capita GDP. However, it is possible to observe that per capita growth in GDP is somewhat lower than aggregate GDP growth during the first half of the century, although this is reversed in the second half. This situation results from population forecasts, which indicate continued growth until peaking in 2046 (see chapter 2). From that year, the population will begin to decrease and will continue to do so until the end of the century.

In the most pessimistic scenario (Scenario 1), per capita GDP would shrink, although it would be practically zero (0.03 percent) for the rest of the century. In contrast, the most optimistic scenario (Scenario 4) presents predicted average growth of 3.3 percent per year for the rest of this century. In figure 9.11, we can appreciate how the different annual growth rates, depending on the scenario, over such a long period, result in completely divergent trajectories for per capita GDP. This outcome illustrates how important the margin of error becomes when forecasting very long-term scenarios.

In summary, from the standpoint of factor accumulation, the conditions for economic growth seem favorable during the next decade and perhaps in the decade after. However, after the 2040s demographic change will begin to undermine the bases of the Uruguayan economy's growth. The depth of impact from demographic trends will fundamentally depend on two crucial elements: the growth rate that is achieved during the window of opportunity and the contribution from TFP. Higher economic growth during the window of opportunity as well as a greater contribution from technological advances will create wealth effects that may enable Uruguay to at least partially offset the decline in the accumulation of physical capital caused by population aging. More moderate economic growth, or even a lower contribution from TFP, would result in demographics expressing itself with greater intensity; thereby lowering the GDP growth rate, not just as a result of a lower contribution from human capital accumulation, but also due to a reduction in the contribution of physical capital.

Intergenerational Transfers and Consumption Patterns

The progress of population aging signifies an increase in the share of the dependent population relative to the economically active population that generates income in the economy. This phenomenon is clearly apparent when we look at the predicted evolution of the dependency ratio (as we did in chapter 2) as well as the trajectory of the economic support ratio (chapter 3).

Forecasts for the economic support ratio until 2100 indicate that the Uruguayan economy will see strong growth in the number of net consumers relative to net workers. This trend is essentially explained by two reasons.

First, population aging will significantly increase the number of dependent persons over age 64. The impact will not be offset by the decrease in dependent persons under age 14. The overall effect is clear when we consider the dependency ratio. Changes in this indicator clearly show how the relative significance of the dependent segments will increase.

Second, the progress of the demographic transition and the solidification of the population aging trend will bring an increase in aggregate consumption. This phenomenon will be directly linked to progressive growth in the segments of the population considered to be net consumers. The older segments of the population have a greater marginal propensity to consume and, therefore, the proportion of income that is spent on consumption increases with age. This aspect is not adequately accounted for in the dependency ratio indicator and means that even if changes occur in the ratio of the dependent population to the economically active population, population aging means that the share of net consumers will rise.

The increase in the number of net consumers relative to net workers generates two important challenges. On one hand, it sets the stage for a scenario in which, all else equal, per capita income will fall. In this context, individuals will have to reduce their consumption or the aggregate savings rate will decrease, which would negatively affect the investment process and therefore growth. This situation was analyzed in greater detail in the previous section, where different scenarios discussed how the growth of net consumers relative to net workers could reduce long-term economic growth.

The results of the simulation exercises indicate that, although population aging depresses the long-term growth rate, the reduction could be offset or at least softened by a more significant increase in incomes during the window of opportunity or through steady growth in TFP.

The principal challenge for public policies is to create a strong process of investment during the next 15 or 20 years, in an attempt to obtain productivity gains and improve the efficiency of production. Taking advantage of these favorable investment conditions should become one of the most important macroeconomic objectives, with significant implications from an economic growth perspective. Attaining improvements in productivity constitutes one of the most effective ways to deal with pressures resulting from growth of consumption without significantly affecting the long-term growth rate.

The second important challenge in this context is to guarantee an intergenerational transfer scheme that ensures the economic well-being of the growing dependent population. Transfer schemes from the economically active population can take various institutional forms and may combine public and private mechanisms. In any case, the growing share of the dependent population will result in an increase in transfer flows from the economically active population. The question of how to finance these transfers will occupy a privileged space in the political and economic debate.

The growing flow of intergenerational transfers that result from the progress of population aging is separate from the institutional setup that is adopted. This means that tensions that emerge will not be resolved with a simple transfer of the administration of resources from the public sphere to the private sphere, or vice versa.

This warning is especially important for Uruguay because in most institutional systems through which intergenerational transfers are carried out, the public sector plays a role, both as the direct administrator of resources and as the regulator of activities through which the services are provided, as is the case with health care services.

Financing the systems that carry out transfers to older adults will be, without a doubt, a fiscal policy challenge. In this context, dimensions related to fiscal sustainability take on special importance.

The results from studies carried out by Bucheli, González, and Olivieri (2010) and Bucheli and González (2011) show that in Uruguay the systems that make transfers to dependent sectors composed of older adults are mostly financed through income from active workers and public transfers. In contrast, in the case of transfers to dependent children and adolescents, private transfers play a role through family ties.

Consequently, despite that social security reforms in 1996 removed from the public sphere a significant portion of the administration of intergenerational income transfers, so reducing the fiscal effects of population aging, we can expect that demographic change will create tensions for public finances. These issues are analyzed in detail in the next section, reviewing the estimates provided in previous chapters.

Demographic Change and Fiscal Policy

We now turn to the effects of the demographic transition on public finances, under the premise that throughout the period under analysis the institutional framework remains unchanged for each component of spending, while the structure of public income also stays the same.

Maintaining the current fiscal structure, both for taxes and in financing public activities across the components of spending, may appear to be an excessively strong assumption when we are analyzing phenomena developed over an extended time. However, this hypothesis has the virtue of enabling us to evaluate the impact of demographic transition in the absence of innovations in fiscal policy. This means that the implications that come out of this analysis should be considered as a sort of "passive forecast." Accordingly, the results discussed in this section should be interpreted as useful inputs for identifying tensions and topics that could form part of the future public policy agenda.

Chapter 3 enabled us to analyze forecasts of the different components of public social spending in a scenario free of policy changes. The results indicate that population aging will produce a significant increase in public social spending as a proportion of GDP by 2100. The estimates suggest that social spending, which in 2014 was slightly above 19.4 percent of GDP,[8] will increase until reaching a level equal to 24 percent of GDP in 2100. Specifically, the results of the simulations show that by the end of the 21st century, the changes in the population will require public social spending to increase by 4.6 percentage points of GDP.

The relative increase in the proportion of public social spending relative to GDP arises from heterogeneous changes in its components. Table 9.3 shows that the components that explain the increase in public spending will be retirement and pension transfers (an increase of 3.7 percent of GDP is expected) and health care spending (an increase of 1.7 percent of GDP is expected). The proportion of "other transfers" will remain essentially unchanged (with a contraction of just 0.1 percent of GDP). In turn, demographic change will result in a reduction of education spending that will reach 0.9 percent of GDP, the product of the expected fall in the young population's share of the total population.

The forecasted behavior indicates that during the first half of the century public social spending as a proportion of income will not expand significantly. For that matter, the estimates show that by 2050 public social spending will contract by about 0.3 percent of current GDP.

The explanation for this behavior is related to the fact that during the first half of the century the fiscal cost of transfers for retirement and pensions will be affected by the gradual transfer of social security payments from the public system administered by the Social Security Bank (Banco de Previsión Social [BPS]

Table 9.3 Public Social Transfers, 2014, 2050, and 2100
percent of GDP

	2014	*2050*	*2100*
Education[a]	3.6	2.8	2.7
Health care	5.2	5.7	6.9
Retirement and pensions	9.2	9.3	13.1
Other transfers	1.3	1.2	1.2
Total	**19.3**	**19.0**	**23.9**

Source: Chapter 3.
a. Assumes that the level of spending per student remains constant during the period.

to the Social Security Savings Fund Administrators (Administradoras de Fondos de Ahorro Previsional [AFAPs]). These transfers were established in the social security reform implemented in 1996. In the second half of the century, when the new social security regime reaches a steady state, demographic change will again put pressure on the public purse and will produce a steady increase in the proportion of spending on these transfers.

Analysis of the forecast trend for public social spending enables us to conclude that, although population aging will put pressure on fiscal policy, the effect will not begin to be felt until the second half of the century. This means that in the most probable scenario the demographic transition will not be particularly relevant from the perspective of the evolution of aggregate public spending.

If coverage is expanded in the education system and per-student spending is increased to close the education gaps (the third scenario in chapter 6), then public spending on education will not drop as a percentage of GDP, and therefore the demographic transition will not free up resources that could be used to meet the needs of the older adult dependent population.

On the contrary, as table 9.4 demonstrates, the scenario with expanding education coverage discussed in chapter 6 entails an increase in public spending through 2100 on the order of 2.3 percent of GDP. In this new scenario, the expected increase in public social spending would be on the order of 7.8 percent of GDP. However, we must consider that the pressure from this component of spending would continue to be very moderate during the first half of the century. The expected increase in public social spending would be 2.4 percentage points of GDP by 2050.

The analysis of the fiscal repercussions of the demographic transition should incorporate the changes in public income that will occur throughout 2015–2100. It is important to keep in mind that Uruguay's current tax structure comprises some direct progressive taxes. The presence of this category, in a time of economic growth, will enable the government to increase fiscal pressure without needing to change tax rates or taxable bases. In effect, the existence of "progressive" rates for individual income taxes (Impuesto a las Rentas de las Personas Físicas [IRPF]) (corresponding to category II) and the existence of the social security assistance tax (Impuesto de Asistencia a la Seguridad Social [IASS])

Table 9.4 Public Social Transfers, Expansion of Education Coverage Scenario, 2014, 2050, and 2100
percent of GDP

	2014	*2050*	*2100*
Education[a]	3.6	5.5	5.9
Health care	5.2	5.7	6.9
Retirement and pensions	9.2	9.3	13.1
Other transfers	1.3	1.2	1.2
Total	**19.3**	**21.7**	**27.1**

Source: Chapters 3 and 6.
a. Assumes expansion of coverage and per-student expenditure (chapter 6).

means that as economic activity expands, the government will collect a growing proportion of GDP. This feature is especially important in the analysis because it contributes to mitigating some of the pressure that the demographic transition will put on public finances.

On the other hand, consumption taxes at present contribute the greatest portion of tax collections, specifically the value added tax (Impuesto al Valor Agregado [IVA]) and the specific internal tax (Impuesto Específico Interno [IMESI]). Thus if there is a significant change in consumption's proportion of GDP, we would need to consider the effect of this on tax collections.

Table 9.5 presents the expected evolution of collections of consumption taxes (IVA and IMESI), the category II IRPF (income tax), and the IASS relative to GDP for each of the scenarios in the previous section.

To the extent that the first and second scenarios did not foresee changes in the human capital stock, the results of the simulations would be compatible with the public spending described in table 9.3. In contrast, the evolution of the human capital stock corresponding to the third and fourth scenarios arises from assuming an expansion of education coverage that is in step with the assumptions for the evolution of spending that were presented in table 9.4.

In all the cases considered here we can expect public income to increase relative to GDP without the need to modify the tax structure. The growth of the economy and the changes in consumption are the factors that explain this behavior. Obviously, the assumptions related to TFP and, therefore, projected economic growth will result in different rates of fiscal pressures in the coming decades.

One result that emerges from the simulation exercises is that the endogenous increase in tax pressure in all the cases enables Uruguay to at least offset a portion of the expected growth in public spending, relieving pressures that the demographic transition will put on the fiscal account balance.

Table 9.5 Collections of IRPF + IASS and IVA + IMESI, 2014, 2050, and 2100
percent of GDP

		2014	*2050*	*2100*
Scenario 1	IVA-IMESI	10.97	11.02	12.70
	IRPF-IASS	2.76	3.80	2.71
	Total	**13.73**	**14.82**	**15.41**
Scenario 2	IVA-IMESI	10.97	10.81	11.69
	IRPF-IASS	2.76	4.63	7.01
	Total	**13.73**	**15.44**	**18.69**
Scenario 3	IVA-IMESI	10.97	10.83	11.96
	IRPF-IASS	2.76	4.56	5.45
	Total	**13.73**	**15.39**	**17.41**
Scenario 4	IVA-IMESI	10.97	10.73	11.09
	IRPF-IASS	2.76	5.11	9.89
	Total	**13.73**	**15.84**	**20.98**

Note: IASS = social security assistance tax (Impuesto de Asistencia a la Seguridad Social); IMESI = specific internal tax (Impuesto Específico Interno); IRPF = individual income tax (Impuesto a las Rentas de las Personas Físicas); IVA = value added tax (Impuesto al Valor Agregado).

For example, in the first and second scenario we expect an increase in public income of 1.7 percent and 5 percent of GDP by 2100, respectively, to attend to the increase in public social spending of 4.6 percent of GDP. This means that in the first scenario population aging would result in a decline in the fiscal balance equivalent to 2.9 percent of GDP, while in the second scenario the fiscal balance would improve to the order of 0.4 percent of GDP.

In turn, in the third and fourth scenarios we expect an increase in public sector income of 3.7 percent and 7.3 percent of GDP, respectively, while public social spending will increase by the equivalent of 7.8 percent of GDP. Consequently, the expansion of education coverage and increase in per-student expenditure would reduce the fiscal balance by 4.1 percent of GDP in the third scenario and by 0.5 percent of GDP in the fourth scenario.

The results of the simulations indicate that the predicted evolution of public income reinforces the idea that the fiscal tensions caused by demographic change will mostly be felt during the second half of the century. In addition, continued economic growth moderates the effects on the fiscal balance because it creates a significant increase in public income relative to GDP.

In short, the simulation exercises allow us to draw two important conclusions. First, it is evident that population aging will put pressure on public spending. Second, the expected increase in spending will not necessarily mean that the tax structure will have to change since the current system will bring an endogenous increase in the tax burden as the economy expands. This increase will offset some, if not all, of the projected growth in public spending attributable to the demographic transition.

The results obtained here indicate that the changes in public spending directly related to population aging do not represent threats to the government's ability to sustain fiscal policy, which means that demographic change by itself is unlikely to provoke changes in the tax system.

Even in the scenarios which forecast a larger shrinkage in fiscal accounts, the deterioration would occur in the second half of the century, which means that the country has a temporary window of a little more than three decades to design and implement reforms that would gradually mitigate the imbalances that the demographic transition would cause in the macroeconomic and fiscal structure of the Uruguayan economy.

Conclusions

The analysis developed in this work enables us to conclude that the progress of the demographic transition will undermine the Uruguayan economy's growth potential relative to its growth during the last decade. However, we must keep in mind that during this recent period human capital made a much higher contribution to growth than during the second half of the 20th century.

In the most pessimistic scenario, the reduction in the "business-as-usual" growth rate with respect to the reference period could surpass 1.5 percent of GDP.

The outcomes of the simulation exercises show that the likely shrinking of economic growth would be moderated significantly through labor force productivity improvements and if the gender gaps in labor force participation were closed. However, population aging will decrease economic growth by a little more than half a percentage point in the best-case scenario.

Predictably, the effects will be moderate until the beginning of the 2040s, but during the second half of the century population aging will significantly narrow the Uruguayan economy's potential for growth.

The results of the simulations indicate that if the country intends to prevent population aging from turning into a bottleneck to improvements in the well-being of future generations, it is essential that during the window of opportunity the country take advantage of the benefits derived from the second growth dividend to make investments that contribute to increasing productivity. One of the principal conclusions originating from this work is that the potential for growth during the window of opportunity depends to a large extent on the ability to sustain the accumulation of physical capital at rates comparable to those recorded in the last decade. This would be the most effective mechanism for mitigating the impact of slowing human capital accumulation.

Higher economic growth during the window of opportunity as well as a larger contribution from technological advances would generate wealth effects, enabling Uruguay to reduce the impact of population aging. In this context, policies aimed at strengthening investment and efforts already deployed to promote technological progress would take on growing importance. Achieving structural reforms that promote efficient allocation of resources and improve the functioning of markets must become pillars of the development strategy, since increasing productivity will be fundamental to preventing population aging from obstructing the potential to improve living conditions in coming decades.

One important challenge is to guarantee a scheme of intergenerational transfers that ensures that the needs of the dependent population will be met. The institutional schemes needed to implement these transfers may combine public and private mechanisms in diverse ways, but we must keep in mind that the growing flow of transfers is kept independent of the adopted institutional setup. The tensions will not be resolved by transferring the administration of resources from the public sphere to the private sphere, or vice versa.

Population aging will put pressure on public social spending, principally in the retirement and pensions category, as well as on health care spending. The expected increases could be financed without the need to increase fiscal pressure. The current tax structure would allow for endogenous increases in the tax burden if the economy keeps growing through to 2100. The analysis developed here indicates that changes in spending directly related to population aging will not threaten the sustainability of fiscal policy.

In conclusion, deterioration of the fiscal balance will lessen as the economy achieves higher growth. Even in the scenarios where fiscal accounts significantly decline, the deterioration would not occur until the second half of the

21st century, which means that there is a window of a little more than three decades to implement initiatives that would gradually alleviate the imbalances that the demographic transition will eventually bring to Uruguay's fiscal structure.

Annex 9A: Marginal Propensity to Save and Income Level per Capita

The positive ratio between per capita income and the marginal propensity to save is empirically consistent with observations from data across countries. For example, figure 9A.1 provides a scatterplot where the x-axis represents the Napierian logarithm of per capita GDP measured in purchasing power parity (PPP) dollars, and the y-axis shows internal savings expressed as a percentage of GDP with data from 2014.

As an ad hoc way of expressing the "wealth effect" on the marginal propensity to save, we utilized the database of countries represented in figure 9A.1 to estimate a coefficient of the elasticity of the marginal propensity to save with respect to per capita GDP.

The estimate of elasticity was performed returning directly to the marginal propensity to save for each country with respect to the Napierian logarithm of per capita GDP in PPP dollars and a constant without adding additional controls. The result of this estimate is included in table 9A.1.

Figure 9A.1 Internal Savings and Logarithm of Per Capita GDP in PPP Dollars

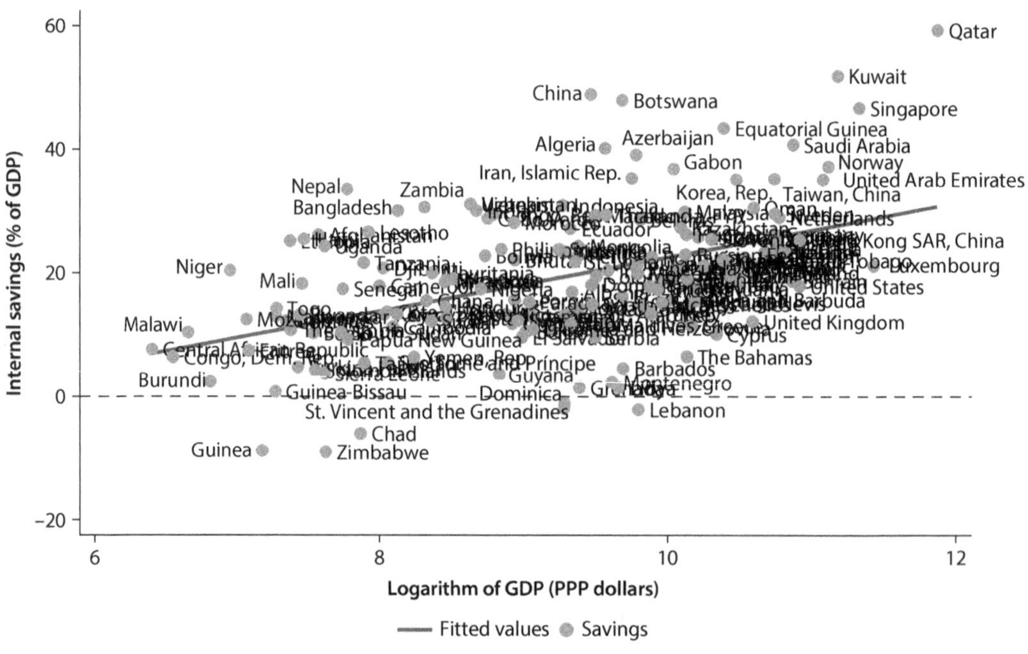

Source: World Economic Outlook database, International Monetary Fund.
Note: PPP = purchasing power parity.

Table 9A.1 Elasticity of the Marginal Propensity to Save with Respect to Per Capita GDP

Savings rate	*Coefficient*	*Standard deviation*	*t*	*P>|t|*	*[95% confidence interval]*	
ln(pbi_pc)	0.3749	0.0060	6.29	0.000	0.02572	0.049246
c	−0.1609	0.5530	−2.91	0.004	−0.270059	−0.051693
No. of observations	166					
F(1, 164)	39.61					
Prob>F	0					
R-squared	0.1946					
Adjusted R-squared	0.1896					
Root mean squared error	0.09046					

Source: Estimates based on International Monetary Fund data.

Annex 9B: Forecasts of IRPF + IASS and IVA + IMESI as a Percentage of GDP

The forecasts of collection of direct taxes that fall directly on individual income were based on a simple methodology using assumptions that could certainly be considered strong or restrictive.

For the case of the (IRPF + IASS)/GDP ratio relative to GDP growth in real terms, we carried out a simple regression between both variables including a constant and did not consider any other control variables.

To estimate the (IVA + IMESI)/GDP ratio, we first calculated the implicit rate for these taxes in 2014 relative to consumption according to the equation 9B.1:

$$t_{IVA+IMESI} = \frac{IVA + IMESI}{C}, \tag{9B.1}$$

where $t_{IVA+IMESI}$ is the tax pressure of these taxes relative to consumption, $IVA + IMESI$ represents the collections of IVA and IMESI in current pesos during 2014, and C represents the economy's aggregate level of consumption, also measured in current pesos.

In order to create the forecasts of tax pressure associated with these taxes relative to GDP, we considered that the implicit rate relative to consumption would remain constant during the entire period under analysis. In this way, the (IVA + IMESI)/GDP ratio would change in the simulations only as a result of changes in the economy's marginal propensity to consume; that is, changes in the c = C/GDP ratio.

Notes

1. Fernando Lorenzo and Gonzalo Zunino, Center for Economic Research. Correspondence to florenzo@cinve.org.uy; zunino.gon@gmail.com.
2. Fanelli (2014) states that in Argentina's case the demographic dividend phase will extend until approximately 2040.

3. Compensation for the capital factor was set at equal to the income from the use surplus and 50 percent of mixed income.
4. The similarity between the observed growth rate and the trend should not be consequential if we keep in mind that the available estimates suggest that in Uruguay the macroeconomic cycle has an average duration of eight years (Kamil and Lorenzo, 1997).
5. TFP's contribution to economic growth in Uruguay is a topic of debate. For a period that covers almost the entire second half of the 20th century, De Brun (2004); Fossati, Mantero, and Olivella (2004); and Oddone and Cal (2007) conclude that TFP's contribution to economic growth was negative. For a similar period, Bucacos (1999), Theoduloz (2005), and Deagosto et al. (2014) find a positive contribution from TFP of between 0.4 and 0.6 percentage points per year. Keep in mind that the econometric estimates on which these authors' estimates are based correspond to a period in which per capita GDP growth barely surpassed 1 percent per year and that the levels of productive investment were consistently below 15 percentage points of GDP. The work of Deagosto et al. (2014) also analyzes TFP's more recent contribution and finds a positive contribution equivalent to 1 percentage point of GDP.
6. We must not lose sight of the fact that according to the lens of analysis used in this work, the human capital stock may be modified both by variations in the number of workers and by variations in their productivity.
7. See chapter 3 for more details.
8. Chapter 3 presents a detailed explanation of the composition of public social spending used here. The structure utilized in this work does not consider some of the categories included in public social spending in the reports released by the Ministry of Social Development (Ministerio de Desarrollo Social [MIDES]).

References

Bucacos, E. 1999. "Fuentes del Crecimiento Económico en Uruguay: 1960–98." *Revista de Economía, Segunda Época* 6 (2): 39–79.

Bucheli, M., and C. González. 2011. "Public Transfer Flow between Generations." In *Population Aging and the Generational Economy: A Global Perspective*, edited by R. Lee and A. Mason, 434–45. Cheltenham, UK: Edward Elgar Publishing.

Bucheli, M., C. González, and C. Olivieri. 2010. "Transferencias del Sector Público a la Infancia y Vejez en Uruguay." *Notas de Población* 90: 163–84.

Carbajal, F., B. Lanzilotta, C. Llambí, and C. Velázquez. 2007. "La Brecha de Producto para Uruguay: Metodologías para Su Estimación y Aplicaciones." Working document, CINVE.

De Brun, J. 2004. "Growth in Uruguay: Factor Accumulation or Productivity Gains?" Inter-American Development Bank, Economic and Social Study Series RE1-04-010.

Deagosto, G., F. Fraga, R. González, G. Oddone, and D. Pirocco. 2014. "Macroeconomía Estructural: Alternativas para el Cambio: Desafíos para el Crecimiento en Uruguay: Una Mirada desde los Fundamentos de Largo Plazo." In *Uruguay + 25*, Working Document 10, Fundación Astur, Montevideo.

Domínguez, M., B. Lanzilotta, S. Rego, and P. Regueira. 2014. "Productividad Total de Factores en Uruguay (1991–2013)." Working document 02/2014, CINVE.

Fanelli, J. M. 2014. "Demografía y Macroeconomía: Oportunidades y Riesgos en la Argentina del Bono." In *Los Años No Vienen Sólos*, edited by M. Gragnolati, R. Rofman, I. Aperlla, and S. Troiano. Buenos Aires: World Bank.

Fossati, F., R. Mantero, and V. Olivella. 2004. "Determinantes del Crecimiento Económico en Uruguay: 1955–2003." Un Análisis de la Productividad Total de los Factores Tesis de Economía de la Facultad de Ciencias Económicas y de Administración, Universidad de la República, Montevideo.

Kamil, H., and F. Lorenzo. 1997. "Caracterización de las Fluctuaciones Cíclicas en la Economía Uruguaya." *Revista de Economía* 5 (1): 83–140.

Lanzilotta, B., and C. Llambí. 2005. "Una Aproximación hacia la Influencia de la Innovación Tecnológica sobre el Crecimiento en Uruguay a través de la Productividad Total de Factores: La Relación entre las Actividades de Innovación y el Ciclo Económico Corto." Instituto de Economía, FCEyA, Universidad de la República, Montevideo.

Mason, A., and R. Lee. 2006. "Demographic Transition and Demographic Dividends in Developed and Developing Countries." United Nations Expert Group Meeting on Social and Economic Implications of Changing Population Age Structure, Mexico City, August 31–September 2.

Oddone, G., and I. Cal. 2007. "El Largo Declive de Uruguay durante el Siglo XX." *América Latina en la Historia Económica* 30.

Solow, R. 1956. "A Contribution to the Theory of Economic Growth." *Quarterly Journal of Economics* 70 (1): 65–94.

Theoduloz, T. 2005. "El Producto Potencial en la Economía Uruguaya: 1978–2003." Jornadas de Economía, Central Bank of Uruguay, Montevideo, August 1–2.

CHAPTER 10

Sources of Growth in a Context of Population Aging

Ignacio Apella[1]

Introduction

The transition to an older population raises questions about the impact it could have on the labor market and the fiscal requirements it will create for the future social protection system. As this book makes clear, Uruguay's demographic transition is advanced and the country faces potentially higher spending to finance retirement and pension transfers and, to a lesser extent, the health care system.

As a whole, the social security system could require around 12.8 percent of gross domestic product (GDP) in 2050 and 17.1 percent in 2100. These amounts are a clear fiscal and economic challenge, the latter because if the current rules remain, the economy will have to direct a greater portion of its output to fund these types of transfers. In turn, the health care system will likely also require more public funds, from about 5.2 percent of GDP in 2013 to 6.8 percent in 2100.

Looking beyond policies focused on containing spending,[2] the demographic transition also increases the challenge of raising the resources to fund potentially higher spending. For this, a country needs to lay the foundations for an economic dynamic that ensures growth in per capita GDP even in a context of an increasing total dependency ratio.

This challenge appears even larger if we consider the general idea that population aging could have negative effects on the economy, including a fall in per capita output, due to the reduction in the labor force and the savings level. If individuals' behavior within each age group were to remain unchanged, the supply of labor and per capita savings would tend to decrease as the proportion of older adults in the population increased. Keeping some factors, like productivity, at their current values, would entail lower per capita GDP growth (Bloom, Canning, and Fink 2011).

However, assuming that the evolution of partial and/or total factor productivity is constant is an assumption that deserves to be debated. In specific terms, the challenge posed by the window of opportunity is to create the necessary conditions so that factor productivity can increase and thus support a steady growth rate of per capita output during the aging phase.

For this reason, the objective of the present chapter is to present a brief discussion related to the factors that would allow the economy to sustain a positive growth rate for per capita output in the context of an aging labor force. In particular, we highlight the importance of the endowments of factors of production, as well as the mechanisms available for increasing the productivity of those factors, to explain the rate of economic growth.

The following section outlines the dilemma posed by the demographic transition in terms of its effects on overall well-being. The third section discusses the areas in which public policy can help. We summarize reflections in the final section.

Aging and the Growth Dilemma

The pessimistic visions related to aging's impact on overall economic well-being relate to the shrinking and aging of the labor force. In this context, the effect of population aging on overall well-being, measured as per capita consumption, is a critical ratio. Other things equal, we might observe a reduction in the endowment of labor and therefore a decrease in per capita output. Additionally, an older labor force raises questions about labor productivity. In particular, a negative correlation between age and labor force productivity would entail lower output per worker.[3] For example, equation 10.1 is useful for understanding the connection between population aging, consumption, and productivity:

$$\frac{C}{N} = \frac{C}{Y}\frac{Y}{L}\frac{L}{N} \tag{10.1}$$

where C is aggregate consumption, Y is GDP, N is population, and L is employment. Population aging has direct and potential effects. On one hand L/N decreases, on the other this could reduce labor productivity (Y/L) as a result of the increase in the average age of L. Clearly, assuming that the proportion of consumption in terms of output (C/Y) is constant, this phenomenon entails lower levels of well-being (C/N).

The sources of economic growth may be organized into two large categories. In one, are those related with the individual contribution of each factor of production, essentially in terms of the endowments of labor and the capital services available. Accordingly, variations in the endowments of factors of production entail movements throughout the production function.

A second set of explanatory factors is those related to productivity increases of the production factors, which entails a shift in the production function.

Generally, productivity refers to the ratio between output and the input(s) of a specific productive process. In connection with this definition, two dimensions are distinguished simultaneously. One is *total factor productivity*—the production increase resulting from improvements in organizing the productive process, independent of the accumulation of factors of production: capital, labor, and inputs. This constitutes a measure of the degree to which economies of scale exist, that is, a situation in which total output grows at a rate more than proportional to the increase in the quantity of all of the factors of production.

In the second dimension, the partial productivity of each factor is defined. Specifically, labor productivity describes the ratio of output arising out of a technological process and the capacity utilized expressed in units of time or the number of individuals involved (Tangen 2005).

Thus, identifying a country's economic growth profile consists of knowing which part of it is correlated with the contribution from factors of production (increases in their endowments) and which with the contribution from the increase in both partial and total factor productivity.

Chapter 7 studied various scenarios of changes in the economic activity rate, and their potential implications for economic growth and changes in productivity. In that exercise, we assumed that the profile of labor productivity by gender, age, and education level remained constant over time and that the demographic transition would entail changes in per capita output as a result of the change in the composition of workers. Even if factor endowments remained constant, because of a potential negative correlation between age and labor force productivity, per capita GDP would maintain a decreasing trend because of the aging of workers.

However, the assumption of the invariability (including decreases) of labor force productivity and total factor productivity could not be considered categorically. The increase of factor productivity, both partial as well as total, constitutes one of the principal challenges that economies passing through the demographic transition face; keeping in mind, above all, that the sources of economic growth are not just associated with the endowments of the factors possessed by the economy, but also with their productivity (quality).

Chapter 9 of this book performs a factorial decomposition of growth during 1997–2014, which incorporates the capital endowment, the labor endowment adjusted for the level of human capital, and a component of technological change. The results suggest that just 53.5 percent of economic growth is explained by factor endowments, with the remaining 46.5 percent resulting from total factor productivity. As a result, it is possible to suggest the existence of other sources of economic growth beyond the total endowment of factors of production, highlighting those that operate both on labor productivity as well as the residual, or total factor productivity.

Sources of Productivity Growth

Based on the previous discussions, it is important to ask what public policy options are available to mitigate the potential adverse effects posed by population aging in terms of the endowment of labor, laying a foundation that would favor sustained growth of per capita output in the long term.

Arguing that population aging has irreversible negative effects on the growth rate of per capita output in an economy as the result of the reduction in the size of the labor force entails assuming that the endowment of factors of production is the only explanatory variable for economic growth. However, since Solow's (1956) first works as well as the subsequent developments of the theory of endogenous growth (Romer 1986; Lucas 1988; Rebelo 1991; among others), signs have suggested that the factors of production are not the only determinant variables, but rather that it is also possible to include the increase in their total productivity.

The pioneering theoretical framework elaborated by Solow (1956) proposes that the growth of per capita output in the long term will exhaust itself unless there are exogenous changes in the level of technological knowledge. The model predicts that if economies only differentiate themselves based on the level of capital stock per capita, in the long term they will exhibit a converging trend in the growth rate and the level of per capita income.

Within this analytical framework, with exogenous technological progress, population aging poses some limitations on the economy's ability to grow insofar as it entails a reduction in the endowment of one of its factors of production, namely labor. This means that the only resource available to sustain economic growth is to increase: (a) the partial productivity of the labor force; or (b) total factor productivity.

Nonetheless, although the growth of total factor productivity is associated with exogenous factors, and is entirely explained by technological change, the neoclassical model provides an estimate of the factors that contribute to the growth of the partial productivity of the labor force.

Assuming a Cobb-Douglas[4] production function, total factor productivity is defined as the difference between the growth of output and the weighted growth of the inputs as it is represented in equation 10.2:

$$\Delta lnA = \Delta lnY - v_k lnK - v_l lnL \tag{10.2}$$

where v_k *and* v_l are the proportion of capital and labor in national income, respectively. The neoclassical standard is that both parameters add to one. Using this assumption, it is possible to identify the sources of the average growth of labor productivity (equation 10.3), defined as output per hour worked (*Y/H*).

$$\Delta lny = \Delta lnY - \Delta lnH \tag{10.3}$$

Thus,

$$\Delta lny = v_k \Delta lnk + v_l \left(\Delta lnL - \Delta lnH\right) + \Delta lnA \tag{10.4}$$

Based on this equation, the growth of output per hour worked (Δ*lny*) depends on four factors. The first is the endowment of labor (Δ*lnL*). The second is the intensity or depth of capital (Δ*lnk*), which captures the increase in the capital stock per hour worked. The third is the growth of the quality of labor, which measures the shift toward workers with higher levels of marginal productivity and is defined as the difference between the increase in labor and the required hours of work. The fourth is the growth of total factor productivity (ΔlnA), which captures the impact of technological change and other factors that affect growth beyond the traditional factors of production, basically based on the creation and exploitation of economies of scale.

This final source of growth drove subsequent developments in the theory of growth. While the traditional theory considered it to be exogenous, in contrast the endogenous growth theory presents arguments which can be used to show that it may be the result of endogenous forces within the process of accumulation itself.

Thus, considering this it is possible to suggest that there are at least four public policy alternatives in the medium and long terms that foment sustained growth in per capita output in a future scenario of population aging. They are (a) the expansion of the economically active population (L); (b) increasing the ratio of capital per worker (K/L); (c) increasing investment in human capital that enables partial labor productivity to improve, that is, reducing H; and (d) creating incentives that favor the generation of knowledge and technological change, enabling the achievement of a constant improvement in the organization of factors such that economic efficiency (A) increases.

Growth of the Economically Active Population

The perception of the impact that the demographic transition will have on the labor market, and the resulting impacts on the level of output and the population's social well-being, has been skeptical. In general, it is assumed that the window of opportunity, or first dividend, which results from the period with a lower demographic dependency ratio, is defined by the age distribution of the population. Thus, as the transition ends, population aging will result in a reduction of the total endowment of labor and consequently will limit the economy's ability to achieve sustained growth of output.

However, the window of opportunity defined in chapter 2 and, based on age groups, loses sight of the decision making that individuals employ themselves, especially as it relates to their participation in the labor market. In effect, it is possible that at least two phenomena provide dynamism to the demographic dividend beyond just the average age of the population: the increase in women's economic participation and the postponement of the retirement age by older adult workers.

The first of these phenomena is associated with women's economic activity. Accordingly, in Uruguay, as well as in much of the world, the increase in the economic activity rate during the last 30 years was mostly the result of the increase of women's labor participation. Chapter 7 identifies the reallocation of resources from the manufacturing industry to the tertiary sector, which increases the demand for women, among the principal factors explaining this behavior. A narrowing of gender salary gaps is another, which affects how domestic tasks and labor force participation are allocated among spouses. The effect of rising women's education should also be considered, as well as the increase of the returns to education since the 1990s, among others.

In the second, both the incentives created by the pension system itself as well as the levels of human capital accumulated during one's working life delay retirement from the labor market for a significant group of older adults, at least partially sustaining the endowment of labor. Accordingly, the rigidities inherent to the contributory pension systems, in eligibility requirements (number of contribution years and age), limit retirement from economic activity. Alternatively, the increase of the formal education rate and the subsequent increase in human capital accumulation increase the probability that older adults will continue to participate actively in the labor market. This latter point is connected to the opportunity cost of accumulated human capital that an individual confronts upon retiring from the labor market, which suggests that the higher the level of education, the more likely the individual will remain in the labor market after reaching the minimum retirement age. In other words, the more capital invested in education, the more individuals will have interest in continuing to receive a return on said capital.

In this context, it is possible to think about reconfiguring the care system and incorporating women to the paid employment system. As we saw in chapter 7, questions arise about the productivity associated with these jobs, as well as applying traditional gender roles within the labor market, including the perpetuation of gender segregation.

As was mentioned in chapter 4, creating incentives, especially financial ones, for the equalization of the legal and actual retirement ages, would enable the country to offset some of the reduction in the labor force. Accordingly, it is possible to assume that the social security system could create incentives to delay retirement through workers' financial earnings. These are made up of two components: the present value of the salary obtained from employment and the higher future social security benefit associated with the "premium" earned from longer contribution periods and fewer years to enjoy the expected benefit.[5]

This incentive operates naturally in the funded regime, insofar as longer contribution favors generation of larger retirement and pension funds, which, along with the number of years as a beneficiary, mean a worker would receive a larger benefit. Additionally, given the Uruguayan social security system mix of two pillars—a pay-as-you-go regime administered by the BPS (Banco de Previsión Social) and an individually funded scheme—it can be expected that the same financial gain will be provided to the benefits paid by the pay-as-you-go regime.

Nonetheless, we cannot forget that the first dividend is *potential* in nature, insofar as taking advantage of it is subject to the conditions of the labor market enabling the maximum utilization of the labor force, not just in number of jobs created, but also in their quality.

Even in a favorable labor market, expanding the labor force participation of groups that have traditionally remained inactive would enable the economy to smooth the potential negative effect on the growth of per capita output, but it does not eliminate that effect in the long term because once all of the inactive resources are exhausted, population aging still results in a lower economic activity rate.

Increasing the Per Capita Capital Stock

The second source of growth of per capita output, the increase in the ratio of capital per worker, could be affected by the demographic changes in two ways. The first, for any equilibrium ratio, is a mechanical adjustment associated with the time that capital stock requires to adapt itself to the changes in the endowment of labor. In the short term, this signifies an increase in the *K/L* ratio as a response to the aging of the population. The second is the change in the long-term equilibrium ratio. This ratio may experience changes as a consequence of various factors, such as the potential changes in the quality of labor—another direct source of growth of labor productivity—and the variations in the global demand profile among sectors that maintain different intensities in the utilization of capital as a factor of production. Accordingly, the changes induced by aging in the consumption profile among sectors with different capital intensities may have implications for labor productivity that are not trivial.[6]

The significance of the increase in capital stock per worker is associated with the concept of the second demographic dividend. The period during which the demographic dividend or window of opportunity occurs is favorable for economic development because the aggregate life-cycle surplus, that is, the sum of the difference between income and consumption of the groups of workers with the capacity to save, enables the economy to increase savings and therefore, by appropriately deploying those savings, to increase investment.

The reduction in the dependency ratio frees up resources for public and private investment in physical capital, allowing per capita income to grow rapidly. This is commonly called the "first demographic dividend."

According to Fanelli (2014), the contribution of the first dividend to economic growth is a phenomenon that, while it lasts a long time, it is also true that it is transitory: during the aging phase, the first dividend reverses itself and exercises its influence by depressing growth. For this reason, the challenge from a public policy perspective consists of channeling said savings to internal investment, thereby enabling the accumulation of physical capital. As a result, each worker will be able to possess more capital in the future and output will therefore increase.

Accordingly, despite the potential reduction of the capacity to save in the future, which is the product of the reduction of the economically active population and therefore of those with the capacity to save, it is possible that the second demographic dividend will appear.

According to Mason and Lee (2011), the second dividend has positive effects on growth associated with the period prior to the aging phase and which are not temporary. This phenomenon essentially operates through the increase of savings and the subsequent accumulation of physical capital and foreign assets. As the capital/labor ratio increases, productivity rises, and as the stock of foreign assets climbs, national income improves.

The forces that give rise to the potential second dividend have to do with the incentives to save during the demographic dividend and with the changes in the proportion of the cohorts that save. The second dividend will only occur if savings behave in such a way that the endowment of capital grows more quickly than actual workers during the window of opportunity. If this occurs, then the benefits will be permanent to the extent that capital stock will be permanently higher. The question that naturally arises in this context is, then, which factors have an effect on aggregate savings during the demographic dividend period. Fanelli (2014) points to at least three mechanisms.

First, the first dividend generates higher income, which can be directed both to consumption as well as to investment in assets. Only when at least a portion of the extra per capita income produced during the window of opportunity is saved and invested, will it strengthen the economy's ability to grow, contributing to the realization of the second dividend.

Second, the second dividend may also be strengthened by generating extra savings associated with the growing primary savings during the window of opportunity. Accordingly, it can be expected that primary savings contribute significantly to the accumulation of assets as the demographic dividend period progresses because the population that has completed or is about to complete their productive years is growing and needs to increase their savings for retirement.

Third, as life expectancy increases it raises the years individuals expect to live after retiring, increasing the resources needed to finance consumption during those extra years.

These impulses to save are inherent to all demographic transitions, and in turn, will have more or less strength as a function of the macroeconomic and structural factors that affect the incentives. Among the factors that should be kept in mind we must mention: the tax pressure on primary savers; family transfers to children and the elderly; and the generosity of the pension system, which determines what proportion of retirement needs is expected to be covered by current transfers instead of assets accumulated during one's economically active period. These elements especially affect the amount of wealth accumulated by the population over 50 years old, which tends to own the largest portion of the economy's assets (IMF 2005).

According to the International Labour Organization (ILO; 2013), the second dividend will emerge to the extent that the institutional and policy frameworks induce individuals, firms, and governments to increase the national savings rate, and that these savings are utilized to fund the accumulation of capital. Otherwise, in a context of low interest rates, undeveloped financial markets, macroeconomic volatility, and limited investment alternatives, it is not likely that the economy will generate enough investments needed to maintain the level of capital accumulation and, therefore, productivity and economic growth.

In this context, the public policy initiatives implemented during the window of opportunity or demographic dividend play an important role. Both the first as well as the second dividends flow from the demographic dividend, and thus it is important to generate conditions that incentivize savings by the economic actors, particularly those that find themselves in the surplus-generating phase of the life cycle.

Human Capital Investment—The Quality of L

The concept of human capital underlies all production functions. We see it implicitly in the traditional growth theory through the concept of the quality of labor (H), and explicitly in the new endogenous growth models as a determinant of technological change (A). Accordingly, the investment directed to improve the labor force's skills and abilities itself constitutes a significant source of growth for per capita output. Within this concept of investment, we can include expenditures directed to fund formal education, labor force training, and even health care.

It is possible to identify two population groups for focusing attention in human capital formation. First, we have the young population passing through the formal education system. To that effect, efforts directed toward this sector not only expand enrollment but also improve education system quality, clearly the objective of human capital formation policy.

During the demographic dividend, the school-age dependency ratio decreases, freeing up resources that, while maintaining the same level of total spending on education, would enable the country to increase per capita investment to improve education quality, both in inputs required and knowledge imparted.

Any initiative that incentivizes investment in education during childhood and youth generates long-term returns in increased abilities, basic and technical, and through the higher productivity achieved, higher labor income is also attained. The expansion of the formal education system does not just entail reaching more of the target population, but also increasing years of study. In general, we can see a trend to delay the age of entry into the labor market by young people, which is associated with longer periods in the formal education system. Fostering this behavior among all youth populations is a clear human capital formation policy.

Yet the young adult population, the group that participates actively in the labor market, must have incentives to continue investing in job training. In other words, current worker participation in continuing education enables them to better adapt to technological change, which is necessary for the economy to maintain, and even increase, labor productivity.

The investment decisions are taken within a process of intertemporal utility maximization, and one of the key variables of this process is the relative prices of the factors. It is possible to expect that the prices of factors of production like interest and salaries will tend to change considerably during the demographic transition. According to Kim and Hewings (2012), in an economy that passes through a process of population aging, the labor force (physical capital) becomes relatively scarce (abundant); therefore the price of labor (physical capital) should move up (down). The implication of these potential changes in relative prices of the factors is that the agents have incentives to increase the time directed to investment in education because we can expect that in the medium and long term, payments to labor will grow relative to those to capital.

Concurrently, it is also possible to find some disincentives associated with the existence of an opportunity cost of investment. Sadahiro and Shimasawa (2002) point out that an increase in the time dedicated to investment in education reduces the amount of time dedicated to work, thus also reducing income and consumption and therefore utility. This is especially likely among those individuals that belong to low-income households. As a consequence of this, spaces are created for public policy to avoid these disincentives.

Seshadri and Yuki (2004) suggest that the transfers directed to financing the education system increase efficiency and reduce inequality in the steady-state equilibrium. The application of a cash transfer directed to finance the opportunity cost of investing in education, both for formal education as well as continuing education processes, represents a tool that incentivizes human capital investment. The principal objective of a policy with these characteristics is to avoid socially suboptimal equilibria in terms of the levels of capital invested.

In the same vein, Becker, Murphy, and Tamura (1990) postulate that there are multiple equilibria in the production of human capital. On one hand, there is the possibility of a downward trend in the profitability of this type of investment, that is, a type of vicious cycle that is characteristic of developing economies in which human capital is scarce. Individuals invest less and less in education because the returns keep falling. Consequently, human capital accumulation tends to dry up.

Alternatively, a situation could occur that exhibits a growing behavior that corresponds to developed countries with high capital stock. These countries experience a type of virtuous cycle because as more resources are invested in human capital, higher returns are obtained, and thus there are incentives to continue investing. In order to cut the vicious cycle, one alternative so that individuals will invest in human capital consists of providing them a subsidy that offsets the decrease in the returns on their investment.

The strategy of subsidizing education could reduce costs and change the decreasing trend in the rate of return on investment in human capital. This subsidy proposal has been formulated by Lucas (1988) and Becker, Murphy, and Tamura (1990) for countries that have scarce capital stock and whose internal rate of return is falling.

In addition to the effect that investing in human capital has on the quality of the labor force, promoting said accumulation during the early stages of life could increase future participation in the labor market among older adults because they would enjoy higher-quality jobs and increased returns.

In terms of the incentives created for the young population, the programs of income transfers to households are a commonly used tool, through which the household's opportunity cost of children attending educational institutions is offset.

Chapter 6 presented various future scenarios, highlighting the increase of the education system's coverage and the improvement in the graduation rate at different education levels. Depending on the scenario upon which we focus, the demographic transition creates an opportunity to increase per-student investment insofar as the school-age dependency ratio is reduced. In order to increase the stock of human capital it is important to reinvest the surplus resources which are freed up in the formal education system.

In terms of the programs that promote continuing education, the basis for these types of initiatives rests on the potential passive behavior that older workers exhibit in the face of this type of investment. It is possible to assume that as the average age of workers increases, they will be less active in terms of the amount of time dedicated to human capital investment as a result of the relatively low marginal returns to education.

This is particularly important because it would occur in a context where the abilities that workers have already acquired in their workplaces would begin to become obsolete as new technologies were introduced. Kim and Hewings (2012) divide skills obsolescence into two categories depending on their cause: "technical" and "economic" obsolescence. The former refers to the natural erosion of skills as individuals age. The latter, in contrast, can be attributed to external causes like technological change and changes in the technical requirements in the productive sector. Thus, population aging in an environment with rapid technological change provokes an accelerated process of technical skills obsolescence at the aggregate level.

Worker training as a policy to increase human capital and offset the fall in productivity associated with aging is becoming more relevant in the debate. Economies with an older age structure began to strongly push these types of interventions during the initial years of the new century, in order to deal with labor supply problems and the fiscal sustainability of pension systems. In particular, European Union countries consolidated experiences from isolated interventions in terms of formal education, adult education, training, and job training in order to get closer to a comprehensive continuing education system, or lifelong learning, that includes all stages of an individual's life cycle.

Heckman, Lochner, and Taber (1998) reveal that the post-school learning process, including the process of learning by doing, represents between one-third and one-half of all of the skills training that the labor force acquires in the modern economy.

This renewed interest in lifelong learning policy was accompanied by the vast production of literature on the empirical estimation of the impacts of education and training programs on worker productivity, measured via salary changes (Blundell et al. 1999; Kuckulenz and Zwick 2003; Carneiro and Heckman 2004; among others). Although all of these studies focus on the experiences of developed countries, they nonetheless offer points of reference for making changes in the productivity profile of those countries that are still passing through the demographic dividend.

In effect, it is possible to find a higher marginal return than in the rich countries that belong to the Organisation for Economic Co-operation and Development (OECD) because of the lower initial endowment of human capital. In addition, during the first half of the current century, it is possible to generate a moderately fast convergence toward patterns of educational achievement, composition of the workforce, and productivity observed in the more developed countries.

Research and Development

The creation of knowledge through explicit research and development activities is an additional extension of capital accumulation that deserves special attention. It has been argued that investment in human capital is an important factor of economic growth, based on the increase in the quality of labor that it entails. Nonetheless, the growth of human capital is not a sufficient condition for self-sustaining growth if a portion of that capital stock is not directed to the creation of knowledge and technological abilities.

Accordingly, it has been argued that part of the growth of per capita output has been explained by total factor productivity. The idea behind this concept is that the factors of production, as a whole, may exhibit increasing marginal returns to scale. In other words, that a proportional increase of all of the factors signifies growth in output that is more than proportional. This is one of the reasons that economies of scale exist in the production function (decreasing average costs).

The effort to improve any productive process seeks as its ultimate goal to improve total factor productivity, and in this way to obtain the same level of output at a lower cost. For this reason, productive sectors' incentive to seek mechanisms that enable improvements in the organization of their factors and in this way to be more efficient is precisely, in aggregate terms, what has been called ΔlnA. In other words, the constant search for technological improvements enables the creation of marginal returns to scale and therefore itself becomes a source of economic growth.

The notion of the creation of technological abilities or innovation attempts to capture this idea and includes not just the creation of new methods of production, but also the activities of purchasing, adapting, and changing of existing technologies (Chudnovsky 1999).

Thus, part of self-sustained growth in output is the result of technological progress as a result of the creation of economies of scale in the production process. But, at the same time, even though growing returns may not be created inside a firm that implements a technological change, it could create growing returns for the whole economy. This is because knowledge, as a factor of production, is nonrival and partially excludable. These characteristics of a public good allow for growing returns to scale at the global level, due to the creation of externalities generated by a firm's research and development and the spillovers that it creates, affecting the stock of knowledge available for the rest of the firms. This argument was proposed by Romer (1986), who incorporated technological change as an additional factor of production into the economic models that place innovation at the center of output growth. In doing this, innovation stops being an exogenous factor, to the extent that we recognized that it is the fruit of the intentional investment of resources by profit-maximizing firms (endogenous).

In this way, technological change is recognized as an essential force for economic growth that incentivizes the continuity of capital accumulation. As a whole, this change and accumulation are responsible for a large part of the increase in the output obtained per hour worked.

This process may occur naturally and endogenously as a result of the incentives in the productive sector. As Schumpeter (1942) points out, the fundamental impulse that sets up and keeps the capitalist machinery moving comes from new products for consumption, new methods of production or transport, and new markets. This process continuously revolutionizes the economic structure from within, destroying the old structure, and creating a new one. This "creative destruction" is the basic fact that takes place in capitalism.

Creative destruction arises out of firms' continuous investment in knowledge and technological innovation, and the same factors that affect investment in general influence the decisions to do so. In fact, the quality of regulation, the protection of property rights, the tax code, the macroeconomic regime, the intensity of competition, and the development of infrastructure affect decisions to invest in innovation, sometimes even more significantly than to invest in fixed capital (OECD 2013).

The characteristics of this type of investment that favor economies of scale, however, also create incentives to arrive at suboptimal levels of investment. This is because the production of knowledge and innovation is developed amid information asymmetry and positive externalities. Market failures create suboptimal equilibria in the social optimum, which justifies state intervention. Accordingly, the principal goals of science and technology policy shift from ensuring a continuous stream of innovations to favoring the diffusion of innovations into the productive structure.

Because knowledge is a nonrival and nonexcludable good, as noted, rival firms can exploit another firm's investment, creating a difference between the private and social returns of the investment. This creates clear disincentives for private investment in knowledge production.

A second characteristic in knowledge production is the degree of uncertainty. According to Hall (2002), the return on investment in innovation is more uncertain and exhibits longer periods of development. This limits investment in this area, especially when the investor and the inventor are different actors. For this reason, the market where investors with the ability to finance projects and inventors meet usually resembles the "market for lemons" described by Akerlof (1970). Investors are more skeptical about financing a project with a high level of uncertainty or demand a higher rate of return, excluding projects with less uncertainty from the market (*the adverse selection problem*). This situation is compounded because innovators may be reticent to reveal detailed information about their projects.

In this context, various restrictions may influence firms' decisions on investment in innovation and knowledge, such as the risk of spillover, the level of human capital, and financing. Although it is not the main purpose of this chapter, we highlight several experiences in developed countries that could help overcome the problems, as revealed in OECD (2005).

The first is achieving long-term consensus in the public and private sectors on the importance of maintaining public support and constantly updating innovation policies.

Additionally, countries should foster adoption of foreign technology, creation of research infrastructure, and investment in human capital. Support for applied research in previously identified strategic sectors, jointly with initial protection of intellectual property rights, should accompany these actions.

A set of policy tools should accompany all of these, such as direct budget transfers to public technological institutions, fiscal incentive schemes for private innovation, financing of mission-driven research programs, and the use of public purchases. According to OECD (2005), in developed countries these tools were continually focused on creating positive externalities, for example through the financing of collaborative investigation and the deployment of multipurpose technologies that are disseminated among different sectors, such as biotechnology and information and communication technologies.

Developing countries face greater restrictions on progress in creating new technologies because of funding restrictions, market size, and risk allocation, as well as the shortfall in the stock of accumulated human capital.

Yet technological progress can still occur. For example, the Republic of Korea more actively adapted foreign technologies through copycat innovation and reverse engineering. To do so, Korean firms began to invest more intensively in the development of local technology, above all through technology licenses and know-how transfer agreements with multinational firms operating in the Republic of Korea.

It is not unusual to hear the argument that developing countries can gain an advantage by adopting and adapting the innovations of developed countries. However, adopting new production technologies is not less complicated than innovation itself. In effect, the availability of key complementary resources, such as human capital, institutions, and natural resources, constitute a key variable for effective and efficient adaptation of new technologies designed in developed countries. For this reason, local investments in learning and innovation are necessary, and because these have the same public good characteristics and information asymmetry that affect investments in innovation in general, they require active state participation in its role as promoter.

Conclusions

Uruguay's demographic transition—and the aging of the labor force and reduction of labor endowments and potential savings it entails—as in all countries in the region, raises questions about its impact on economic growth. These concerns are justified by the traditional argument that maintains that economic growth is a function of the endowments of factors of production, labor, and capital, in addition to a residual component commonly called total factor productivity.

However, the sources of economic growth do not end with the factor endowments, but rather include the partial productivity of each factor of production as well as total productivity. This means that increasing factor productivity is the principal challenge faced by economies that find themselves passing through the demographic transition.

For this reason, this chapter has discussed four medium- and long-term public policy alternatives that would foster sustained growth of per capita output, even amid population aging. Some of these are directly linked to the factor endowment and others with productivity.

A first alternative consists of expanding the economically active population. As a short- and medium-term policy, one suggestion is to create the conditions so that those population groups that have been traditionally inactive (women and older adults) can be incorporated into economic activity. This would allow the country to moderate the medium-term effects of the decrease in the size of the labor force as a result of aging. The increase in the economically active population in Uruguay in recent years is the result of women's entry into the labor market. The creation of incentives for equality of activities and salaries, as well as complementary services, would allow women to participate even more. Among older adults, clear incentives exist—associated with the higher stock of human capital older workers possess—to delay the age of retirement from the labor market; financial "premiums" could strengthen these incentives.

Nonetheless, this strategy enables the country to smooth the effects of the reduction of the labor force in the medium term, but not in the long term. Once all of the inactive groups have been incorporated to the economically active population, however, the average age of workers will, of course, continue to rise, meaning that labor force productivity will have to partially determine the rate of growth of output.

A second dimension that favors a positive per capita output growth rate is the increase in the capital endowment per worker, which favors an increase in labor productivity. Uruguay finds itself in a moderately favorable situation to arrive at the aging phase with a higher capital endowment. This is the result of the boom period that it is experiencing, during which a larger quantity of primary savers exists. For this reason, taking advantage of the demographic dividend entails creating the incentives, both from the labor market as well as from the financial system, to increase the savings level and therefore investment and the accumulation of physical capital. In effect, effort should be directed to reducing the lack of productive employment opportunities, while at a time when a significant portion of the labor force is either looking for work or is made up of low-skilled workers, with low-quality jobs in the informal economy and very low salaries. Similarly, conditions in the financial market need attention, including in respect for property rights, asset placement alternatives, and interest rates, which are fundamental for creating incentives to save and reduce the elevated propensity to consume.

Additionally, considering not just the endowment of labor but also its quality, a third area of action emerges in the need to generate conditions for increased accumulation of human capital. Human capital, understood as workers' cognitive and technical abilities, is a feature that directly determines the labor force's productivity. The stock of human capital is created based on a process of investment decisions undertaken by economic actors themselves, who must face a certain opportunity cost. For this reason, any policy initiative directed to reducing said opportunity cost and improving the quality of the labor force's education should be considered a priority to foster sustained growth.

Finally, the continuous creation of new knowledge or technological change is the fourth factor that conditions economic growth, and is produced through investments in research and development, which enables the economy to improve efficiency in the utilization of the factors of production. In this context, the medium-term challenge consists of creating the necessary conditions that incentivize a higher level of investment in these types of activities, which will enable constant improvement in organizing the factors of production, such that economies of scale are created and exploited.

Progress entails the genuine creation of new knowledge (basic science) and admits those activities associated with the adoption and adaptation of technological changes developed in developed countries. In effect, during the first phase of strengthening the innovation system we emphasize the activities associated with copycat innovation and reverse engineering of inventions created in developed countries. This requires the active participation of the private sector, by taking risks, and the state, through programs that foster and promote local technological capacity through the provision of technology licenses and know-how transfer agreements with multinational firms operating in the country.

In summary, the demographic transition toward an older population is gradual but certain. It pressures expenditures in certain social sectors—such as pensions and health care—as the age profile increases. Nonetheless, beyond the level of fiscal and economic effort that a society must undertake to finance rising spending, the important point is that these changes are accompanied by the economy's ability to face higher spending levels, that is, the growth of per capita output. Accordingly, throughout the chapter we have proposed alternative sources of growth, such as the accumulation of physical and human capital and investment in research and development, in which public policy can help maintain economic dynamism that will enable output to increase steadily.

Notes

1. Ignacio Apella, World Bank, Social Protection and Labor Global Practice. Correspondence to iapella@worldbank.org.
2. These types of initiatives are more feasible in the pension system than in the health care system, to the extent that it is not plausible to reduce health care spending, but rather just postpone it.
3. Although various studies have supported this hypothesis, they also emphasize that the effect of aging on productivity is related to the type of occupation, and that the

productivity-age connection is not static, but rather it changes according to the labor market's requirements (Skirbekk 2003).

4. $Y = A.K^{v_k}L^{v_l}$ where v_k and v_l add up to one.
5. For examples see Stock and Wise (1990) and Gruber and Wise (2002).
6. If the consumption profile varies by age group and we assume that demand from older adults is mostly directed to goods and services whose production process is capital intensive, then population aging will entail a change in the overall demand profile toward capital-intensive sectors, creating aggregate incentives for the accumulation of capital and therefore an increase in the *K/L* ratio. For more detail see Guest (2011).

References

Akerlof, G. 1970. "The Market for Lemons: Quality Uncertainty and Market Mechanism." *Quarterly Journal of Economics* 84 (3): 488–500.

Becker, G., K. Murphy, and R. Tamura. 1990. "Human Capital, Fertility and Economic Growth." *Journal of Political Economy* 98 (5): 12–37.

Bloom, D., D. Canning, and G. Fink. 2011. "Implication of Population Aging for Economic Growth." NBER Working Paper 16705, National Bureau of Economic Research, Cambridge, MA. http://www.nber.org/papers/w16705.

Blundell, R., L. Dearden, C. Meghir, and B. Sianesi. 1999. "Human Capital Investment: The Returns from Education and Training to the Individual, the Firm and the Economy." *Fiscal Studies* 20 (1): 1–24.

Carneiro, P., and J. Heckman. 2004. "Human Capital Policy." In *Inequality in America: What Role for Human Capital Policies?*, edited by J. Heckman, A. Krueger, and B. Friedman. Cambridge, MA: MIT Press.

Chudnovsky, D. 1999. "Políticas de Ciencia y Tecnología y el Sistema Nacional de Innovación en Argentina." *Revista de la CEPAL* 67 (Abril): 153–71.

Fanelli, J. 2014. "Demografía y Macroeconomía: Oportunidades y Riesgos en la Argentina del Bono." In *Los Años No Vienen Solos: Oportunidades y Desafíos Económicos de la Transición Demográfica en Argentina*, edited by M. Gragnolati, R. Rofman, I. Apella, and S. Troiano, 373–411. Buenos Aires: World Bank.

Gruber, J., and D. Wise. 2002. "Social Security Programs and Retirement around the World: Micro Estimation." NBER Working Paper 9407, National Bureau of Economic Research, Cambridge, MA.

Guest, R. 2011. "Population Ageing, Capital Intensity and Labour Productivity." *Pacific Economic Review* 16 (3): 371–88.

Hall, B. 2002. "The Financing of Research and Development." *Oxford Review of Economic Policy* 18 (1): 35–51.

Heckman, J., L. Lochner, and C. Taber. 1998. "Explaining Rising Wage Inequality: Exploration with a Dynamic General Equilibrium Model of Labor Earnings with Heterogeneous Agents." *Review of Economic Dynamics* 1 (1): 1–58.

ILO (International Labour Organization). 2013. "Empleo y Protección Social en el Nuevo Contexto Demográfico." ILO, Geneva.

IMF (International Monetary Fund). 2005. *Households Balance Sheets: Global Financial Stability Report*. Washington, DC: IMF.

Kim, T., and G. Hewings. 2012. "Endogenous Growth in an Aging Economy: Evidence and Policy Measures." *Annals Regional Science* 50: 705–30.

Kuckulenz, A., and T. Zwick. 2003. "The Impact of Training on Earnings: Differences between Participant Groups and Training Forms." ZEW Discussion Paper 03–57, Centre for European Economic Research, Mannheim, Germany.

Lucas, R. 1988. "On the Mechanics of Economic Development." *Journal of Monetary Economics* 22: 3–42.

Mason, A., and R. Lee. 2011. *Population Aging and the Generational Economy: A Global Perspective*. Cheltenham, UK: Edward Elgar.

OECD (Organisation for Economic Co-operation and Development). 2005. *Innovation Policy and Performance: A Cross-Country Comparison*. Paris: OECD.

———. 2013. "Knowledge-Based Capital, Innovation and Resource Allocation." In *Supporting Investment in Knowledge Capital, Growth and Innovation*. Paris: OECD Publishing.

Rebelo, S. 1991. "Long-Run Policy Analysis and Long-Run Growth." *Journal of Political Economy* 99 (3): 500–21.

Romer, P. 1986. "Increasing Return and Long-Run Growth." *Journal of Political Economy* 94 (5): 1002–37.

Sadahiro, A., and M. Shimasawa. 2002. "The Computable Overlapping Generations Model with an Endogenous Growth Mechanism." *Economic Modelling* 20: 1–24.

Schumpeter, J. 1942. *Capitalism, Socialism, and Democracy*. New York: Harper and Row.

Seshadri, A., and K. Yuki. 2004. "Equity and Efficiency Effects of Redistributive Policies." *Journal of Monetary Economics* 51: 1415–47.

Skirbekk, V. 2003. "Age and Individual Productivity: A Literature Survey." MPIDR Working Paper 28, Max Planck Institute for Demographic Research, Rostock, Germany.

Solow, R. 1956. "A Contribution to the Theory of Economic Growth." *Quarterly Journal of Economics* 70: 65–94.

Stock, J., and D. Wise. 1990. "Pension, the Option Value of Work, and Retirement." *Econometrica* 58 (5): 1151–80.

Tangen, S. 2005. "Demystifying Productivity and Performance." *International Journal of Productivity and Performance Management* 54 (1): 34–46.

Environmental Benefits Statement

The World Bank Group is committed to reducing its environmental footprint. In support of this commitment, the Publishing and Knowledge Division leverages electronic publishing options and print-on-demand technology, which is located in regional hubs worldwide. Together, these initiatives enable print runs to be lowered and shipping distances decreased, resulting in reduced paper consumption, chemical use, greenhouse gas emissions, and waste.

The Publishing and Knowledge Division follows the recommended standards for paper use set by the Green Press Initiative. The majority of our books are printed on Forest Stewardship Council (FSC)–certified paper, with nearly all containing 50–100 percent recycled content. The recycled fiber in our book paper is either unbleached or bleached using totally chlorine-free (TCF), processed chlorine-free (PCF), or enhanced elemental chlorine-free (EECF) processes.

More information about the Bank's environmental philosophy can be found at http://www.worldbank.org/corporateresponsibility.

green press INITIATIVE

www.ingramcontent.com/pod-product-compliance
Lightning Source LLC
LaVergne TN
LVHW080642011026
849160LV00014B/1299